CompTIA A+® Certification Practice Exams

Second Edition

(Exams 220-801 & 220-802)

James Pyles
Mike Chapple
Michael Pastore

New York Chicago San Francisco Lisbon London Madrid
Mexico City Milan New Delhi San Juan Seoul Singapore Sydney Toronto

The **McGraw-Hill** Companies

Cataloging-in-Publication Data is on file with the Library of Congress

McGraw-Hill books are available at special quantity discounts to use as premiums and sales promotions, or for use in corporate training programs. To contact a representative, please e-mail us at bulksales@mcgraw-hill.com.

CompTIA A+® Certification Practice Exams, Second Edition (Exams 220-801 & 220-802)

1234567890   DOC DOC   1098765432

ISBN: Book p/n 978-0-07-179227-1 and CD p/n 978-0-07-179228-8
of set 978-0-07-179230-1

MHID: Book p/n 0-07-179227-9 and CD p/n 0-07-179228-7
of set 0-07-179230-9

Associate Acquisitions Editor Meghan Riley Manfre	**Technical Editor** Chris Crayton	**Production Supervisor** James Kussow
Editorial Supervisor Jody McKenzie	**Copy Editor** Lisa McCoy	**Composition** Cenveo Publisher Services
Project Manager Vastavikta Sharma, Cenveo Publisher Services	**Proofreader** Claire Splan	**Illustration** Cenveo Publisher Services
Acquisitions Coordinator Stephanie Evans	**Indexer** James Minkin	**Art Director, Cover** Jeff Weeks

As always, to my lovely wife, Lin; my three terrific children, David, Michael, and Jamie; my wonderful daughter-in-law, Kim; and my loving grandson, Landon. You all make life sweet.
—James

To George Parker and James Cooper. Thank you for your service.
—Mike

ABOUT THE AUTHORS

James Pyles (CompTIA A+, CompTIA Network+) works as a consultant, author, editor, and technical writer. He has been involved in numerous Ethernet rollout projects, software and hardware installations, and upgrades, as well as Windows and UNIX operating system upgrades. James has provided support services for a city government IT department and a wireless network vendor, and supported a usability lab for Hewlett-Packard. He has served as a technical writer for EmergeCore Networks, Aquent Studios, and iAnywhere/Sybase, and as a developmental editor for Global Support Content Operations at Hewlett-Packard.

James has authored and technically edited several books on CompTIA A+, Microsoft Office SharePoint, and GIMP. He has also been a contributor to *Linux Pro Magazine* and Ubuntu User magazine. James has bachelor's degrees in psychology and computer network support and a master's degree in counseling. He currently works as a technical writer at Keynetics, Inc., in Boise, Idaho.

Mike Chapple, Ph.D., is an information technology professional and concurrent assistant professor with the University of Notre Dame. He has over 15 years of experience in information security in the public, private, and nonprofit sectors. Mike is the author of a dozen books, including the *CISSP Study Guide, Information Security Illuminated,* and *SQL Server 2008 for Dummies.* He is a frequent contributor to SearchSecurity.com, serves as the About.com Guide to Databases, and teaches several information security courses.

Michael Pastore (CompTIA A+, CompTIA Network+, CompTIA Security+, MCP) has been writing computer books for more than 15 years and has been involved in IT for more than 30 years in roles ranging from network technician to president of an IT training school. Michael's writing background includes experience as a contributor to *Computerworld* and a columnist for Leap-it.com. Throughout the course of his career, Michael has served as a faculty member at several IT institutes, including the University of Phoenix and DeVry University.

About the Technical Editor

Chris Crayton (CompTIA A+, CompTIA Network+, MCSE) is an author, editor, technical consultant, and trainer. Chris has worked as a computer and networking instructor at Keiser University; as network administrator for Protocol, an eCRM company; and as a computer and network specialist at Eastman Kodak. He has authored several print and online books on PC repair, CompTIA A+, CompTIA Security+, and Microsoft Windows Vista. Chris has served as technical editor on numerous professional technical titles for many of the leading publishing companies, including *CompTIA A+ Certification All-in-One Exam Guide*, *Mike Meyers' CompTIA A+ Guide to Managing and Troubleshooting PCs, Third Edition Test Bank*, and also *Mike Meyers' CompTIA Network+ Certification Passport*.

About LearnKey

LearnKey provides self-paced learning content and multimedia delivery solutions to enhance personal skills and business productivity. LearnKey claims the largest library of rich streaming-media training content that engages learners in dynamic media-rich instruction, complete with video clips, audio, full-motion graphics, and animated illustrations. LearnKey can be found on the Web at www.LearnKey.com.

It Pays to Get Certified

In a digital world, digital literacy is an essential survival skill. Certification proves you have the knowledge and skill to solve business problems in virtually any business environment. Certifications are highly valued credentials that qualify you for jobs, increased compensation, and promotion.

LEARN		CERTIFY	WORK

IT is Everywhere	IT Knowledge and Skills Get Jobs	Job Retention	New Opportunities	High Pay-High Growth Jobs
IT is mission critical to almost all organizations and its importance is increasing.	Certifications verify your knowledge and skills that qualifies you for:	Competence is noticed and valued in organizations.	Certifications qualify you for new opportunities in your current job or when you want to change careers.	Hiring managers demand the strongest skill set.
• 79% of U.S. businesses report IT is either important or very important to the success of their company	• Jobs in the high growth IT career field • Increased compensation • Challenging assignments and promotions • 60% report that being certified is an employer or job requirement	• Increased knowledge of new or complex technologies • Enhanced productivity • More insightful problem solving • Better project management and communication skills • 47% report being certified helped improve their problem solving skills	• 31% report certification improved their career advancement opportunities	• There is a widening IT skills gap with over 300,000 jobs open • 88% report being certified enhanced their resume

CompTIA A+ Certification Advances Your Career

- **The CompTIA A+ credential**—provides foundation-level knowledge and skills necessary for a career in PC repair and support.

- **Starting Salary**—CompTIA A+ Certified individuals can earn as much as $65,000 per year.

- **Career Pathway**—CompTIA A+ is a building block for other CompTIA certifications such as Network+, Security+, and vendor-specific technologies.

- **More than 850,000**—individuals worldwide are CompTIA A+ certified.

- **Mandated/Recommended by organizations worldwide**—such as Cisco and HP and Ricoh, the U.S. State Department, and U.S. government contractors such as EDS, General Dynamics, and Northrop Grumman.

- **Some of the primary benefits individuals report from becoming CompTIA A+ certified are:**
  - More efficient troubleshooting
  - Improved career advancement
  - More insightful problem solving

CompTIA Career Pathway

CompTIA offers a number of credentials that form a foundation for your career in technology and that allow you to pursue specific areas of concentration. Depending on the path you choose to take, CompTIA certifications help you build upon your skills and knowledge, supporting learning throughout your entire career.

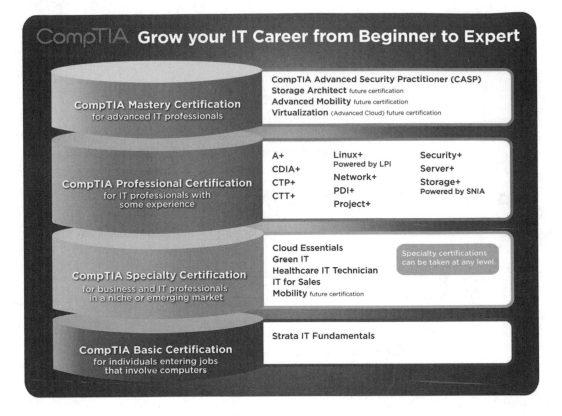

Steps to Getting Certified and Staying Certified

1. **Review exam objectives.** Review the certification objectives to make sure you know what is covered in the exam:
www.comptia.org/certifications/testprep/examobjectives.aspx

2. **Practice for the exam.** After you have studied for the certification, take a free assessment and sample test to get an idea what type of questions might be on the exam:
www.comptia.org/certifications/testprep/practicetests.aspx

3. **Purchase an exam voucher.** Purchase your exam voucher on the CompTIA Marketplace, which is located at: www.comptiastore.com

4. **Take the test!** Select a certification exam provider and schedule a time to take your exam. You can find exam providers at the following link: www.comptia.org/certifications/testprep/testingcenters.aspx

5. **Stay certified!** Continuing education is required. Effective January 1, 2011, CompTIA A+ certifications are valid for three years from the date of certification. There are a number of ways the certification can be renewed. For more information go to: http://certification.comptia.org/getCertified/ steps_to_certification/stayCertified.aspx

Join the Professional Community

The free online IT Pro Community provides valuable content to students and professionals. Join the IT Pro Community:

http://itpro.comptia.org

Career IT job resources include:

- Where to start in IT
- Career assessments
- Salary trends
- U.S. job board

Join the IT Pro Community and get access to:

- Forums on networking, security, computing, and cutting-edge technologies
- Access to blogs written by industry experts
- Current information on cutting-edge technologies
- Access to various industry resource links and articles related to IT and IT careers

Content Seal of Quality

This courseware bears the seal of CompTIA Approved Quality Content. This seal signifies this content covers 100 percent of the exam objectives and implements important instructional design principles. CompTIA recommends multiple learning tools to help increase coverage of the learning objectives.

Why CompTIA?

- **Global recognition**—CompTIA is recognized globally as the leading IT nonprofit trade association and has enormous credibility. Plus, CompTIA's certifications are vendor-neutral and offer proof of foundational knowledge that translates across technologies.
- **Valued by hiring managers**—Hiring managers value CompTIA certification because it is vendor- and technology-independent validation of your technical skills.
- **Recommended or required by government and businesses**—Many government organizations and corporations (for example, Dell, Sharp, Ricoh, the U.S. Department of Defense, and many more) either recommend or require technical staff to be CompTIA certified.
- **Three CompTIA certifications ranked in the top 10**—In a study by DICE of 17,000 technology professionals, certifications helped command higher salaries at all experience levels.

How to Obtain More Information

Visit CompTIA online
Go to www.comptia.org to learn more about getting CompTIA certified.

Contact CompTIA
Please call 866-835-8020, ext. 5 or e-mail questions@comptia.org.

Join the IT Pro Community
Go to http://itpro.comptia.org to join the IT community to get relevant career information.

Connect with CompTIA
Find us on Facebook, LinkedIn, Twitter, and YouTube.

CAQC Disclaimer

The logo of the CompTIA Approved Quality Content (CAQC) program and the status of this or other training material as "Authorized" under the CompTIA Approved Quality Content program signifies that, in CompTIA's opinion, such training material covers the content of CompTIA's related certification exam.

CONTENTS

ACKNOWLEDGMENTS

First off, we want to say "thanks" again to Carole Jelen at Waterside for continuing to keep us busy with projects. We also want to thank the fine folks at McGraw-Hill, including Acquisitions Editor Meghan Riley Manfre, who welcomed us to this project, and Acquisitions Coordinator Stephanie Evans, who has been riding shotgun beside us on every chapter. Of course, we want to acknowledge the tireless efforts of Chris Crayton, who with laser-like precision has kept the technical accuracy of all our material up to snuff. Thanks to everyone else at McGraw-Hill for all of your good work and keen insights. Without a team, no book would ever be possible. Cheers.

—James Pyles and Mike Chapple

This book exists because of the patience and kindness of everyone around me, my family and my friends, everyone who depends on me, and everyone upon whom I depend. Thank you all for continuing to show me that life is an adventure and each day is a new wonder.

—James Pyles

This book is only possible due to the loving support of my family. Without the help of my wife, Renee, I never would have been able to carve out the time to get this book finished. My sons, Richard, Matthew, and Christopher, provide a constant source of enthusiasm and inspiration. Thank you all for your support.

—Mike Chapple

W elcome to *CompTIA A+ Certification Practice Exams, Second Edition,* or rather, one of the vital steps in studying for and successfully sitting the CompTIA A+ 220-801 and 220-802 exams. This book and the accompanying electronic practice exam content feature more than 1000 detailed questions and answers that are designed to help prepare you to become CompTIA A+ certified *and* hone your knowledge in the areas related to hardware and software maintenance and repair and computer desktop support.

In This Book

Within this book you will find practice exam questions that mirror the actual multiple-choice exam questions in content, style, tone, format, and difficulty. For each multiple-choice question you will find an explanation for both the correct *and* incorrect answers, allowing you to test the information you know and learn the information you don't.

Note: This book does not include simulations of the new performance-based question type. For more information on this new question type, please see the Introduction.

In Every Chapter

This book is organized for efficiency so that you can make the most of the time you spend studying. Take a look at what you'll find in every chapter:

- Every chapter begins with **Certification Objectives**—what you need to know in order to pass the section of the exam dealing with the chapter topics. These objectives are the vendor-given exam objectives covered in the chapter.
- **Practice Exam Questions,** 7 to 25 unique questions, are included in every chapter. By answering these questions you will test your knowledge while familiarizing yourself with the format of the multiple-choice portion of the exam.

- The **Quick Answer Key** follows the Practice Exam Questions and allows you to easily check your answers.
- The **In-Depth Answers** at the end of every chapter provide the opportunity to learn not only why one answer choice is correct but why the others are not.

Pre-Assessment Tests

This book features two pre-assessment tests included as Appendices A and B. The pre-assessment tests will gauge your areas of strength and weakness prior to beginning your studies.

Practice Exams

Of the 1000+ questions included in this book, 600 are organized into six practice exams.

Objective Map

At the end of the Introduction you will find an Objective Map. This map has been constructed in the form of a table to allow you to reference the official certification exam objectives and refer to the order in which these objectives are covered in this book. The objectives are listed with the corresponding book chapter and question number reference.

On the CD-ROM

Included on the CD-ROM you will find two practice exams hosted in a software test engine and a link to download two additional practice exams. For more information on the CD-ROM, please see the About the CD-ROM appendix at the back of the book.

Using This Book

This book was developed and written in conjunction with the *CompTIA A+ Certification Study Guide, Eighth Edition (Exams 220-801 & 220-802)*, by Jane and Charles Holcombe. These books were designed to work together as a comprehensive program for self-study, but both books are discrete and complete test prep guides.

Study Strategies

This book can be used in a number of ways. The most obvious method is to go through the book cover to cover, testing yourself from one subject to the next. Since each chapter can contain a mix of 220-801 and 220-802 objective content, you can test your understanding in specific areas, such as motherboards and processors or upgrading PC components, as they are applied in both exams.

Another strategy is to take the practice questions by exam objective. For example, both Chapters 4 and 6 contain content for Objective 801:1.3: Compare and contrast RAM types and features. You can find a list of the objectives covered in each chapter at the beginning of each chapter as well as in the Objective Map included at the end of the Introduction. You may also just want to test yourself on a specific topic such as security. In that case, you can cover all of the practice questions in Chapters 15 and 17 to determine your readiness in this area.

Whichever method you decide to employ, it is recommended that you begin with the pre-assessment tests. By taking the pre-assessment tests first you will identify your areas of strength and weakness and be able to use the results to inform your studies.

Taking the Practice Exams

In addition to the questions contained in Chapters 1–21, there are an additional 600 multiple-choice practice exam questions divided among the six practice exams. Two of these exams are included as Appendices C and D, two are available on the book's accompanying CD-ROM, and two are available for download. Each practice exam contains 100 multiple-choice questions representing the exam objectives for either the 220-801 or 220-802 exam.

The practice exam content is randomized within each individual practice exam, so these exams are a great way to test your exam readiness without being able to anticipate the question content. Simply select a practice exam that covers either the 220-801 or 220-802 content and then progress through the exam questions, assessing your skills.

INTRODUCTION

ompTIA A+ certification is the starting point for a career in IT support. Per CompTIA, "Successful candidates will have the knowledge required to assemble components based on customer requirements, install, configure and maintain devices, PCs and software for end users, understand the basics of networking and security/forensics, properly and safely diagnose, resolve and document common hardware and software issues while applying troubleshooting skills. Successful candidates will also provide appropriate customer support; understand the basics of virtualization, desktop imaging, and deployment."

There are no required prerequisites for CompTIA A+ certification, but CompTIA does recommend 12 months of hands-on experience in the lab or field. Certification candidate job roles include technical support specialist, field service technician, IT support technician, IT support administrator, and IT support specialist.

The CompTIA A+ Certification 2012 Exams

The 2012 CompTIA A+ certification track consists of two exams: the CompTIA A+ 220-801 Exam and the CompTIA A+ 220-802 Exam. Candidates are required to pass both exams in order to achieve the certification.

The CompTIA A+ 220-801 Exam

The CompTIA A+ 220-801 Exam consists of five domains (categories). CompTIA represents the relative importance of each domain within the body of knowledge required for an entry-level IT professional taking this exam.

1.0 PC Hardware	40%
2.0 Networking	27%
3.0 Laptops	11%
4.0 Printers	11%
5.0 Operational Procedures	11%

1.0 Operating Systems	33%
2.0 Security	22%
3.0 Mobile Devices	9%
4.0 Troubleshooting	36%

The CompTIA A+ 220-802 Exam

The CompTIA A+ 220-802 Exam consists of four domains. CompTIA represents the relative importance of each domain within the body of knowledge required for an entry-level IT professional taking this exam.

Computerized Testing

For many certifying bodies, the most practical way to administer exams on a global level is through Pearson VUE testing centers, which provide proctored testing services for many companies, including CompTIA. In addition to administering the tests, Pearson VUE scores the exam and provides statistical feedback on each section of the exam to the companies and organizations that use their services.

Exam Structure

Previously, the CompTIA A+ exams were composed solely of 100 multiple-choice questions. For the first time the 2012 exams will be composed of a mix of question types, including multiple-choice and performance-based questions.

For the multiple-choice questions, most questions will have only a single correct answer. Some others will have multiple correct answers, in which case, the question will include a note such as "Select two."

The performance-based questions will be hands-on simulation questions. For more information on the performance-based questions, please visit the CompTIA Website at www.comptia.org. There you will find more information on the exams, including their passing scores, and additional practice exam questions.

Signing Up

After all your hard work preparing for the exams, signing up will be a very easy process. You can register for the exams online at www.vue.com/comptia or by calling the Pearson VUE test center nearest you.

Note: Effective July 9, 2012, the CompTIA A+ exams are exclusively available through Pearson VUE testing centers. The CompTIA exams are no longer available through Prometric testing centers.

Taking the Exams

The best method of preparing for the exams is to create a study schedule and stick to it. You can brush up on good study techniques from any quality study book from the library, but some things to remember when preparing and taking the exams are

- Get a good night's sleep. Don't stay up all night cramming. If you don't know the material by the time you go to sleep, your head won't be clear enough to remember it in the morning.

- Arrive at the test center a few minutes early. You don't need to feel rushed right before taking an exam.

- Don't spend too much time on one question, but be warned, unanswered questions do count against you. Assuming you have time left when you finish the other questions, you can return to the marked questions for further evaluation.

- If you don't know the answer to a question, think about it logically. Look at the answers and eliminate the ones that you know can't possibly be the answer. This may leave you with only two possible answers. Give it your best guess if you have to, but you can resolve most of the answers to the questions by process of elimination.

- No books, calculators, laptop computers, or any other reference materials are allowed inside the testing center. The tests are computer based and do not require pens, pencils, or paper, although some test centers provide scratch paper to aid you while taking the exam.

Good luck! Once you pass your exams and earn the title of CompTIA A+ Certified your value and status in the IT industry increase. CompTIA A+ certification carries an important proof of skills and knowledge level that is valued by customers, employers, and professionals in the computer industry.

Exam 220-801

Official Objective	Chapter Nos.	Question Nos.
1.0 PC Hardware		
1.1 Configure and apply BIOS settings	3	1, 2, 3, 4, 5, 6, 7, 8, 9, 10
	App A	35
	App C	56, 63, 73, 84, 85, 97, 98, 99
1.2 Differentiate between motherboard components, their purposes, and properties	3	11, 12, 13, 14, 15, 16, 17, 18
	6	1, 2, 3, 4
	App A	26
	App C	46, 47
1.3 Compare and contrast RAM types and features	4	1, 2, 3
	6	5
	App A	14, 15, 16, 17
	App C	25

Official Objective	Chapter Nos.	Question Nos.
1.4 Install and configure expansion cards	4 6 App A App C	4, 5 6 18, 37 26, 27, 64, 74, 76, 77
1.5 Install and configure storage devices and use appropriate media	4 6 App A App C	6, 7, 8, 9, 10, 11 7 22, 23, 38, 39 23, 28, 29, 32, 33, 34, 35, 36, 37, 38, 39, 40, 41, 42, 43, 44, 45, 50, 72, 75
1.6 Differentiate among various CPU types and features and select the appropriate cooling method	3 6 App A App C	19, 20, 21, 22 8, 9, 10, 11 34 65, 66
1.7 Compare and contrast various connection interfaces and explain their purpose	4 App A App C	12, 13 25, 42, 49 9
1.8 Install an appropriate power supply based on a given scenario	5 App A App C	1, 2, 3, 4 50 86, 87, 88
1.9 Evaluate and select appropriate components for a custom configuration to meet customer specifications or needs	5 6 App A	5, 6, 7, 8 12, 13, 14, 15 19
1.10 Given a scenario, evaluate types and features of display devices	5 App A App C	9, 10, 11, 12 41 89, 90
1.11 Identify connector types and associated cables	4 5 App A	14, 15 13, 14, 15, 16, 17, 18, 19 36
1.12 Install and configure various peripheral devices	5 App A App C	20, 21, 22, 23, 24, 25, 26, 27, 28, 29 21, 24, 51, 52, 53, 54, 55, 57, 68, 69, 91, 92, 93
2.0 Networking		
2.1 Identify types of network cables and connectors	14 App A	1 6
2.2 Categorize characteristics of connectors and cabling	14 App A App C	2, 3 9 14, 15

Official Objective	Chapter Nos.	Question Nos.
4.2 Given a scenario, install and configure printers	21 App A App C	5, 6, 7, 8 27 94, 95, 96
4.3 Given a scenario, perform printer maintenance	21 App A App C	9, 10, 11, 12 28, 29, 30 67
5.0 Operational Procedures		
5.1 Given a scenario, use appropriate safety procedures	1 App A App C	1, 2, 3, 4, 5, 6, 7 45 70, 78, 79, 80
5.2 Explain environmental impacts and the purpose of environmental controls	1 App A App C	8, 9, 10, 11, 12, 13, 14 43 71, 81, 82, 83
5.3 Given a scenario, demonstrate proper communication and professionalism	1 App A App C	15, 16, 17, 18, 19, 20 48 60
5.4 Explain the fundamentals of dealing with prohibited content/activity	1 App A App C	21, 22 40, 44 58, 59

Exam 220-802

Official Objective	Chapter Nos.	Question Nos.
1.0 Operating Systems		
1.1 Compare and contrast the features and requirements of various Microsoft operating systems	2 10 App B	1, 2, 3, 4, 5, 6, 7, 8, 9, 10, 11, 12, 13, 14, 15, 16, 17, 18, 19, 20, 21, 22 1, 2, 3 36
1.2 Given a scenario, install and configure the operating system using the most appropriate method	9 10 App B App D	1, 2, 3, 4, 5 4, 5, 6 30 53, 54, 76, 77, 78
1.3 Given a scenario, use appropriate command-line tools	10 13 App B App D	7, 8, 9 1, 2, 3, 4 2, 31, 32 52

Official Objective	Chapter Nos.	Question Nos.
1.4 Given a scenario, use appropriate operating system features and tools	9 10 13 App B App D	6, 7, 8, 9 10, 11, 12 5, 6, 7, 8 33, 34, 35, 37, 38, 39, 40 15, 46, 55, 62, 79
1.5 Given a scenario, use Control Panel utilities (the items are organized by "classic view/large icons" in Windows)	7 9 App D	15, 16 11, 12, 13, 14, 15 26, 48, 49, 50, 56, 57, 58, 59, 60, 61, 63, 64, 65, 74, 75
1.6 Set up and configure Windows networking on a client/desktop	19 App B App D	1, 2, 3, 4, 5, 6, 7, 8, 9, 10 13, 22, 23, 25 31, 32, 33, 34, 35, 36, 39, 40
1.7 Perform preventive maintenance procedures using appropriate tools	13 App D	9, 10, 11, 12 72, 73
1.8 Explain the differences among basic OS security settings	10 19 App D	13, 14, 15 11, 12, 13, 14, 15 12, 23, 27, 30, 37, 38, 47
1.9 Explain the basics of client-side virtualization	8	1, 2, 3, 4, 5, 6, 7, 8
2.0 Security		
2.1 Apply and use common prevention methods	17 App B App D	1, 2, 3, 4, 5, 6 1, 6, 8, 11, 12, 17 9, 13, 44, 45
2.2 Compare and contrast common security threats	17 App B App D	7, 8, 9, 10 20 14, 18, 19, 24, 51
2.3 Implement security best practices to secure a workstation	18 App B App D	16, 17 9, 10, 18, 19 16, 17
2.4 Given a scenario, use the appropriate data destruction/disposal method	17 App B	11 7
2.5 Given a scenario, secure a SOHO wireless network	15 App D	11, 12 1
2.6 Given a scenario, secure a SOHO wired network	15 App D	13, 14 2
3.0 Mobile Devices		
3.1 Explain the basic features of mobile operating systems	20 App D	1, 2, 3 4, 5

Official Objective	Chapter Nos.	Question Nos.
3.2 Establish basic network connectivity and configure e-mail	20 App B	4, 5, 6 47, 49, 50
3.3 Compare and contrast methods for securing mobile devices	20 App D	7, 8, 9, 10 10, 25
3.4 Compare and contrast hardware differences in regard to tablets and laptops	20 App D	11, 12 34
3.5 Execute and configure mobile device synchronization	20 App B App D	13, 14, 15 48 29
4.0 Troubleshooting		
4.1 Given a scenario, explain the troubleshooting theory	11	1, 2, 3
4.2 Given a scenario, troubleshoot common problems related to motherboards, RAM, CPU, and power with appropriate tools	11 App B App D	4, 5, 6, 7 3, 41, 42, 43, 45 11, 80, 81, 100
4.3 Given a scenario, troubleshoot hard drives and RAID arrays with appropriate tools	11 App B App D	8, 9, 10, 11 44, 46 82, 83, 84, 87, 97, 98, 99
4.4 Given a scenario, troubleshoot common video and display issues	11 App B App D	12, 13, 14, 15 21, 26 85, 86
4.5 Given a scenario, troubleshoot wired and wireless networks with appropriate tools	16 App B App D	1, 2, 3, 4, 5, 6, 7, 8, 9, 10, 11, 12 4, 5, 14, 15, 16, 24 3, 7, 8, 41, 42
4.6 Given a scenario, troubleshoot operating systems with appropriate tools	13 App B App D	13, 14, 15 27, 28, 29 20, 43, 69, 70, 71, 88, 89
4.7 Given a scenario, troubleshoot common security issues with appropriate tools and best practices	18 App D	1, 2, 3, 4, 5, 6, 7, 8, 9, 10, 11, 12, 13, 14, 15 6, 21, 22, 28
4.8 Given a scenario, troubleshoot and repair common laptop issues while adhering to the appropriate procedures	12	1, 2, 3, 4, 5, 6, 7, 8, 9, 10, 11, 12, 13, 14, 15
4.9 Given a scenario, troubleshoot printers with appropriate tools	21 App D	13, 14, 15 66, 67, 68, 90, 91, 92, 93, 94, 95, 96

1

Operational Procedures

QUESTIONS

While it's considered a minor province in the realm of an A+ technician, following proper safety procedures is a must in terms of maintaining a good reputation, keeping a stellar safety record, and showing respect for your customers. While it's impossible to avoid all accidents, your customers will appreciate you treating them, and their equipment, with respect, and not frying the motherboard of their new PC just because you forgot to take electrostatic discharge (ESD) precautions. Also, while you likely choose this career path because you're good with machines, the people who own those machines are human. You'll need to be just as proficient communicating with them as you are in using the command line or comprehending a computer's binary language.

Objective 801: 5.1   Given a Scenario, Use Appropriate Safety Procedures

1. You need to work on the inside of a customer's PC, but you forgot to bring any ESD safety equipment with you to the work site. What can you do to minimize the likelihood of damaging the computer's interior when you open the case?

    A. After opening the computer case, briefly grip the metal frame of the PC to equalize the static potential between you and the machine.

    B. After opening the computer case, keep one part of your body touching the computer case panel to continually equalize the static potential between you and the machine.

    C. Before opening the computer case, grip the exterior of it to equalize the static potential between you and the machine.

    D. It is too dangerous to work inside a computer case without a proper ESD mat and strap to ground both yourself and the PC. Go back to your shop and get your safety equipment before proceeding.

2. You work for a small city IT department, and you and a coworker are decommissioning a number of older computers, including their power supplies. Your coworker starts to disassemble one of the power supply units "to see what makes it tick." You immediately stop him because of the danger involved. Which statement is true and should be considered first when working on a power supply unit?

    A. You should unplug the power supply from its power source before opening the case to avoid electrical shock.

    B. You should remove the power supply from the computer before opening the case to avoid damaging the computer.

    C. Never open a power supply without special equipment and special training because you could ruin the power supply's internal connections.

    D. Never open a power supply without special equipment and special training because the stored charge in even an unplugged power supply is dangerous.

3. You have just replaced a CPU fan on a PC and you have powered up the device without replacing the case cover to make sure the fan is spinning up properly. You have grounded the device and yourself using an ESD mat and strap, and reach into the machine to make some small adjustments. Of the following, what are the primary safety concerns? (Choose all that apply.)

    A. Your ring and necklace could cause an electrical problem or personal hazard if caught on running machinery.

    B. Your shirt sleeves could cause a personal hazard if caught on running machinery.

    C. Your ESD strap could cause an electrical problem if it enters the case of a running computer.

    D. Running a computer without the PC case cover could cause the CPU to overheat, resulting in a fire hazard.

4. You work for a small city IT department, and you and a coworker are decommissioning a number of older computers, including their power supplies. Your coworker wants to take one of the power supplies and put it into a new PC she's building at her workbench. Could there be a problem with this practice?

    A. No, all power supplies work with all computer components.

    B. Yes, the power supply may not fit in the case of the computer she's building due to a form factor mismatch, but other than that, the practice should be okay.

    C. Yes, the power supply specifications may not match the components in the computer she's building.

    D. No, the power supply has a selector switch so that your coworker can set its specifications to match the computer she's building.

5. You are adding several new servers to the server room for your company's main office, including the networking cables from the servers to the patch panel. Of the following, what is the primary safety concern when laying network cable?

    A. Manage the cables and remove them from areas where people need to walk so that they don't present a tripping hazard.

    B. Manage the cables so that they don't present an electrical shock hazard.

    C. Manage the cables so that they don't present an ESD hazard to the servers.

    D. Manage the cables so that they are organized and labeled by patch panel port number and server type.

6. You work for a small city IT department, and you notice another technician reaching up on a shelf above him, trying to pull down a large carton of printer paper. What immediate hazard does this represent?

A. The carton may fall on top of the technician.

B. The technician may hurt his lower back when lifting the carton.

C. The technician may hurt his knees when pulling on the carton.

D. There is no hazard. The technician is executing a proper procedure.

7. You work for a small city IT department, and a fellow technician has been tasked with disposing of a collection of obsolete cathode ray tube (CRT) monitors. You ask him about his disposal plan, and he tells you he's going to load the monitors into the back of his truck and take them to a large, industrial dumpster. How do you respond?

A. You say this is an adequate plan.

B. You explain that CRT monitors contain lead and that the city must store them indefinitely due to the environmental hazard.

C. You explain that CRT monitors contain lead and that he must use a licensed recycling company for disposal.

D. You explain that CRT monitors contain lead and that he must mail the monitors back to the manufacturer for disposal.

Objective 801: 5.2   Explain Environmental Impacts and the Purpose of Environmental Controls

8. You work for a small city IT department, and you and another tech are reviewing the inventory of the different chemicals used by your department. Your coworker comes across a sticker on one of the chemical containers similar to the accompanying image. What do you tell him this design means?

A. This is a NiCd sticker indicating this chemical is used to clean nickel cadmium battery contacts.

B. This is a NiMH sticker indicating this chemical is used to clean nickel metal hydrate battery contacts.

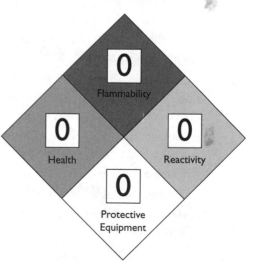

C. This is an MSDS sticker indicating general information about the chemical, including potential hazards.

D. This is the manufacturer's proprietary sticker, indicating the general characteristics of the chemical.

9. You are preparing to replace a faulty PCI Express network interface card (NIC) with a new expansion card in a customer's PC. In order to avoid damaging the new card, how should you store it until you are ready to install it in the computer?

A. Place it on the top of your workbench until you are ready to install it.

B. Place it in an antistatic bag until you are ready to install it.

C. Place it in a box of other PCI Express cards until you are ready to install it.

D. Place it in your toolkit until you are ready to install it.

10. You are conducting a routine tune-up on a customer's computer. When you open the computer case, you notice that a great deal of dust has built up inside the PC and it is clogging the various fans and components inside the computer. Of the following, which are the safest methods of removing the dust? (Choose two.)

A. Use a can of compressed air to blow the dust out of the computer case.

B. Use a cotton rag lightly coated with an ammonia-based cleaner to wipe the dust out of the computer case.

C. Use the smallest extension on the hose of a home electric vacuum cleaner to suck the dust out of the computer case.

D. Use a battery-operated vacuum cleaner especially designed for use inside a computer to suck the dust out.

11. You work for a small city IT department and are teaming with another technician to service the computers and laser printers in the accounting office over the weekend. When the other technician opens her toolkit, you notice she has a small supply of face masks in the kit. When you ask her about them, she explains the circumstances under which she uses them and why working on devices in an area with good ventilation is important. Of the following, which are good reasons to use face masks and to maintain good air flow when working on computers and printers? (Choose two.)

A. Laser printer toner is made up of very fine clay, pigment, and resin, and can be dangerous if inhaled.

B. Dust inside computer cases is toxic and can be dangerous if inhaled.

C. Computer components release gases that are toxic and can be dangerous if inhaled.

D. Dust and other debris inside computer cases can potentially cause coughing and choking if inhaled.

12. A sales rep at your company is in the habit of leaving his laptop computer in his car overnight during the winter and then bringing it into the office in the morning and starting it up first thing. It's been getting below freezing for the past several nights. As an IT technician responsible for maintaining your office's computers, what are your concerns regarding this practice? (Choose all that apply.)

    A. The sudden change in temperature from being very cold to the sudden heating that occurs when the laptop is powered up could warp the laptop's motherboard.

    B. The long-term exposure to cold could cause delicate electronic components to snap or crack when suddenly exposed to a warm office environment.

    C. The sudden shift from a cold to a warm environment could cause condensation to build up inside the laptop resulting in damage to the laptop when power is applied.

    D. Laptops are completely intolerant of cold, and overnight exposure to freezing temperatures will almost certainly cause the LCD screen to become damaged.

13. You are supporting a SOHO (small office/home office) customer who complains that his computer spontaneously reboots several times a week. This is usually the sign of a dying power supply in the PC, but you've tested it and the power supply is fine. You notice that the customer has his computer, printer, and other electronic devices plugged into a simple power strip. You are also aware that the customer lives in an area that is prone to electrical power fluctuations. Why is this a clue as to the cause of the computer's rebooting problem?

    A. Power strips do not protect against power surges, which are a likely cause of computer reboots.

    B. Power strips do not protect against power sags and brownouts, which are a likely cause of computer reboots.

    C. When a power strip has gone bad, it can cause any computer attached to it to spontaneously reboot.

    D. A simple power strip cannot support the power demands of even one computer and it should be replaced with a more advanced power strip.

14. You work for a small city IT department and you have been given the responsibility of disposing of a supply of damaged and worn-out computer components, including motherboards and old CRT monitors. Part of your task is to research and comply with any local government regulations regarding recycling and disposing of such units. What is your first step in correctly disposing of these items?

    A. Use the local phone book and look under the local government listings for recycling.

    B. Call the hardware vendors for each of the components you need to dispose of and acquire a list of correct recycling procedures.

    C. Use the Internet to access the Environmental Protection Agency Website and discover the proper disposal method.

    D. All recycling centers are required, by law, to accept and properly dispose of computer components, so just take the items to your nearest recycler.

Objective 801: 5.3   Given a Scenario, Demonstrate Proper Communication and Professionalism

15. You are at a customer's home attempting to manage a severe malware infection on the customer's computer. With the customer watching, you use several methods of removing the malware. Unfortunately, most of the methods you use don't remove the malware successfully. You feel yourself becoming frustrated and are annoyed that the customer continues to stand behind you and watch you work. The customer repeatedly asks you what's taking so long. How do you respond?

    A. Maintaining a positive attitude, you calmly explain the situation to the customer, describing the methods you are using to correct his computer, including the likelihood of success for each method and about how long your work should take.

    B. Maintaining a positive attitude, you ask the customer to step out of the room so that you can concentrate more freely on restoring his computer.

    C. You describe to the customer the sorts of Websites he likely had to visit to so badly infect his computer and suggest that his Web surfing habits are what caused the problem in the first place.

    D. You step outside so that you can cool off.

16. You have made several appointments with home and small business customers estimating the time of each visit based on the customer's initial requests. Just before lunch, you encounter a problem with a customer's computer that puts you two hours behind your schedule. You are already late for your next visit and still have to finish the current job. What do you do?

    A. Finish the current job and get to the next customer as quickly as you can.

    B. Finish the current job and call the next customer to reschedule for tomorrow so that you can keep the rest of today's scheduled appointments on time.

    C. Call your next customer and explain that you'll be late, notify them of your estimated arrival time, and then finish the current job.

    D. Tell the current customer that you will be back tomorrow to finish their job and leave so that you can keep the rest of your schedule.

17. You work for a company that provides computer and network support services to home and small business customers. You are supervising a new technician who just started providing services to several home customers this week. You have received several phone complaints about the new technician today, describing him as unprofessional. Of the following, what behaviors described to you could account for valid customer dissatisfaction? (Choose two.)

    A. The technician took several lengthy phone calls and texts from family and friends while at the home of customers, interrupting his repair activities.

    B. The technician took a friend with him on his home visits to "show him the ropes" of the computer repair business.

   C. The technician took periodic breaks during the day to use the restroom.

   D. The technician called his spouse during a home visit, saying he was running late in his schedule and asking her to pick up their child after school.

18. You are attempting to work with a home customer who has a complaint about her computer, but you are having difficulty understanding the nature of the complaint in terms you can comprehend. What can you do to gain a better understanding of the customer's perception of the computer problem? (Choose all that apply.)

   A. Ask open-ended questions rather than questions that require the customer to answer either "yes" or "no" so that she has the opportunity to explain the problem fully and in her own words, and acknowledging any issues that require you to be culturally sensitive.

   B. Once the customer states her computer's problem, restate the problem in your own words to verify that you correctly comprehend what she has told you.

   C. Advise the customer to explain the problem with her computer in as formal and as technical a language as possible, so you can completely understand what is happening.

   D. Have the customer sit at her computer and show you what she does to produce the conditions leading to the problem behavior by the PC.

19. You are considering starting your own home and small business computer and network support business. While you know a great deal about the technology involved, you are a little unclear about the business end of things. Of the following, what are elements you may want to include in your business? (Choose three.)

   A. Time and cost estimate sheets

   B. An invoice of services and parts

   C. A customer questionnaire about their computer problems

   D. Customer confidentiality sheet for the customer to sign

20. You are performing a data restore on a home customer's computer after a crash when you notice a large amount of unprotected information about the customer's banking practices, PayPal transactions, and other confidential data, including the customer's Social Security number. What should you do?

   A. Nothing. It's the customer's data. Restore it and ignore it.

   B. Advise the customer that this data could potentially be located and copied from his computer and advise him of what security measures he should take to protect his data.

   C. Make a personal backup of this data and take it back to your shop, just in case the customer loses it in the future.

   D. Place this data in an encrypted directory on the computer and then tell the customer what you did and why.

Objective 801:5.4   Explain the Fundamentals of Dealing with Prohibited Content/Activity

21. You work for a small city IT department and you have just finished reinstalling an application that had become corrupted on a computer used in the finance department. In the process of testing the application by opening various documents and graphics files, you discover numerous files containing adult material, the possession of which on work computers is strictly prohibited by company policy. What is the first action you must take in response to this discovery?

A. Identify the specific nature of the material, verifying that it is in violation of company policy and/or law.

B. Report the discovery through the proper channels as established by policy.

C. Create copies of the adult material to be presented to the proper authority such as the HR department.

D. Immediately power down the computer and remove it to a secure location as established by policy.

22. You work for the IT department of a company that has developed a Software as a Service (SaaS) product that is designed to protect hospitals and other medical agencies from having sensitive patient data being accessed by unauthorized individuals over the Internet. Your company's product is highly competitive, and the development details of the product are formally considered trade secrets. You have been conducting routine maintenance on your company's e-mail server and discovered that one employee has been sending a large number of confidential company documents as e-mail attachments to an unknown third party, which is a violation of the trade secrets provisions of your company's policies. Specifically in terms of documenting this situation for personnel action and legal purposes, what are your duties? (Choose all that apply.)

A. Fill out an incident report or otherwise document all of the steps you took to discover this information and how you determined who was involved in the improper behavior.

B. Document any personal knowledge you have of the suspected offender prior to this incident, including personal opinions and suspicions.

C. Document your actions after discovering the incident, being specific as far as who you notified and who was responsible for taking whatever further action was deemed necessary by policy and/or law.

D. Copy any files and logs from the e-mail server at the direction of the proper authority and give them to that authority as established by company policy.

QUICK ANSWER KEY

1. A	9. B	17. A, B
2. D	10. A, D	18. A, B, D
3. A, B	11. A, D	19. A, B, C
4. C	12. B, C	20. B
5. A	13. B	21. A
6. A	14. A	22. A, C, D
7. C	15. A	
8. C	16. C	

IN-DEPTH ANSWERS

1. ☑ **A.** While it's best practice to always use an ESD strap and mat to minimize the potential of damaging the electrical components inside the machine, after opening the case, you can briefly grip the unpainted metal frame of the computer case to dissipate any static electricity before putting your hands inside the machine.

    ☒ **B, C,** and **D** are incorrect. **B** is incorrect because continually touching the case panel won't dissipate your static electrical potential, or if it does, the process should only take a moment and not require continual contact. **C** is incorrect because the exterior of the case is often plastic and not metal, and touching the plastic case won't dissipate static electricity. **D** is incorrect because, while it is the ideal solution in one sense, you can reasonably work inside a computer by touching the metal frame first, and your customer may not want to wait for you to retrieve your ESD mat and strap to ground yourself and the PC.

2. ☑ **D.** A power supply, even when completely unplugged and removed from a computer, stores enough electrical energy in its capacitors to deliver a severe and even fatal shock. Never open a power supply unless you have had special training and have the proper equipment.

    ☒ **A, B,** and **C** are incorrect. **A** is incorrect because unplugging the power supply from an electrical socket or power strip doesn't remove the danger of electrical shock, since the unit's capacitors store a large electrical charge. **B** is incorrect because the primary danger in opening a power supply is not to the computer. **C** is incorrect because the primary danger in opening a power supply isn't to the power supply's internal connections.

3. ☑ **A** and **B.** Loose sleeves, a ring, or loose jewelry such as a necklace dangling inside the case of a running computer could be caught on moving parts or accidentally come in contact with electrical components inside the PC, which could injure you and damage the computer.

    ☒ **C** and **D** are incorrect. **C** is incorrect because an ESD strap is designed to be used inside of a computer case and to prevent electrical mishaps. **D** is incorrect because running a computer without its cover in place may reduce the potential for the CPU and other components from overheating. However, it is not recommended that a computer be allowed to run for more than a short time without the cover in place due to the risk of accidentally touching and damaging an internal component.

4. ☑ **C.** The power specifications of the power supply and motherboard may not match. This could result in the computer being unable to boot if the power produced by the power supply is insufficient or the computer's electronic components being "fried" from too much power.
☒ **A, B,** and **D** are incorrect. **A** is incorrect because there is no such thing as a "one size fits all" power supply. **B** is incorrect because a form factor "mismatch" isn't the only problem with putting a "random" power supply in a computer. **D** is incorrect because the power supply's selector switch is used to set the power supply to use different electrical output types used in different parts of the world, not to select between different motherboard specifications.

5. ☑ **A.** The primary safety concern when laying networking cable is to make sure the cable is out of the way and doesn't present a tripping hazard.
☒ **B, C,** and **D** are incorrect. **B** is incorrect because networking cable typically doesn't carry electrical current unless it's specifically for PoE (Power over Ethernet). **C** is incorrect because network cables cannot present an electrostatic discharge hazard to servers. **D** is incorrect because, while correctly labeling network cables is desirable, it's not a safety concern.

6. ☑ **A.** The most immediate hazard is that the technician may lose his grip and cause the heavy carton to fall on him. To avoid this, if necessary, a ladder can be used so that the carton can be pulled at chest level and then lowered. If the carton is heavy, the technician should ask someone else for help with this task, or a special piece of equipment may have to be used to grip and move the carton.
☒ **B, C,** and **D** are incorrect. **B** is incorrect because a lower back injury is more likely when moving a heavy object off the floor without bending at the knees. **C** is incorrect because a knee injury isn't a very immediate danger in this circumstance. **D** is incorrect because the technician is not performing the task in the safest manner available.

7. ☑ **C.** CRT monitors contain lead and other hazardous materials and must be disposed of in a manner that is environmentally safe. Usually, a licensed recycling center will be able to safely manage these materials.
☒ **A, B,** and **D** are incorrect. **A** is incorrect because it is illegal to dispose of hazardous materials by putting them in landfill trash. **B** is incorrect because there are safe ways of disposing of CRT monitors, and the city doesn't have to store them indefinitely. **D** is incorrect because, unless the manufacturer specifically offers a recycling program for their old CRT monitors, mailing this equipment to them isn't a suitable disposal method.

8. ☑ **C.** The MSDS (Material Safety Data Sheet) sticker indicates the general characteristics of the chemical, particularly regarding any safety or disposal issues. An MSDS document is a standard form that also contains this information and provides data on how to handle and work with chemicals in a safe way. Other information may include melting point, boiling point, flash point, toxicity, health effects, reactivity, and health treatment requirements.

☒ **A, B,** and **D** are incorrect. **A** and **B** are incorrect because the sticker does not specify the use of this chemical as a battery contact cleaner. **D** is incorrect because this sticker is not specific to a particular chemical manufacturer.

9. ☑ **B.** The safest way to store an expansion card until you are ready to install it in a computer is in a specialized antistatic bag or similar container. This will protect the delicate components in the card from ESD damage.

☒ **A, C,** and **D** are incorrect. **A** is incorrect because if the card is placed on a workbench for any length of time, it is vulnerable to ESD damage and possibly dust contamination. **C** is incorrect because placing a collection of expansion cards together haphazardly in a box will likely result in several of the cards being damaged. **D** is incorrect because contact with the tools and other objects in the toolkit are likely to damage the card.

10. ☑ **A and D.** A can of compressed air is the most common safe method of removing dust and debris from the inside of a computer case. Make sure you hold the can upright when in use to avoid any liquids or chemicals used for the propellant from being leaked into the PC case. If you are going to use a vacuum cleaner inside a computer, only use one that is especially made for this purpose, as it will not cause a dangerous static discharge near computer components.

☒ **B and C** are incorrect. **B** is incorrect because an ammonia-based cleaner could severely damage computer components. Also a cotton rag likely will contain lint, which can damage components as well. **C** is incorrect because an electric home vacuum cleaner will create static electricity, which will damage computer components.

11. ☑ **A and D.** The toner in laser printers is composed of very fine particles of clay mixed with pigments and resin, and may cause choking or other respiratory problems if inhaled. Dust inside a computer case may also cause similar breathing problems.

☒ **B and C** are incorrect. **B** is incorrect because while dust may cause some breathing problems, it is not toxic. **C** is incorrect because electrical components inside a computer case do not routinely emit toxic gases.

12. ☑ **B and C.** The sudden change in temperature, while unlikely to cause the motherboard to warp, could result in some of the more delicate components in the laptop to break. Also, humidity is a great concern in this situation, and the sudden temperature change could result in condensation forming inside the laptop. Once it is powered up, this could result in short-circuiting inside the laptop, destroying the computer.

☒ **A and D** are incorrect. **A** is incorrect because such a temperature change, while not ideal, is unlikely to cause the motherboard to warp. **D** is incorrect because computers tend to be more tolerant of cold than heat, so it is not a foregone conclusion that being left in a car in winter conditions overnight will result in LCD screen damage.

13. ☑ **B.** Power sags or dips are the most likely cause of computer reboots in this situation, and a power strip cannot protect against variability in power flow, since it is basically just an extension cord with multiple plug-ins. It should be replaced with a surge protector or better yet, an uninterruptable power supply (UPS), which can treat power variability and provide the customer's computer with a very even power flow. It can also provide battery backup in the event of a brownout or blackout.

    ☒ **A, C,** and **D** are incorrect. **A** is incorrect because, although a power strip does not protect against power surges, power sags are a more likely cause of computer reboots. **C** is incorrect because if the power strip had gone bad, no power at all would be supplied to the computer. **D** is incorrect because a power strip of any kind should be able to support one or more computers.

14. ☑ **A.** Since you need information about local government regulations, start by contacting a local recycling provider listed in the government pages of the phone book and acquire the proper information from them.

    ☒ **B, C,** and **D** are incorrect. **B** is incorrect because the various hardware vendors for all of the items requiring disposal are unlikely to have information about your local recycling regulations. **C** is incorrect because the national EPA Website is not likely to contain information about local disposal regulations for computer components. **D** is incorrect because your local regulations may not allow you to simply drop off computer components at any recycling center.

15. ☑ **A.** Even when you feel frustrated over the difficulty of a technical repair job, maintain a calm and positive attitude. There are some situations where the customer may expect you to quickly and easily repair their computer problem when, in fact, it will be a rather lengthy process. Describing the situation in a professional manner will help the customer to have more realistic expectations and reduce the amount of stress you feel at having to "perform."

    ☒ **B, C,** and **D** are incorrect. **B** is incorrect because the customer may feel entitled to watch you work on his property and asking him to leave the room could damage his trust in your abilities. **C** is incorrect because, even if the customer did directly cause the problem with the computer, blaming the customer does not communicate a professional attitude. **D** is incorrect because ignoring the customer's query and leaving the room just to decrease your anxiety won't communicate confidence and professionalism.

16. ☑ **C.** If you are going to be unavoidably late to an appointment, call the person and explain that you are running late and, if appropriate, why. If you can, let them know your new estimated arrival time and then finish the current job. While it's ideal to always be on time for all appointments, you will sometimes encounter a repair problem that takes longer than expected, disrupting the rest of your schedule. As best as you can, try to schedule appointments so that you have a reasonable expectation of being on time for each visit.

☒ **A, B,** and **D** are incorrect. **A** is incorrect because your next customer is expecting you at a specific time. If you simply don't show up on time, they have no way of knowing if you are going to be late and, if so, how late, so they can, if necessary, make other arrangements in their own schedule. **B** is incorrect because it is unfair and unreasonable to expect your next customer to wait a day for a service that was scheduled today. Also, many people often have to disrupt their work schedule to make such appointments and you would be further interrupting your customer's schedule by making such a request. **D** is incorrect because it is unfair and unreasonable to make your current customer wait for repairs that were supposed to be finished today, just so you can keep the rest of your schedule.

17. ☑ **A and B.** While the occasional important or even emergency phone call from family or a friend may be unavoidable, continuing to run your social life while you are supposed to be working will communicate unprofessionalism and disrespect, and it will certainly put you behind schedule. Also, taking unauthorized individuals on the job with you is inappropriate and most likely a violation of company policy. In addition, having a friend present will likely result in a great deal of time-consuming social interaction that will interrupt work activities.

☒ **C and D** are incorrect. **C** is incorrect because it is reasonable for a person to use the restroom during various break periods in the work day. **D** is incorrect because, occasionally, a technician may need to make brief contact with a family member in order to ensure that an important responsibility is met. These calls need to be kept as brief as possible.

18. ☑ **A, B,** and **D.** If you ask customers "yes" or "no" questions about the computer problem, you are imposing your assumptions about the problem by the nature of your questions. Letting the customer explain things in her own way may take a little longer, but you'll get a better idea of what she experiences with her computer. Repeating what she has said using your own words verifies that you have correctly understood her description and comprehend what the problem is from her viewpoint. Sometimes just having the customer show you what the problem is by reproducing it on the computer is a fast and efficient way to get to the core of the problem. Also, if any cultural differences between you and the customer are involved in any communication difficulties, be sensitive to these needs rather than expecting the customer to conform to your culture's communications style.

☒ **C** is incorrect because you are asking the customer to explain things using your vocabulary, which may be difficult or impossible for her.

19. ☑ **A, B,** and **C.** It's helpful to look at other businesses that are similar to yours and that you use as a customer and see what forms and practices you have come to expect. You may want to develop an estimates form so that you can give written notice to a customer of the repairs you intend to do and the estimated cost before work begins. You may also want to give customers a written invoice of all the work you have done on their computer broken down by parts and labor. While interviewing a customer about their computer problems is the usual way to learn more about their situation, you can also e-mail them a brief questionnaire for them to fill out before your first visit, so you can get a better idea of the situation.

    ☒ **D** is incorrect because customers aren't expected to keep anything about your work or practice confidential, and certainly they aren't expected to sign such a statement.

20. ☑ **B.** No information on a computer connected to a network and especially to the Internet is absolutely safe, and the data you found could be used by an unscrupulous person to remove money from the customer's accounts and to steal the customer's identity. Let the customer know the risk involved and suggest appropriate security measures.

    ☒ **A, C,** and **D** are incorrect. **A** is incorrect because the customer may not know the risk of allowing sensitive information to remain in an unprotected state on his computer. **C** is incorrect because you have no legal or ethical right to take personal information about a customer and store it without his knowledge and consent. **D** is incorrect because you should inform the customer of any security risks, offer security options, and then let the customer make the final decision. It's unprofessional and unethical for you to make such security decisions for a customer and then later inform the customer of your decision about his data.

21. ☑ **A.** Your first response when you become aware of any forbidden material on a work computer or any suspicious behavior by coworkers in relation to the company's technology is to identify the specific nature of the material or behavior, verifying that it is actually prohibited by policy and/or law. After this, your duties then include reporting that material or behavior and then preserving the evidence, such as confiscating the computer or copying logs, which is done in accordance to company policy and at the direction of the proper company authority such as the head of IT or HR.

    ☒ **B, C,** and **D** are incorrect. **B** is incorrect because you must first identify the specific nature of the material. **C** and **D** are incorrect because after identifying the material, you must report the incident through the proper channels and then receive instructions regarding the actions to be taken to preserve evidence.

22.   ☑   **A, C,** and **D.** If your company has a formal incident report form, you will be required to complete it, detailing everything you did to discover the improper behavior and how you determined who committed the potential breach. This is important, as accusing someone of a violation of company policy as well as illegal behavior can have serious consequences, so the evidence that supports the allegations must be clearly established. Preserving evidence properly is important so that it can be established how information was managed at each step after the initial discovery of inappropriate activity. This reduces the likelihood that it could be tampered with, damaged, or lost if the chain of evidence is not maintained. Also, any specific data, such as logs or other documentation, should be copied and given to the person or group authorized to take any subsequent steps in this matter, which can include the HR department, any internal security group, and law enforcement.

☒   **B** is incorrect because your personal opinions of anyone suspected of a policy or legal violation are not relevant as evidence and may actually result in legal difficulties if the suspect can state that they have been accused because you, as a company employee, were biased against them.

2

Operating System Fundamentals

❑ **802: 1.1** Compare and contrast the features and requirements of various Microsoft operating systems.

QUESTIONS

As an A+ technician, you are expected to have a basic understanding of the various Microsoft Windows operating systems, from Windows XP to Windows 7, including upgrade paths, user interfaces, system requirements, and so on. Some of the most common questions and issues your customers will have are Windows related.

Objective 802: 1.1 Compare and Contrast the Features and Requirements of Various Microsoft Operating Systems

1. You have a customer who makes extensive use of the Windows Sidebar tool in Windows Vista to dock features such as Calendar, Contacts, and Stocks. He has upgraded his computer to Windows 7 and now can't find the Stocks gadget. What do you tell him?

   A. Microsoft added some gadgets to the Windows 7 Sidebar but permanently removed others, including Stocks.

   B. The Stocks gadget is not available by default in the Windows 7 Sidebar as it was in Windows Vista, but can be downloaded for free from the Microsoft Gadgets Gallery.

   C. The Stocks gadget is not available by default in Windows 7 as it was in Windows Vista, but can be downloaded from a third-party vendor for a small fee.

   D. The Windows Sidebar feature was removed from Windows 7.

2. You have a customer who is considering upgrading from Windows Vista to Windows 7. She particularly likes the Windows Aero interface and asks you what has been changed in Aero for Windows 7. What do you say? (Choose two.)

   A. Aero Peek was added.

   B. Aero Snap was added.

   C. Live thumbnails were added.

   D. Live icons were added.

3. You are having a discussion with another tech about the level of security Windows runs during the installation of application software. The other tech criticizes Windows for automatically installing software with the permission levels of the user logged on, which is almost always as an administrator. What Windows security feature do you mention that limits application software installation to standard user privileges until an administrator authorizes increased permission levels?

   A. Sysinternals

   B. UAC

   C. Wininternals

   D. WinXPatch

4. You are reviewing the system requirements for different Windows operating system versions. Of the following, which hard drive space requirements are correct?

   A. Windows 7 Professional requires 2 GB hard disk space for the 32-bit version and 16 GB for the 64-bit.

   B. Windows XP Home requires at least 1.5 GB of available hard drive space.

   C. Windows XP Professional requires at least 2.5 GB of available hard drive space.

   D. Windows Vista Home Basic requires a 40 GB hard drive with at least 15 GB of available space.

5. You have a customer using a Windows XP Professional computer and he wants to know if he can perform a direct upgrade to any version of Windows 7. What do you tell him?

   A. He can upgrade Windows XP Professional to Windows 7 Professional, Enterprise, or Ultimate.

   B. He can upgrade Windows XP Professional to Windows 7 Professional or Enterprise.

   C. He can upgrade Windows XP Professional to Windows 7 Professional.

   D. A direct upgrade from Windows XP Professional to any version of Windows 7 is unsupported.

6. You have a customer who received a PC running 64-bit Windows Vista as a gift from a family member. She doesn't understand what "64-bit" is supposed to mean. What do you tell her? (Choose two.)

   A. A 64-bit computer can process information faster than a 32-bit computer.

   B. A 64-bit computer can support both 32-bit and 64-bit device drivers.

   C. A 64-bit computer can support all 32-bit and 64-bit applications.

   D. A 64-bit computer can address more than 4 GB of memory.

7. You have a customer using a 64-bit Windows Vista computer who tries to run a program and gets an error message saying the program cannot start or run due to incompatibility with 64-bit versions of Windows. What happened?

   A. He's trying to run a 32-bit program on 64-bit Windows Vista.

   B. He's trying to run a 32-bit program using 64-bit device drivers on 64-bit Windows Vista.

   C. He's trying to run a 64-bit program using 32-bit device drivers on 64-bit Windows Vista.

   D. He's trying to run a program that is only compatible with Windows XP on 64-bit Windows Vista.

8. You have a customer using a Windows 7 computer who tried to run a program that ran effectively on his Windows XP machine but now refuses to run on Windows 7. What is the most direct solution that will most likely allow him to run the program on his current platform?

   A. He can install a virtual Windows XP machine on Windows 7 to run the program.

   B. He can try to find a version of the program that will run on Windows 7.

   C. He can continue to use the program on a Windows XP machine.

   D. He can run the program in Windows Compatibility Mode.

9. You have a customer who uses a Windows 7 computer but is unfamiliar with some of the symbols and applets on the notification area. She sees what looks like a small flag in the notification area on the right as depicted in the accompanying screenshot. What does it mean?

   A. You click the flag to show hidden icons.

   B. You click the flag to show warning messages.

   C. You click the flag to show just the desktop.

   D. You click the flag to open the Control Panel.

10. You have a customer who used to use the Virtual Folders feature for Windows Explorer in Windows XP. She now has a Windows 7 computer, which uses Libraries in Windows Explorer instead of Virtual Folders. She is unfamiliar with this new feature. Of the following, which do you tell her are the default Windows 7 libraries? (Choose three.)

    A. Documents

    B. Music

    C. Templates

    D. Videos

11. You have a customer who wants to buy a new Windows 7 computer but who needs to run some applications that will only operate on Windows XP. What do you suggest as a solution to this customer?

    A. You tell the customer to purchase Windows 7 Home Premium edition or higher, since those editions come with XP Mode, which is a virtual Windows XP environment that will allow the customer to run the required applications.

    B. You tell the customer to purchase Windows 7 Professional edition or higher, since those editions will allow him to download and install Windows XP Mode and Virtual PC and will allow the customer to run the required applications.

    C. You tell the customer to purchase Windows 7 Enterprise edition or higher, since those editions come with XP Mode, which is a virtual Windows XP environment that will allow the customer to run the required applications.

    D. You tell the customer to purchase Windows 7 Ultimate, since it is the only edition of the Windows 7 operating system that comes with XP Mode, which is a virtual Windows XP environment that will allow the customer to run the required applications.

12. You have a customer who has just replaced her Windows XP computer with a Windows 7 computer. She went into the Control Panel of the Windows 7 computer, but didn't understand the views available. Of the following, what are the view options in a Windows 7 Control Panel? (Choose three.)

A. Category view
B. Classic view
C. Large icons
D. Small icons

13. You work for a small city IT department and are watching another, more experienced technician manually create a backup copy of data on a volume of a Windows 7 computer. This backup technology can use a hardware provider that abstracts the functionality to the operating system to manage the data copy process. The technician opens a command prompt window as an administrator and types the command "vssadmin list providers" to display all installed hardware providers on the Windows 7 machine. Which backup method is this technician using?
    A. Easy Transfer
    B. Restore Point
    C. Shadow Copy
    D. System Restore

14. You have a customer who wants to use the latest version of the BitLocker drive encryption utility on her Windows Vista Enterprise edition computer to encrypt the data on a USB thumb drive. What do you tell her?
    A. You tell her that she will be able to successfully use BitLocker on Windows Vista Enterprise for this task.
    B. You tell her that she will only be able to do this on a Windows Vista Ultimate edition computer.
    C. You tell her that she will only be able to do this on a Windows 7 computer.
    D. You tell her that BitLocker cannot encrypt removable drives, regardless of which Windows operating system platform is used.

15. You work for the IT department of a small city, and one of the people in accounting needs a quick way to improve disk read performance on his Windows 7 computer. You suggest using Windows ReadyBoost. What is required to use ReadyBoost?
    A. An external storage device such as a USB thumb drive or SD card with at least 256 MB storage capacity
    B. An external storage device such as a USB thumb drive or SD card with at least 4 GB storage capacity
    C. A separate volume on an internal hard drive with at least 256 MB storage capacity
    D. A separate volume on an internal hard drive with at least 4 GB storage capacity

16. You have a customer who uses Windows Vista and wants to use an antispyware program. Your customer is concerned about price and asks you to suggest an effective software product for a minimal cost. You know that Windows Defender will suit your customer's needs. What do you tell her?

A. Windows Defender is an antispyware program that is free and built into Windows Vista.

B. Windows Defender is an antispyware program that is a free download for Windows Vista from Microsoft.

C. Windows Defender is an antispyware program that can be downloaded from Microsoft for Windows Vista for a modest fee.

D. Windows Defender is an antispyware program that can be downloaded from a third-party vendor for Windows Vista for a modest fee.

17. You are performing a check of the security systems on a customer's Windows Vista computer. You open the Windows Security Center in the Control Panel. Of the following options, which security essentials can you turn on, off, or modify the settings for in Security Center? (Choose all that apply.)

A. Automatic Updating

B. Backup and Restore

C. Firewall

D. Malware Protection

18. You have just purchased a 64-bit Windows 7 Ultimate computer and are familiarizing yourself with how the directory structure is laid out. As you examine the OS (C:) directory, which folders do you find are located there by default? (Choose all that apply.)

A. Drivers

B. Microsoft Office

C. PerfLogs

D. Program Files (x86)

19. You work for a small city IT department and you are training a new intern in your department. You decide to show her the different methods of opening the Event Viewer on a Windows 7 computer. Of the following, which methods will cause Event Viewer to be opened? (Choose all that apply.)

A. Open Control Panel, double-click Administrative Tools, and then double-click Event Viewer.

B. Click the Start button, type **event viewer** in the Search box, and then click Event Viewer.

C. Click the Start button, type **event viewer** in the Search box, and then click View Event Logs.

D. Click the Start button, type **cmd** in the Search box, right-click cmd.exe, select Run As Administrator, and then at the control prompt, type **event viewer**.

20. You have an older game on your Windows 7 computer that will only run under Windows XP Service Pack 2. You want to run it using Compatibility Mode, which will allow the game to behave as if it were running on a Windows XP machine with Service Pack 2. What is the correct method of getting this game to run as desired?

A. Go into Control Panel, open Programs and Features, right-click the desired program, and then click Compatibility Mode.

B. Go into Control Panel, open Programs, right-click the desired program, and then click Use An Older Program With This Version Of Windows.

C. Go to the location of the program's executable file, right-click this file, click Properties, and then on the Compatibility tab, select Run This Program In Compatibility Mode For and then select Windows XP (Service Pack 2) in the menu.

D. Go to the location of the program's executable file, right-click this file, click Compatibility Mode, select Run this program in compatibility mode, and then select Windows XP Service Pack 2.

21. You want to modify the appearance of the taskbar at the bottom of your Windows 7 machine's screen. Where can you perform this task? (Choose three.)

A. Right-click the taskbar and click Properties.

B. Open the Control Panel and click Taskbar And Start Menu.

C. Right-click the Computer icon on the desktop and click Properties.

D. Right-click the Windows Start button and click Properties.

22. You are discussing the differences between 32-bit bus and 64-bit bus Windows operating systems for Windows Vista and Windows 7 with a customer who is trying to decide which OS to select for a new computer. One of the differences you describe is that 64-bit operating systems are able to use more RAM than 32-bit operating systems. You show your customer a chart of the different versions of Windows Vista and Windows 7 and the amount of memory they use. Your customer asks why Windows Vista Starter and Windows 7 Starter editions only have a single RAM amount limit, regardless of the bus type. What do you tell him?

A. Starter editions only come as 32-bit operating systems.

B. Starter editions only come as 64-bit operating systems.

C. Starter editions can only use the same amount of memory, regardless if they are 32-bit or 64-bit.

D. Starter editions are only installed on computers with motherboards that support up to 2 GB of memory, regardless if the operating system is 32-bit or 64-bit.

QUICK ANSWER KEY

1.	B	**9.**	B	**17.**	A, C, D
2.	A, B	**10.**	A, B, D	**18.**	A, C, D
3.	B	**11.**	B	**19.**	A, B, C
4.	B	**12.**	A, C, D	**20.**	C
5.	D	**13.**	C	**21.**	A, B, D
6.	A, D	**14.**	C	**22.**	A
7.	A	**15.**	A		
8.	D	**16.**	B		

IN-DEPTH ANSWERS

1. ☑ **B.** Microsoft added some gadgets to the Windows 7 Sidebar and removed others, including Stocks, but Stocks can be downloaded for free from the Microsoft Gadgets Gallery site.

   ☒ **A, C,** and **D** are incorrect. **A** is incorrect because, although Stocks is not available by default for Sidebar, it can be downloaded and installed for free. **C** is incorrect because the Stocks gadget is available as a free download from Microsoft. **D** is incorrect because the Sidebar feature is present in Windows 7.

2. ☑ **A** and **B.** In Windows 7, Microsoft added a number of new Aero features, including Aero Peek, which lets you hover over a taskbar icon to show a thumbnail of the program, and Aero Snap, which causes a window to resize and to occupy different areas of the screen depending on where you drag the window. Other features include Aero Shake and an improved Aero blur effect.

   ☒ **C** and **D** are incorrect because they were standard features of Aero in Windows Vista.

3. ☑ **B.** UAC, or User Account Control, is a technology introduced with Windows Vista and continues to be used with Windows 7. UAC notifies the computer user when an application is trying to be installed or run and will only let that application have access to the system with standard user privileges until a user with administrator rights gives the application an increase in rights for installation or so it can run.

   ☒ **A, C,** and **D** are incorrect. **A** is incorrect because Sysinternals is a part of the Microsoft TechNet Website that offers technical resources and utilities designed to troubleshoot Windows problems. **C** is incorrect because Wininternals is fictitious. **D** is incorrect because WinXPatch is a third-party Windows Registry "tweaking" tool used to perform Windows security upgrades.

4. ☑ **B.** Windows XP Home requires at least 1.5 GB of available space on the hard disk. Keep in mind these are the bare minimum requirements. To use any of these systems under normal, production conditions, you'll need more hard drive space.

   ☒ **A, C,** and **D** are incorrect. **A** is incorrect because Windows 7 requires 16 GB available hard disk space for the 32-bit version and 20 GB for the 64-bit version. **C** is incorrect because the hard drive space requirements for Windows XP Professional are identical to those of Windows XP Home. **D** is incorrect because Windows Vista Home Basic requires a 40 GB hard drive with at least 20 GB of available space.

5. ☑ **D.** There is no direct upgrade path for any version of Windows XP to any version of Windows 7. The most common upgrade paths to Windows 7 are from their equivalent versions in Windows Vista. This means, for example, Windows Vista Business, Enterprise, and Ultimate (SP1 and 2) can upgrade to Windows 7 Professional, Enterprise, and Ultimate, respectively.

   ☒ **A, B,** and **C** are incorrect because there is no direct upgrade path for any version of Windows XP to any version of Windows 7.

6. ☑ **A** and **D.** 64-bit processors provide better performance and data throughput than 32-bit processors, resulting in their performing the same tasks faster. A 32-bit computer can address up to 4 GB of physical memory, while a 64-bit computer can address much more. Often 32-bit architectures are referred to as x86, a term derived from successors of the early 8086 processors (all ending in the number "86"). The term x86-64, or usually just x64, is used to differentiate between 32-bit and 64-bit processing platforms.

   ☒ **B** and **C** are incorrect. **B** is incorrect because 32-bit device drivers are not supported on a 64-bit architecture. **C** is incorrect because not all 32-bit software applications are able to run natively on a 64-bit computer.

7. ☑ **A.** This error message appears when a program or feature cannot start because it is a 32-bit application that is trying to run on but is not compatible with a 64-bit environment.

   ☒ **B, C,** and **D** are incorrect. **B** is incorrect because a 32-bit program doesn't use 64-bit drivers. **C** is incorrect because a 64-bit program doesn't use 32-bit drivers. **D** is incorrect because the program would be able to run on most 32-bit Windows systems and is not specifically designed for Windows XP.

8. ☑ **D.** Windows Compatibility Mode allows you to run legacy programs on Windows 7 in an environment compatible with an earlier version of Windows such as Windows XP. This isn't an absolute solution since 9 out of 10 times, the Compatibility Assistant will run and suggest running the program in a virtual machine (VM) and point you to download XP Mode and a virtual software program.

   ☒ **A, B,** and **C** are incorrect. **A** is incorrect because, while it would work if he installed a virtualization application on his computer, it is not the most direct method. **B** is incorrect because, although it would work if he could find a compatible version of the program, it isn't the most direct method. **C** is incorrect because he wouldn't be running the program on his current platform.

9. ☑ **B.** Clicking the flag shows any available warning messages such as those involving configuring backup settings or Windows Update. You can also open the Action Center, which will show you the warning messages in more detail and lets you solve problems on the computer detected by the Action Center.

   ☒ **A, C,** and **D** are incorrect because clicking the flag will perform none of those actions. Click the arrow pointing up that's at the left of the flag to show hidden icons. Right-click the system tray and then click Show The Desktop to show the desktop. Click the Windows button and then click Control Panel to show the Control Panel.

10. ☑ **A, B,** and **D.** Windows 7 comes with four libraries by default: Documents, Music, Pictures, and Videos. Libraries aren't associated with specific folders on the Windows 7 computer, but rather they contain links to files and folders anywhere on the hard drive and local network. You can also create custom libraries.

    ☒ **C** is incorrect because it is not a default library on Windows 7.

11. ☑ **B.** Virtual PC and Windows XP Mode are downloads available for Windows 7 Professional, Ultimate, and Enterprise. They can be installed to provide a virtual environment that will allow the customer to run Windows XP–compatible applications.

    ☒ **A, C,** and **D** are incorrect. **A** is incorrect because XP Mode is not available for Windows 7 Home Premium. **C** and **D** are incorrect because XP Mode is available for Windows 7 Professional as well as Windows 7 Enterprise and Windows 7 Ultimate editions.

12. ☑ **A, C,** and **D.** While Category view is still present, your other view choices in the Windows 7 Control Panel are "classic" views using either large or small icons.

    ☒ **B** is incorrect because there is no single Classic View option for Control Panel in Windows 7.

13. ☑ **C.** Shadow Copy is a method of taking an automatic or manual backup or snapshot of data on a specified volume of a computer. It uses the Volume Snapshot Service (VSS), which was originally used on Windows XP and Windows Server 2003. Running the command "vssadmin list providers" will return the Provider type, which is System, by default; the Provider ID number; and the version of the Shadow Copy provider.

    ☒ **A, B,** and **D** are incorrect. **A** is incorrect because Easy Transfer is a Windows 7 feature that allows you to transfer files from one computer to another if you are switching or upgrading from one computer to another. **B** is incorrect because a restore point is a specific condition of a computer used by the System Restore utility, which is available with Windows XP and up, to roll back the operating system files, programs, and so forth, to a previous state, but is not a backup or snapshot technology. **D** is incorrect because System Restore uses restore points to roll back a Windows operating system to a previous state.

14. ☑ **C.** The latest version of BitLocker, which is included on Windows 7 and Windows Server 2008 R2, can encrypt removable drives. These encrypted removable drives can be read but not written to by Windows XP using the Microsoft BitLocker To Go Reader application.

☒ **A, B,** and **D** are incorrect. **A** and **B** are incorrect because the versions of BitLocker on Windows Vista Enterprise and Ultimate editions cannot encrypt removable drives. **D** is incorrect because BitLocker on Windows 7 and Windows Server 2008 R2 can encrypt removable drives.

15. ☑ **A.** The Windows ReadyBoost feature uses external drives such as USB flash drives, SD (secure digital) cards, and CF (compact flash) cards to improve disk read performance. The external storage device requires a minimum storage capacity of 256 MB with at least 64 KB of free space. Performance enhancement of SSD drives is not supported. Windows 7 will disable ReadyBoost if an SSD drive is being used.

☒ **B, C,** and **D** are incorrect. **B** is incorrect because only 256 MB storage is required. **C** and **D** are incorrect because ReadyBoost uses external drives, not a volume on an internal drive.

16. ☑ **B.** While Windows Defender antispyware software is built into Windows 7, it is a free download for Windows XP and Windows Vista.

☒ **A, C,** and **D** are incorrect. **A** is incorrect because Windows Defender is not built into Windows Vista. **C** is incorrect because Microsoft does not charge a fee for downloading Windows Defender. **D** is incorrect because Windows Defender is produced by Microsoft and not a third-party vendor, and Microsoft does not charge for this product.

17. ☑ **A, C,** and **D.** The Windows Security Center in Windows Vista allows you to turn on, off, or configure the Windows Firewall, automatic updating, malware protection, and other security settings, which includes restoring Internet security settings and restoring User Account Control settings.

☒ **B** is incorrect because Backup and Restore for Windows Vista cannot be configured from the Security Center.

18. ☑ **A, C,** and **D.** Directories included in the C: drive in 64-bit Windows 7 Ultimate, by default, include Drivers, PerfLogs, Program Files, Program Files (x86), and Users. You can see all of these folders in Windows Explorer if Show Hidden Files, Folders, And Drives is selected in Advanced Settings under the View tab in Folder Options.

☒ **B** is incorrect because the Microsoft Office directory is located in Program Files and Program Files (x86).

19. ☑ **A, B,** and **C.** You can access the Event Viewer by opening Administrative Tools in the Control Panel and then double-clicking the Event Viewer applet. You can also use the Search box to search for "event viewer" and click Event Viewer under Programs, or View Event Logs under Control Panel.

☒ **D** is incorrect because Event Viewer cannot be opened from the command prompt, even when run as an administrator. If you attempt this, you will receive an error message stating "event" is not recognized as an internal or external command, operable program, or batch file.

20. ☑ **C.** You must use Compatibility Mode from the Properties box of the .exe, .bat, .cmd, or .msi file of the program you want to run under an older version of Windows.

☒ **A, B,** and **D** are incorrect. **A** is incorrect because right-clicking a program name in Programs and Features does not allow you to run Compatibility Mode. **B** is incorrect because this set of steps only works in Windows Vista. **D** is incorrect because the option to run Compatibility Mode does not appear when you right-click the .exe file.

21. ☑ **A, B,** and **D.** Perform any of these actions to open the Taskbar and Start Menu Properties dialog box. If you right-click the Windows Start button, you will have to select the Taskbar tab, as the dialog box will open by default on the Start Menu tab.

☒ **C** is incorrect because right-clicking the Computer icon on the desktop and selecting Properties will not allow you to select taskbar properties.

22. ☑ **A.** Starter editions for Windows Vista and Windows 7 only come as 32-bit operating systems, so memory access is limited by that factor. Windows Vista Starter edition has a 1 GB RAM limit, while Windows 7 Starter edition has a 2 GB RAM limit.

☒ **B, C,** and **D** are incorrect. **B** is incorrect because Starter editions only come in 32-bit versions. **C** is incorrect because Starter editions do not come in 64-bit versions, only in 32-bit versions. **D** is incorrect because Starter editions of Windows Vista and Windows 7 are capable of being installed on PCs using a variety of different motherboards and their RAM usage limitations are not restricted solely by motherboard type.

3

Personal Computer Components: Motherboards and Processors

❑   **801: 1.1**   Configure and apply BIOS settings.

❑   **801: 1.2**   Differentiate between motherboard components, their purposes, and properties.

❑   **801:1.6**   Differentiate among various CPU types and features, and select the appropriate cooling method.

❑   **801:2.10**   Given a scenario, use appropriate networking tools.

QUESTIONS

Becoming a CompTIA A+ technician requires that you have a good grounding in the components and types of devices found in a PC system. The two primary components in PC systems are motherboards and CPUs (central processing units). Configuring BIOS settings is also vital, as those settings tell the computer how to manage PC hardware without the involvement of the operating system. Finally, it is important when performing basic networking tasks to know how to use all of the relevant tools.

Objective 801: 1.1   Configure and Apply BIOS Settings

1. You want to check to make sure your Windows 7 computer motherboard is using the latest BIOS version. What is the easiest way of determining the current version of your computer's BIOS?

    A. By pressing the ESC, F1, or F7 key and entering the BIOS setup.

    B. By opening the computer case and checking the specific make and model of the computer's motherboard.

    C. By going to the computer manufacturer's Website and looking up the version of BIOS your computer used when you purchased it.

    D. By typing **msinfo32** into the Search box in Windows.

2. You have determined that the motherboard of your Windows 7 computer requires a BIOS update to fix a bug and to allow it to use a faster CPU. For modern computers, what are your options for flashing the BIOS? (Choose all that apply.)

    A. Download the BIOS update executable file to your computer's hard drive and execute it from within Windows 7.

    B. Download the BIOS update executable to a USB flash drive and execute it from a command-line window.

    C. Download the BIOS update executable to a floppy diskette and execute it from the A:/ drive.

    D. Download the BIOS update executable to the CMOS chip and execute it from within the BIOS setup.

3. You are in the advanced section of the BIOS configuration utility on your computer and you notice that you can adjust the timings for the DRAM on your PC. In most cases, what is the default setting for DRAM memory timing?

    A. Auto

    B. DDR

    C. SPD

    D. The highest timing that your memory is capable of, expressed as a digital value

4. You are in the BIOS setup on your computer and are reviewing the different drive settings that are available. Of the following, which settings can you change in the BIOS? (Choose all that apply.)

A. The sequence in which the computer will look to different drives for the operating system boot sector

B. The ATA and PIO modes for parallel hard drives and optical drives on the computer

C. Enabling and disabling SATA drive channels

D. Setting the computer to use only ATA drives, only SATA drives, or both

5. You are in the BIOS setup on your computer and you notice that you can enable and disable both video and sound on the PC. Since both of these features seem to be required on a computer, why would you need to disable either of them?

A. If you have integrated video and sound on your computer and you want to upgrade these features by adding extension cards, you will need to disable the onboard video and sound controller and enable the new cards.

B. Video and sound are disabled when a computer is shipped from the factory and must be enabled in the BIOS before the computer is used for the first time.

C. If your video or sound card goes bad, you must disable these features in the BIOS before removing the old cards and replacing them with working hardware.

D. Enabling and disabling video and sound are only performed at the factory for testing purposes and you will never need to access these settings as a computer user or technician.

6. You are in the BIOS setup on your computer when a friend, who knows very little about PCs, notices that there are settings for date/time and clock speeds. He wants to know what the difference is between these two types of settings. What do you tell him?

A. You say that they are two redundant methods of setting the computer's internal clock.

B. You say that date/time manually sets the date and time the computer uses and clock speed sets the interval the clock waits between seconds.

C. You say that date/time only sets the format by which the computer displays date and time and clock speed controls the data transfer rate of the hard drive.

D. You say that date/time sets the date and time the computer recognizes as the present and clock speed controls the frequency by which the CPU processes instructions.

7. You want to run several different virtual machines on your Windows 7 computer but you need to enable virtualization in your computer's BIOS. You enter the BIOS setup and on the advanced screen, switch the setting for virtualization from disabled to enabled. After you are finished, you reboot the computer, but after Windows 7 loads, virtualization is still not enabled. What could have caused this? (Choose all that apply.)

A. You forgot to save your BIOS settings.

B. You should have let the computer boot into Windows 7 immediately after making changes in the BIOS rather than rebooting it.

C. You should have turned the computer off for several minutes and then restarted it after enabling virtualization in the BIOS.

D. You forgot to reset the BIOS administrator password before rebooting.

8. You work for a small city IT department and you are reviewing computer security procedures with other members of the IT team. One of your coworkers asks which form of security authenticates the hardware rather than the user. What do you tell her?

A. The BIOS user password

B. The BIOS supervisor password

C. The lojack system

D. TPM

9. You work for a small city IT department and you are reviewing BIOS monitoring and testing features. In your review, which of the following do you discover is the most common BIOS testing feature?

A. CPU temperature

B. Fan speeds

C. POST

D. Voltage

10. You work for a small city IT department. You have installed a new sound card in a computer used by the finance department and have rebooted the computer. You see a message displayed on the screen stating: "Alert! Cover was previously removed." What is causing this message to appear?

A. Chassis intrusion detection has been enabled in the BIOS.

B. The CPU temperature monitor in the BIOS detected a temperature variance based on the computer cover recently being open.

C. The lojack system is enabled in the BIOS.

D. This is a normal feature of the POST test in the latest BIOS versions.

Objective 801: 1.2 Differentiate Between Motherboard Components, Their Purposes, and Properties

11. You are working on a PC for a customer who has complained that his computer won't start. You suspect that there may be a loose connection or component on the motherboard. The customer believes that the motherboard in his computer is ATX, but when you open up the PC's case, you find out this isn't true. What tells you the motherboard is not an ATX form factor?

A. The board does not support standard ATX processors.

B. USB support is included.

C. It is too small physically to be an ATX board.

D. It uses a single power supply connection.

12. You are building a custom PC for a client and are using a motherboard that measures 6.7 by 6.7 inches and is designed to be passively cooled since the motherboard uses very little power. Of the following, which motherboard form factor are you installing?

A. ATX.

B. Micro-ATX.

C. ITX.

D. It is impossible to tell from the limited information available.

13. The PCI NIC card on a customer's computer has failed, and you have been tasked with replacing it. The computer is several years old and uses a PCI bus. The customer wants you to use a newer PCI Express card for the replacement because he has heard the PCI Express standard allows for faster data transfers and he believes it will give him a faster network and Internet connection. What do you tell him?

A. You tell the customer that PCI and PCI Express cards can use the same slots on the motherboard and the data transfer rates will give him a faster network connection.

B. You tell the customer that PCI and PCI Express cards are not compatible and cannot use the same slots, but if they could, he would experience faster network and Internet speeds.

C. You tell the customer that PCI and PCI Express cards are not compatible and cannot use the same slots, but if they could, he would not experience faster network and Internet speeds.

D. You tell the customer that PCI and PCI Express cards are really the same and PCI Express is just a lighter-weight card than PCI.

14. You are working on an older laptop adding a new Wi-Fi expansion card. The slot you are using on the motherboard can use cards that comply with the PCI v 2.2 standard and uses a 32-bit bus. Of the following, which is the most likely expansion slot you are using to install this card?

A. Mini PCI

B. PCI

C. PCI Express

D. PCI-X

15. You are working on an older computer that supports the AGP bus, and are replacing a faulty video card. The card you're installing is AGP 8x. How can you be sure that the AGP slot on the motherboard is correct for the expansion card?

A. AGP 8x slots are larger than AGP 2x and 4x slots and can only allow AGP 8x cards to be installed.

B. AGP 8x slots are larger than AGP 2x and 4x slots, but if the card is a different size, the 8x slot can accept smaller cards.

C. AGP slots are all the same size but the pin-outs for 2x, 4x, and 8x are completely different, so you will have to check the label on the slot to make sure it can take an AGP 8x card.

D. AGP slots are all the same size and the only difference between 2x, 4x, and 8x is the transfer rate speeds.

16. Which chipset on a motherboard is traditionally responsible for connecting AGP and DRAM buses directly to the CPU?

A. CMOS

B. CNR

C. Northbridge

D. Southbridge

17. You are working inside a computer with an ATX motherboard and are trying to differentiate between connectors. You see a large power connector with 24 pins. What type of connector is it?

A. It is a power connector for an ATA hard drive.

B. It is a power connector for the CPU.

C. It is the power connector for the motherboard.

D. It is the power connector for the audio card fan.

18. You work for a small city IT department and are training a new intern on computer basics. Using the accompanying illustration, which choice correctly identifies all of the buttons and lights found on the front of a computer case?

A. 1 is the hard drive power light, 2 is the computer power button, 5 are FireWire connectors, and 6 are the microphone and speaker ports.

B. 1 is the hard drive activity light, 2 is the reset button, 3 is the power button, and 5 are the USB ports.

C. 2 is the power button, 3 is the reset button, 4 is the hard drive activity light, and 5 are the USB ports.

D. 1 is the hard drive activity light, 3 is the power button, 5 are the network cable connections, and 6 are the microphone and speaker ports.

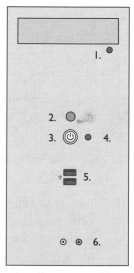

Objective 801: 1.6 Differentiate Among Various CPU Types and Features and Select the Appropriate Cooling Method

19. You are working on a customer's computer in her small business environment. It is a very old unit and is used as a simple print server. You are replacing the CPU assembly. Given the age of the computer, which of the following do you expect to be part of the CPU cooling solution? (Choose all that apply.)

   A. Fans

   B. Heat sink

   C. Liquid cooling

   D. Thermal paste

20. A customer of yours has expressed an interest in Intel's Hyper-Threading technology, which allows a single CPU to execute two threads or two sets of instructions at the same time, and asks if you can install an Intel Hyper-Threading CPU into his PC. You explain that his computer must possess a number of technologies that support Hyper-Threading, including which of the following? (Choose three.)

   A. A chipset that supports Hyper-Threading

   B. A system BIOS that supports Hyper-Threading

   C. A system CMOS that supports Hyper-Threading

   D. An operating system that supports Hyper-Threading

21. You are installing a Core i7 CPU in a computer you are building for a customer. What CPU socket type will the Core i7 most likely require on the motherboard?

   A. AM2

   B. AM3

   C. FM1

   D. 1366

22. You are evaluating CPU speeds and particularly the process of how a CPU can retrieve requested data from cache and memory. Of the following, which has the fastest data retrieval time and why?

   A. L1 cache is fastest because it's on the CPU.

   B. L1 cache is fastest because it's smallest.

   C. L2 cache is fastest because it's bigger than L1 cache.

   D. L3 cache is fastest because it works independently of L1 and L2.

Objective 801: 2.10 Given a Scenario, Use Appropriate Networking Tools

23. You work for a small city IT department and you are working with a team that is installing network cabling for a new wing in city hall. You are currently working with a device that has two physical components. Both units are small and can fit into the palm of your hand. The larger of the two units has two ports for RJ45 connectors and LEDs numbered one through eight. The second unit has a single port for an RJ45 connector and it also has LEDs numbered one through eight. Of the following, which device are you working with?

A. Cable tester

B. Multimeter

C. Toner probe

D. Loopback plug

QUICK ANSWER KEY

1.	D	9.	C	17.	C
2.	A, B	10.	A	18.	B
3.	A	11.	C	19.	A, B, D
4.	A, B, C	12.	C	20.	A, B, D
5.	A	13.	B	21.	D
6.	D	14.	A	22.	B
7.	A, C	15.	D	23.	A
8.	D	16.	C		

IN-DEPTH ANSWERS

1. ☑ **D.** The easiest way to determine the BIOS version on a Windows 7 computer is to type **msinfo32** in the Search box. That opens the System Information screen. Look for the BIOS Version/Date entry in the list to determine the BIOS maker, version, and date of the BIOS.

   ☒ **A, B,** and **C** are incorrect. **A** is incorrect because, while you can learn the version of the BIOS in the BIOS setup, it is not the easiest way to acquire this information. It should also be noted that, depending on your computer's BIOS, you can enter the BIOS setup through a number of different keys, such as pressing F1, F7, F10, ESC, or DEL. **B** is incorrect because you cannot tell the current version of BIOS your motherboard is using by looking at the motherboard. **C** is incorrect because, while you will be able to locate the latest BIOS version your computer uses at the manufacturer's site, you will not be able to tell what version it was using at the time you originally purchased your computer.

2. ☑ **A and B.** For modern computers, you can go to the computer manufacturer's Website and look up the make and model of your computer, then find the latest BIOS update. You can either download the executable to a directory on your hard drive and double-click it to start the update, or download it to a USB flash drive and execute it from the command line. Make sure to follow the manufacturer's instructions in each case, since the update process will vary from one vendor to another.

   ☒ **C and D** are incorrect. **C** is incorrect because modern computers typically don't come with a floppy diskette drive, and current methods of updating the BIOS don't require the use of floppy diskettes. **D** is incorrect because, while the CMOS chip stores basic configuration information for the computer, it cannot be used to store a BIOS update executable and to update the BIOS.

3. ☑ **A.** In most computer BIOS setups, the timing setting for memory is set to Auto, which allows the computer system to select the most optimal speed to use to ensure stability. This is probably not the fastest speed of which your memory is capable.

   ☒ **B, C,** and **D** are incorrect. **B** is incorrect because DDR stands for double data rate, which is a type of DRAM, but not the default setting for memory timing. **C** is incorrect because SPD stands for serial presence detect and is a feature available on all DDR memory modules and allows BIOS to more easily configure the computer to optimize DDR memory. **D** is incorrect because the default is set to the timing that is the most stable for your computer, which is usually not the fastest.

4. ☑ **A, B,** and **C.** The BIOS will allow you to set the boot order sequence for your computer so that specific drives are accessed first, second, third, and so on. For instance, a BIOS boot sequence can be set to look to boot the OS from a removable drive, then the optical drive, and then the hard drive. Parallel drives, also called ATA drives, can be set to use either ATA or PIO modes, which controls the data transfer rate. If your computer uses SATA drives, you can set which channels are active so that if you have two SATA drives installed on your computer, you can enable just the channels those two drives utilize.

    ☒ **D** is incorrect because there is no BIOS setting that lets you choose to have your computer access ATA vs. SATA drives or a combination of both. The ability for a computer to use different drive types is dependent both on the BIOS and the adapters available on the motherboard, but this specific BIOS selection screen is not available.

5. ☑ **A.** Some computers come with video and sound integrated in the motherboard; however, the quality and features of these controllers are limited. If you want to upgrade video and sound using extension cards, you will need to disable the onboard controllers and enable the video and sound cards you're installing in the BIOS setup.

    ☒ **B, C,** and **D** are incorrect. **B** is incorrect because video and sound features are not disabled for shipping. If they were, then when you took delivery of a computer, you would have to manually enter the BIOS and enable video and sound before the computer became usable. **C** is incorrect because you can remove a defective video or sound card from a computer without first disabling those cards in the BIOS. The BIOS should automatically detect when you exchange cards, but on some occasions, you may have to enter the BIOS and enable the new device if the computer doesn't recognize the new card. **D** is incorrect because enabling and disabling devices is not just a task performed by the computer maker for testing purposes.

6. ☑ **D.** You can set the date and time in the BIOS so the computer's date and time will match the "present." Clock speed has nothing to do with date and time, and this BIOS setting controls how fast the CPU is able to process instructions within the limits of the processor's physical abilities.

    ☒ **A, B,** and **C** are incorrect. **A** is incorrect because the date/time and clock speed settings control totally different features. **B** is incorrect because while the first part of the answer is true, clock speed doesn't literally control how fast the computer's internal clock processes seconds. **C** is incorrect because date/time sets the actual date and time for the computer, not the format by which the date and time is displayed, and clock speed does not set the hard drive's data transfer rate.

7. ☑ **A** and **C.** The most common reason a change in the BIOS doesn't take effect is because users forget to save their BIOS settings before exiting the BIOS. Also, the enabling process for virtualization typically requires that the computer be completely shut down for several minutes and then a "cold restart" of the machine is performed.

   ☒ **B** and **D** are incorrect. **B** is incorrect because the proper procedure does not require booting immediately into the operating system after enabling virtualization in the BIOS. **D** is incorrect because enabling virtualization does not require setting or resetting any password in the BIOS.

8. ☑ **D.** TPM, or trusted platform module, is a specialized chip installed on a computer motherboard that stores specific information about the computer system, such as a digital certificate or encryption keys, and protects the computer's data from being accessed both due to physical theft and an external hack over the network. This allows the hardware to be authenticated rather than the user.

   ☒ **A, B,** and **C** are incorrect. **A** is incorrect because setting the user password in the BIOS just prevents an unauthorized user from booting the system. **B** is incorrect because setting the supervisor password just prevents someone from accessing or changing BIOS settings. **C** is incorrect because the lojack system allows a computer that has been physically stolen to be located using GPS technology.

9. ☑ **C.** POST, or power-on self-test, is the most common BIOS testing feature and is available in all versions of BIOS. This collection of tests runs every time you power up your computer and checks for the presence and status of a variety of devices and components; if an error is found, the BIOS provides an auditory or visual notification.

   ☒ **A, B,** and **D** are incorrect because, while most BIOSs can monitor these factors in a computer, the POST is by far the single most common test run by BIOS.

10. ☑ **A.** The intrusion detection/notification system in the BIOS has been enabled and has detected that the case was recently opened, which is correct since you just opened and closed the case to replace a faulty internal component. Most of the time, this feature is disabled in the BIOS and is only enabled if there is a significant threat that the computer may be stolen or physically accessed by an unauthorized person.

    ☒ **B, C,** and **D** are incorrect. **B** is incorrect because the CPU temperature monitor will only send an alert if the CPU temperature exceeds proscribed limits. **C** is incorrect because the lojack system allows a computer to be tracked via GPS but sends no alerts about the case being opened. **D** is incorrect because this is not a normal feature of POST in any version of BIOS.

11. ☑ **C.** The ITX motherboard is physically smaller than an ATX board, and this should be immediately noticeable to an experienced technician.
☒ **A, B,** and **D** are incorrect because ITX boards, in general, support the same processor types as ATX boards, both boards support USB integration, and both boards use a single power connector.

12. ☑ **C.** The ITX or Mini-ITX motherboard form factor is just slightly smaller than the Micro-ATX and is screw-compatible. It is specifically designed for low power consumption and for that reason, often can be passively cooled.
☒ **A, B,** and **D** are incorrect. **A** is incorrect because the full-size ATX motherboard measures 12 × 9.6 inches and is an older motherboard form factor, not specifically designed for low power use. **B** is incorrect because the Micro-ATX is just slightly larger than the ITX and is backward compatible with the ATX form factor. **D** is incorrect because the information available is enough to determine that the board you were working with is an ITX motherboard.

13. ☑ **B.** PCI and PCI Express are incompatible standards, with PCI cards using parallel data transfers and PCI Express using serial communications. The card slots are not compatible; however, a PCI Express network card would allow for faster speeds than an analogous PCI card due to faster PCIe bus speeds, even if the network throughput capacity of the two cards were identical.
☒ **A, C,** and **D** are incorrect. **A** is incorrect because PCI and PCI Express slots are not compatible and the difference in data transfer rates will not affect network speeds. **C** is incorrect because the difference in PCI and PCI Express data transfer rates does make a difference in network speeds. **D** is incorrect because PCI and PCI Express are not the same standard and "Express" doesn't mean a lighter-weight card.

14. ☑ **A.** The Mini PCI is an expansion bus that is used in laptops, and the cards and slots are about a quarter the size of their regular PCI counterparts. This slot cannot be accessed from outside the laptop, and you must install expansion cards in this sort of slot directly on the motherboard.
☒ **B, C,** and **D** are incorrect. **B** is incorrect because laptop motherboards do not accommodate full-sized PCI slots. **C** is incorrect because PCI Express slots are not an add-on to the PCI v 2.2 standard. **D** is incorrect because PCI-X slots are most commonly found on servers and are double-wide versions of PCI slots.

15. ☑ **D.** AGP 2x, 4x, and 8x all refer to the transfer speeds at which the devices run on the AGP interface. The slots are all the same size.
☒ **A, B,** and **C** are incorrect. **A** and **B** are incorrect because all AGP slots and cards are the same size. **C** is incorrect because there is no pin-out difference between devices and slots in relation to different AGP transfer speeds.

16. ☑ **C.** The Northbridge bus typically manages communications directly between AGP, PCI Express, and the Southside bus. The Northside bus is directly connected to the CPU, while the Southside bus relies on the Northside bus for that connection.

    ☒ **A, B,** and **D** are incorrect. **A** is incorrect because the CMOS is a low-energy chipset and in computers is responsible for providing power to store basic instructions that allow a computer to boot. **B** is incorrect because CNR stands for Communication and Networking Riser and is a type of riser card used on ATX motherboards to add expansion cards. **D** is incorrect because the Southside chipset is not directly connected to the CPU and handles all the I/O functions on a computer, such as audio and USB.

17. ☑ **C.** On an ATX motherboard, the main ATX power connector has 24 pins.

    ☒ **A, B,** and **D** are incorrect. **A** is incorrect because the power connector for an ATA hard drive has four pins. **B** is incorrect because the power connector for the CPU has eight pins. **D** is incorrect because audio cards typically don't require cooling fans.

18. ☑ **B.** 1 is the hard drive activity light, 2 is the reset button, 3 is the power button, 4 is the power light, 5 are the USB ports, and 6 are the microphone and speaker ports.

    ☒ **A, C,** and **D** are incorrect because not all of the items on the front of the computer are correctly identified.

19. ☑ **A, B,** and **D.** On older computers especially, CPU cooling is made up of a heat sink and a cooling fan designed to direct heat away from the CPU. The cooling unit is bonded to the top of the CPU by thermal paste, which directs heat from the CPU to the heat sink unit.

    ☒ **C** is incorrect because CPU liquid cooling is a newer technology you would not expect to find in older PCs.

20. ☑ **A, B,** and **D.** According to the Intel Hyper-Threading Technology Web page, in addition to installing a processor that supports Intel HT Technology, an HT-enabled chipset, an HT-enabled system BIOS, and an enabled/optimized operating system are required.

    ☒ **C** is incorrect because the CMOS is the chip that contains the BIOS settings, but only the BIOS needs to be HT enabled.

21. ☑ **D.** The Core i7 processor will require an Intel 1366 socket on the motherboard. Given the options, this should be fairly obvious if you know the Core i7 is an Intel chip, since most Intel socket types tested for in this part of the A+ exam use three- or four-digit identifiers except for the LGA socket type.

    ☒ **A, B,** and **C** are incorrect because AMD socket types are usually given identifiers that use two letters and then a number, such as AM2, AM3, and FM1. Exceptions are the 940 and F sockets.

22. ☑ **B.** The speed of data retrieval from the CPU cache is dependent on the size of the cache and not its location. L1 cache yields faster retrieval times because of its smaller size.
☒ **A, C,** and **D** are incorrect. **A** is incorrect because cache data retrieval isn't primarily affected by the cache being on or off the CPU chip. **C** is incorrect because data is retrieved more quickly from a smaller-sized cache than from a larger-sized cache. **D** is incorrect because L3 cache works with L1 and L2 caches to improve performance, not independently of them.

23. ☑ **A.** A network cable tester is designed to verify that a length of Ethernet cable has the correct pin-out and is carrying current correctly across all pins. One end of the cable is connected to a port on the larger unit, and the other end of the cable attaches to the port on the smaller device. If the pin-out is correct, all of the LEDs on both devices will illuminate. This device is often used to test Ethernet cables you have manually constructed.
☒ **B, C,** and **D** are incorrect. **B** is incorrect because a multimeter is a single device, somewhat larger than the cable tester devices, with two probes, and is used to test electronic devices to verify they are generating specific amounts of current. **C** is incorrect because a toner probe is designed to determine connectivity between two network or telephone ports. If, for instance, you are unsure which network port near a user's desk is associated with a cable connection in a network closet or server room, you can use this device to make the determination. A correct match will result in a tone being emitted by the device, which is what gives the unit its name. **D** is incorrect because in networking, a loopback plug is typically inserted into a computer's Ethernet port to perform a loopback test of the networking circuitry.

4

Personal Computer Components— Storage, Memory, and Adapters

QUESTIONS

There are a wide variety of internal components that make up a standard computer system, and as an A+ technician, you are responsible for understanding the nature of these various components, including storage, memory, and adapters.

Objective 801:1.3   Compare and Contrast RAM Types and Features

1. You are reviewing the characteristics of memory module slots in desktop computers and are currently describing a memory slot that uses a 64-bit path and takes non-Rambus memory. Of the following, which slot are you describing?

   A. DIMM
   B. SIMM
   C. SO-DIMM
   D. RIMM

2. You work for a small city IT department, and you are currently upgrading a PC to use SDRAM DDR3 memory. There are a number of sticks of SDRAM sitting on your workbench, but it looks like someone mixed the various types of SDRAM DDR such that DDR1, DDR2, and DDR3 sticks are not stored separately. Since you want to use DDR3 for your current job, how can you tell which SDRAM sticks are DDR3? Use the accompanying illustration for comparison.

   A. DDR3 sticks have a notch at the bottom of the module that's a little over 7 cm from the left side of the module, as in the first or top stick in the illustration.
   B. DDR3 sticks have a notch at the bottom of the module that's almost exactly 7 cm from the left side of the module, as in the second stick in the illustration.
   C. DDR3 sticks have a notch at the bottom of the module that's about 5½ cm from the left side of the module, as in the third stick in the illustration.
   D. DDR3 sticks have a notch at the bottom of the module that's about 2 cm from the left side of the module, as in the fourth or bottom stick in the illustration.

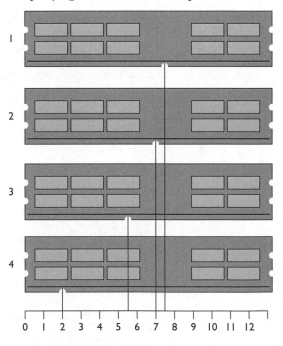

3. You are upgrading the memory of several laptop computers in your shop for different customers. You notice that some of the SODIMM slots are slightly wider than others. What accounts for there being two different widths of SODIMM slots?

    A. The smaller slots take 30-pin SODIMMs for a 32-bit data bus, and the larger slots take 72-pin SODIMMs for a 64-bit data bus.

    B. The smaller slots take 168-pin SODIMMs for a 32-bit data bus, and the larger slots take 184-pin SODIMMs for a 64-bit data bus.

    C. The smaller slots take 72-pin SODIMMs for a 32-bit data bus, and the larger slots take 144-pin SODIMMs for a 64-bit data bus.

    D. The smaller slots take 184-pin SODIMMs for a 16-bit data bus, and the larger slots take 214-pin SODIMMs for a 32-bit data bus.

Objective 801: 1.4   Install and Configure Expansion Cards

4. You are in the process of building a customized PC for a customer and are about to install the expansion cards in the expansion card slots. In the accompanying diagram, based on size, shape, and location, which are the most likely slots in which to install expansion cards?

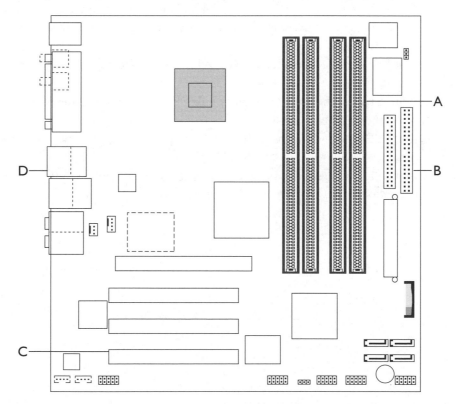

    A. Install the cards here.

    B. Install the cards here.

    C. Install the cards here.

    D. Install the cards here.

5. You are working on the interior of an older computer that does not have its modem or audio interfaces integrated into the PC, but rather, they are located on a riser card that is mounted in a slot containing two rows of 23 pins per row. What sort of card are you looking at?

    A. AGP

    B. AMR

    C. CNR

    D. PCMCIA

Objective 801: 1.5   Install and Configure Storage Devices and Use Appropriate Media

6. A customer is considering buying a new computer and asks you about the advantages of solid-state drives (SSDs). She has heard they are quieter and faster, but is concerned that they will not permanently save her data the way a hard disk drive (HDD) typically does. What do you tell her?

    A. You say that SSDs use the same technology as HDDs and the only difference is the bus speed, allowing for faster data transfers.

    B. You say that SSDs use the same technology as HDDs and the only difference is that the read/write heads are more efficient.

    C. You say that SSDs use flash memory that retains information, even when power is not supplied to the computer, so her data will be safe.

    D. You say that SSDs use flash memory and as long as power is supplied to the computer, her data will be safe.

7. You have a customer who asks you to build him several Windows 7 64-bit custom PCs for his home business. He requires a great deal of storage space on each computer's magnetic hard disk drive (HDD) and is concerned about how much space Windows 7 requires on a hard drive on a 64-bit system. He asks if it's possible to build computers that can store 1 terabyte (TB) or more of data per HDD and still satisfy the hard drive space needs of Windows 7 64-bit. What do you tell him?

    A. You tell him that Windows 7 64-bit requires 16 GB of space, but that the largest hard drive currently available is 900 GB.

    B. You tell him that Windows 7 64-bit requires 16 GB of space and that the largest hard drive currently available is 1 TB.

    C. You tell him that Windows 7 64-bit requires 20 GB of space and that the largest hard drive currently available is 1.5 TB.

    D. You tell him that Windows 7 64-bit requires 20 GB of space and that the largest hard drive currently available is 4 TB.

8. A customer tells you that his brother-in-law recently installed a second hard disk drive in the customer's computer to add storage capacity. At first, it seemed as if everything was fine, but when your customer tried to watch a DVD movie on his computer, the DVD drive wouldn't open. The computer seems to be working fine otherwise. Without opening the case, what is the most likely problem?

    A. The second HDD is setting up electrical interference, preventing the DVD drive from turning on and running.

    B. When the second HDD drive was installed, the power cable to the DVD drive was probably loosened or detached accidentally.

    C. Modern motherboards can only support one HDD and one DVD drive, so the customer's brother-in-law must have unplugged the DVD drive from the motherboard and plugged the second HDD into the DVD's controller.

    D. After the second HDD was installed, the customer's brother-in-law forgot to reboot the system to reset the BIOS to enable using two HDDs and one DVD.

9. One of your customers needs to have a failed CD drive in her computer replaced. She typically uses the CD drive to copy pictures of her grandkids and other family members to CD-RW discs so that she can distribute them to family and friends. You know she'll need her CD burning software updated to work with the replacement since her computer is older, but she's concerned about the cost of buying software on top of the hardware replacement. What do you tell her? (Choose two.)

   A. You tell her that she has no choice but to buy the CD drive replacement and the CD burning software as separate purchases in order to be able to burn CDs on her computer again.

   B. You tell her that you can replace the hardware and that you can download the CD burning software as freeware.

   C. You tell her that the CD burning software comes with the CD drive replacement.

   D. You tell her that you can install the CD burning software on her computer from your personal copy of Nero.

10. One of your customers regularly watches movies using his laptop's built-in DVD drive but is starting to collect some Blu-ray Discs. He asks you if you could replace the DVD player with a Blu-ray drive. His laptop is less than a year old. What do you tell him?

    A. You tell him that you should be able to install a Blu-ray drive that's compatible with his laptop.

    B. You tell him that the only way he can play Blu-ray Discs on his laptop is to use an external Blu-Ray unit via a USB cable.

    C. You tell him that Windows systems cannot currently play Blu-ray Discs.

    D. You tell him that currently Blu-ray technology isn't compatible with laptops.

11. A customer has asked you to install a Blu-ray drive in her PC so that she can watch movies with the best-quality images. Her computer is a few years old and is running Windows Vista. You suggest that you may need to perform some other upgrades so that she can get the most out of the Blu-ray experience. Of the following, what upgrades might be necessary? (Choose three.)

    A. Her computer might need more RAM.

    B. Her computer might need a CPU upgrade.

    C. Her computer might need a video and sound card upgrade.

    D. Her computer might need a hard drive upgrade.

801: 1.7   Compare and Contrast Various Connection Interfaces and Explain Their Purpose

12. You have a customer who wants to buy an external hard drive that has a storage capacity in the 500 GB range and can connect to computers using a wide variety of interfaces. What do you tell him are the most likely types of interfaces available for such drives? (Choose three.)

A. ATA/IDE

B. USB 3.0

C. FireWire 400

D. eSATA

13. You have a customer who has heard of devices that can be "hot-swapped" on a computer and asks if this is something new. What do you tell her?

A. You tell her that a special class of devices has just been released that can be plugged in and removed from a computer without powering down the computer.

B. You tell her that such devices have been around for years, typically in the form of USB storage and other devices.

C. You tell her that only nonstorage USB devices such as USB mice and USB microphones have this capacity.

D. You tell her no such devices exist.

801: 1.11   Identify Connectors and Associated Cables

14. You get a call from a customer who is helping her father set up an older computer a friend gave him. She was looking at the back of the computer before setting it up and noticed a pair of connectors, one purple and one green, similar to the ones on the accompanying photograph.

They appear to be for a keyboard and mouse, but she has always used USB keyboards and mice. What do you tell her about these connections?

A. They are PS/2 connectors originally used to connect keyboards and mice to PCs.

B. They are PS/3 connectors originally used to connect keyboards and mice to PCs.

C. They are DIN connectors originally used to connect keyboards and mice to PCs.

D. They are auxiliary (AUX) keyboard and mice connectors that can be used in an emergency if the USB bus should fail on the PC.

15. One of your home user customers has just purchased his first new computer in several years, and when he attempted to use a parallel cable to connect his aging printer to his new PC, he was distressed to find that the computer had no parallel port. What are your customer's options? (Choose three.)

A. The customer could buy a new printer, since they are relatively inexpensive and it is likely the customer's current printer is on its last legs.

B. The customer could buy a USB-to-parallel printer cable and then use one end of the cable to attach to the parallel port of the printer and the other side of the cable to connect to a USB port on the PC.

C. The customer could buy a PCI Express parallel card that you could install in his PC to add a parallel port to his computer.

D. The customer could buy a new printer, since modern computers are unable to connect to obsolete parallel buses.

QUICK ANSWER KEY

1.	A	**6.**	C	**11.**	A, B, C
2.	C	**7.**	D	**12.**	B, C, D
3.	C	**8.**	B	**13.**	B
4.	C	**9.**	B, C	**14.**	A
5.	B	**10.**	A	**15.**	A, B, C

IN-DEPTH ANSWERS

1. ☑ **A.** DIMM memory slots use a 64-bit data transfer bus.

   ☒ **B, C,** and **D** are incorrect. **B** is incorrect because SIMM slots only use a 32-bit data bus. **C** is incorrect because SODIMM slots are specifically found in laptops and other portable devices. **D** is incorrect because RIMM slots specifically take Rambus memory modules.

2. ☑ **C.** DDR3 sticks have a notch at the bottom of the module that's just slightly over 5 cm from the left side of the stick.

   ☒ **A, B,** and **D** are incorrect. **A** is incorrect because it most closely resembles a stick of SDRAM DDR1 memory. **B** is incorrect because it most closely resembles a stick of SDRAM DDR2 memory. **D** is incorrect because it is a fictitious illustration and description and does not resemble any type of SDRAM memory.

3. ☑ **C.** Typically, SODIMM slots taking 72-pin modules have a 32-bit memory bus and are about 2.35 inches long, and slots taking 144-pin modules have a 64-bit memory bus and are about 2.66 inches long. Newer 204-pin SODIMMs can contain DDR3 SDRAM, with specifications such as PC3-6400, PC3-8500, PC3-10600, and PC3-12800.

   ☒ **A, B,** and **D** are incorrect because SODIMMs do not come in any of the pin arrays described for the stated memory bus widths.

4. ☑ **C.** Expansion card slots come in groups but are not as long as memory module slots. Expansion slots are also located so that the connectors of these cards can protrude from the back of the computer, allowing connections to be made.

   ☒ **A, B,** and **D** are incorrect. **A** is incorrect because, based on their length, they are most likely memory slots. **B** is incorrect because, based on size and pin configuration, these are most likely connections for hard drives or floppy drives. **D** is incorrect because, based on size and location, they are most likely integrated connections for USB, serial, or NIC ports.

5. ☑ **B.** You are looking at an AMR or audio/modem riser card, which was used on motherboards using Pentium III, Pentium 4, and other Intel CPUs and designed to act as an extension to the motherboard and save space. AMR (Audio Modem Riser) has been superseded by ACR (Advanced Communication Riser) and CNR (Communications and Network Riser) risers, and riser technology in general is on the decline, replaced by PCI Express or components integrated on the motherboard.

   ☒ **A, C,** and **D** are incorrect. **A** is incorrect because AGP is not a riser card and is used primarily for graphics cards. **C** is incorrect because although it is a riser card, it has two rows of 30 pins. **D** is incorrect because PCMCIA cards are inserted in laptops and similar mobile devices to add functionality such as modems or NIC cards.

6. ☑ **C.** Modern SSDs use NAND-based flash memory, which can retain data even when no power is supplied to the computer, so information stored on an SSD will not be lost the way that volatile random-access memory is lost once power is no longer supplied.

☒ **A, B,** and **D** are incorrect. **A** and **B** are incorrect because SSDs use solid-state memory to store persistent data and microchips are used rather than moving parts such as read/write heads. **D** is incorrect because SSDs using solid-state memory can store persistent data when power is no longer supplied to the computer.

7. ☑ **D.** Windows 7 64-bit requires 20 GB (minimum) of hard drive space, and as of March 2012, the largest magnetic HDD available was 4 TB, so this would be the best option to satisfy the customer's requirements.

☒ **A, B,** and **C** are incorrect. **A** and **B** are incorrect because Windows 7 64-bit requires 20 GB of space, not 16 GB, and because larger hard drives are available. **C** is incorrect because larger HDD storage capacities are currently available and this option just barely meets the customer's requirements.

8. ☑ **B.** The most likely cause is, during the installation of the second HDD, the power cable to the DVD drive was either loosened or detached accidentally. Once the power cable is correctly inserted in the DVD drive, the unit will work fine.

☒ **A, C,** and **D** are incorrect. **A** is incorrect because an HDD does not produce any type of interference that would prevent a DVD drive from receiving power and opening. **C** is incorrect because there should be two HDD controllers on the motherboard and HDDs use different controllers than do DVD drives. **D** is incorrect because rebooting a computer does not reset the BIOS.

9. ☑ **B** and **C.** You can download a freeware version of CD burning software such as FinalBurner Free, but when you buy a replacement CD drive, it likely comes with CD burning software, such as Nero, included in the price.

☒ **A** and **D** are incorrect. **A** is incorrect because CD burning software often comes with the CD drive when you purchase the hardware. **D** is incorrect because it is unethical and probably illegal to install a copy of software licensed only for your personal use on another person's PC.

10. ☑ **A.** Blu-ray drive units are currently available for laptops, and it is possible to install a Blu-ray drive as requested.

☒ **B, C,** and **D** are incorrect. **B** is incorrect because, in addition to using an external Blu-ray drive, you can install an internal unit. **C** is incorrect because Blu-ray technology is available for PC computers. **D** is incorrect because Blu-ray technology can be used with laptops.

11. ☑ **A, B,** and **C.** Blu-ray support is resource intensive, so the computer may need more RAM and a faster CPU. To get the best video and sound quality from Blu-ray playback, the video card and sound card may also need to be upgraded.

    ☒ **D** is incorrect because upgrading the hard drive shouldn't have any impact on the Blu-ray experience.

12. ☑ **B, C,** and **D.** Although USB is the most common interface for external hard drives, FireWire, including FireWire 400, and eSATA can also be found.

    ☒ **A** is incorrect because ATA/IDE is a common interface for internal hard drives but is never found as a solution to attach an external hard drive to a computer.

13. ☑ **B.** USB storage and other devices are typically hot-swappable, but at least on Windows computers, it is best to use the "safely remove hardware" option before removing a USB device such as a thumb drive.

    ☒ **A, C,** and **D** are incorrect. **A** is incorrect because USB and other hot-swappable devices have been around for a long time. **C** is incorrect because you can hot-swap both USB storage and nonstorage devices. **D** is incorrect because hot-swappable devices do indeed exist.

14. ☑ **A.** PS/2 connectors were introduced in 1987 and used to connect keyboards (purple) and mice (green) to computers. Many computers still have these connectors, but more and more often, customers use USB or wireless connections for keyboards and mice, so some users may be completely unaware of PS/2 connectors.

    ☒ **B, C,** and **D** are incorrect. **B** is incorrect because PS/3 typically stands for PlayStation 3. **C** is incorrect because DIN connectors were superseded by PS/2 connectors. **D** is incorrect because the primary purpose of PS/2 connectors is not as an emergency keyboard and mouse connection in the event that a PC's USB bus should fail.

15. ☑ **A, B,** and **C.** It's likely that the customer's printer is fairly old and he should consider replacing it with a newer printer that uses a USB connection. However, if he wants to keep the printer, he can either buy an inexpensive USB-to-parallel printer cable to make the connection or he can have you install a PCI Express parallel card to add a parallel port to his computer.

    ☒ **D** is incorrect because there are options to connect a modern computer with no parallel port and an older printer that uses a parallel port.

5

Power Supplies, Display Devices, and Peripherals

QUESTIONS

It's important to understand the functions and variations among different PC components and between different PCs. As part of those tasks, you'll need to know how to select and install a computer power supply based on different requirements. You'll also need to know how to construct a custom computer that meets a customer's specifications. Additionally, you will need to know how to differentiate between different display devices and how to select between various cable and connector types. Finally, you will be required to understand how to install and configure numerous peripheral devices for computers.

Objective 801: 1.8   Install an Appropriate Power Supply Based on a Given Scenario

1. You have installed a new power supply in a computer and are connecting the different power supply connectors to the motherboard, drives, and devices. Of the following connectors, which ones have four pins? (Choose all that apply.)

   A. Floppy
   B. Molex
   C. PCIe
   D. SATA

2. You are installing a new power supply into an older computer. The power supply connector for the motherboard has 24 pins, but the power connector on the motherboard has only 20 pins. You've located a 20-to-24 pin converter so you can make a power connection from the power supply to the motherboard, but you are aware that four leads from the power supply are not able to connect to the motherboard. What are these "extra" four pins for?

   A. To power SATA drives
   B. To power the PCIe bus
   C. To provide more power to the motherboard
   D. To provide more power to the CPU

3. You are building a custom computer for a client using a Micro-ATX motherboard. The power supply you are installing was designed for an ATX motherboard. Will there be any problem with the power supply connectors?

   A. No, most Micro-ATX motherboards use the same power connectors as ATX motherboards.
   B. Yes, you must use a power supply that is specifically designed for the Micro-ATX since the power connectors are not backward compatible.

C. Yes, but you can use an adapter connector to make the ATX power supply work with the Micro-ATX motherboard.

D. The ATX power supply and the Micro-ATX motherboard may or may not work together, depending on which company made each unit. You will have to consult with the documentation that came with the power supply and motherboard to make sure.

4. You are installing a power supply into a computer you are custom making for a customer. The computer's power supply must support an unusually large number of peripheral devices. When considering this requirement, what key factor does the power supply you selected need to possess?

A. It must be the largest physical size to put out the most power.

B. It must produce higher wattage to support more devices.

C. It must have the most connectors to support the most devices.

D. It must possess an 8-pin CPU connector rather than a 4-pin CPU connector to optimize processing requests from so many devices.

Objective 801: 1.9   Evaluate and Select Appropriate Components for a Custom Configuration to Meet Customer Specifications or Needs

5. You are building several customized computers for different customers who have unique computing needs. Of the following computers you are building, which ones will require high-end and/or specialized video? (Choose all that apply.)

A. An audio/video editing workstation

B. A gaming PC

C. A graphic design workstation

D. A virtualization workstation

6. You are building several customized computers for different customers who have unique computing needs. You are purchasing several powerful processors, one for each of the computers you are building. Of the following, which PC or workstation types will require these high-end processors? (Choose all that apply.)

A. An audio/video editing workstation

B. A gaming PC

C. A graphic design workstation

D. A home theater PC

7. You are building several custom computers for customers with different computing needs. You have installed a Gigabit NIC into a computer and are configuring it to use a RAID array. What are you building?

    A. A gaming PC

    B. A home server PC

    C. A home theater PC

    D. A thin client

8. You are building several custom computers for customers with different computing needs. You are working on a system that primarily is responsible for running all of the standard desktop applications used in a business setting, even when the network is down. Of the following, what type of computer are you working on?

    A. Home server PC

    B. Thick client PC

    C. Thin client PC

    D. Virtualization workstation

Objective 801: 1.10   Given a Scenario, Evaluate Types and Features of Display Devices

9. You are building a custom computer to a client's specifications and you are at the point of choosing an appropriate monitor. Your client needs a monitor that works without a backlight, can display deep black levels, can natively process digital signals, and can achieve a high contrast ratio in a dark room. The screen must also be physically thin and lightweight. Of the following, which monitor type best fits the customer's requirements?

    A. CRT

    B. LCD

    C. LED

    D. OLED

10. You are building a custom computer to a client's specifications and you are at the point of choosing an appropriate monitor. Your customer will be using his computer almost exclusively for gaming and watching movies, and it will not be used for surfing the Web or other typical end-user tasks. Power consumption and heat generation are not concerns for this customer and neither is cost. Of the following, which screen will best fit his needs?

    A. LCD

    B. LED

    C. Plasma

    D. Projector

11. You are building a custom computer to a client's specifications and you are at the point of choosing an appropriate monitor. The customer needs a projector monitor to display slideshows, videos, and other content during business conferences. She requires a projector that has a very large number of physical pixels in its fixed array. Of the following, which feature is being described?

   A. Brightness/lumens

   B. Native resolution

   C. Resolution

   D. Refresh rate

12. You are setting up a customer's Windows 7 computer to use dual monitors. Of the following, which are valid monitor combinations to choose for this setup? (Choose all that apply.)

   A. Two CRT monitors

   B. Two LCD monitors

   C. One CRT and one LCD monitor

   D. One LCD and one privacy/antiglare monitor

Objective 801: 1.11 Identify Connectors and Associated Cables

13 Of the following display connector types, which ones can use both single and dual link? (Choose all that apply.)

   A. DVI-A

   B. DVI-B

   C. DVI-D

   D. DVI-I

14. Of the following, which connector types are most associated with coaxial cable? (Choose all that apply.)

   A. BNC

   B. DB-15

   C. Din-6

   D. RCA

15. You are using a type C connector with a 19-pin configuration to attach a portable DVD player to a laptop. Of the following, what connector and cable type are you most likely using?

   A. DB-15 connector with a VGA cable

   B. miniHDMI connector with an HDMI cable

   C. RCA connector with a RGB cable

   D. RJ-45 connector with Ethernet cable

16. You are going through an old box of different types of cable and you find one that has a yellow RCA connector. You recognize the cable as the type that carries a signal format for analog television pictures on a single channel before those signals are combined with sound signals. Of the following, which cable type are you handling?

    A. Component
    B. Composite
    C. DisplayPort
    D. S-video

17. You are attempting to locate a specific port on the back of a computer. You come across a port that looks like the accompanying illustration. What is this port?

    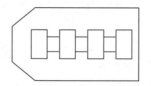

    A. IEEE1394
    B. Parallel
    C. PS/2
    D. Serial

18. You are working with a hard drive connector that uses 7 pins for data and 15 pins for power. What hard drive connector or connectors are you using? (Choose all that apply.)

    A. eSATA
    B. PATA
    C. SATA
    D. USB

19. You are working with a computer that has a 68-pin male connector. Of the following choices, which connector type are you working with?

    A. Audio
    B. Floppy
    C. RJ-45
    D. SCSI

Objective 801: 1.12   Install and Configure Various Peripheral Devices

20. You have a customer who typically uses a USB keyboard and mouse, but would like the freedom of using wireless input devices so that she can do without the wires. Her USB keyboard and mouse just plugged in and worked. Will she need to do any additional configuration or add any components or parts for her wireless keyboard and mouse?

   A. No, she should just put the keyboard and mouse near her computer, turn them on, and they will work.

   B. Yes, she will need to plug in a USB transmitter to the computer, which will send out a signal to the receiver in the keyboard and mouse as well as electrical power.

   C. Yes, she will need to plug in a USB transmitter to the computer and put batteries in the keyboard and mouse; then the units will receive a wireless signal from the transmitter.

   D. Yes, she will need to plug in a USB transmitter to the computer and put batteries in the transmitter, keyboard, and mouse; then the units will receive a wireless signal from the transmitter.

21. You have a small business customer who wants you to install a barcode scanner on his computer so that he can use it to scan items for sale. Of the following, what is true about installing a barcode scanner on a computer? (Choose two.)

   A. You can connect the barcode scanner via a 40-pin parallel port.

   B. You can connect the barcode scanner via a USB port.

   C. Barcode scanners are plug and play and require no software configuration.

   D. Barcode scanners require software to be installed on the computer to understand the meaning of the barcodes.

22. You have a customer who wants you to install a Webcam so that she can video-chat with her sister in New Zealand. She has purchased the Webcam, and it meets the requirements for her computer. What has to happen next?

   A. You must have the customer create an account for chat such as Yahoo! Messenger or Skype before you can install the Webcam.

   B. You must install the Webcam before the customer can create an account for chat such as Yahoo! Messenger or Skype.

   C. The customer can have a chat account before you install the Webcam, or you can install the Webcam and then have the customer create the chat account.

   D. Webcams can only communicate over the Internet for chat using AOL Instant Messenger, so she must specifically install that chat client.

23. You have a customer who makes extensive use of digital photography but also dictates notes for the photographs on her computer. She wants to keep both the USB digital camera and her USB microphone plugged in to her PC almost all the time and asks if this will cause any technical problems. What do you tell her?

A. You say she can leave the USB connections for the camera, microphone, and other devices plugged in full time and it won't cause any problems.

B. You say that the USB camera and microphone won't cause a problem with each other, but they may interfere with any printers connected to the PC via USB.

C. You say that she can only have either the camera or the microphone plugged into her computer via USB at any one time.

D. You say that it's okay to have them both plugged in at one time as long as she doesn't try to do any sound recording with the microphone at the same time she's actively uploading photos from the camera.

24. You have a customer who wants to connect a MIDI keyboard to his computer, be able to play the keyboard, and have the input managed by the computer's MIDI sound card. What are some of the necessary steps? (Choose two.)

A. The keyboard can connect to the computer using the 15-pin connector on the back of the MIDI sound card.

B. Connect the 5-pin MIDI OUT connector from the computer to the MIDI IN port on the keyboard.

C. You should install software for the keyboard on the computer if using a USB connection.

D. You should install software for the keyboard on the computer if using an eSATA connection.

25. You have a customer who bought a computer and a fingerprint reader from the same computer vendor at the same time. The computer and fingerprint reader are designed to work together. He installed the hardware and software, and while the device appears in the Control Panel of the Windows computer, when he tries to use the device, he gets an error message saying it is not connected to the computer. He has verified that all the connections are firmly in place and that he followed all of the instructions to the letter when installing the device. What is the best first step to take in order to find a solution?

A. You uninstall and reinstall the device and the software.

B. You go to the Windows Update site and look for updated drivers for the device.

C. You contact Microsoft Windows customer support for assistance.

D. You contact the computer hardware vendor's customer support for assistance.

26. One of your customers asked you to install a touch screen monitor on her computer. You are going through the instructions prior to performing the installation. Of the following, what do you discover? (Choose two.)

   A. A VGA or DIVX video cable may be used with the touch screen.

   B. Serial cables cannot be used with a touch screen.

   C. You may need to connect the mouse to the touch screen.

   D. The touch screen will not work until you install all of the software on the accompanying disc.

27. A customer uses one PC for his home business. He has a second small PC he'd also like to use, but he doesn't have a lot of room on his desk for an additional monitor, keyboard, and mouse. You suggest a small, two-port KVM (Keyboard Video Mouse) switch so that the customer can use one monitor, keyboard, and mouse and just switch between the two PCs whenever he needs to do so. How do you connect the KVM switch to the computers?

   A. The KVM comes with two pairs of identical, specialized cables to make the connections between the switch and the two PCs.

   B. The KVM comes with two pairs of MicroTCA cables to make the connection between the switch and the two PCs.

   C. The KVM comes with two pairs of FireWire cables to make the connection between the switch and the two PCs.

   D. The KVM comes with two pairs of SATA cables to make the connection between the switch and the two PCs.

28. You have a customer who wants to minimize the amount of wires he has connected to his computer and requires devices that can be connected to his Windows 7 PC using wireless and USB connections. He is a digital artist and an avid gamer and requires high-quality devices for his activities. Of the following, which devices are capable of being connected to his computer with USB and via Wi-Fi and provide for his specific needs? (Choose all that apply.)

   A. Digitizer

   B. Gamepad

   C. Joystick

   D. Monitor

29. You have a customer who wants to be able to use a variety of connection types for peripheral devices and is looking for devices that can be connected to a PC using IEEE 1394 (FireWire), USB, and Wi-Fi. Of the following, which devices can commonly use all three connections? (Choose all that apply.)

   A. Camcorder

   B. Printer

   C. Scanner

   D. Speakers

QUICK ANSWER KEY

1.	A, B	11.	B	21.	B, D
2.	C	12.	A, B, C	22.	C
3.	A	13.	C, D	23.	A
4.	B	14.	A, D	24.	A, B
5.	A, B, C	15.	B	25.	D
6.	B, C	16.	B	26.	A, C
7.	B	17.	A	27.	A
8.	B	18.	A, C	28.	A, B, C
9.	D	19.	D	29.	A, D
10.	C	20.	C		

IN-DEPTH ANSWERS

1. ☑ **A** and **B.** Although they are different sizes, the power supply Molex and floppy drive connectors both use four pins.
    ☒ **C** and **D** are incorrect. **C** is incorrect because the PCIe connectors use 6/8-pin attachment. **D** is incorrect because the SATA connector attaches using what appears to be a slot but actually uses 15 pins.

2. ☑ **C.** The power supply is new and designed to provide power to modern motherboards and so uses a modern 24-pin power connector. Older PCs have motherboards with only 20-pin power connectors because their power requirements weren't quite as robust as newer computers. The "extra" four pins are to provide for the additional power requirements of modern boards.
    ☒ **A, B,** and **D** are incorrect because SATA drives, PCIe, and CPUs all use their own dedicated power connectors from the power supply.

3. ☑ **A.** The Micro-ATX board was made to be backward compatible with the ATX board so you should be able to safely use the ATX power supply with the Micro-ATX motherboard.
    ☒ **B, C,** and **D** are incorrect. **B** and **C** are incorrect because the Micro-ATX power connector is backward compatible with the ATX power connector. **D** is incorrect because that kind of variability between ATX and Micro-ATX power connectors does not exist.

4. ☑ **B.** More devices require more wattage to be produced by the power supply. Each device uses a rated number of watts and, by calculating the total amount of watts used by all devices, you should be able to determine the required wattage output of the needed power supply.
    ☒ **A, C,** and **D** are incorrect. **A** is incorrect because physical size does not mean the power supply actually produces more power. **C** is incorrect because just having more connectors doesn't mean that the power supply will produce sufficient wattage for all of the PC's devices. **D** is incorrect because, while having the correct CPU power connector is important, it's not a critical factor in selecting a power supply that can support a large number of devices.

5. ☑ **A, B,** and **C.** Graphic, CAD, and CAM workstations require high-end or specialized video capacities in order to design and produce professional graphics projects. Audio/ video editing workstations also have special video needs in order to edit and produce video projects such as films or similar deliverables. Gaming PCs require high-end video abilities to process the demanding visual component of modern computer games.
    ☒ **D** is incorrect because virtualization workstations, which are designed to run multiple virtual computers in one or more virtual network environments, primarily require large amounts of RAM and a high number of CPU cores to satisfy each virtual machine's resource requirements. This type of computer does not require a greater-than-average video capacity.

6. ☑ **B** and **C.** Both the gaming PC and graphic design workstation will require powerful processors to manage the large amount of data produced in modern PC gaming and in graphic project design.

    ☒ **A** and **D** are incorrect. **A** is incorrect because audio/video editing usually requires a specialized audio/video card; a large, fast hard drive; and typically dual monitors, but it does not require high-end processing power. **D** is incorrect because a home theater PC requires specialized surround-sound audio, HDMI output, a TV tuner card, and a compact HTPC form factor, but does not use an unusually high amount of processing power.

7. ☑ **B.** A home server PC is typically used to provide server-grade services to a home or small office environment and may be used for file and print sharing or media streaming. Since several PCs will be accessing this device, it will require a Gigabit NIC to respond to multiple network requests. If it will be managing large amounts of data, and particularly if data redundancy is important, a RAID array may be required.

    ☒ **A, C,** and **D** are incorrect. **A** is incorrect because a gaming PC, while it has special requirements such as a high-speed CPU and superior cooling abilities, does not typically need both an especially fast NIC and RAID. **C** is incorrect because a home theater PC also does not require a fast NIC or RAID. **D** is incorrect because thin client computers are designed to run with a minimum of hardware, sometimes without even an onboard hard drive, depending on external systems, such as a server, for data storage and even an operating system.

8. ☑ **B.** A thick client PC is another term for what you might think of as an "ordinary" computer. Most users in an office environment use a thick client to operate typical desktop applications, which can be run even if the network is temporarily down.

    ☒ **A, C,** and **D** are incorrect. **A** is incorrect because the primary purpose of a home server PC is to provide file, print, media streaming, and other server-type services to multiple computers in a home or small office environment. Also, this type of PC cannot serve its function if the network is down since no client computers could access the server. **C** is incorrect because thin clients require a network connection to access most of the basic functions, including storage and sometimes even the operating system. It is unlikely to be able to function in the absence of a network connection and is typically used to provide access to only basic applications. **D** is incorrect because a virtualization workstation's primary function is to support multiple virtual computers in a virtual network environment, not to support desktop applications.

9. ☑ **D.** OLED, or organic light-emitting diode, is a type of LED screen that uses emissive electroluminescent layers made of organic compounds. OLEDs work without a backlight and can display deep black levels better than LCD screens can. It can also achieve a higher contrast ratio in a dark room than an LCD and uses less light per area than an inorganic LED.

   ☒ **A, B,** and **C** are incorrect. **A** is incorrect because CRT, or cathode ray tube, screens meet none of the requirements, process analog signals natively, and are large and bulky. **B** is incorrect because the LCD, or liquid crystal display, screen uses a backlight and does not meet several other requirements. **C** is incorrect because the inorganic LED screen uses a backlight.

10. ☑ **C.** While plasma screens are not optimal for typical computer use, they do provide excellent results when used for gaming or viewing films. They do generate a great deal of heat and are not particularly power efficient, but the customer is not concerned about these characteristics. Plasma screens can also be quite costly.

   ☒ **A, B,** and **D** are incorrect. **A** and **B** are incorrect because while they both produce good images, they are not as optimized for gaming and film viewing as plasma. They are also more cost effective, produce less heat, and consume less power, so they would be a better selection for customers who have concerns in these areas. **D** is incorrect because a projector screen is best used to direct the visual output of a computer onto an external screen or white board for viewing by a number of people, such as in a conference or business meeting. The image is suboptimal for gaming and film viewing.

11. ☑ **B.** Projectors use microdisplays, which can be LCD panels or DLP (digital light processing) chips that have a fixed array of pixels. This is the native resolution of the projector, which is also called physical resolution, and the projector can never display more actual pixels than it has on its panel or chips.

   ☒ **A, C,** and **D** are incorrect. **A** is incorrect because brightness or lumens is the amount of actual light produced by the projector or any other display and has nothing to do with the fixed number of pixels. **C** is incorrect because resolution is the signal format of the computer being sent to the display. Computers are capable of a variety of resolution formats, including the maximum resolution, which is the highest resolution signal the projector is able to process and display. **D** is incorrect because the refresh rate is the number of times per second that an image is "drawn" onto the display and is expressed as a scanning frequency.

12. ☑ **A, B,** and **C.** Although it is common to use two LCD flat-screen monitors in a dual monitor setup, you can use any two functional monitors.

☒ **D** is incorrect because a privacy/antiglare monitor is most likely an LCD monitor and is a feature rather than a type of monitor screen. Privacy/antiglare is a feature for a monitor that ensures anyone attempting to look at a monitor image from any angle other than straight on will not be able to view the image.

13. ☑ **C** and **D.** Both DVI-D (digital) and DVI-I (digital and analog) connectors can use single and dual link.

☒ **A** and **B** are incorrect. **A** is incorrect because DVI-A (analog) is incapable of using dual link. **B** is incorrect because this is a fictitious connector type.

14. ☑ **A** and **D.** BNC, or Bayonet Neill-Concelman, connectors are a very common type of radio frequency (RF) connector used with coaxial cable, a type of shielded cable associated with radio, television, and other radio-frequency equipment. RCA connectors are most associated with common audio and video cables, originally used for phonograph connections but also commonly used for VHS and DVD connections to televisions. They are commonly used with coaxial cables

☒ **B** and **C** are incorrect. **B** is incorrect because DB-15 is a type of D-subminiature connector characterized by its "D" shape and associated with a number of different cable types. **C** is incorrect because the Din-6 connector is a type of mini-DIN multipin electrical connector used for a variety of applications, cables, and port types.

15. ☑ **B.** miniHDMI connectors are typically used with portable devices such as laptops to connect to digital audio/video sources such as DVD players, camcorders, and video game consoles using HDMI cables. This connector type uses a 19-pin configuration.

☒ **A, C,** and **D** are incorrect. **A** is incorrect because the DB-15 connector uses a 15-pin connection. **C** is incorrect because RCA connectors use a single pin connection and are not specific to portable devices. **D** is incorrect because this connector and cable type is more typically used for network rather than audio/video connections.

16. ☑ **B.** Composite video cable is designed to carry the video-only portion of an analog television signal on a single channel and is recognized by its yellow RCA connector.

☒ **A, C,** and **D** are incorrect. **A** is incorrect because component video cable can carry analog video signals split into two or more component channels. Like composite cables, they use RCA connectors but of varying colors. **C** is incorrect because DisplayPort is a connector type and not a cable, and is used to connect a video source to a display device, such as connecting a PC to a monitor. **D** is incorrect because S-video, or separate video, is a cable type designed to carry analog video signals on two channels.

17.   ☑   **A.** This is a typical FireWire IEEE 1394 port based on its shape and configuration.
☒   **B, C,** and **D** are incorrect. **B** is incorrect because parallel ports are longer and contain either 25 or 36 pins. **C** is incorrect because these are round connectors used for keyboards and mice and have six round pins and one rectangle pin. **D** is incorrect because serial ports come in different shapes, including oblong and round, but typically have 9 or 25 pins.

18.   ☑   **A** and **C.** Both the SATA and eSATA connectors use 7 pins for data and 15 pins for the power connection.
☒   **B** and **D** are incorrect. **B** is incorrect because the IDE connector has 40 pins and the EIDE connector has 44 pins. Both drives take a four-pin power connector. **D** is incorrect because USB connectors use four pins.

19.   ☑   **D.** This is most likely an HD68 male used for ultra-wide SCSI-3/Ultra2 LVD SCSI. This connector can be either internal or external. It looks similar to the HD50 SCSI connector, but can be differentiated by size, with the HD50 being 1⅜" (36mm) long and the HD68 being 1⅞" (47mm) long.
☒   **A, B,** and **C** are incorrect. **A** is incorrect because an audio jack on a computer is usually just a single port. **B** is incorrect because a floppy connector has 34 pins, both on the end and middle connectors on the floppy ribbon cable. **C** is incorrect because the RJ-45 connector looks like a larger version of a telephone cable connector and has eight pins.

20.   ☑   **C.** The wireless USB transmitter unit gets power from the PC, but the keyboard and mouse take batteries (usually AA) for power. The keyboard and mouse will then receive a signal from the transmitter and be able to communicate with the computer. Rarely will you need to install drivers, but a disc typically comes with the wireless keyboard and mouse kit if they are needed.
☒   **A, B,** and **D** are incorrect. **A** is incorrect because the keyboard and mouse can't form a "relationship" with the computer just by sitting next to it. **B** is incorrect because the USB transmitter doesn't send out electrical power through the air to the keyboard and mouse, just a wireless signal. **D** is incorrect because the USB transmitter gets power from the PC and does not need batteries.

21.   ☑   **B** and **D.** You can attach a barcode scanner to a computer using either a USB or a serial connection, and software needs to be installed on the computer so that it understands the meaning of the barcodes and how to process the data.
☒   **A** and **C** are incorrect. **A** is incorrect because you cannot connect a barcode scanner to a computer using a 40-pin parallel port, though you can make the connection using a serial port. **C** is incorrect because without software, the hardware components may scan barcodes, but the computer won't understand the input or how to process it.

22. ☑ **C.** It doesn't matter if you install the Webcam first or if the customer creates the chat account first, but after the Webcam is installed, it will still need to be configured to use the customer's preferred chat client before communication over the Internet can proceed.
☒ **A, B,** and **D** are incorrect. **A** and **B** are incorrect because the order of installation is irrelevant. It only matters that both must be installed on the computer before the Webcam can be configured to use the chat client. **D** is incorrect because Webcams can use many other chat clients besides AOL Instant Messenger.

23. ☑ **A.** You can leave multiple USB devices connected to a computer on a long-term basis without causing any problems.
☒ **B, C,** and **D** are incorrect. **B** is incorrect because having a USB camera or microphone plugged into a PC will not cause a problem with a USB printer or any other device also connected to the computer. **C** is incorrect because you can have multiple USB devices plugged into a computer at the same time without problems. **D** is incorrect because you can actively use a USB camera, a microphone, and other devices at the same time on a computer without problems.

24. ☑ **A** and **B.** You can connect a MIDI keyboard to a computer via a 15-pin connector on a MIDI sound card, but you'll also have to make the necessary connections via the 5-pin MIDI ports on the computer and keyboard. The MIDI connection will likely require that drivers and other software be installed on the computer, but the MIDI port connections and software are likely not required if you are connecting the keyboard to the computer via USB.
☒ **C** and **D** are incorrect. **C** is incorrect because it is unlikely you'll have to install software on the computer if connecting the keyboard to the PC via USB. **D** is incorrect because eSATA ports are designed to recognize external SATA drives, not MIDI keyboards.

25. ☑ **D.** Since the customer purchased the computer and fingerprint reader to use together and the hardware vendor also supplied all of the software and drivers for the fingerprint reader, the best first step is to contact the hardware vendor's customer support for assistance. Often, they are aware of any problems with their hardware and software and can quickly suggest a solution.
☒ **A, B,** and **C** are incorrect. **A** is incorrect because, although this is a common troubleshooting strategy, it may or may not work, and contacting customer support under these circumstances may yield faster results. **B** and **C** are incorrect because Microsoft didn't produce the software for this product and is not responsible for finding or developing a solution.

26. ☑ **A** and **C.** While touch screens made by different vendors may have slightly different installation instructions, a touch screen can connect to a computer using a VGA or DIVX cable, as well as USB or serial connections. Some touch screens require that the mouse be connected to a port on the touch screen.

☒ **B** and **D** are incorrect. **B** is incorrect because some touch screens can connect to a computer via a serial cable. **D** is incorrect because some touch screens may work as soon as they are connected to the computer and turned on, but you should still install the required software.

27. ☑ **A.** You must use the two pairs of KVM cables, which come with connectors for the keyboard, mouse, and monitor ports on the backs of both PCs, allowing them to connect to a set of ports on the KVM device.

☒ **B, C,** and **D** are incorrect because you cannot use MicroTCA, FireWire, SATA, or any other cables besides the KVM cables to make the proper connections. Note that Micro Telecommunications and Computing Architecture (MicroTCA) is emerging as a form factor for low-end equipment such as cellular base stations and access equipment, and no, it's not covered on the A+ exam.

28. ☑ **A, B,** and **C.** Digitizers, such as graphics tablets for artists, and gamepads come with both USB and wireless connections. There also are a few joysticks, typically flight sticks that are both USB and wireless as well.

☒ **D** is incorrect because, although there are monitors that can be connected to a computer using wireless and USB connections, for an avid gamer, the USB connection would produce a suboptimal display.

29. ☑ **A** and **D.** There are camcorders and speakers on the market that are capable of all three of these connection types, but it requires a bit of shopping.

☒ **B** and **C** are incorrect because, while printers and scanners typically offer both USB and wireless connection types, it is rare that these devices use IEEE1394 (FireWire) for connections to a PC, if at all.

6

Installing and Upgrading PC Components

❑   **801: 1.2**   Differentiate between motherboard components, their purposes, and properties.

❑   **801: 1.3**   Compare and contrast RAM types and features.

❑   **801: 1.4**   Install and configure expansion cards.

❑   **801: 1.5**   Install and configure storage devices and use appropriate media.

❑   **801: 1.6**   Differentiate among various CPU types and features and select the appropriate cooling method.

❑   **801: 1.9**   Evaluate and select appropriate components for a custom configuration to meet customer specifications or needs.

QUESTIONS

While it's important to understand the functions and variations among different PC components, the heart of your work is actually installing and upgrading different devices in computers. You need to be able to demonstrate the ability to install and configure different storage devices, motherboards, processors, and other PC equipment. You also need to be able to design custom configurations to meet customer needs.

Objective 801: 1.2 Differentiate between Motherboard Components, Their Purposes, and Properties

1. You are configuring an older motherboard that uses jumper settings and have looked up the manual for the particular motherboard on the manufacturer's Website to determine how to use the jumpers to create a particular configuration. Of the following, which are valid uses for motherboard jumper settings? (Choose three.)
   A. CPU make and model
   B. I/O voltage
   C. System bus speed
   D. CMOS battery reset

2. You have determined that the CMOS battery in a customer's computer is dying and you need to replace it. Before replacing the battery, what are some of the tasks you need to perform? (Choose three.)
   A. You need to go into the BIOS and write down the current settings for the computer.
   B. You need to locate and write down all of the information about the battery.
   C. You need to click the Windows button, right-click Computer, click Properties, and then write down all the information about the computer's operating system, RAM, and CPU.
   D. You need to determine if the CMOS battery can be replaced or if you can only add a replacement battery on the motherboard.

3. You have a customer who wants you to build her a customized PC. She has some technical knowledge and wants you to explain what component or property of a motherboard defines its bus speed. What do you tell her?
   A. The front-side bus determines the bus speed.
   B. The back-side bus determines the bus speed.
   C. The Northbridge chipset determines the bus speed.
   D. The Southbridge chipset determines the bus speed.

4. You are in the process of building a customized PC for a customer and are about to install the SDRAM modules. In the accompanying diagram, based on size, shape, and location, which are the most likely slots in which to install SDRAM modules?

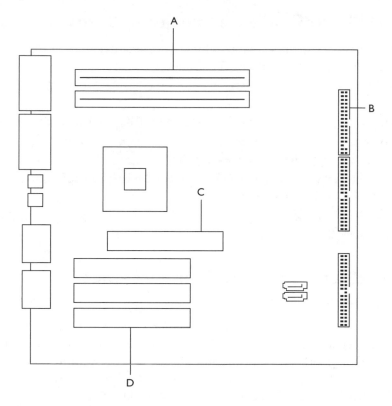

A. Install the SDRAM here.
B. Install the SDRAM here.
C. Install the SDRAM here.
D. Install the SDRAM here.

Objective 801: 1.3 Compare and Contrast RAM Types and Features

5. You are building a customized PC for a customer and are in the process of inserting the memory modules on the motherboard, which has four memory slots. This is a 64-bit system, and you plan to install Windows 7 Professional on the computer once the hardware is built. Of the following options, which one most correctly describes the theoretical amount of memory you can install?

A. The most you can install is 1 GB of RAM in each memory slot for Windows 7 Professional.
B. The most you can install is 2 GB of RAM in each memory slot for Windows 7 Professional.

C. The most RAM supported by Windows 7 Professional is 192 GB.

D. The most RAM supported by Windows 7 Professional is 512 GB.

801: 1.4 Install and Configure Expansion Cards

6. You are building a customized PC that uses Intel APIC architecture and that will run Windows 7 to test modern and older I/O interfaces in computing. To that end, you are installing PCI Express cards for FireWire, USB, parallel, and serial ports. Should you expect any IRQ conflicts when you power up the computer?

A. Plug-and-play specifications have done away with IRQs, so feel free to install the cards.

B. Once you install the cards and power up the computer, you must go into Device Manager in Windows and resolve the inevitable IRQ conflicts.

C. The architecture for this computer uses 24 IRQs with an extra 8 IRQs to route PCI interrupts and avoid conflicts, so you should be okay.

D. Once you install the cards and power up the computer, you must go into the Program Files folder and view and resolve any potential IRQ conflicts.

801: 1.5 Install and Configure Storage Devices and Use Appropriate Media

7. You are helping a friend modify a computer on which to test RAID 1, or mirroring. In order to do this, you've been asked to install a SATA RAID X4 controller card into a PCI Express slot in the computer's motherboard. The machine already has the operating system installed on the first SATA drive, and after installing the computer, you will install a second SATA drive to be used as the "mirror." What SATA controller ports should be used?

A. Plug the first drive in port 1 and the second drive in port 2.

B. Plug the first drive in port 2 and the second drive in port 1.

C. Plug the first drive in port 2 and the second drive in port 3.

D. Use any of the four ports on the SATA RAID controller.

801: 1.6 Differentiate among Various CPU Types and Features and Select the Appropriate Cooling Method

8. Your customer has requested that you upgrade his computer with a newer triple-core CPU and asks what his options are. You research triple-core CPUs on the market and tell him he has his choice of which of the following processor types? (Choose two.)

A. AMD Athlon II triple-core processor

B. AMD Opteron triple-core processor

C. AMD Phenom triple-core processor

D. AMD Sempron triple-core processor

9. You are building a customized PC for a customer using a new ASUS Xtreme Design Core Unlocker motherboard that takes an AMD Phenom II X4 945 Deneb 3.0 GHz processor. What CPU socket does this motherboard have that is specifically designed to be used with Phenom II processors?

A. Socket AM1

B. Socket AM2

C. Socket AM3

D. Socket AM4

10. You are building a customized PC for a customer who requires a processor with six cores, a clock speed of 2.8 GHz, and a total L2 and L3 cache of 9 MB. Of the following, which processor meets these specific requirements?

A. AMD Phenom II 1090T

B. AMD Phenom II 1055T

C. Intel Core i7 930

D. Intel Core i5 750

11. You are discussing with a customer the advantages of moving from 32-bit processing to 64-bit processing on a personal computer, and being skeptical, your customer asks you to name one disadvantage of 64-bit processing. Of the following, what do you say?

A. 64-bit processing can use no more physical memory than 32-bit processing.

B. 64-bit CPUs are still less available than 32-bit CPUs.

C. 64-bit processing requires more memory for the same amount of data than 32-bit processing.

D. Data encryption software actually executes faster in 32-bit processing than in 64-bit processing.

801: 1.9   Evaluate and Select Appropriate Components for a Custom Configuration to Meet Customer Specifications or Needs

12. You are building a customized PC for a customer who is an avid gamer. This sort of PC usually requires a lot of power, so you are installing a power supply to provide the power output typically used in higher-end gaming machines. Of the following, which type of power supply should you install?

A. 100–300 W

B. 300–500 W

C. 500–800 W

D. 800–1400 W

13. You are designing a custom system for a customer who intends to use it to host a virtualization platform. Which of the following performance characteristics is most important to maximize?

   A. Powerful CPU
   B. High-end video
   C. High-quality sound
   D. Compact form factor

14. You have a customer who is interested in having you construct a custom computer for viewing and editing high-definition videos, but wants to know which connector should be installed to accept digital video using a single cable for any uncompressed TV or PC video format and that always carries audio content. What do you tell him?

   A. The best connector for this purpose is VGA.
   B. The best connector for this purpose is HDMI.
   C. The best connector for this purpose is S-Video.
   D. The best connector for this purpose is DVI.

15. You are building a custom PC for a customer and are currently attempting to install an AMD Athlon 64 processor on the motherboard. You discover that the CPU is incompatible with the processor socket on the brand-new motherboard. You look at the motherboard's manual and see that the socket is Socket AM3, which is compatible with AMD Phenom, Athlon, and Sempron processors; however, the pin count is different between the AMD Athlon 64 CPU you are trying to install and the Socket AM3. What is the most likely problem?

   A. The AMD Athlon 64 is an older chip compatible with the Socket AM2 and Socket AM2+. The Socket AM3 is not backwardly compatible and will not accommodate the CPU you're trying to install.
   B. The AMD Athlon 64 is compatible with a Socket AM3a, but the motherboard you have has an AM3b socket, suitable only for multithreading processors.
   C. The AMD Athlon 64 is a "cutting edge" CPU, and even though you are working with a brand-new motherboard, it does not have the compatible Socket AM4 with the correct pin count required for such new technology.
   D. The AMD Athlon 64 is an older chip, but the Socket AM3 should be backwardly compatible and allow the CPU to be installed. You likely have a faulty chip with a missing pin.

QUICK ANSWER KEY

1.	B, C, D	6.	C	11.	C
2.	A, B, D	7.	A	12.	D
3.	A	8.	A, C	13.	A
4.	A	9.	C	14.	B
5.	C	10.	B	15.	A

IN-DEPTH ANSWERS

1. ☑ **B, C,** and **D.** You can use jumpers on some motherboards to set the I/O voltage and system bus speed. You can also sometimes use a jumper setting to clear the CMOS chip and reset the BIOS configuration if a problem occurred after flashing the BIOS that made the computer unable to boot.

    ☒ **A** is incorrect because, although you can use a jumper setting to configure the core voltage for a CPU, you can't use jumpers to set a motherboard to use a specific make and model of processor.

2. ☑ **A, B,** and **D.** Once you remove the CMOS battery, the BIOS settings will be lost, so before replacing the battery, go into the BIOS and write down the settings. You'll need to restore them once the new battery is in place. You will also need to record all the information about the battery, such as voltage, wiring, and so on, so you can make sure you buy and install the correct replacement. Some motherboards don't let you remove the old battery but allow you to add a replacement battery, which usually also requires that you set a jumper on the motherboard so that the motherboard knows to use the replacement battery.

    ☒ **C** is incorrect because information on the computer's operating system, RAM, and CPU, as found in the Properties setting for the computer in Windows, is irrelevant. The BIOS information about the computer's settings is what will be lost and what will need to be reset when the CMOS battery is replaced.

3. ☑ **A.** The speed of a motherboard is usually measured in megahertz (MHz) and is determined by the front-side bus, which connects the CPU to the Northbridge chipset.

    ☒ **B, C,** and **D** are incorrect. **B** is incorrect because the back-side bus connects the CPU with the cache and does not determine the motherboard bus speed. **C** is incorrect because the Northbridge chipset manages communications with the CPU, RAM, PCI Express cards, and so on, but does not determine overall motherboard bus speed. **D** is incorrect because the Southbridge is the chipset that manages communications with slower devices in a computer, such as PCI and PCI-Express devices; it does not determine the overall motherboard bus speed.

4. ☑ **A.** Typically, DRAM slots on a motherboard are among the longest slots and tend to come in pairs. Of the available slots in the diagram, these are the most likely candidates for memory slots.

    ☒ **B, C,** and **D** are incorrect. **B** is incorrect because based on the size, location, and pin arrangement, these slots most likely are hard drive or floppy drive controllers. **C** is incorrect because it is a single slot, and based on its size and shape, it is most likely an expansion card slot such as an AGP slot. **D** is incorrect because based on size and shape, these slots are most likely expansion card slots such as PCI or PCI-Express slots.

5. ☑ **C.** A 64-bit Windows 7 Professional machine can support up to 192 GB of memory in theory; however, it is unlikely that you would ever actually install that much memory. In theory, 64-bit computers can support up to 16 exabytes of RAM, but a physical limit of 4 petabytes has been imposed due to size limitations on physical memory chips. Operating systems, even if 64-bit, impose further limitations on the amount of memory they can address.

☒ **A, B,** and **D** are incorrect. **A** is incorrect because Windows 7 Professional can support more than 4 GB of memory. **B** is incorrect because Windows 7 can use more than 8 GB of memory. **D** is incorrect because even if the 64-bit hardware can address 512 GB of memory, the Windows 7 Professional operating system cannot.

6. ☑ **C.** Newer Intel APIC architecture computers use 24 IRQs, including 8 IRQs designed to avoid conflicts on the PCI bus. IRQ conflicts are much rarer than in the early days of personal computing.

☒ **A, B,** and **D** are incorrect. **A** is incorrect because IRQs, or interrupt requests, have not been eliminated in modern computing technology. **B** is incorrect because it is not inevitable that there will be IRQ conflicts that will require a manual resolution. **D** is incorrect because even if there are conflicts, you would not resolve them in Windows by going to Program Files, as this folder usually contains configuration files for software applications installed on the computer.

7. ☑ **A.** The best configuration is to connect the drives in order, with the primary drive connected to port 1 and the secondary, or mirror, drive connected to port 2.

☒ **B, C,** and **D** are incorrect because even though this type of card supports up to four SATA drive connections for different RAID implementations, it is best to connect the drives in sequential order.

8. ☑ **A** and **C.** Both the AMD Athlon II and Phenom processor lines offer triple-core options.

☒ **B** and **D** are incorrect because the AMD Opteron and Sempron processor lines do not offer triple-core options.

9. ☑ **C.** AMD's Socket AM3 line was designed to be used for Phenom II processors.

☒ **A, B,** and **D** are incorrect. **A** and **D** are incorrect because there are no AMD sockets named Socket AM1 or Socket AM4. **B** is incorrect because Socket AM2 doesn't have the correct key placement and doesn't support the AM3 processor-integrated memory controller.

10. ☑ **B.** Of the available choices, only the AMD Phenom II 1055T meets each of the stated customer requirements.

☒ **A, C,** and **D** are incorrect. **A** is incorrect because its clock speed is higher than required at 3.2 GHz. **C** is incorrect because it has only four cores and a total cache of 8 MB. **D** is incorrect because the processor has only four cores, a clock speed of 2.66 GHz, and a total cache of 8 MB.

11. ☑ **C.** The same amount of data consumes more memory space in 64-bit processing than in 32-bit processing, increasing memory requirements and possibly making less efficient use of processor cache.

   ☒ **A, B,** and **D** are incorrect. **A** is incorrect because 64-bit processing can use much more physical memory than 32-bit processing. **B** is incorrect because 64-bit CPUs are abundant in the marketplace. **D** is incorrect because data encryption software can execute three to five times faster in 64-bit environments than in 32-bit environments.

12. ☑ **D.** Higher-end gaming machines use power supplies that have an output of 800–1400 W, although the very highest-end units can put out 2 kW, but those are used mainly for servers.

   ☒ **A, B,** and **C** are incorrect. **A** and **B** are incorrect because very small form-factor systems typically use 300 W, while an average PC will use around 500 W. **C** is incorrect because lower-end gaming machines use 500–800 W power supplies.

13. ☑ **A.** The most important characteristics for a virtualization workstation are maximum RAM and a powerful CPU.

   ☒ **B, C,** and **D** are incorrect. **B** and **C** are incorrect because audio and video requirements are not significant for a virtualization system. **D** is incorrect because virtualization workstations do not have specific size requirements.

14. ☑ **B.** HDMI, or High-Definition Multimedia Interface, is a compact multimedia connector used to transmit and receive uncompressed digital data and is an alternative to analog methods such as coax cable, S-Video, and VGA. It comes in a variety of connector types that represent the HDMI 1.0, HDMI 3.0, and HDMI 4.0 specifications.

   ☒ **A, C,** and **D** are incorrect. **A** and **C** are incorrect because they are analog connectors. **D** is incorrect because, although it is a digital media connector, it can, but doesn't always, carry audio data.

15. ☑ **A.** The AMD Athlon 64 chip is a slightly older CPU and is generally compatible with Socket AM2 and Socket AM2+ but not Socket AM3, which is suitable for newer AMD Athlon II CPUs, among other processors.

   ☒ **B, C,** and **D** are incorrect. **B** is incorrect because there are no such sockets as Socket AM3a and AM3b. **C** is incorrect because the Athlon 64 is not a brand-new, "cutting edge" chip. **D** is incorrect because the Socket AM3 is not backwardly compatible with the Socket AM2.

7

Installing and Configuring Laptops

QUESTIONS

As an A+ technician, you will be expected to have the specialized skills to troubleshoot laptops when something goes wrong and to prevent problems from happening in the first place.

Objective 801:3.1 Install and Configure Laptop Hardware and Components

1. You have a customer who wants you to upgrade his laptop's wireless card. He has purchased a Mini PCI Express 802.11b, 802.11g, 802.11n wireless card with two antennas for this purpose. You review the documentation for the card and laptop and then assemble your tools and the material that came with the wireless card. Of the following, what will you likely need and need to do to install the card? (Choose three.)

   A. You will need a flat tool such as a very small flathead screwdriver.
   B. You will need a soldering iron to solder the card into the expansion slot.
   C. You will need to connect the two antennas to the card.
   D. You will need the installation disc for the wireless card.

2. You are in the process of upgrading the video card in a customer's laptop. You've consulted the laptop's documentation, determined that the video card in this laptop can be upgraded, and have selected an appropriate card. For the installation process, what are you likely to have to remove from the laptop to get to the video card slot? (Choose three.)

   A. The battery
   B. The keyboard
   C. The optical drive
   D. The CPU

3. A customer has lost several keys off her laptop keyboard over time and asks you to replace the keyboard. In order to completely remove the old keyboard so you can replace it with the new one, what will you likely have to disconnect or remove? (Choose two.)

   A. The data cable between the keyboard and the laptop's motherboard
   B. The power cable between the keyboard and the laptop's power supply
   C. The screws and tabs securing the keyboard to the laptop
   D. The warranty seal attaching the keyboard to the laptop frame

4. You have a customer who brings his new laptop to you and shows you a crack he accidentally caused. The crack is about half an inch long next to the touchpad. The laptop works fine and there is no internal damage. What can you do to repair this type of problem? (Choose two.)

   A. Use epoxy on the underside of the crack.
   B. Buy a replacement part on eBay.

C. Replace the laptop.

D. Solder the crack.

5. You have a customer who is complaining that the touchpad on her Windows 7 laptop isn't responding. What can you do to diagnose the problem? (Choose three.)

A. Go into Control Panel.

B. Go into Device Manager.

C. Check the internal touchpad connection.

D. Check the internal keyboard connection.

6. You have a customer who complains the sound quality of his laptop's internal speakers has degraded markedly in the past few weeks. You know it's very easy to "blow out" laptop internal speakers, so you'll need to replace the speakers. What is the process for installing replacement speakers in a laptop?

A. Internal laptop speakers cannot be replaced because they're integrated into the laptop frame. The customer needs to use headphones or external speakers.

B. Internal laptop speakers are integrated into the laptop's sound card, so you'll have to replace both.

C. Internal laptop speakers are fairly easy to replace as long as you get speakers that are a proper fit for the laptop.

D. The sound quality of even the best-quality internal laptop speakers is very poor. Your customer's best bet is to replace the internal speakers with external speakers for better sound.

7. You have a laptop customer who has added a number of external peripheral devices, a Mini PCI Express sound card, and a PCMCIA wireless network adapter, all within the past few days. Now he says his laptop won't start. What troubleshooting steps can you take to diagnose the problem? (Choose two.)

A. Reinstall the operating system and then reboot the computer to see if it starts.

B. Reinstall all applications and then reboot the computer to see if it starts.

C. Remove all peripheral devices and then add them back one at a time, seeing if the computer starts each time you add a device.

D. Use a multimeter to check the power adapter brick connections and cords to see if they're supplying power.

8. You work for a small city IT department and have just received a new, unformatted laptop hard drive from the manufacturer that you need to use as a replacement in a damaged unit. You take all appropriate safety precautions, assemble the required tools, and replace the damaged laptop's hard drive. You then boot the laptop to test it. What do you expect to happen?

A. You expect to see the laptop boot into the operating system.

B. You expect to see a message saying that there is no operating system present.

    C. You expect to see a message saying the operating system needs to be configured.

    D. You expect that you will receive a message saying the BIOS needs to be installed.

9. You have just installed a stick of SODIMM memory in a customer's computer, and when you try to start the unit, the laptop fails to power up. What do you suspect?

    A. A bad SODIMM stick

    B. A bad battery

    C. A bad motherboard

    D. A bad display driver

Objective 801: 3.2 Compare and Contrast the Components Within the Display of a Laptop

10. A customer complains that the image on her laptop display screen is garbled and indistinct. You aren't sure if this is a display screen problem, a video card problem, or some other issue. What methods of testing do you use? (Choose two.)

    A. Attach an external monitor using the laptop's external video connector.

    B. Reseat the memory modules.

    C. Open the laptop and check the LCD inverter connections.

    D. Open the laptop and check the LCD cable connections.

11. Which of the following technologies is most commonly used to light the LCD screens on full-sized laptop computers?

    A. Plasma

    B. LED

    C. OLED

    D. AMOLED

Objective 801: 3.3 Compare and Contrast Laptop Features

12. You have a customer who complains that her Windows laptop's built-in wireless network card isn't working. What can you do to diagnose this problem? (Choose three.)

    A. Check the manual Wi-Fi on-and-off switch on the laptop.

    B. Check Device Manager and see if any warning or error messages are listed for the wireless network adapter.

    C. Check the internal and, if present, external wireless antenna connections to make sure they are secure.

    D. Check the power lead from the motherboard to the wireless adapter.

13. You get a call from a customer who says that her laptop fans are running all of the time while she's using her laptop. You investigate and discover she uses the laptop primarily late in the evening after she's gotten ready to go to bed. What do you suspect?

    A. The laptop has been on all day and has been accumulating heat.

    B. She is using the laptop in bed and the sheets and blankets on the bed are blocking the laptop's cooling vents.

    C. The laptop's cooling fans are going bad.

    D. The battery is overheating.

14. You have a user who is trying to decide between purchasing a port replicator or a more expensive docking station. You explain that they have some common features, but which of the following would normally only be found in a docking station?

    A. Monitor connection

    B. USB port

    C. Power connection

    D. Optical drive

Objective 802: 1.5   Given a Scenario, Use Control Panel Utilities

15. You are talking to a customer about his new Windows 7 laptop, and he asks about a feature he has noticed that combines hibernation and sleep on the device. What is this feature?

    A. Hybrid Sleep

    B. Hybrid Hibernate

    C. Sleep

    D. Standby

16. Which of the following Windows 7 power plans offers laptop users full performance while conserving power when the system is idle?

    A. High Performance

    B. Power Saver

    C. Laptop

    D. Balanced

QUICK ANSWER KEY

1.	A, C, D	**7.**	C, D	**13.**	B
2.	A, B, C	**8.**	B	**14.**	D
3.	A, C	**9.**	A	**15.**	A
4.	A, B	**10.**	A, D	**16.**	D
5.	A, B, C	**11.**	B		
6.	C	**12.**	A, B, C		

IN-DEPTH ANSWERS

1. ☑ **A, C,** and **D.** Depending on the design of the laptop, you will likely need to remove the laptop's keyboard to gain access to the Mini PCI Express slot for the wireless card. Sometimes you use a tab to release the keyboard from the laptop frame, but must still use a thin, flat tool to pry the keyboard up from the frame. Some wireless cards have both main and auxiliary antenna connectors, and both need to be attached. Once you have physically installed the card, you will still need to use the installation disc to configure the card for the laptop.
    ☒ **B** is incorrect because it is unlikely that you'll need to solder a Mini PCI Express card into an expansion slot.

2. ☑ **A, B,** and **C.** It is standard to remove the battery before beginning any sort of repair or upgrade on a laptop to prevent accidentally powering up the laptop. Very often, you'll need to remove the keyboard to gain access to the laptop's internal components. It is also common to have to remove the optical drive to access the video card.
    ☒ **D** is incorrect because it's unlikely you'll have to remove the CPU in order to gain access to the video card.

3. ☑ **A** and **C.** A keyboard can be attached to a laptop by a combination of screws and tabs that will need to be removed to free the keyboard. If the screws come in different sizes, you can keep them organized by putting the like screws in small paper cups and labeling each cup to indicate where the screws need to be placed upon reassembly. The keyboard is connected to the motherboard by a wide data cable. Sometimes you'll need a small plastic "pick" to press the latches securing the cable to the motherboard to release the cable.
    ☒ **B** and **D** are incorrect. **B** is incorrect because there is no power cable attached to the keyboard and no internal power supply in the laptop. **D** is incorrect because the "warranty seal" is fictitious.

4. ☑ **A** and **B.** You can disassemble the laptop to remove the plastic piece and then carefully apply epoxy to the underside of the crack to repair it if the crack isn't too big. If the damage is more extensive, you can purchase a replacement part. While it's usually recommended to buy replacement parts from the manufacturer, often you can find the same part at a better price on eBay.
    ☒ **C** and **D** are incorrect. **C** is incorrect because the laptop is new and otherwise working well and the damage to the plastic part is not severe. **D** is incorrect because soldering plastic not only won't repair the damage, but hot solder will create more extensive damage to the plastic and probably to the internal components beneath the crack as well.

5. ☑ **A, B,** and **C.** In Control Panel, click Hardware And Sound, then Mouse, and click the Pointer Options tab to view and adjust the touchpad settings. In Device Manager, expand Mice And Other Pointing Devices and then double-click Touch Pad to access the Touch Pad Properties dialog box. From here, you can determine if the device is working and update the drivers if necessary. The touchpad is a replaceable device, and sometimes the connection to the motherboard can become loose. Check and make sure the cable connection is secure.

    ☒ **D** is incorrect because the keyboard connection should not affect the touchpad.

6. ☑ **C.** While replacing a laptop's internal speakers is more or less an easy process, the most difficult part is finding speakers that will properly fit in the laptop.

    ☒ **A, B,** and **D** are incorrect. **A** is incorrect because laptop speakers are not integrated into the laptop. **B** is incorrect because laptop speakers are not integrated into the laptop's sound card. **D** is incorrect because, while you will get better sound quality from external speakers, if you have a laptop because it's portable, having to carry external speakers around is inconvenient.

7. ☑ **C** and **D.** Since the problem started after the customer added a number of devices, begin by removing all the added peripherals and see if the computer boots. If it does, try adding each peripheral back one at a time, starting the computer each time, until you find the problem device. If the computer doesn't start, you can use a multimeter to check the power adapter components and see if the problem is there.

    ☒ **A** and **B** are incorrect. **A** is incorrect because not only is reinstalling the operating system an extreme diagnostic method, most likely a problem with the operating system wouldn't result in the computer completely failing to boot. **B** is incorrect because there's no indication that the problem is application related.

8. ☑ **B.** If you installed an unformatted hard drive in a laptop, when you boot the machine, you'll receive a message stating that no operating system is present. You will need to format the drive and install an operating system.

    ☒ **A, C,** and **D** are incorrect. **A** and **C** are incorrect because, if the drive is unformatted, the operating system will not be present on the hard drive. **D** is incorrect because the BIOS is installed in the motherboard and not the hard drive, so it is already present.

9. ☑ **A.** Since the most recent change you made to the laptop was installing a SODIMM stick, it is likely this is the cause of the boot failure. Remove the new SODIMM stick and try booting the computer again to test this theory.

    ☒ **B, C,** and **D** are incorrect. **B** is incorrect because having the battery fail just after you installed a memory stick would be coincidental. Also, you can partially test this theory by plugging the laptop into a power strip and seeing if it will power up. **C** is incorrect because it's unlikely that the motherboard will fail just after installing a new SODIMM module unless you did something to damage the motherboard during the process. **D** is incorrect because, while a bad driver can cause a computer to fail to boot, it isn't a very likely occurrence.

10. ☑ **A** and **D.** Attach an external monitor to the laptop via the VGA port. If the image on the external monitor is fine, the problem is related to the screen. If it's not, the problem is probably the video card. Open the laptop to check the connections between the LCD screen and the motherboard. If that fixes the problem, it was a loose connection. If not, it's probably the video card or a bad screen.

☒ **B** and **C** are incorrect. **B** is incorrect because poorly seated memory modules will not cause this specific problem. **C** is incorrect because an LCD inverter problem would cause the screen to appear very dim or black, not produce a garbled image.

11. ☑ **B.** Full-size laptops most often use liquid crystal display (LCD) technology for their screens. These displays are lit by light-emitting diodes (LEDs).

☒ **A, C,** and **D** are incorrect. **A** is incorrect because plasma displays are not used in laptop devices. **C** and **D** are incorrect because OLED and AMOLED technology are typically used in smaller form-factor devices, such as tablets and smartphones.

12. ☑ **A, B,** and **C.** Laptops often have manual switches that let you turn Wi-Fi on or off. They can be physical switches on the laptop case or keyboard shortcuts. Check the documentation for your specific laptop make and model to find the Wi-Fi on/off switch. Checking Device Manager will show you if there are any error messages associated with the wireless adapter, including whether it requires a driver update. Internal and external wireless antennas can become disconnected, resulting in this sort of problem. Verify that all physical connections are secure.

☒ **D** is incorrect because there is no separate power lead for a built-in wireless adapter from the motherboard.

13. ☑ **B.** People commonly use their laptops in bed, but the presence of thick blankets or other bedding can block the cooling fan vents, causing the machine to overheat and the fans to continually run to try to cool the unit.

☒ **A, C,** and **D** are incorrect. **A** is incorrect because under normal circumstances, the laptop cooling system should keep the laptop interior cool, even if the unit has been running all day. Also, most laptops are set to go into some form of Sleep mode, which drastically reduces the machine's heat output if left unused for long periods of time, so heat wouldn't have "accumulated" by the evening when the customer started using the laptop. **C** is incorrect because, although possible, the circumstances of the problem strongly indicate a situational rather than a systemic problem. **D** is incorrect because it is unlikely the battery is overheating under these circumstances.

14. ☑ **D.** Port replicators typically include all of the ports commonly found on a laptop computer, allowing for permanent connections to devices on a user's desk. Port replicators do not include storage devices, optical drives, or expansion slots that are commonly found in docking stations.

☒ **A, B,** and **C** are incorrect because port replicators typically include monitor connections, USB ports, and power connections.

15. ☑ **A.** Hybrid Sleep is a feature introduced with Windows Vista and continued in Windows 7 for laptops that saves any open documents and programs to memory and to your hard disk, and then puts your computer into a low-power state as in normal Sleep/ Standby state. An advantage of Hybrid Sleep is that if a power failure occurs, Windows can restore your work from your hard disk.

☒ **B, C,** and **D** are incorrect. **B** is incorrect because Hybrid Hibernate is a not a Windows feature. **C** is incorrect because Sleep is more commonly known as Standby and stores information to memory. **D** is incorrect because standby is another term for "Sleep" and stores open documents and other data into memory.

16. ☑ **D.** The Balanced power plan in Windows 7 offers the best performance trade-off for laptop users. It provides a good mix of system performance and power efficiency.

☒ **A, B,** and **C** are incorrect. **A** is incorrect because the High Performance power plan consumes a large amount of power. **B** is incorrect because it is only appropriate when you need to squeeze every last bit of battery time out of your laptop. **C** is incorrect because there is no Laptop power plan in Windows 7.

8

Client-Side Virtualization

❑   **802: 1.9**   Explain the basics of client-side virtualization.

QUESTIONS

Earlier in the world of computing there was software and it ran on hardware and that was that. While computer virtualization has existed for many years now, recently it has become extremely common for a large portion of server and client computing systems to run in virtual environments. With virtualization a single piece of hardware can support multiple servers and client computers for both testing and production purposes. While the A+ exams don't expect you to be a virtualization guru, you must know the basics of supporting virtual client-side computing.

Objective 802: 1.9 Explain the Basics of Client-Side Virtualization

1. You run an IT company that supports small to mid-range business clients and specializes in client-side virtualization. You have several customers who would benefit from running virtual computers rather than multiple hardware computers. Of the following, which customers would benefit from using client-side virtualization? (Choose all that apply.)

   A. A customer with a limited budget who needs to test applications they are developing on multiple x86 operating systems and multiple versions of the same x86 operating system.

   B. A customer with a limited budget who needs to test the Web application they are developing on multiple Web browsers and multiple versions of the same Web browser on Windows 7.

   C. A customer with a limited budget who needs to test new network configurations between multiple x86 desktop operating systems in a secure environment that doesn't affect their production computing platform.

   D. A customer with a limited budget who needs to run multiple server clients for their DHCP, DNS, FTP, print, and database needs of their business.

2. You are teaching a course on basic computing and your topic for today is computer virtualization basics. Your students are well versed in hardware computing but have only a limited grasp on virtual computing. The question of the hypervisor comes up. How do you best describe what a hypervisor is to a group inexperienced with virtual machines? (Choose all that apply.)

   A. Software that supports desktop virtualization

   B. A virtual machine monitor (VMM)

   C. A virtual machine

   D. Allows multiple virtual machines to run on the same computer

3. You have a client who wants to run Windows XP Mode on her Windows 7 computer in order to run business applications that will only run on Windows XP. You tell her you must download and install Windows XP Mode and Windows Virtual PC onto her machine but must first make sure her computer meets the resource requirements. When you check, what do you find are the resource requirements for Windows Virtual PC?

A. 1 GHz 64-bit processor

B. 2 GB memory or higher recommended

C. Recommended 30 GB hard disk space per virtual Windows environment

D. Windows 7 Professional or Windows 7 Ultimate

4. You are teaching a class on beginning virtualization at your local community college. A student asks about the difference between virtualization and emulation. You explain that an emulator allows a person to run an operating system on hardware with which it is completely incompatible. Virtualization, on the other hand, uses emulators to create virtual machines that are compatible with the underlying hardware. Of the following, what do you say about emulator requirements?

A. Emulators need more computing resources than hypervisors.

B. Hypervisors need more computing resources than emulators.

C. Emulators and hypervisors need the same computing resources.

D. Emulators consume no computing resources at all.

5. You have installed a virtualization application on your Windows 7 host computer and you have just installed a Windows XP guest computer and a Windows Vista guest computer to use for testing different applications your small business develops, including e-mail client apps. Your Windows 7 host computer is secure with antivirus, antispam, the onboard Windows firewall, and other security features, but you are concerned about your virtual machines. Of the following, what security measures should you take for your Windows guest systems? (Choose all that apply.)

A. You should install an antivirus program on each guest machine.

B. You should install an antispam program on each guest machine.

C. You should enable Windows Firewall or install a third-party firewall program on each guest machine.

D. Each guest machine is protected by the security measures implemented on the host computer, so no additional steps need to be taken to protect your guest machines.

6. You are teaching a class on beginning virtualization at your local community college. You are discussing the networking requirements for desktop virtualization, which include running a hypervisor and guest operating system on a desktop machine. Of the following, what are reasons why having an Internet connection is required for desktop virtualization? (Choose all that apply.)

   A. The easiest way to obtain a hypervisor is by downloading it over the Internet.

   B. To download updates for the host and guest operating systems.

   C. To update the hypervisor to the latest version.

   D. To run your hypervisor on a remote server.

7. You work for an IT company that supports small business and home computer users. You are reviewing the requirements for Microsoft Virtual PC 2007 for a small business customer who wants to use virtual machines on a number of his current computers. Of the following, which host computer operating systems do you tell the customer will natively support Microsoft Virtual PC 2007? (Choose all that apply.)

   A. Windows XP

   B. Windows Vista

   C. Windows 7

   D. Linux

QUICK ANSWER KEY

1. A, C
2. A, B, D
3. B

4. A
5. A, B, C

6. A, B, C
7. A, B, C

IN-DEPTH ANSWERS

1. ☑ **A** and **C.** A client who needs to run multiple operating systems and multiple versions of the same operating system for testing purposes would greatly benefit by running several virtual machines, each with a different OS platform, on a single hardware computer or on just a few hardware computers. A customer can also create a small virtual network of client machines on a single piece of hardware. Both scenarios would allow the clients to achieve their business goals while conserving financial resources by not making hardware purchases for each client computer required.

    ☒ **B** and **D** are incorrect. **B** is incorrect because you can install multiple Web browsers on a single Windows 7 machine and would need only a few Windows 7 computers to run multiple versions of multiple Web browsers. **D** is incorrect because the customer requires that a server-side virtualization environment be configured and you support client-side virtualization.

2. ☑ **A, B,** and **D.** A hypervisor is software that allows virtual machines to be created. It is also referred to as a virtual machine monitor (VMM). The hypervisor allows multiple guest operating systems to run on the same hardware computer.

    ☒ **C** is incorrect. A hypervisor is software that allows the creation of virtual machines, but it is not the virtual machine itself.

3. ☑ **B.** 2 GB of memory or more are required to run Windows Virtual PC.

    ☒ **A, C,** and **D** are incorrect. **A** is incorrect because you can use 1 GHz 32-bit or 64-bit processor, not just a 64-bit processor. **C** is incorrect because 15 GB or more hardware drive space is recommended per virtual Windows environment. **D** is incorrect because supported operating systems are Windows 7 Home Basic, Home Premium, Enterprise, Professional, and Ultimate, not just Professional and Ultimate.

4. ☑ **A.** Emulators need more computing resources than hypervisors, and operating systems typically run slower in an emulator than on the original hardware.

    ☒ **B, C,** and **D** are incorrect. **B** is incorrect because the opposite is true. **C** is incorrect because emulators need more resources than hypervisors. **D** is incorrect because emulators do consume computing resources.

5. ☑ **A, B,** and **C.** Each guest machine acts as an independent network device in relation to the host machine's security methods. You will need to install or enable all of the security applications on your guest Windows machines as if they were stand-alone host machines, including antivirus, antispam, and firewall applications.

    ☒ **D** is incorrect because the security measures running on the host machine will not protect the guest operating systems.

6. ☑ **A, B,** and **C.** A hypervisor is just like any other type of software and can be downloaded and updated over the Internet. Also, both the host and guest operating systems need updates, which requires an Internet connection.

   ☒ **D** is incorrect because the setup for running desktop virtualization being discussed requires that the hypervisor run on the local host desktop machine, not a remote server.

7. ☑ **A, B,** and **C.** Microsoft Virtual PC will run on most editions of Windows, including Windows XP, Windows Vista, and Windows 7.

   ☒ **D** is incorrect because Microsoft Virtual PC 2007 is not natively supported on Linux.

9

Upgrading, Installing, and Configuring Windows

❑ **802: 1.2** Given a scenario, install and configure the operating system using the most appropriate method.

❑ **802: 1.4** Given a scenario, use appropriate operating system features and tools.

❑ **802: 1.5** Given a scenario, use Control Panel utilities (the items are organized by "classic view/large icons" in Windows).

QUESTIONS

As an A+ technician, you will need to be proficient in managing the Windows operating system, including methods of installing, upgrading, and configuring Windows. This includes the ability to use different methods for booting Windows, employing different installation and upgrade types, performing tasks using native Windows administrative tools, and knowing how all of the options in the Control Panel operate. The questions in this chapter will hone those skills.

Objective 802: 1.2   Given a Scenario, Install and Configure the Operating System Using the Most Appropriate Method

1. You want to be able to boot a computer to Windows 7 using a USB thumb drive. The drive will need to be formatted to use the NTFS file system before it can be used as a boot device. To format the thumb drive, you connect it to a USB port on your computer, enter Device Manager, and then, under Disk Drives, right-click the flash drive and select properties. Of the following options, which one correctly describes the computer where you are performing this task?
   A. You must perform this action only if you are using a Windows XP computer to format the flash drive.
   B. You must perform this action only if you are using a Windows Vista computer to format the flash drive.
   C. You must perform this action only if you are using a Windows 7 computer to format the flash drive.
   D. You must perform this action on any Windows operating system version to format the flash drive.

2. The system files on your Windows 7 computer have become corrupt, making it almost impossible to boot your PC. You need to keep the programs and data files intact on your Windows 7 computer but perform an installation that will restore the Windows 7 system files to their original state. Of the following, which installation method should you choose?
   A. Unattended installation
   B. Upgrade
   C. Clean install
   D. Repair installation

3. You want to convert the basic disk on a Windows XP Home computer to a dynamic disk, but when you go through the conversion routine, the option isn't available. You perform some research and discover the reason. What is the problem?

   A. The disk drive contains corrupt system files preventing the conversion from a basic to a dynamic disk.

   B. Drives cannot be converted from basic to dynamic disks. You can only configure a dynamic disk when you partition a drive for the first time.

   C. This action is only supported for Windows XP Professional and later versions of Windows.

   D. You can only perform this action on hard drives installed in Windows Vista and Windows 7 computers.

4. You want to convert one of the hard disks in your Windows 7 computer to NTFS, but first you need to know what file system is currently being used on the drive. Of the following options, which ones can you use to determine this? (Choose all that apply.)

   A. Open a command prompt, navigate to the appropriate drive, and then type **sfc /?** to run the system file checker.

   B. Click the Windows Start button, click Computer, right-click the desired drive, select Properties, and look under File System on the General tab.

   C. Click the Windows Start button, click Computer, right-click the desired drive, select Properties, and look under File System on the Hardware tab.

   D. In Control Panel, click Administrative Tools, click Computer Management, click Disk Management, and look in the File System column for the desired disk in the main pane.

5. You have heard that different computer manufacturers install a factory recovery partition on Windows 7 computers to be used if there is a problem. You don't believe the company that made your computer did this. You investigate to see if Microsoft provides a recovery partition for Windows 7. What do you find out?

   A. Microsoft does not provide a recovery partition for any edition of Windows.

   B. Microsoft provided a recovery partition for the Windows Recovery Environment (WinRE), which only shipped with Windows Vista and was available on the Windows Vista installation disc. It was not continued for Windows 7.

   C. Microsoft provides this feature on all editions of Windows 7 computers in a 200 MB partition if the computer is using a single partition on its disk drive.

   D. Microsoft provides this feature, but only on the Windows 7 installation disc.

Objective 802: 1.4 Given a Scenario, Use Appropriate Operating System Features and Tools

6. You are performing some maintenance tasks on a Windows 7 computer for a client. You click the Windows Start button, click Control Panel, double-click Administrative Tools, and then double-click Computer Management. Of the following, which tasks can you successfully perform with this utility? (Choose all that apply.)

  A. You can click Disk Management under Storage and view the properties of any volume operating on the computer.

  B. You can click Device Manager under System Tools and update driver software for various devices on the computer.

  C. You can click Programs And Features under System Tools to uninstall different applications on the computer.

  D. You can click Network And Sharing Center under Networking to view active networks for the computer.

7. You believe your Windows 7 computer is having a problem with one of the programs that loads when the computer first starts. Your computer is on and operating now, but you want to use the MSCONFIG tool to disable one or more applications and then reboot to see if that makes a difference. How can you use the MSCONFIG utility to accomplish this task?

  A. In the MSCONFIG tool, click the Boot tab and then under Startup Item, deselect the check boxes for each of the programs you want to disable upon the next reboot of the computer.

  B. In the MSCONFIG tool, click the Boot.ini tab and then under Startup Item, deselect the check boxes for each of the programs you want to disable upon the next reboot of the computer.

  C. In the MSCONFIG tool, click the Startup tab and then under Startup Item, deselect the check boxes for each of the programs you want to disable upon the next reboot of the computer.

  D. Windows 7 does not have the MSCONFIG tool. It was discontinued after Windows XP.

8. There appears to be a rogue process, possibly malware, running on a customer's Windows XP machine. You want to stop the process without affecting the overall performance of the computer. How can you do this?

  A. Open Task Manager, select the Applications tab, select the process, and click End Task.

  B. Open Task Manager, select the Processes tab, select the process, and click End Process.

  C. Open Task Manager, select the Performance tab, select the process, and click Stop Program.

  D. Open the command-line window and use the killtask utility to kill the process.

9. Normally, when disks and partitions are added in Windows, Windows takes care of assigning drive letters; however, you want to change the drive letters on a client's computer to fit the requirements of their small business. How can you do this?

   A. In the Computer Management utility, click Disk Management, right-click the desired drive in the top main pane, and then click Change Drive Letter And Paths.

   B. In the Computer Management utility, click Disk Management, right-click the desired drive in the top main pane, click Properties, and then on the General tab, change the drive letter and path under Drive Letter.

   C. Click the Windows Start button, right-click Computer, click Properties, and on the General tab, change the drive letter and path under Drive Letter.

   D. Click the Windows Start button, click Computer, right-click the desired drive, click Properties, and on the General tab, change the drive letter and path under Drive Letter.

10. You are sitting at the keyboard of a Windows 7 computer at work and you want to use a graphical interface to make a remote login connection with a server in the IT room so you can perform some routine maintenance tasks. Which run-line utility should you use?

    A. CMD

    B. SERVICES.MSC

    C. MMC

    D. MSTSC

Objective 802: 1.5   Given a Scenario, Use Control Panel Utilities (the Items Are Organized by "Classic View/Large Icons" in Windows)

11. You are setting up a dial-up connection for a rural customer who is using a Windows 7 computer. You know you must configure the connection by clicking the Setup button on the Internet Properties box as shown in the accompanying screenshot. How do you get to this dialog box? (Choose all that apply.)

    A. In Control Panel in Category View, click Network And Internet, click Network And Sharing Center, click Internet Options, and then, on the Internet Properties box, click the Connections tab.

    B. In Control Panel in Category View, click Network And Internet, click HomeGroup, click Internet Options, and then, on the Internet Properties box, click the Connections tab.

C. In Control Panel in Category View, click Network And Internet, click Internet Options, and then, on the Internet Properties box, click the Connections tab.

D. In Control Panel in Large Or Small Icons View, click Network And Sharing Center, click Internet Options, and then, on the Internet Properties box, click the Connections tab.

12. You notice on your Windows 7 computer that file extensions are not displayed and you are concerned about not being able to see the file extensions of e-mail attachments, as this could pose a security risk. How can you cause file extensions to be displayed?

A. Go into Control Panel and select Folder Options.

B. Click Start, right-click Computer, click Properties, and in the left-hand menu in the System window, select File Options.

C. In the Start menu, right-click Documents and select File Options.

D. There is no way to override this default behavior in Windows 7.

13. You are performing maintenance services on a customer's Windows XP machine and you have opened Control Panel and double-clicked the Add Or Remove Programs applet to uninstall an application the customer no longer uses. After uninstalling the program, you plan to perform other tasks in this tool. Of the following, what can you do inside Add or Remove Programs on Windows XP? (Choose all that apply)

A. You can view which Windows Updates are installed on the computer.

B. You can add or remove Windows components such as Internet Explorer and Windows Messenger.

C. You can specify which programs are accessible from the Start menu and desktop.

D. You can select which programs will load when Windows XP starts up.

14. You have a customer who uses Windows Vista and has complained of numerous difficulties on her computer. You decide to go into Control Panel and open the Problem Reports and Solutions tool in order to investigate. You see a list of problems that have occurred on the computer presented in tabular format. What columns are available that present information? (Choose all that apply.)

A. The Product column shows which device or component has had a problem.

B. The Problem column describes the problem.

C. The Solutions column offers the most likely solution to the problem.

D. The Date column tells you the date and time the problem happened.

15. You work for the operations department in your company, and a user in the accounting department needs to be able to access a Windows Server 2008 machine that has been configured to provide remote applications specific to her job. The server has already been prepared, but you must configure the user's Windows 7 machine to access these applications. You go into Control Panel and click RemoteApp and Desktop Connections. What is the next step you must take?

A. Click Set Up A New Connection With RemoteApp And Desktop Connections.

B. In the Connection URL field, add the URL for the server and directory that the user must access, and then click Next.

C. Type the IP address of the desired server in the available field and then click Next.

D. When the list of available computers and servers on the network appears, navigate to the desired server and double-click it.

QUICK ANSWER KEY

1. A	6. A, B	11. A, C, D
2. D	7. C	12. A
3. C	8. B	13. A, B, C
4. B, D	9. A	14. A, B, D
5. C	10. D	15. A

IN-DEPTH ANSWERS

1. ☑ **A.** You only need to perform these specific steps if you are formatting a USB drive for NTFS on a Windows XP computer. On Vista and Windows 7, you can format a USB drive directly in the Computer dialog box.

   ☒ **B, C,** and **D** are incorrect. **B** and **C** are incorrect because the process for formatting a USB drive on Windows Vista and Windows 7 can be done directly through Computer. Click the Windows Start button, click Computer, right-click the USB drive, and then click Format to begin. **D** is incorrect because you only need to perform the formatting in Device Manager on a Windows XP computer.

2. ☑ **D.** The Windows 7 Startup Repair tool allows you to basically copy over the current Windows 7 system files with the original Windows 7 files, while leaving any installed application software and data intact.

   ☒ **A, B,** and **C** are incorrect. **A** is incorrect because an unattended installation is a method of installing Windows that does not require a person to be at the computer to perform interactive configuration tasks during the installation routine. **B** is incorrect because an upgrade installation is one where you are upgrading an earlier version of Windows, such as Windows Vista, to a later version, such as Windows 7. **C** is incorrect because a clean install is performed on a computer that either has never had an operating system installed before or one where you want to totally overwrite everything on the hard drive, including the existing operating system, all application software, and all data files.

3. ☑ **C.** For Windows XP, this action is only supported on Windows XP Professional, but not on Windows XP Home.

   ☒ **A, B,** and **D** are incorrect. **A** is incorrect because corrupt system files are not a likely cause of not seeing the option to convert a basic disk to a dynamic disk on a Windows computer. **B** is incorrect because there is a process for converting basic disks to dynamic disks. **D** is incorrect because this process can also be performed on Windows XP Professional, not just Windows Vista and Windows 7.

4. ☑ **B and D.** You can determine what file system a drive is using either by right-clicking the drive in the Computer Properties box and looking under File System on the General tab, or in the Disk Management tool, the file system will be displayed for each drive on the computer in the File System column in the main pane of the utility.

   ☒ **A and C** are incorrect. **A** is incorrect because this command will only result in the "help" content being displayed for system file checker. It does not provide information about file system types. **C** is incorrect because the Hardware tab shows all of the drives and drive types but not the file systems they use.

5. ☑ **C.** This feature is available for all editions of Windows 7. If the disk drive is using a single partition, the recovery partition is stored in a 200 MB partition. If the computer is using multiple partitions, the recovery environment is stored in a folder in the root of your installation drive, such as C:\Recovery.

   ☒ **A, B,** and **D** are incorrect. **A** is incorrect because Microsoft does provide a recovery partition for both Windows Vista and Windows 7. **B** is incorrect because, while the information about Windows Vista is true, Microsoft continued to provide a recovery partition option for Windows 7. **D** is incorrect because the recovery partition is available on the Windows 7 computer on the hard drive, not the Windows 7 installation disc, which users often aren't provided with when purchasing a Windows 7 computer.

6. ☑ **A** and **B.** Both the Disk Management and Device Manager options are available in the left sidebar of the Computer Management utility.

   ☒ **C** and **D** are incorrect because Programs and Features and Network and Sharing Center are available as applets in the Control Panel but not in the Computer Management tool.

7. ☑ **C.** In the Search box, type **msconfig** and then press ENTER. When the MSCONFIG tool opens, click the Startup tab and deselect any check box next to an application you want to be disabled on the next startup. Click OK to close the tool, and then reboot the computer.

   ☒ **A, B,** and **D** are incorrect. **A** is incorrect because the Boot tab lists the operating system that loads upon boot and provides you with options for safe boot, boot log, and other diagnostic and repair tools associated with the boot process. **B** is incorrect because the boot. ini tab does not exist in MSCONFIG on Windows 7. **D** is incorrect because MSCONFIG does exist in Windows 7.

8. ☑ **B.** In Task Manager on the Processes tab, you can select a specific process in the list and click the End Process button to stop the process. You'll receive a warning message dialog box stating that ending a process could make your system unstable. Click OK to end the process.

   ☒ **A, C,** and **D** are incorrect. **A** is incorrect because you can only end running applications on the Applications tab but not all processes running on the computer. **C** is incorrect because you can only observe graphic depictions of CPU and page file usage on the Performance tab. **D** is incorrect because the killtask command-line utility is fictitious. Ending a process is possible using the taskkill utility on the command line.

9. ☑ **A.** The only way to change the drive letter for a particular drive or partition mentioned here is by using Disk Management in the Computer Management utility.

☒ **B, C,** and **D** are incorrect. **B** is incorrect because this set of steps takes you to the General tab of the properties box of the selected drive, which does not let you change the drive's letter. **C** is incorrect because right-clicking Computer and then clicking Properties takes you to the System Properties box, which allows you to view information about your computer and to access various tools, but not change a specific disk or partition drive letter. **D** is incorrect because this also takes you to the General tab of the properties box of the selected drive, which does not let you change the drive's letter.

10. ☑ **D.** Typing **mstsc** in the Search box and pressing ENTER opens the Remote Desktop Connection tool, which will allow you to make a remote connection to the server as long as you have the correct login credentials and the name of the server.

☒ **A, B,** and **C** are incorrect. **A** is incorrect because this will open a command prompt, which will not offer you a graphical interface to remotely connect to the server; however, with the correct commands, you could make a remote connection and perform tasks on the server at the prompt. **B** is incorrect because the Services tool allows you to start, stop, and configure the various services running on the Windows 7 computer. **C** is incorrect because the Microsoft Management Console is a tool that lets you add snap-ins to the console to perform a number of computer management tasks.

11. ☑ **A, C,** and **D.** To reach the Internet Properties dialog box, in Control Panel Category view, click Internet Options on the Network And Internet screen and then click the Connections tab. After clicking Setup, if the computer hasn't yet been connected to the Internet, you will be able to enter the required phone number provided by the ISP for the computer to use to connect to a dial-up connection. Enter a user name and password, give the connection a name, and then click Connect. Once the computer connects to the Internet, you can exit the wizard. The Network and Sharing Center has an Internet Options link in the lower-left sidebar.

☒ **B** is incorrect because there is no Network and Internet applet in Control Panel; it's called Network and Sharing Center. Also, after clicking HomeGroup, there is no option to click Internet Options.

12. ☑ **A.** Open Control Panel, open Folder Options, click the View tab, and clear the Hide Extensions For Known File Types check box. However, you must open Control Panel in View By: Large Or Small Icons, not Category, to see the Folder Options applet.
    ☒ **B, C,** and **D** are incorrect. **B** is incorrect because the File Options selection does not appear in the System window. **C** is incorrect because there is no File Options selection when you right-click Documents in the Start menu. **D** is incorrect because there is a method of showing file extensions in Windows 7.

13. ☑ **A, B,** and **C.** In Add or Remove Programs, click the Show Updates check box to see which Windows updates are installed. Click Add/Remove Windows Components to install or uninstall a variety of Windows components on the computer. Click Set Program Access And Defaults to decide which program configuration to use to specify default programs for various activities, including which programs will automatically appear in the Start menu and on the desktop.
    ☒ **D** is incorrect because you cannot perform this task from Add or Remove Programs. You can open MSCONFIG and on the Startup tab, select the check boxes for the installed programs you want to start when the computer loads Windows XP.

14. ☑ **A, B,** and **D.** The Product column gives you the name of the device or component that is having the problem, such as a mouse, video card, or even the operating system. The Problem column lists a short summary of the problem, and the Date column lists the date and time the problem happened. You can select the check box by one or more items in the list and then click the Check For Solutions button to try and find a way to fix the problems listed.
    ☒ **C** is incorrect because there is no Solutions column. Select the check box next to the problem item in the list, and then click Check For Solutions to find one or more possible ways to fix the problem.

15. ☑ **A.** Click the Set Up A New Connection With RemoteApp And Desktop Connections link. You will be taken to a screen where you can enter the specific URL to the server and directory on the server where the desired applications are installed.
    ☒ **B, C,** and **D** are incorrect. **B** is incorrect because this field can only be accessed after you click the Set Up A New Connection With RemoteApp And Desktop Connections link. **C** and **D** are incorrect because these options are not part of the RemoteApp and Desktop Connections tool, either as a first step or in any of the subsequent steps to creating a connection.

10

Disk and File Management

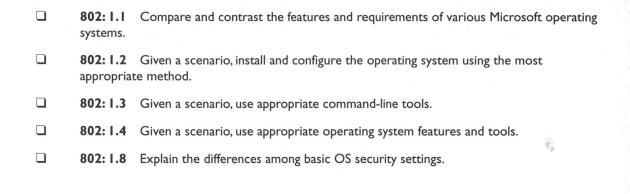

CERTIFICATION OBJECTIVES

❑   **802: 1.1**   Compare and contrast the features and requirements of various Microsoft operating systems.

❑   **802: 1.2**   Given a scenario, install and configure the operating system using the most appropriate method.

❑   **802: 1.3**   Given a scenario, use appropriate command-line tools.

❑   **802: 1.4**   Given a scenario, use appropriate operating system features and tools.

❑   **802: 1.8**   Explain the differences among basic OS security settings.

QUESTIONS

Disk and file management have changed significantly with the different Windows operating systems and, as an A+ computer technician, you will be expected to be able to understand disk and file management in the various editions of Windows. This includes using the command line and other utilities, as well as understanding file system security. Also, although NTFS is widely used in Windows, you'll still need to be familiar with the features and limitations of FAT32 and other file systems. You will also need to know how to compare and contrast different features available in the various editions of the Windows operating system. The questions in this chapter will sharpen your knowledge in these areas and more.

Objective 802: 1.1   Compare and Contrast the Features and Requirements of Various Microsoft Operating Systems

1. You have a customer who is considering upgrading from Windows Vista to Windows 7. She particularly likes the Windows Aero interface and asks you what has been changed in Aero for Windows 7. What do you say? (Choose two.)

    A. Aero Peek was added.

    B. Aero Snap was added.

    C. Live thumbnails were added.

    D. Live icons were added.

2. You are trying to navigate the file system of a Windows computer. In the left side of the screen you currently have open, under Other Places, you see options for My Documents, Shared Documents, and Control Panel. What screen are you looking at and on what operating system?

    A. You are on the Computer screen in Windows 7.

    B. You are on the Computer screen in Windows Vista.

    C. You are on the Libraries screen in Windows XP.

    D. You are on the My Computer screen in Windows XP.

3. On your Windows 7 Professional computer, you have right-clicked the taskbar and selected Properties to view the Taskbar And Start Menu Properties dialog box. On the Start Menu tab, what do you expect to see? (Choose all that apply.)

    A. Options for Start menu and Classic Start menu

    B. An option to set the Power button action

    C. Options under Privacy that let you choose how recently opened programs and items are displayed

    D. An option that says How Do I Change The Way The Start Menu Looks?

Objective 802: 1.2   Given a Scenario, Install and Configure the Operating System Using the Most Appropriate Method

4. You have a customer using a Windows XP Home computer and during routine maintenance, you discover that his computer uses the FAT32 file system. You discuss the advantages of converting to the NTFS file system. What are some of the advantages you mention? (Choose all that apply.)

    A. NTFS has better security than FAT32.

    B. NTFS is compatible with non-Windows computers and FAT32 is not.

    C. NTFS supports file compression and FAT32 does not.

    D. NTFS volumes can be converted to FAT32 volumes without losing data.

5. You are installing Windows XP on a computer for a small business customer who needs to run legacy applications only supported on XP. You insert the Windows XP CD into the computer's optical drive and begin the installation process. The customer wants NTFS as the file format rather than FAT32, and you notice that you are given the options of NTFS File System (Quick) and NTFS File System. Why would you choose the Quick option?

    A. Choose the Quick option if you want to skip scanning the BIOS for errors before formatting the disk.

    B. Choose the Quick option if you want to skip scanning the hard drive for viruses before formatting the disk.

    C. Choose the Quick option if you want to skip scanning the hard drive for bad sectors before formatting the disk.

    D. Choose the Quick option to double the write speed of the hard drive in the BIOS so the disk will be formatted twice as fast.

6. You are familiarizing yourself with all of the different file systems supported by Windows 7. You understand the basics of FAT32 and NTFS but still need to learn about CDFS on Windows. Of the following, what do you discover is true about CDFS?

    A. CDFS was designed to replace FAT32 but was made obsolete by NTFS.

    B. CDFS is the next generation of file system that will replace NTFS.

    C. CDFS is the CD/DVD file system reader used in Windows 7.

    D. CDFS is a file system only used on non-Windows operating systems and is not supported in Windows 7.

Objective 802: 1.3   Given a Scenario, Use Appropriate Command-Line Tools

7. You are managing a group of text files from the command line on a Windows XP computer. You want to copy a version of the win.ini file you've written to the default location of the win.ini file in the Windows directory, and you want to overwrite the file without receiving the prompt asking if you want to perform the overwrite. Which of the following commands should you use?

   A.   copy win.ini c:\windows /a

   B.   copy win.ini c:\windows /b

   C.   copy win.ini c:\windows /v

   D.   copy win.ini c:\windows /y

8. You work for a small city IT department and are managing a group of files and folders on a Windows 7 computer with the XCOPY command-line utility. A newly hired tech sees what you are doing and asks you why you are using XCOPY rather than the copy command. What do you tell her?

   A.   XCOPY is more powerful than copy and is able to move files, directories, and even entire drives from one location to another.

   B.   The copy command does not function on Windows 7 and was replaced by XCOPY.

   C.   The copy command can only copy files within the same directory, while XCOPY can move files across different directories.

   D.   XCOPY is just an alias for the copy command. There's no difference between them and you just prefer the XCOPY alias.

9. You are using the format command at the command line to format a floppy diskette on an old Windows XP machine. You want to add a label called "floppy" when formatting the disk. What is the proper command and switch to do this?

   A.   format a: /a:floppy

   B.   format a: /f:floppy

   C.   format a: /q:floppy

   D.   format a: /v:floppy

Objective 802: 1.4 Given a Scenario, Use Appropriate Operating System Features and Tools

10. An accountant at the company you work for routinely saves his files on the C: drive of his Windows Vista machine in a folder called Records; however, his C: drive is getting full. He has another drive on his machine, the E: drive, that has plenty of room, but he prefers to save all of his financial work records in the Records directory on the C: drive. You suggest that you could create an empty folder in Records called Financial, format it for NTFS, and then mount the E: drive to the Financial folder. This will let the accountant continue to save to the same directory he always does, but his files will actually be stored on the E: drive. How are you going to mount the E: drive to the Financial folder after it is created and formatted?

   A. In Computer Management, click Disk Management, right-click the desired drive, and then click Change Drive Letter And Paths.

   B. In Computer Management, click Disk Management, right-click the desired drive, and then click Mount In This NTFS Folder.

   C. In Disk Management, click Computer Management, right-click the desired drive, and then click Change Drive Letter And Paths.

   D. In Disk Management, click Computer Management, right-click the desired drive, and then click Mount In This NTFS Folder.

11. You have a customer who says the C: drive on her Windows 7 computer is filling up and she needs more space. You suggest that you could possibly extend the partition on her drive, increasing the space, but you'll need to look in the Disk Management utility to see if this is possible. What is the one thing you must see in Disk Management that will make it possible to extend the partition on her C: drive?

   A. There must be free, unused space on any hard drive in the computer so you can extend the partition.

   B. There must be free, unused space on the hard drive where the partition exists so you can extend the partition.

   C. There must be another partition that is not completely full so you can extend the partition into the unused space of the other partition.

   D. The Extend feature must be installed and enabled in Disk Management so you can extend the partition.

12. You have a Windows 7 computer with a single hard drive, the C: drive, that is formatted as a single partition. You want to split the partition on your hard drive into two partitions, one for the OS and one for data. To do that, you must first shrink the partition to create space for a second partition. What limits how much the Shrink tool can shrink the data on the C: drive?

    A. The Shrink tool will only be able to shrink the partition until it encounters unmovable files.

    B. The Shrink tool will only be able to shrink the partition until it encounters the programs and data stored on the C: drive.

    C. The Shrink tool will only be able to shrink the partition until it encounters the part of the C: drive containing the operating system.

    D. You cannot shrink the partition that contains the operating system.

Objective 802: 1.8   Explain the Differences Among Basic OS Security Settings

13. You are setting up a Windows 7 computer for a customer who will be using it in her small home office. In creating her user account, you recommend a specific permission level for her account. Of the following, which account in Windows 7 do you recommend she use for day-to-day operations?

    A. Administrator

    B. Power User

    C. Guest

    D. Standard user

14. You have been newly hired as a desktop support tech for a medium-size business. You are looking on your Windows 7 work computer at the share permissions for various folders that contain sensitive material and you notice that the default Everyone group has Full Control permissions on all of those folders. You ask your supervisor if this is a good idea and she explains why the information can't actually be accessed by everyone. Of the following, what does she say that tells you how security is maintained for those shared folders?

    A. The computer uses the NTFS file system, and NTFS permissions for those folders are set to Restrict for all groups and individuals except the IT department group, which has Allow permissions.

    B. The computer uses the NTFS file system, and NTFS permissions for those folders are set to Deny for all groups and individuals except the IT department group, which has Full Control permissions.

    C. The computer uses the FAT32 file system, and FAT32 permissions for those folders are set to Restrict for all groups and individuals except the IT department group, which has Allow permissions.

    D. The computer uses the FAT32 file system and FAT32 permissions for those folders are set to Deny for all groups and individuals except the IT department group, which has Full Control permissions.

15. You are providing technical support for a small business customer. She has a shared folder on her Windows 7 computer that she wants her two part-time employees to be able to access and read the files it contains, but she doesn't want them to be able to open any of the subdirectories in the folder. What do you tell her about her request?

    A. You can set this up only in Share permissions.

    B. You can set this up only in NTFS permissions.

    C. You can set this up only in CDFS permissions.

    D. This specific type of sharing cannot be configured, regardless of file system type.

QUICK ANSWER KEY

1.	A, B	**6.**	C	**11.**	B
2.	D	**7.**	D	**12.**	A
3.	B, C, D	**8.**	A	**13.**	D
4.	A, C	**9.**	D	**14.**	B
5.	C	**10.**	A	**15.**	B

IN-DEPTH ANSWERS

1. ☑ **A** and **B.** In Windows 7, Microsoft added a number of new Aero features, including Aero Peek, which lets you hover over a taskbar icon to show a thumbnail of the program, and Aero Snap, which causes a window to resize and to occupy different areas of the screen depending on where you drag the window. Other features include Aero Shake and an improved Aero blur effect.

   ☒ **C** and **D** are incorrect because they were standard features of Aero in Windows Vista.

2. ☑ **D.** When you click the Start button in Windows XP and then click My Computer, you are taken to the My Computer screen. In the sidebar under Other Places, you can see options for My Network Places, My Documents, Shared Documents, and Control Panel.

   ☒ **A, B,** and **C** are incorrect. **A** is incorrect because the Computer screen in Windows 7 only shows Documents under Libraries in the sidebar but not My Documents or Shared Documents. **B** is incorrect because the Computer screen in Windows Vista displays Documents, Pictures, and Music as options under Favorite Links in the sidebar. **C** is incorrect because there is no Libraries screen in Windows XP.

3. ☑ **B, C,** and **D.** On the Start Menu tab in the Taskbar And Start Menu Properties dialog box in Windows 7, you can use the Power button action drop-down menu to select what you want to happen when you press the power button. You can also select check boxes under Privacy that let you control how or if recently opened programs and items will be shown on the Start menu and taskbar, and you can click a link that will let you customize the appearance of the Start menu. None of these specific options appear in the same dialog box in Windows XP; however, there is a Customize button that does appear in this dialog box in both operating systems.

   ☒ **A** is incorrect because these options appear on the Start Menu tab for Windows XP but not in Windows 7.

4. ☑ **A** and **C.** NTFS supports individual NTFS folder and file permissions so that even if someone can log on to your computer, they can't necessarily access all of the files and folders on the computer. Also, NTFS supports file compression as well as encryption.

   ☒ **B** and **D** are incorrect. **B** is incorrect because NTFS is only compatible with Windows XP, Vista, and 7, while FAT32 is compatible with non-Windows computers. **D** is incorrect because while FAT32 volumes can be converted to NTFS, NTFS volumes can't be converted to FAT32 without losing data.

5. ☑ **C.** If you choose the Quick option, the formatting process will remove all files from the selected partition but will not scan the disk for bad sectors as the "regular" formatting process does. Only use the Quick option if the hard disk has been previously formatted and you are sure the drive has not been damaged. Selecting the Quick option for FAT32 does the same thing; skip the process of scanning for bad sectors prior to formatting the partition.
   ☒ **A, B,** and **D** are incorrect. **A** and **B** are incorrect because the regular process of formatting a disk for NTFS does not include scanning the BIOS for errors or scanning the hard disk for viruses. **D** is incorrect because choosing the Quick option does not double the write speed of the hard disk in the BIOS.

6. ☑ **C.** CDFS is the driver that allows data on CDs and DVDs to be read in different versions of Windows, including Windows 7. It is also used on other operating systems such as Linux.
   ☒ **A, B,** and **D** are incorrect. **A** and **B** are incorrect because CDFS does not replace either FAT32 or NTFS file systems. **D** is incorrect because CDFS is supported on both Windows and non-Windows operating systems.

7. ☑ **D.** If you use the /y switch with the copy command, it suppresses the prompt to confirm that you want to overwrite the existing destination file.
   ☒ **A, B,** and **C** are incorrect. **A** is incorrect because the /a switch indicates an ASCII text file. **B** is incorrect because the /b switch indicates a binary file. **C** is incorrect because the /v switch verifies that new files are written correctly.

8. ☑ **A.** XCOPY.exe is an external command, meaning it runs "outside" of cmd.exe, while copy runs "inside" cmd.exe. XCOPY is more powerful, possessing more features and switches and can copy files, directories, and even entire drives from one location to another.
   ☒ **B, C,** and **D** are incorrect. **B** is incorrect because copy does function on Windows 7. **C** is incorrect because the copy command can copy files from one part of a directory to another. **D** is incorrect because there is a big difference between copy and XCOPY in terms of features and capacities.

9. ☑ **D.** The /v switch used with a label name such as /v:floppy provides a label for the volume being formatted. If you don't use the /v switch with the format command, you will be prompted for a volume label after formatting is complete.
   ☒ **A, B,** and **C** are incorrect. **A** is incorrect because the /a switch, used with a value, specifies the unit size allocated on the volume to be formatted for FAT32 or NTFS volumes. If you don't use this switch, format will use the volume size as the unit size. Valid values are bytes per cluster, such as 512, 1024, 2048, 4096, and so on. **B** is incorrect because the /f switch, used with a value, indicates the size of the floppy diskette to format. **C** is incorrect because the /q switch performs a quick format of the volume, deleting the file table and root directory on a previously formatted volume but not performing a sector check for errors.

10. ☑ **A.** The correct process in Windows Vista is to open Administrative Tools in Control Panel, open System And Maintenance, open Administrative Tools, and then open Computer Management. Then in the left pane, under Storage, click Disk Management. Right-click the drive you want to mount, such as the E: drive, and then click Change Drive Letter And Paths. Click Add, click Mount In This NTFS Folder, and then either use the Browse feature to browse to the desired folder on the C: drive or type the path to the folder in the available field. Click OK and then click OK again to finish.

    ☒ **B, C,** and **D** are incorrect. **B** is incorrect because you must click Change Drive Letter And Paths and then click Add before the Mount In This NTFS Folder option appears. **C** and **D** are incorrect because Disk Management is located in Computer Management, not the other way around.

11. ☑ **B.** The one thing that must be present in order for you to extend a partition is free, unused space on the hard disk where the partition exists. If there is no unused space on the same disk, there is no place where you can extend the partition.

    ☒ **A, C,** and **D** are incorrect. **A** is incorrect because the unused space must be on the same disk as the partition you want to extend. **C** is incorrect because you cannot extend a partition into another partition. **D** is incorrect because the extend feature exists by default in Windows 7 as a Disk Management utility.

12. ☑ **A.** Anyone who has defragmented a hard drive in Windows knows that there are files on the drive that have a fixed position and cannot be moved. The Shrink tool can shrink the excess space on the partition until it encounters an unmovable file. Then the shrink process stops.

    ☒ **B, C,** and **D** are incorrect. **B** and **C** are incorrect because the shrink process will cease once it encounters the first unmovable file on the drive, which will most likely happen before it encounters the data, programs, and operating system occupying the drive. **D** is incorrect because you can shrink the partition containing the operating system.

13. ☑ **D.** Users should primarily access their Windows 7 computers as standard users. They can log on, run applications, customize the settings that apply to their account, save files, and so on, but cannot make system-wide changes to the computer. If their account should be compromised, although they may lose data, the compromised account can't be used to set policies, edit the registry, create other users and groups, and so on.

    ☒ **A, B,** and **C** are incorrect. **A** is incorrect because using the Administrator account for day-to-day use increases the likelihood that the account could be compromised. The Administrator account should only be used to make system-wide changes, not for routine tasks. **B** is incorrect because there is no option to create a Power User account in Windows 7. **C** is incorrect because the Guest account allows very limited access to the computer and Guests cannot save data and account settings, so for day-to-day business or personal use, it is ineffective.

14. ☑ **B.** When both share and NTFS permissions are set on a shared folder, the more restrictive share settings will be the ones that apply to the folder. In this case, the NTFS Deny setting applied to all groups and individual users will have dominance over the Share settings that let the Everyone group have Full Control. Of course, the file system for the computer must be NTFS for NTFS folder security to be present.

   ☒ **A, C,** and **D** are incorrect. **A** is incorrect because there is no Restrict or Allow setting in NTFS share permissions. **C** and **D** are incorrect because in a FAT32 file system, you only have one method of setting up shared folders. If the Everyone group has Full Control permissions, you would not be able to set the Everyone group to Deny as well.

15. ☑ **B.** In NTFS Advanced Security Settings for a shared folder, you can edit the permission entry properties for a group or individual so that they can only access and read in a specific shared folder but not access any subdirectories contained in that same folder.

   ☒ **A, C,** and **D** are incorrect. **A** is incorrect because regular share permissions do not have this ability. **C** is incorrect because CDFS is the file system reader for CDs and DVDs and is not used to set directory share permissions. **D** is incorrect because NTFS has this capacity.

11

Troubleshooting, Repair, and Maintenance of PCs

QUESTIONS

As a computer technician, you will be expected to solve a wide variety of problems with PCs, including hard drive failures and video problems, as well as issues with motherboards, RAM, and CPUs. You will also need to be well versed in how to solve such problems using troubleshooting theory. The questions in this chapter will sharpen your skills in troubleshooting PC technology.

Objective 802: 4.1   Given a Scenario, Explain the Troubleshooting Theory

1. According to CompTIA's theory of troubleshooting, during which of the following steps should you "question the obvious"?
    A. Identify the problem.
    B. Establish a theory of probable cause.
    C. Test the theory to determine cause.
    D. Establish a plan of action to resolve the problem and implement the solution.
    E. Verify full system functionality and, if applicable, implement preventive measures.
    F. Document findings, actions, and outcomes.

2. You have a customer who says she can't open her Word files on her work computer and is having difficulty articulating what the problem is more specifically. How can you learn more useful information about the problem so you can understand the best troubleshooting response? (Choose all that apply.)
    A. Ask the customer a series of specific questions about the problem that require yes or no answers.
    B. Ask the customer a series of open-ended questions that allow the customer to explain the problem using her own words.
    C. Ask investigative questions, such as "when did you first notice the problem" and "has anything recently changed on your computer."
    D. Ask the customer to sit at her computer and show you what she was doing when the problem first started happening.

3. You have a customer who says she can't open her Word files on her work computer. You have questioned her and acquired valuable diagnostic information and are forming a theory as to the most likely causes. How can you begin testing your theories to see if you can solve the problem?
    A. Order your theories from most likely cause to least likely cause.
    B. Test the first theory that comes to mind.
    C. Test the most likely cause of the problem from the customer's point of view.
    D. Reboot the computer as the most likely way to solve the problem.

4. You have discovered the cause of a customer's problem opening Word documents on her computer and confirmed the nature of the problem by testing it. What general steps should you take to solving the problem?

   A. Take the necessary actions to fix the problem based on your conclusion and then close the case.

   B. Take the necessary actions to fix the problem, have the customer confirm that she can open Word documents, and then close the case.

   C. Take the necessary actions to fix the problem, have the customer confirm that she can open Word documents and use other Microsoft Office tools, and then close the case.

   D. Take the necessary actions to fix the problem and then have the customer use Word and perform other normal work tasks to make sure that her computer is functioning normally.

Objective 802: 4.2   Given a Scenario, Troubleshoot Common Problems Related to Motherboards, RAM, CPU, and Power with Appropriate Tools

5. You have a customer who complains that his Windows XP Professional computer keeps locking up randomly. It had been performing slowly, especially during file transfers across the network, the past few weeks before the first lockup. After a hard reboot, the computer seems fine with no indication of a problem until the next lockup. The user hasn't installed any new hardware or software recently, and there doesn't appear to be a pattern to the lockups such as using a particular application or device. You check Event Viewer, but absolutely no error messages appear for the lockup events, which means the operating system kernel was completely unaware of the lockup occurrences. Of the following, what is the most likely cause?

   A. Bad video card memory

   B. A corrupted copy of Microsoft Office

   C. Bad RAM

   D. Antivirus software consuming all computer resources

6. You notice an odd "burnt plastic" smell coming from one of your computers. What would most likely be the cause?

   A. The hard drive is overheating.

   B. The plastic PC case is overheating.

   C. A capacitor on the motherboard could be overheating.

   D. The cables on the power supply are overloaded.

7. A customer complains that after his brother-in-law installed a new IDE hard drive in his older computer, the hard drive light stays on all the time, even when the computer is idle. The computer seems to run fine otherwise. What do you suspect?

   A. Insufficient RAM

   B. A dying power supply

   C. Hard drive LED connection problem on the motherboard

   D. Malfunctioning extension card

8. A user calls you saying that whenever she turns on her computer it beeps three times and shuts down. How can you find out what this means? (Choose three.)

   A. Check the motherboard manual that came with the computer.

   B. Check the quick start guide that came with the computer.

   C. Search the Internet for the computer's BIOS type.

   D. Search the Internet for the meaning of the beep code.

Objective 802: 4.3   Given a Scenario, Troubleshoot Hard Drives and RAID Arrays with Appropriate Tools

9. A customer complains that she is hearing clicking and scraping noises coming from the drive bay area of her computer. This is a classic symptom of a drive failure. Of the following, what drives can exhibit this symptom? (Choose two.)

   A. Flash

   B. PATA

   C. SATA

   D. SSD

10. You have a customer who complains that his Windows XP computer has blue-screened. You reboot the computer to view the blue-screen message, but it appears only for a few seconds before the computer attempts to restart. You need the blue screen to persist so you can see the error messages displayed. How can you accomplish this?

    A. Take a screenshot of the blue-screen image in the moment that it appears on the monitor.

    B. On the Advanced tab of the System Properties box, click the Startup And Recovery Settings button and then clear the Automatically Restart check box.

    C. In All Programs under Accessories, click System Tools, select System Restore, and then clear the Automatically Restart check box.

    D. In Control Panel, open Administrative Tools, then open Computer Management, click Actions, click All Tasks, and on the Advanced tab of the All Tasks box, click the Startup And Recovery Settings button and then clear the Automatically Restart check box.

11. You suspect that the hard drive on your Windows 7 computer may contain errors, and you want to use a utility that will not only check for errors but possibly fix them. Of the following, what is the best tool you can use to accomplish this task?

    A. CHDKS

    B. CHKDSK

    C. FORMAT

    D. FDISK

12. After electricity has been restored to your neighborhood after a power failure, you start your Windows 7 computer only to receive a message that a serious error has occurred and prompting you to boot into System Recovery using the Windows 7 install disc to repair the damage. What are valid options when using System Recovery that may help fix the problem? (Choose all that apply.)

    A. Booting normally.

    B. Run the Startup Repair wizard.

    C. Use Diskpart.

    D. Power down the computer and check for loose power connections to the hard drive.

Objective 802: 4.4   Given a Scenario, Troubleshoot Common Video and Display Issues

13. You work for a small city IT department and you get a call from a person in the mayor's office complaining her computer's monitor is bad and needs to be replaced. You take a look at the monitor and the power button on the unit is dark, indicating that it is not receiving any power. What could be the problem? (Choose two.)

    A. The power cable could be unplugged.

    B. The power cable could be damaged.

    C. The monitor cable could be unplugged.

    D. The monitor cable could be damaged.

14. You have an old Windows XP Professional computer you keep for testing purposes. Its monitor recently failed, so you connected an old CRT monitor to the computer. However, upon restarting the computer, the monitor presents only a black image and will only work when you use VGA mode. Attempting to change the resolution or depth in VGA mode causes the screen to go black again. What is the most likely problem?

    A. The refresh rate set in Display Properties isn't supported by the monitor.

    B. The resolution set in Display Properties isn't supported by the monitor.

    C. The cable from the computer to the monitor is damaged.

    D. The power cable for the monitor is damaged.

15. You get a call from a customer who was just given a used computer by his brother for his ten-year-old son to use for his school homework. Your customer says the image on the computer's monitor seems dim compared to the other computers he uses at home and work. With only this information available, what is the most likely cause?

    A. The older computer uses a CRT monitor, which habitually provides a dim image compared to newer LCD monitors.

    B. The older computer's monitor cable is damaged, resulting in loss of data being sent from the computer's video card to the monitor.

    C. The older computer's older monitor has lost its sharp image as a result of the passage of time.

    D. The older computer's video card is faulty and needs to be replaced.

16. You are working with a home customer with an older Windows XP computer. The computer uses a CRT monitor, and you have determined that the monitor needs to be degaussed using the monitor's onboard degaussing utility. What led you to this conclusion?

    A. The monitor image is discolored.

    B. The monitor image is distorted.

    C. The monitor image is flickering.

    D. The monitor image contains numerous dead LCD pixels.

QUICK ANSWER KEY

1.	B	**7.**	C	**13.**	A, B
2.	B, C, D	**8.**	A, C, D	**14.**	A
3.	A	**9.**	B, C	**15.**	C
4.	D	**10.**	B	**16.**	A
5.	C	**11.**	B		
6.	C	**12.**	B, C		

IN-DEPTH ANSWERS

1. ☑ **B.** The most likely or probable cause isn't necessarily the correct one. When you are developing your theory of what caused the problem, you should question what seems like the most obvious cause in order to develop alternate causes in the case where a less likely problem is actually the cause.

   ☒ **A, C, D, E,** and **F** are incorrect. **A** is incorrect because when you are identifying the problem, you are still in the process of discovering what the presenting issue is with the computer. Until you've done this, you cannot question the obvious cause. **C** is incorrect because you have to question the obvious cause and develop a theory before you can perform any testing. **D** is incorrect because by the time you are developing a corrective plan for the problem, you should have already questioned the most likely cause. **E** is incorrect because by the time you are verifying that your corrections worked, you are long past questioning the problem's cause. **F** is incorrect because once you get to the point of documenting your findings, you have already questioned the most and less likely causes of that problem.

2. ☑ **B, C,** and **D.** Open-ended questions give the customer the opportunity to describe the problem in their own words, providing details about their observations that can provide valuable diagnostic information. Also asking about what the customer was doing and what has recently changed on the computer will provide clues as to the behaviors and environment of the computer that could be contributing to the problem. Sometimes when a customer has difficulty in articulating a problem, it helps if you ask them to show you what they were doing when the problem first occurred.

   ☒ **A** is incorrect because asking closed-ended questions requiring only yes and no answers does not give the customer the opportunity to explain the details of the problem, and answers are based on the assumptions you are making when you are asking the questions.

3. ☑ **A.** Once you've gathered enough information about the problem and you have begun to form theories as to the probable causes, order the theories from most likely to have caused the problem to least likely to have caused the problem, and then test the most likely cause.

   ☒ **B, C,** and **D** are incorrect. **B** is incorrect because testing the first theory that occurs to you is not an orderly way to test problems and will likely lengthen the amount of time it takes to find the problem and fix it. **C** is incorrect because the customer's assessment of the most likely cause may not take into account details that only you as a computer technician would be aware of. **D** is incorrect because while rebooting is often the default method of fixing problems with Windows, it is not using your best judgment and troubleshooting skills.

4. ☑ **D.** Although performing the actions necessary to fix the problem are probably all you need to do, you should still have the customer not only test the application that was experiencing difficulties working, but perform her other regular work functions to verify that this problem wasn't related to a larger set of issues on the computer.

   ☒ **A, B,** and **C** are incorrect. **A** is incorrect because even once you've made the corrective actions, you don't really know if there are problems still happening on the computer. **B** and **C** are incorrect because these address the immediate problem but do not take into account the possibility that the problem with Word could be related to a larger set of issues, not only with Microsoft Office, but with other features on the computer.

5. ☑ **C.** This problem can be difficult to diagnose and often requires a third-party utility or the computer manufacturer's diagnostic tools suite to discover a bad memory module.

   ☒ **A, B,** and **D** are incorrect. **A** is incorrect because bad video card memory typically results in unusual visual indicators on the monitor. **B** is incorrect because the errors don't always occur when the customer is using Office, and application-related errors would show up in Event Viewer. **D** is incorrect because the problem doesn't always occur when the antivirus program is running, and application errors would show up in Event Viewer.

6. ☑ **C.** A chip or capacitor on the motherboard can produce a unique and pungent smell, kind of like burning plastic when it's overheating. In all likelihood the motherboard will have to be replaced.

   ☒ **A, B,** and **D** are incorrect. **A** is incorrect because it's unlikely the hard drive would overheat and produce such an odor. **B** is incorrect because it's unlikely that the plastic case of the computer could overheat to the point of burning. **D** is incorrect because the power supply wouldn't produce so much power that it would "overload" the cables and cause them to melt.

7. ☑ **C.** The LED connector is attached to the wrong two pins on the motherboard, resulting in the HDD LED being constantly on.

   ☒ **A, B,** and **D** are incorrect because faults in those components wouldn't result in the hard drive light being always on, especially because there are no other symptoms displayed by the computer.

8. ☑ **A, C,** and **D.** The motherboard manual that came with the computer should have a list of beep codes for you to reference. Also searching the Internet for either the BIOS type or beep code should provide the correct answer.

   ☒ **B** is incorrect because the quick start guide that came with the computer usually only includes enough information to set the computer up after it has been removed from its box.

9. ☑ **B** and **C.** Both parallel and serial ATA drives can exhibit these symptoms when on the verge of a mechanical failure, and these symptoms can be caused by a failed spindle motor, head crash, or broken actuator. Advise the customer to turn off her computer immediately. Failures such as these are an excellent reason to back up your valuable computer data often.

    ☒ **A** and **D** are incorrect. **A** is incorrect because a failing USB flash drive doesn't usually make symptomatic sounds. **D** is incorrect because a Solid-State Drive has no moving parts and wouldn't make mechanical sounds when dying.

10. ☑ **B.** In Windows XP, right-click My Computer on the Start menu, click Properties to open the System Properties box, click the Advanced tab, and click the Settings button under Startup And Recovery. On the Startup And Recovery dialog box, in the System Failure area, clear the Automatically Restart check box and then click OK. Restart the computer and when the blue screen appears, it should persist because the computer will not attempt to restart upon experiencing a failure.

    ☒ **A, C,** and **D** are incorrect. **A** is incorrect because you will not be able to access a utility that can take a screenshot on a computer if the operating system can't load, particularly if the blue screen is only present for a brief moment. **C** is incorrect because there is no Automatically Restart check box on the Welcome To System Restore screen. **D** is incorrect because clicking All Tasks produces a menu, not a dialog box, and the menu does not lead to an option to clear the Automatically Restart check box.

11. ☑ **B.** CHKDSK, or "check disk," is a command prompt utility used to check file system integrity on hard disks containing Windows operating systems. The tool can potentially fix logical file system errors.

    ☒ **A, C,** and **D** are incorrect. **A** is incorrect because CHDKS is not a valid utility. **C** is incorrect because FORMAT is used to prepare a hard disk for data storage by creating a file system on the disk drive. **D** is incorrect because FDISK is used to partition hard disks.

12. ☑ **B** and **C.** The Startup Repair wizard available in System Recovery can help in fixing a number of issues that can cause serious boot errors, including repairing a missing boot partition. You can also run Diskpart from the command prompt in System Recovery to repair a disk-partitioning error, including selecting the correct partition on a computer's drive as the boot partition.

    ☒ **A** and **D** are incorrect. **A** is incorrect because after a serious boot error, trying to boot normally into the operating system is unlikely to be effective. **D** is incorrect because it is not a System Recovery solution, and a loose power connection is unlikely to result in the inability of a computer to locate its boot partition.

13. ☑ **A and B.** In this circumstance, the power cable could be unplugged. Also, if the cable extends underneath the user's desk, it's not uncommon for cables to be run over by chair wheels or repeatedly stepped on, causing damage that would result in no power getting to the monitor.

☒ **C and D** are incorrect because an unplugged or damaged monitor cable connecting the monitor to the computer would still allow power to go to the monitor, which would be indicated, if turned off, by the monitor power button glowing amber.

14. ☑ **A.** The most likely problem is the refresh rate set in Windows is not supported by the older CRT monitor. Go into Display Properties, click the Settings tab, click the Advanced button, and then on the Monitor tab, set the refresh rate to its lowest setting, which should be 60 Hz.

☒ **B, C,** and **D** are incorrect. B is incorrect because any attempt to change the resolution results in a black screen. C is incorrect because a damaged cable from the computer to the monitor would most likely result in no image at all, including VGA mode. D is incorrect because a damaged monitor power cable would most likely result in no power being delivered to the monitor.

15. ☑ **C.** Monitors lose their sharpness and vividness of color over time and the image they produce gradually begins to fade.

☒ **A, B,** and **D** are incorrect. A is incorrect because a CRT monitor does not produce a dramatically dimmer image compared to an LCD monitor, although LCD monitors generally provide a crisper image. B is incorrect because a damaged monitor cable would not result in the image being dimmer but otherwise unchanged. D is incorrect because a faulty video card would result in either a distorted image or no image, but not a dimmer image on the monitor.

16. ☑ **A.** CRT monitors are subject to discoloration around the edges of the screen due to magnetic interference. It is common for CRT monitors to have a built-in degaussing mechanism to remove the magnetic interference and restore the true color to the monitor. The process typically takes just a few seconds.

☒ **B, C,** and **D** are incorrect. B and C are incorrect because a CRT screen that needs to be degaussed does not appear distorted or flicker. D is incorrect because CRT screens do not use pixels to render an image. Lines are "drawn" onto the screen by an electron gun, which causes phosphors on the screen to light up, producing images with a combination of red, green, and blue.

12

Troubleshooting and Preventive Maintenance for Laptops

❑ **802: 4.8** Given a scenario, troubleshoot and repair common laptop issues while adhering to the appropriate procedures.

QUESTIONS

Mobile computers are ubiquitous in the world, and they present special challenges when a problem occurs. As an A+ technician, you will be expected to be equally adept at diagnosing and repairing problems with laptops as you are with desktop computers. This chapter will help you develop your laptop troubleshooting and repair skills.

Objective 802: 4.8   Given a Scenario, Troubleshoot and Repair Common Laptop Issues While Adhering to the Appropriate Procedures

1. A customer complains that his laptop's battery isn't recharging when it's plugged into a wall socket. He knows the wall socket is good because he's plugged a lamp into it and the lamp lit up. What else could you check to verify that a laptop battery is charging?

   A. The battery indicator in the Windows notification area
   B. The light on the AC adapter "brick"
   C. The indicator gauge on the battery itself
   D. Power Options in Control Panel

2. A customer complains that he gets no image on the display screen when he opens his laptop lid and presses the power button. What could be causing this behavior? (Choose all that apply.)

   A. The LCD lid "close" switch could be stuck.
   B. The customer may not be pressing down on the power button long enough or with sufficient pressure to signal the computer to start.
   C. The Display Mode may be set to use an external monitor.
   D. A memory module could have gone bad.

3. A customer complains that the image on her laptop display screen is garbled and indistinct. You aren't sure if this is a display screen problem, a video card problem, or some other issue. What methods of testing should you use? (Choose all that apply.)

   A. Attach an external monitor to the VGA port on the laptop.
   B. Reseat the memory modules.
   C. Open the laptop and check the FL inverter connections.
   D. Open the laptop and check the LCD cable connections.

4. You have a customer who has added a number of external peripheral devices, a Mini PCI Express sound card, and a PCMCIA wireless network adapter, all within the past few days. Now he says his laptop won't start. What troubleshooting steps would you take to diagnose the problem? (Choose two.)

A. Reinstall Windows and then reboot the computer to see if it starts.

B. Reinstall Microsoft Office and then reboot the computer to see if it starts.

C. Remove all peripheral devices and then add them back one at a time, seeing if the computer starts each time you add a device.

D. Use a multimeter to check the power adapter brick connections and cords to see if they're supplying power.

5. You have a customer who complains that her laptop's built-in wireless network card isn't working. What can you do to diagnose this problem? (Choose three.)

A. Check the manual Wi-Fi on and off switch on the laptop.

B. Check Device Manager and see if any warning or error messages are listed for the wireless network adapter.

C. Check the internal and, if present, external wireless antenna connections to make sure they are secure.

D. Check the power lead from the motherboard to the wireless adapter.

6. You need to almost completely disassemble a customer's laptop computer in order to upgrade the CPU on the motherboard. You are preparing a list of tasks to perform that will ensure that you'll be able to disassemble and reassemble the laptop successfully. Of the following, which is the first thing you should do?

A. Document and label cable and screw locations.

B. Organize parts.

C. Refer to manufacturer documentation.

D. Use appropriate hand tools.

7. You have a customer who complains that when she is using her laptop to type a Word document or edit a spreadsheet document, the cursor jumps to an unexpected part of the document, causing her to make mistakes. This happens only intermittently and with a variety of applications where she has to do a lot of keyboarding. You ask her to demonstrate this by typing in a Word document. After watching her for a few minutes, what do you suspect is the cause of the problem?

A. Sticking keys on the keyboard

B. A bad connection between the keyboard and the motherboard

C. Accidental brushing against the touchpad during typing

D. Accidental pressing of the CAPS LOCK key during typing

8. You have a customer who says that a few of the keys on his laptop's keyboard are sticking periodically, causing those letters to be repeated when he's creating documents or writing e-mails. What methods are commonly used to fix this problem? (Choose all that apply.)

   A. Remove the keys that are sticking from the keyboard and clean the area where the keys connect to the keyboard contacts.

   B. Turn the laptop upside down over a waste basket and gently shake the unit, dislodging the dirt from the keyboard.

   C. Use a can of compressed air to blow dirt and dust out from between the keys on the keyboard.

   D. Use an antistatic vacuum unit to suck the dirt and dust out from between the keys on the keyboard.

9. You have a customer who uses a Bluetooth mouse with her keyboard because she finds it easier than the laptop's touchpad. The mouse has suddenly stopped working. What could be causing this problem? (Choose all that apply.)

   A. The batteries in the mouse may be dead.

   B. The laptop's Bluetooth antenna may have been accidentally disabled.

   C. The selector switch on the mouse may have accidentally been turned from the Bluetooth position to the Wi-Fi position.

   D. The mouse was placed too far away from the laptop and is out of range of the laptop's Bluetooth antenna.

10. You have a customer who has connected an external monitor to his laptop, but after the laptop and monitor are turned on, no image appears on the external monitor. Of the following, what should you check? (Choose all that apply.)

    A. Make sure the power cable is correctly connected to the external monitor and plugged into a good power strip or surge protector.

    B. Make sure the monitor cable is correctly attached to the monitor and to the laptop.

    C. Toggle the Display Mode key on the monitor to verify it is set to use the laptop as a display source.

    D. Toggle the Display Mode key on the laptop to verify it is set to use an external monitor.

11. You need to upgrade the CPU on a customer's laptop and realize that to reach the CPU, you need to almost completely disassemble the laptop. You are concerned about keeping track of all of the different laptop parts and ensuring that you will be able to correctly reassemble the unit. What steps should you take to keep the parts organized and assist you in reassembly? (Choose all that apply.)

    A. Consult any documentation you have available about the construction of the laptop.

    B. Keep screws and clips in different paper cups, with each cup labeled for what the screws or clips are used for.

    C. Label cables using masking tape and a marker by their use.

    D. Label each of the tools you use to disassemble the laptop by their function.

12. You have a customer who complains that whenever she's typing in a Word document, creating an e-mail, or performing some similar task, when she presses some of the letter keys, numbers are created instead. What should you check?

    A. Look and see if the NUM LOCK light is on.

    B. Look and see if the CAPS LOCK light is on.

    C. Toggle the Display Mode key.

    D. Toggle the on/off switch for the Wi-Fi antenna.

13. You have a customer who just got a new Windows 7 laptop and who has connected it to the 802.11n wireless network in his home. The connection seems to work for a while, but then periodically drops the connection. He has another wireless laptop at home that he has used for a few years and never had a problem, so he's fairly sure it's not the wireless router. What should you try to fix the problem with the new laptop? (Choose all that apply.)

    A. Disable and then enable the new laptop's wireless card.

    B. Install the latest drivers for the new laptop's wireless card.

    C. Disable the laptop's onboard firewall.

    D. Reset the wireless router back to its default settings.

14. You have a Windows 7 laptop customer who travels a great deal for business and must take her laptop with her. She complains that even though she confirms that the laptop battery is fully charged using the laptop's battery indicator, when she turns off the laptop while traveling for long periods, by the time she turns it back on again, the battery is significantly drained or even completely empty of power. She also mentions that the laptop seems warm, even when shut down and sitting in its carrying case for long periods of time. What do you suspect? (Choose all that apply.)

    A. The battery is faulty and it isn't really charging when the customer thinks it is.

    B. When she presses the power switch to turn the laptop off, the laptop is configured to go into Sleep mode, which consumes some battery power and will eventually drain the battery.

    C. When she presses the power switch to turn the laptop off, the laptop is configured to go into Standby mode, which consumes some battery power and will eventually drain the battery.

    D. The battery is faulty and overheating, even when the laptop is turned off, and should be replaced.

15. You have a customer who says that the keyboard on his old Windows XP laptop has stopped working. You check the laptop, and the keyboard appears to be completely dead. Of the following, what troubleshooting methods can you use to investigate the problem? (Choose all that apply.)

A. Plug an external USB keyboard into the laptop and see if it works.

B. Check Device Manager and see if any keyboard error messages appear.

C. Open the laptop and check the keyboard power cable connection.

D. Open the laptop and check the keyboard data cable connection.

QUICK ANSWER KEY

1.	A	**6.**	C	**11.**	A, B, C
2.	A, B, C	**7.**	C	**12.**	A
3.	A, C, D	**8.**	B, C, D	**13.**	A, B
4.	C, D	**9.**	A, B, D	**14.**	A, B, D
5.	A, B, C	**10.**	A, B, D	**15.**	A, B, D

IN-DEPTH ANSWERS

1. ☑ **A.** You can check the battery indicator in the Windows notification area to see if the battery is charging.

   ☒ **B, C,** and **D** are incorrect. **B** is incorrect because the light indicates that power is reaching the adapter, but there still could be a problem between the adapter and the battery. **C** is incorrect because the battery may have a light indicating it is charging, but not an actual gauge that measures how much of a charge it is carrying. **D** is incorrect because Power Options in Control Panel will let you configure power settings for the laptop, but it will not show you if the battery is actively charging.

2. ☑ **A, B,** and **C.** If the LCD lid "close" switch gets stuck, the screen backlight won't be on. There will still be a very faint image on the screen, but it is usually too faint for most people to see. If you just briefly and lightly press the power button, it may not make full contact and the laptop won't be powering up. The screen is blank because the laptop is still off. If the customer recently used the laptop with an external monitor, the Display Mode for the laptop may still be set to use an external monitor rather than the laptop's onboard display screen.

   ☒ **D** is incorrect because a bad memory module would result in other problems and issue a beep code, but would not likely result in the customer getting no image on the display screen.

3. ☑ **A, C,** and **D.** Attach an external monitor to the laptop via the VGA (or other available video type) port. If the image on the external monitor is fine, the problem is related to the screen. An inverter problem usually causes a screen to appear very dim and indistinct, if not blank, though it may not cause a "garbled" image. If it's not, the problem is probably the video card. Open the laptop to check the connections between the LCD screen and the motherboard. If that fixes the problem, it was a loose connection. If not, it's probably the video card or a bad screen.

   ☒ **B** is incorrect because poorly seated memory modules will not cause this specific problem.

4. ☑ **C** and **D.** Since the problem started after the customer added a number of devices, begin by removing all the added peripherals and see if the computer boots. If it does, try adding each peripheral back one at a time, starting the computer each time, until you find the problem device. If the computer doesn't start, you can use a multimeter to check the power adapter components and see if the problem is there.

   ☒ **A** and **B** are incorrect. **A** is incorrect because not only is reinstalling Windows an extreme diagnostic method, but most likely, a problem with Windows wouldn't result in the computer completely failing to boot. **B** is incorrect because there's no indication that the problem is Microsoft Office related.

5. ☑ **A, B,** and **C.** Laptops often have manual switches that let you turn Wi-Fi on or off. They can be physical switches on the laptop case or keyboard shortcuts. Check the documentation for your specific laptop make and model to find the Wi-Fi on/off switch. Checking Device Manager will show you if there are any error messages associated with the wireless adapter, including whether it requires a driver update. Internal and external wireless antennas can become disconnected, resulting in this sort of problem. Verify that all physical connections are secure.

☒ **D** is incorrect because there is no separate power lead for a built-in wireless adapter from the motherboard.

6. ☑ **C.** The first thing you should always do when you are about to attempt such an ambitious task is to consult the available documentation. This can include the documents that came with the laptop and those you can find on the Internet, most likely at the laptop maker's Website. Become thoroughly familiar with the parts involved and any instructions involving the steps for taking apart and putting back together the laptop before proceeding.

☒ **A, B,** and **D** are incorrect. **A** is incorrect because you will want to consult the documentation first. Afterward you will want to note the actual locations of any external screws and latches, and then, only after opening the laptop up, will you be able to label cables and other internal components. **B** is incorrect because this step will only occur after you've disassembled the laptop. **D** is incorrect because you will only begin selecting and using tools once you've reviewed the documentation.

7. ☑ **C.** It's not uncommon for a person to accidentally brush their fingers over the touchpad while typing. Depending on the sensitivity of the touchpad, this can result in the cursor suddenly jumping from one part of the screen or document being worked on to another. The solution would be to adjust the sensitivity of the touchpad so that a light touch would not move the cursor.

☒ **A, B,** and **D** are incorrect. **A** is incorrect because sticking keys would result in the same letter or symbol being reproduced in the document or the letter or symbol not being produced, but would not make the cursor suddenly move to a different area. **B** is incorrect because a bad keyboard connection to the motherboard would probably result in the keyboard not working at all. **D** is incorrect because accidentally pressing the CAPS LOCK key would result in all letters being capitalized during typing.

8. ☑ **B, C,** and **D.** Dirt, dust, and sometimes bits of food get stuck between and underneath keys, causing them to stick. To repair the problem, you need to use one or more methods of removing the debris and freeing the stuck keys. When turning the laptop upside down over a waste basket, make sure the keyboard is directly over the receptacle. When using compressed air, make sure not to tip the can too far over and spill propellant on the keyboard.

Also, try and angle the can so you are blowing debris out of the keyboard rather than wedging it tighter in between the keys. Only use vacuum units that are antistatic and approved for use in and around computers.

☒ **A** is incorrect because once a key is removed from a laptop keyboard, it is extremely difficult to reattach. Removing keys is not a common method of solving this problem, although some technicians will risk it if they feel confident in their ability to reattach the key or there is just no other way to solve the sticky keys problem.

9. ☑ **A, B,** and **D.** The most common problem in this scenario is that the batteries in the mouse need to be changed out for new ones. Otherwise, the on-off switch for the laptop's Bluetooth antenna may have been set accidentally to the off position. It is possible for the mouse to be placed out of range of the Bluetooth signal and still be within arm's reach.

☒ **C** is incorrect because Bluetooth mice do not come equipped with a selector switch that lets you choose a Wi-Fi option.

10. ☑ **A, B,** and **D.** Cable problems are the most common cause of display issues; however, the Display Mode key on the laptop may not be set to use an external monitor.

☒ **C** is incorrect because you use the Display Mode key on the laptop, not an external monitor, to verify it is set to use an external monitor.

11. ☑ **A, B,** and **C.** Often the manufacturer's documentation will be a great assistance in helping you understand how different parts of the laptop fit together and in what order to assemble them. Keeping screws, clips, and other small pieces in individual paper cups or similar containers labeled by function and type will help you remember where each of these components are used when it comes time to put the laptop back together. Also, labeling cables by type and where they are used in the laptop will be very useful.

☒ **D** is incorrect because you shouldn't need to label your tools since you should know the difference between how and when to use a screwdriver rather than a pair of tweezers, and so on.

12. ☑ **A.** If the NUM LOCK key is on, it means the laptop customer may have turned on an embedded keypad feature available in the laptop, resulting in numbers being entered in place of some letters.

☒ **B, C,** and **D** are incorrect. **B** is incorrect because the CAPS LOCK light just indicates that the letters being typed will be capitalized. **C** is incorrect because the Display Mode key controls the type of monitor display the keyboard will use (onboard or external). **D** is incorrect because the Wi-Fi antenna switch controls whether Wi-Fi on the laptop is on or off, but it won't affect the function of different keys on the keyboard.

13. ☑ **A** and **B.** Sometimes disabling and enabling the wireless card will do the trick, but the more likely problem is that the wireless card requires updated drivers. Keep in mind that wireless problems can be caused by a wide variety of factors and what is listed here are just a few of the more common causes.

    ☒ **C** and **D** are incorrect. **C** is incorrect because if the firewall were on, it would either block the signal all of the time or allow it all of the time. **D** is incorrect because the customer said that he was sure the router wasn't the problem, and there is another laptop in the same environment that is having no problems maintaining a connection to the router. If the router was the problem, you'd expect that both laptops would be having connection issues.

14. ☑ **A, B,** and **D.** Windows laptops can be configured to perform several actions when the power button is pressed to shut off the computer. In this case, it's likely that pressing the power button sends the unit into Sleep mode, which still consumes power and keeps the laptop warm. Eventually, this will drain the battery completely, unless the customer plugs the computer into a power outlet periodically. Also, a faulty battery could account for the problem.

    ☒ **C** is incorrect because there is no Standby mode that can be configured for a Windows 7 laptop. That was last available in Windows XP.

15. ☑ **A, B,** and **D.** If you can use a USB keyboard with the laptop, the problem is probably keyboard or motherboard related. Checking Device Manager will show any warnings or errors associated with the keyboard, such as needing updated drivers (assuming the keyboard shows up as installed), and opening the laptop will let you verify that the problem isn't a loose or disconnected data cable link between the motherboard and keyboard.

    ☒ **C** is incorrect because there is no separate power cable connection between the motherboard and keyboard.

13

Troubleshooting and Preventive Maintenance for Windows

QUESTIONS

Microsoft Windows desktop and server computers remain dominant in the home and business market, so when something goes wrong with a Windows computer, you, as an A+ computer technician, will be expected to troubleshoot and repair the problem. You will also be expected to anticipate problems in Windows before they happen and to maintain computers so that these problems are less likely to occur. The following questions will help test your skills in these areas.

Objective 802: 1.3 Given a Scenario, Use Appropriate Command-Line Tools

1. You have a customer whose Windows XP computer has experienced a serious problem. You have booted into the Recovery Console and are reviewing your options for repair. Of the following, which tool is available in the Recovery Console that will directly help address hard drive and boot problems?

   A. BOOTREC

   B. DISKPART

   C. ROBOCOPY

   D. TLIST

2. You are on the command line of a Windows 7 computer and you want to use a command that will scan all protected system files and replace incorrect versions with correct Microsoft versions. Of the following, which command would you use?

   A. CD

   B. MD

   C. RD

   D. SFC

3. The Notepad utility is not responding on your Windows 7 computer. You want to terminate the process for notepad.exe on the command line. What is the correct command to use?

   A. process -k notepad.exe

   B. k notepad.exe

   C. kill /im notepad.exe

   D. taskkill /im notepad.exe

4. You have a customer whose Windows XP computer has experienced a serious problem. You have booted into the Recovery Console and are reviewing your options for repair. Of the following, which utility can you use to repair the master boot record of the computer's boot partition?

A. Fdisk
B. Fixboot
C. Fixmbr
D. Format

Objective 802: 1.4   Given a Scenario, Use Appropriate Operating System Features and Tools

5. You suspect that one of the software applications that starts on a Windows XP computer when the operating system loads is causing a problem. Which run-line utility do you launch to see a list of startup programs? (Choose all that apply.)

A. DXDIAG
B. MSCONFIG
C. MSINFO32
D. REGEDIT

6. You just launched the MSCONFIG utility on a Windows XP computer in order to see a list of the various help and diagnostic programs in Windows. Which tab do you have to click to see a list of these programs, and where you can launch programs on the list?

A. General
B. Services
C. Startup
D. Tools

7. You suspect that a process running on a Windows 7 computer has its priority set too high and you want to change its priority setting. How can you do this in Task Manager?

A. On the Application tab, right-click the application and then click Set Priority.
B. On the Processes tab, right-click the process and then click Set Priority.
C. On the Application tab, double-click the application and then click Set Priority.
D. On the Processes tab, double-click the process and then click Set Priority.

8. You want to see which process is associated with a specific application that is running on your Windows 7 computer. How do you do this?

   A. On the command line, type **PID** and press ENTER to see a list of all running applications and their associated processes.

   B. On the command line, type **top** and press ENTER to see a list of all running applications and their associated processes.

   C. In Task Manager, on the Applications tab, right-click the application and then select Go To Process to be taken to the specific process on the Processes tab associated with the application.

   D. In Task Manager, on the Processes tab, right-click the process and select Application to be taken to the specific application on the Applications tab that's associated with the process.

Objective 802: 1.7 Perform Preventive Maintenance Procedures Using Appropriate Tools

9. You want to automate a number of maintenance tasks on a customer's Windows XP computer. Of the following, which tasks can you schedule to run automatically using Windows XP native tools? (Choose all that apply.)

   A. Backups

   B. CHKDSK

   C. Defragmentation

   D. Windows Updates

10. You want to configure System Restore on a customer's Windows XP computer. When you open the System dialog box and select the System Restore tab, what options can you configure? (Choose all that apply.)

    A. You can turn System Restore on and off for all drives on the computer.

    B. If the computer has more than one drive, you can turn System Restore on or off for a specific drive.

    C. You can set how much disk space is used for System Restore.

    D. If the computer has more than one drive, you can configure System Restore to use one disk to store System Restore Points for all disks on the computer.

11. You previously created a recovery image for your Windows 7 computer and stored the image on an external hard drive. Your Windows 7 computer has just crashed and cannot boot from the hard drive. You want to restore your computer from the recovery image. What will the recovery image restore? (Choose all that apply.)

A. The Windows 7 operating system

B. The System Settings

C. All files that existed at the time the computer crashed

D. All programs that were installed on the computer at the time the image was made

12. You have a customer who wants to know how often she should defrag the hard disk on her Windows 7 computer. What do you tell her?

A. Daily

B. Weekly

C. Monthly

D. Depends on usage

Objective 802: 4.6   Given a Scenario, Troubleshoot Operating System Problems with Appropriate Tools

13. You have a customer whose Windows 7 computer has experienced a serious problem. You have booted into System Recovery and are reviewing your options for repair. Of the following, which are available selections in the System Recovery Options menu? (Choose all that apply.)

A. Command Prompt

B. Startup Repair

C. System Restore

D. System Repair

14. You get an error message saying, "Application error when you click Product Updates" on your Windows 7 computer. You do a bit of research and determine that you can resolve the problem with a Windows utility that registers and unregisters OLE controls such as DLL or ActiveX Controls. Of the following, which is the proper tool?

A. FIXMBR

B. REGSVR32

C. REGEDIT

D. SFC

15. You want to launch the SFC utility to scan your Windows 7 computer for suspected corrupt Windows system files. You open the command prompt, type **sfc /scannow**, and press ENTER, but the scan doesn't begin. What happened?

A. The /scannow command switch is invalid.

B. You did not run the command prompt as an administrator.

C. You can only run this command in the GUI from inside Control Panel.

D. You can only run this command at the command prompt once you are in Windows 7 System Recovery.

QUICK ANSWER KEY

1.	B	**6.**	D	**11.**	A, B, D
2.	D	**7.**	B	**12.**	D
3.	D	**8.**	C	**13.**	A, B, C
4.	C	**9.**	A, D	**14.**	B
5.	B, C	**10.**	A, B, C	**15.**	B

IN-DEPTH ANSWERS

1. ☑ **B.** DISKPART is used in Recovery Console for adding and deleting partitions.
   ☒ **A, C,** and **D** are incorrect. **A** is incorrect because BOOTREC is a Windows Vista and Windows 7 recovery environment tool and is not available in Windows XP. **C** is incorrect because ROBOCOPY is a command-line utility that has copying abilities exceeding the copy and xcopy commands, but is not specifically part of the Recovery Console. **D** is incorrect because TLIST is a tool that prints a list of tasks to stdout (standard output) and can determine a process ID, but is not part of Recovery Console.

2. ☑ **D.** SFC, or System File Checker, is a command-line utility that lets you scan for and restore corrupt Windows system files.
   ☒ **A, B,** and **C** are incorrect. **A** is incorrect because the CD command is used to change directories on the command line. **B** is incorrect because the MD command is used to make directories on the command line. **C** is incorrect because the RD command is used to remove directories on the command line.

3. ☑ **D.** The taskkill command is a utility supported on the Windows command line that allows you to kill a process. To kill the process by name, use the /im, or image name, switch and then the name of the process, such as notepad.exe.
   ☒ **A, B,** and **C** are incorrect. **A** and **B** are incorrect because "process -k" and "k" are fictional commands. **C** is incorrect because the "kill" command is not supported on the Windows command line.

4. ☑ **C.** Fixmbr is a Recovery Console utility that can write a new master boot record to a specified hard drive on a computer.
   ☒ **A, B,** and **D** are incorrect. **A** is incorrect because Fdisk is a command-line utility used for disk partitioning. **B** is incorrect because Fixboot is used to write new boot-sector code to the system partition. **D** is incorrect because Format is a command-line tool used to format a drive with a specific file system.

5. ☑ **B** and **C.** Running either MSCONFIG or MSINFO32 in the Run box on a Windows XP computer will show you which programs start when the OS loads, although MSINFO32 provides a more concise list. Once MSCONFIG is open, click the Startup tab to locate which programs are starting with the OS. In MSINFO32, expand Software Environment and then click Startup Programs to see the list.
   ☒ **A** and **D** are incorrect. **A** is incorrect because DXDIAG is the DirectX Diagnostic Tool. **D** is incorrect because REGEDIT is used to edit the Windows Registry.

6.   ☑   **D.** Click the Tools tab to see a list of help and diagnostic utilities. Select a specific tool, and then click the Launch button to open the tool.
  ☒   **A, B,** and **C** are incorrect. **A** is incorrect because this tab lets you select the Startup method for Windows and launch System Restore. **B** is incorrect because this displays a list of services running on the machine and lets you enable or disable these services. **C** is incorrect because this tab lists the different applications that start when Windows loads and lets you enable or disable them.

7.   ☑   **B.** Right-clicking the desired process on the Processes tab will open a menu. Select Set Priority and then click the desired priority for the process.
  ☒   **A, C,** and **D** are incorrect. **A** is incorrect because right-clicking an application on the Application tab will open a menu, but there is no option on the menu to set the priority of the process that is running behind the application. **C** is incorrect because double-clicking the application moves the running application to the front of all the open screens on the computer. **D** is incorrect because double-clicking a process doesn't do anything.

8.   ☑   **C.** Right-clicking the application will open a menu, and when you click the Go To Process option, you will be taken to the Processes tab with the desired process selected in the list.
  ☒   **A, B,** and **D** are incorrect. **A** and **B** are incorrect because these commands are not supported on the Windows command line. **D** is incorrect because the option to select an application on the menu after right-clicking a process is not present.

9.   ☑   **A** and **D.** You can use the Windows Backup Wizard to schedule backups to run automatically, and you can set Automatic Updates to download and install Windows Updates automatically on a specific schedule.
  ☒   **B** and **C** are incorrect. **B** is incorrect because when you run CHKDSK, either on the command line or in the GUI, the utility will run the next time you restart Windows. **C** is incorrect because the defragmentation utility in Windows XP cannot be set to run automatically, only manually.

10.   ☑   **A, B,** and **C.** You can either turn System Restore on or off for all disks on the computer or for specific disks on the computer, if there is more than one disk present. You can also set how much disk space System Restore uses on each hard disk.
  ☒   **D** is incorrect because you cannot set System Restore to use only a single disk to store all restore points for all disks on the computer. Each disk must store its own restore points.

11.   ☑   **A, B,** and **D.** The recovery image will restore the Windows 7 operating system and all system settings, applications, and files as they were when the recovery image was made.
  ☒   **C** is incorrect because all files will be restored as they existed when the recovery image was made, not as they were at the time the computer crashed.

12. ☑ **D.** There is no one set frequency at which to defrag a computer's hard drive. If files are created and edited frequently and programs are installed and/or removed frequently, then you should defrag more often. If files and programs are modified less frequently or very infrequently, then the defrag frequency should be much less.

    ☒ **A, B,** and **C** are incorrect because the frequency at which you defrag your computer's hard drive depends on how often files and programs are modified on a computer. The more often the computer's drive is accessed and modified, the more often it should be defragged.

13. ☑ **A, B,** and **C.** The System Recovery Options menu lists Startup Repair, System Restore, System Image Recovery, Windows Memory Diagnostic, and Command Prompt.

    ☒ **D** is incorrect because System Repair is not a selection on the System Recovery Options menu in Windows 7.

14. ☑ **B.** REGSVR32 is a command-line tool that registers and unregisters OLE controls as command components in the registry and can be used to repair the problem referenced in the question.

    ☒ **A, C,** and **D** are incorrect. **A** is incorrect because FIXMBR is a tool that repairs the master boot record on a computer's hard drive. **C** is incorrect because REGEDIT is used to edit the Windows Registry. **D** is incorrect because SFC is used to scan a Windows computer for corrupt system files and to restore them.

15. ☑ **B.** To run this command at the command prompt, you must run the command prompt as an administrator. In the Windows 7 search box, type **cmd**, right-click the command prompt icon that appears in the list, and click Run As Administrator.

    ☒ **A, C,** and **D** are incorrect. **A** is incorrect because the switch is valid. **C** is incorrect because you cannot run this command in the GUI. **D** is incorrect because you can run this command at the command prompt without using System Recovery.

14

Network Basics

QUESTIONS

Computer networking is a specialized area in the realm of computing involving many different protocols, devices, and software types, yet it is also the core of how and why people use computers, both at home and at work. Part of installing and configuring a computer as an A+ technician is making sure the computer can connect to other computers on the local network and to the Internet. To do this, you have to maintain a basic understanding about how networking computers works.

Objective 801: 2.1   Identify Types of Network Cables and Connectors

1. You are reviewing the different connector types used to plug data cables into the modem and network interface card ports in the back of your computer. Of the following, which are the correct connectors for each port? (Choose two.)

    A. RJ-11 connectors are used for phone modem ports.

    B. RJ-45 connectors are used for network interface card ports.

    C. RJ-45 connectors are used for phone modem ports.

    D. RJ-11 connectors are used for network interface card ports.

Objective 801: 2.2   Categorize Characteristics of Connectors and Cabling

2. You work for a small city IT department, and you are helping to string network cable for a new building under construction. The cables lead from the various patch panels in the walls and are used by computers; they travel to the server room by way of the empty space above the ceiling tiles. This empty space also contains the air conditioning and heating ducts. What type of cable is designed for use in this empty space?

    A. Coaxial

    B. Plenum

    C. STP

    D. UTP

3. You work for a small city IT department, and you are helping to string network cable for a new building under construction. You are stringing UTP cable for Gigabit Ethernet. Of the following options, which cable types could you use? (Choose two.)

    A. CAT3

    B. CAT5

C. CAT5e
D. CAT6

Objective 801: 2.3 Explain Properties and Characteristics of TCP/IP

4. You have a customer who has asked you to create a small network of three computers for his home office. All of the computers will need to have their network addressing information configured using static, rather than dynamic, addressing. Of the following, what addressing information can you configure for the computer? (Choose three.)
   A. The computer's IP address and subnet mask
   B. The address of the default gateway
   C. The address of the preferred DHCP server
   D. The address of the preferred DNS server

5. You are describing the basic concept of network classes to a group of high school students attending a technology workshop. In a standard IPv4 (Internet Protocol version 4) networking structure, network addressing classes are defined by the number of networks allowed within a class and the number of node addresses allowable within each individual network. The fewer networks per class, the more addresses are available within each network. Of the following, which class is commonly used for networking in home and small office environments and uses the fewest number of addresses per individual network?
   A. Class A
   B. Class B
   C. Class C
   D. Class D

6. You are describing the differences between IPv4 (Internet Protocol version 4) and IPv6 (Internet Protocol version 6) addressing to a group of high school students attending a technology workshop. Of the following, which are true statements about IPv4 and IPv6 addressing? (Choose two.)
   A. The IPv4 address size is 32 bits, and it uses decimal values to indicate addresses.
   B. The IPv4 address size is 32 bits, and it uses hexadecimal values to indicate addresses.
   C. The IPv6 address size is 128 bits, and it uses decimal values to indicate addresses.
   D. The IPv6 address size is 128 bits, and it uses hexadecimal values to indicate addresses.

Objective 801: 2.4 Explain Common TCP and UDP Ports, Protocols, and Their Purpose

7. You are configuring an FTP client application on your computer so that you can transfer data from your computer to your company's FTP server for storage. You enter the IP address of the server host and your user name. What do you enter when prompted for a port number?

   A. 21
   B. 25
   C. 80
   D. 110

8. You are reviewing the well-known port numbers for common protocols used in networking. The HTTP protocol is normally used for Web connections, but HTTPS is used for more secure Web transactions, such as online banking transactions. What port number does HTTPS use?

   A. 53
   B. 23
   C. 110
   D. 443

9. You are giving a presentation at a technology workshop and speaking to a group of high school students. You are currently discussing the issue of hostname–to–IP address translation such as www.google.com to 74.125.19.147. What service provides this type of translation?

   A. DNS
   B. LDAP
   C. SMB
   D. SNMP

10. You are providing support to a client who needs to find a secure method to connect to a Linux server and issue commands. What protocol should you recommend?

    A. Telnet
    B. SSH
    C. SFTP
    D. RDP

11. Which of the following statements about the TCP and UDP protocols are correct? (Choose two.)

    A. TCP is a connection-oriented protocol.
    B. UDP is a connection-oriented protocol.
    C. TCP provides guaranteed delivery of packets.
    D. UDP provides guaranteed delivery of packets.

Objective 801: 2.5   Compare and Contrast Wireless Networking Standards and Encryption Types

12. You have a customer who wants to install a wireless network in his home so that members of his family can surf the Web wirelessly on their laptops. He asks which of the wireless standards provides the greatest speed. What do you say?

   A.   802.11a

   B.   802.11b

   C.   802.11g

   D.   802.11n

Objective 801: 2.7   Compare and Contrast Internet Connection Types and Features

13. You have a customer who is about to retire to a rural area of your state and asks you to recommend a broadband Internet connection type that will work best in a sparsely populated area. What do you tell him?

   A.   DSL is his best option.

   B.   Cable is his best option.

   C.   Satellite is his best option.

   D.   Fiber-optic is his best option.

Objective 801: 2.8   Identify Various Types of Networks

14. You are reviewing network type characteristics with another technician in your workplace. In discussing a WAN vs. a LAN, what do you say is true? (Choose two.)

   A.   A LAN, or large area network, uses leased lines to connect computers in distant locations such as different cities.

   B.   A LAN, or local area network, is a collection of networked computers in a single room or a group of rooms in a building.

   C.   A WAN, or wide area network, is made up of numerous different local network segments and can stretch across large distances.

   D.   A WAN, or wide area network, uses switches but not routers.

15. In what type of network topology are all systems on the network connected to a central node?

   A.   Mesh

   B.   Ring

   C.   Star

   D.   Bus

Objective 801: 2.9 Compare and Contrast Network Devices, Their Functions, and Features

16. You work for a small city IT department and are networking a new wing at the main branch of the city library. You need a networking device that can connect numerous computers on a single segment and can offer dedicated lines between any two nodes, providing the full bandwidth of the network between them. Of the following, which devices would be most appropriate to perform this function?

    A. Hub

    B. Switch

    C. Router

    D. Bridge

17. You have a small-business customer who wants to use a voice over IP (VoIP) system and subscribe to this service through his ISP using DSL. What special piece of equipment will need to be installed to provide signal conversion between the analog and digital networks?

    A. NAS

    B. Modem

    C. Access point

    D. Firewall

18. Which of the following functions are typically found in an Internet appliance? (Choose two.)

    A. Web browser

    B. E-mail client

    C. Command shell

    D. SSH client

QUICK ANSWER KEY

1. A, B	**7.** A	**13.** C
2. B	**8.** D	**14.** B, C
3. C, D	**9.** A	**15.** C
4. A, B, D	**10.** B	**16.** B
5. C	**11.** A, C	**17.** B
6. A, D	**12.** D	**18.** A, B

IN-DEPTH ANSWERS

1. ☑ **A** and **B.** Although these cable connector types look very similar, an RJ-11 connector is smaller and is used for ordinary telephone cables. An RJ-45 connector is slightly larger and is used for standard network ports.

   ☒ **C** and **D** are incorrect because they indicate the wrong connector types for telephone and network ports.

2. ☑ **B.** Plenum cable is named for the plenum space used to string the cable from network ports, up above the ceiling tiles, to the server room or network closet. Plenum cable must meet specific standards, such as being jacketed in fire-retardant plastic or low-smoke polyvinyl chlorine (PVC).

   ☒ **A, C,** and **D** are incorrect. **A** is incorrect because coaxial cable, which uses BNC connectors and F-connectors, like the type used to connect television sets for cable TV service, does not meet the specific requirements for use in the plenum space. **C** is incorrect because STP, or shielded twisted-pair, cable is a network cable type made up of twisted pairs of wires wrapped in foil shielding to provide more reliable data communications and does not meet plenum cable standards. **D** is incorrect because UTP, or unshielded twisted-pair, cable is made up of twisted pairs of wires wrapped in a plastic outer layer and does not meet plenum cable standards. UTP is also not considered as reliable as STP for data communication.

3. ☑ **C** and **D.** CAT5e cabling supports a maximum data transmission rate of 1 Gbps, as does CAT6 cabling. Both have maximum segment lengths of 100 meters (328 feet).

   ☒ **A** and **B** are incorrect. **A** is incorrect because CAT3 is commonly used for analog voice communications and has a maximum bandwidth of 16 MHz. **B** is incorrect because CAT5 cabling supports a maximum transmission speed of 100 Mbps. As with other UTP cables, CAT3 and CAT5 cables are limited to 100 meter (328 foot) segments.

4. ☑ **A, B,** and **D.** With statically assigned IP addressing, you can manually enter the IP address, subnet mask, and default gateway address, which is the address of the router or broadband modem that lets the computer connect outside the local network. You can also manually enter the IP addresses for the preferred DNS server and the alternate DNS server. DNS servers provide hostname–to–IP address translation, so when you type www.google.com in your Web browser's address bar, DNS can look up the IP address for Google.com and resolve the two.

   ☒ **C** is incorrect because if you are manually configuring the computer's IP addressing data, you don't need to configure it for the DHCP server IP address, since DHCP is the service that provides IP addressing information to computers dynamically.

5. ☑ **C.** Class C allows a total of 2,097,152 networks and 256 addresses per network. It is commonly used in small business and home networks.

   ☒ **A, B,** and **D** are incorrect. **A** is incorrect because it allows a total of only 128 networks and 16,777,216 addresses per network. **B** is incorrect because it allows a total of 16,384 networks and 65,536 addresses per network. **D** is incorrect because it is reserved for multicast, which allows a message sent by a single network node to be received by numerous destination computers at the same time. Class D is not used to provide IP addresses to computers. There is also a Class E network, but it is a reserved range of addresses and is not used in production environments.

6. ☑ **A** and **D.** The IPv4 address size is limited to 32 bits, which is of concern since the total number of addresses could actually be exhausted due to the exponential explosion of device types that require networking. IPv4 addresses are expressed in four octets of numerical values separated by periods, such as 192.168.0.1. The IPv6 address size is 128 bits, which may well provide an almost inexhaustible number of network addresses. Such addresses are expressed in hexadecimal values separated by colons, such as 2001:0DB8:FE01: AC10:0000:0000:0000:0000. The trailing zeros can be omitted in the actual address.

   ☒ **B** and **C** are incorrect. **B** is incorrect because IPv4 addresses are expressed in numeral values. **C** is incorrect because IPv6 addresses are expressed in hexadecimal values.

7. ☑ **A.** Port number 21 is the well-known port number used by the FTP service to transfer data.

   ☒ **B, C,** and **D** are incorrect. **B** is incorrect because port 25 is the well-known port number for the SMTP outgoing mail service. **C** is incorrect because port 80 is the well-known port number for the HTTP protocol for Web connections. **D** is incorrect because port number 110 is the well-known port number for POP3 incoming mail service.

8. ☑ **D.** HTTPS stands for Hypertext Transfer Protocol Secure, which combines the Hypertext Transfer Protocol with SSL/TLS to provide encrypted communication in Web exchanges. HTTPS uses well-known port number 443.

   ☒ **A, B,** and **C** are incorrect. **A** is incorrect because port 53 is the well-known port number for DNS, or the Domain Name Service. **B** is incorrect because port 23 is the well-known port number for Telnet, which is a network protocol used to provide a bidirectional interactive terminal connection between remote hosts. **C** is incorrect because port 110 is the well-known port number for the POP3 incoming mail service.

9. ☑ **A.** DNS, or Domain Name Service, provides hostname–to–IP address translation on the Internet.

   ☒ **B, C,** and **D** are incorrect. **B** is incorrect because LDAP, or the Lightweight Directory Access Protocol, provides directory access over the network. **C** is incorrect because the Server Message Block (SMB) protocol is used for file sharing. **D** is incorrect because the Simple Network Management Protocol (SNMP) is used to manage network devices.

10. ☑ **B.** The Secure Shell (SSH) protocol provides encrypted connections to remote servers and works at the command line.

    ☒ **A, C,** and **D** are incorrect. **A** is incorrect because Telnet does not provide an encrypted, secure connection and is vulnerable to eavesdropping. **C** is incorrect because SFTP is used for file transfers only and does not provide command-line access. **D** is incorrect because RDP is a proprietary Microsoft protocol that does not run on Linux.

11. ☑ **A and C.** The Transmission Control Protocol (TCP) provides reliable, guaranteed delivery of packets across a network. It is a connection-oriented protocol that requires setting up connections between systems before transferring data.

    ☒ **B and D** are incorrect. **B** is incorrect because the User Datagram Protocol (UDP) is connectionless. **D** is incorrect because UDP does not contain mechanisms that guarantee packet delivery.

12. ☑ **D.** 802.11n devices support speeds over 100 Mbps at a range of over 200 feet using the 2.4 and 5 GHz frequency bands.

    ☒ **A, B,** and **C** are incorrect. **A** is incorrect because 802.11a networks only provide 54 Mbps of throughput. They operate at ranges of up to 115 feet using the 5 GHz band. **B** is incorrect because 802.11b networks support a maximum of 11 Mbps throughput on the 2.4 GHz band with a maximum range of 115 feet. **C** is incorrect because 802.11g networks have a maximum speed of 54 Mbps on the 2.4 GHz band with a range of 125 feet.

13. ☑ **C.** Satellite broadband connections are the best option in a sparsely populated, rural area for high-speed Internet connections. The other broadband connection types require that the receiver be within a certain distance of the provider, which is unlikely in a rural area. Satellite provides Internet and television signals, but the broadband connection will be substantially slower than either DSL or cable, while still about ten times as fast as a dial-up connection. Satellite service can be disrupted by severe weather conditions. Fiber-optic connections have recently become a viable option for the home user and can deliver both Internet and VoIP (Voice over IP) services at speeds far faster than DSL or cable, but this type of connection still requires the customer and provider to be within a specific distance from each other and is not a good fit for a rural environment.

    ☒ **A, B,** and **D** are incorrect because they all require the customer to be within a specified distance of the broadband provider, which is unlikely in a sparsely populated rural area.

14. ☑ **B and C.** A LAN, or local area network, is usually a small collection of computers on a single network segment, with computers attached to each other through one or more switches. You can find LANs in a home, small office, or office building. A WAN, or wide area network, can encompass many network segments, routing traffic across large distances using leased lines or public telephone lines. The largest WAN in the world is the Internet.

    ☒ **A and D** are incorrect. **A** is incorrect because LANs do not span great distances using leased lines and the "L" in LAN doesn't stand for "Large." **D** is incorrect because WANs use routers to direct traffic across numerous, dissimilar networks, including the Internet.

15. ☑ **C.** In a star network topology, all systems are connected to a central hub that repeats transmissions to other hosts.
     ☒ **A, B,** and **D** are incorrect because the mesh, ring, and bus topologies do not use a central controller. In some cases, these topologies can be combined with a star topology to form a hybrid network.

16. ☑ **B.** A switch is a device used to connect numerous computers together in the same network segment and that allows the full bandwidth of the network to be used between any two network nodes connected to the switch.
     ☒ **A, C,** and **D** are incorrect. **A** is incorrect because although a hub allows numerous computers to be connected together on the same network segment, a hub shares the total bandwidth of the network among all the connected nodes at once. Switches are almost exclusively used in place of hubs in modern networking. **C** is incorrect because a router allows two or more dissimilar network segments to be connected, routing traffic from a source network to any one of several destination networks. **D** is incorrect because a bridge is used to connect two network segments together.

17. ☑ **B.** The modem's modulation and demodulation services provide translation between the digital data network in the office and the analog telephone network.
     ☒ **A, C,** and **D** are incorrect. **A** is incorrect because Network Attached Storage (NAS) provides centralized storage for network users. **C** is incorrect because an access point is used to create a wireless network. **D** is incorrect because firewalls are used to secure network connections but do not perform conversion.

18. ☑ **A** and **B.** Internet appliances are special-purpose computers designed to provide Internet access and little else. They typically provide access to the Web and e-mail.
     ☒ **C** and **D** are incorrect. **C** is incorrect because Internet appliances typically do not provide command-line access. **D** is incorrect because SSH clients are not normally found in Internet appliances.

15

Installing a Small Office/Home Office (SOHO) Network

❑ **801: 2.6**   Install, configure, and deploy a SOHO wireless/wired router using appropriate settings.

❑ **801: 2.10**   Given a scenario, use appropriate networking tools.

❑ **802: 2.5**   Given a scenario, secure a SOHO wireless network.

❑ **802: 2.6**   Given a scenario, secure a SOHO wired network.

QUESTIONS

While some A+ technicians may work exclusively in large and midsized enterprises, many also must work in small office and home office environments. The skills required to manage and maintain these networks can vary significantly from those used in larger organizations.

Objective 801: 2.6   Install, Configure, and Deploy a SOHO Wireless/Wired Router Using Appropriate Settings

1. Your customer wants you to set up a wireless network for her office. She works with confidential business documents and wants to make sure no one in the other offices in her building will be able to connect to her wireless network and compromise her security. You suggest WPA2 as a security method, but she asks for additional measures. Of the following, which do you suggest? (Choose three.)

    A. Disabling DHCP
    B. Disabling SSID broadcasts
    C. Enabling MAC address filtering
    D. Enabling WEP in addition to WPA2

2. You have a customer who wants you to update the settings on the firewall built into the broadband modem his office uses to connect to the Internet. He wants to allow Web traffic in and out of his office network but specifically wants to prevent employees in his network from being able to upload data from the network to FTP servers on the Internet. You enter the broadband modem's graphical setup utility and access the firewall rules screen. Of the following, what rule will meet your customer's requirements?

    A. Allow inbound traffic on port 80 and deny inbound and outbound traffic on port 21.
    B. Allow inbound and outbound traffic on port 80 and deny inbound and outbound traffic on port 21.
    C. Deny inbound and outbound traffic on port 80 and deny inbound and outbound traffic on port 21.
    D. Allow inbound and outbound traffic on port 80 and deny outbound traffic on port 21.

3. One of your business office customers needs to test different online games and has asked you to open the required port on the firewall in the company's broadband modem so that an internal user can connect to one particular online game, but not to other online games. The firewall already blocks the port numbers of the games that are not required. The testing should only be allowed on one computer with the IP address of 192.168.0.5 in the customer's office. The customer also wants the port to the online game to be open only when the test is actually being conducted, rather than having the port open all the time. Of the following, what solution will meet the customer's requirements?

A. Port assignment

B. Port forwarding

C. Port rules

D. Port triggering

4. You are creating a wireless network for a small office environment in the United States and are configuring the access point. You choose to use the faster 802.11n wireless standard to ensure maximum throughput and want to use a 40 MHz wide channel that is least likely to be subject to interference from other wireless networks. What wireless channel should you use for this network?

A. 1

B. 3

C. 11

D. 13

5. You are configuring a combination firewall, router, and wireless access point for a small office environment. The office has one web server that must be accessible to the general public over the Internet. Where should you place this server?

A. Private network

B. Intranet

C. Internet

D. DMZ

Objective 801: 2.10 Given a Scenario, Use Appropriate Networking Tools

6. You are working on a new job as an A+ technician and are asked to assist the wiring crew as they prepare the data network for a new building. The network technician hands you the tool shown here and asks you to go get a replacement from the supply manager. When you get there, what tool do you ask the supply manager to give you?

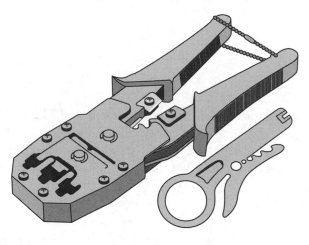

   A. Toner probe
   B. Crimper
   C. Multimeter
   D. Stripper

7. You have a box full of coaxial network terminators that are unlabeled, so you are unsure whether they are 50-ohm or 75-ohm terminators. What tool can you use to identify them?

   A. Multimeter
   B. Crimper
   C. Stripper
   D. Toner probe

8. You are wiring a new network jack in a building where existing wire is already pulled. You are having difficulty identifying which wire to connect to the switch in the data closet. What tool can you use to assist with this task?

   A. Multimeter
   B. Crimper
   C. Stripper
   D. Toner probe

9. You are constructing a wireless network for one floor of an office building containing numerous work areas for users. There are four self-contained cubicle areas on the floor, and users on the entire floor must be able to use the wireless network. The area of the floor in the accompanying illustration is 300 × 300 feet, and the access points you are using have a range of between 100 and 150 feet. Based on the placement of access points in the illustration, what would be the minimum number and position of access points to allow all users on the floor equal wireless network access?

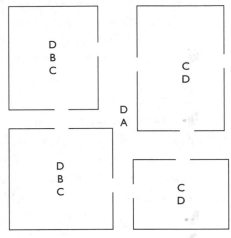

A. You only need one access point in the center of the area to equally cover the entire floor.

B. Two access points on one side of the floor will be able to cover the entire floor.

C. Four access points will be able to cover the entire floor with sufficient overlap of the signal that none of the users will suffer from lack of access.

D. Five access points, one in each area and one in the center of the floor, are necessary to guarantee maximum coverage with the minimum number of access points.

10. You are running Ethernet cable for a business customer in a building under construction. The cabling on the floor you're working on is being brought down from the plenum space through a column in the center of the room as shown in the accompanying illustration. The floor you are working on is 600 × 600 feet. You know that Ethernet cable has a length limitation before you have to start using switches or repeaters. Assuming the column is the starting point, how many repeating devices will you need to sufficiently cable this floor so that all of the cubicle areas in the diagram will be able to be sufficiently wired?

A. Zero. If you're starting the cabling at the center of the room, each cable length from the center should be sufficient.

B. Two. Cable lengths to the two areas on the right should be sufficient, but the two areas on the left are too far away.

C. Four. Although cable lengths seem sufficient, remember, you'll be routing cables into numerous different individual cubicles, so the length won't be straight end-to-end.

D. Eight. You'll need two switches or repeaters in each cubicle area, since the maximum effective length of each Ethernet cable segment is only 50 meters.

Objective 802: 2.5   Given a Scenario, Secure a SOHO Wireless Network

11. You are creating a wireless network for a small business that will be providing wireless networking for their customers. The business wants to provide access without asking customers to enter a password but would also like to limit the use of the network by people in adjoining businesses. What actions can you take to help with this requirement? (Choose two.)

     A. Adjust the radio's power level to the minimum required to cover the business.

     B. Use static IP addresses.

     C. Implement WPA encryption.

     D. Adjust the radio antennas to control the broadcast pattern.

12. You are installing a wireless network in a retail store that will only use the network to connect two cash registers at the front of the store with the server in the back of the store. What security measures can you use? (Choose three.)

     A. Secure the network with WEP.

     B. Use static IP addresses.

     C. Implement WPA2 encryption.

     D. Firewall the network from the Internet.

Objective 802: 2.6   Given a Scenario, Secure a SOHO Wired Network

13. You are securing a network for a branch office of your business and wish to take appropriate measures to prevent unauthorized use of the wired network. Which of the following actions should you take? (Choose three.)

     A. Enable WPA2 encryption.

     B. Disable unused switch ports.

     C. Employ MAC filtering.

     D. Assign static IP addresses.

14. You are assisting a network engineer with a security assessment of the network switches in your organization. Which of the following things should you check? (Choose two.)

     A. The switch is housed in a physically secure location.

     B. The switch is enabled to use WPA2 encryption.

     C. The administrative password for the switch has been changed from the default value.

     D. The switch is set to block all network traffic on port 80.

QUICK ANSWER KEY

1. A, B, C
2. D
3. D
4. C
5. D

6. B
7. A
8. D
9. D
10. C

11. A, D
12. B, C, D
13. B, C, D
14. A, C

IN-DEPTH ANSWERS

1. ☑ **A, B,** and **C.** Disabling the DHCP service on the wireless access point or router and configuring all the customer's wireless devices with manual IP addresses is one way to prevent unauthorized wireless devices from being dynamically assigned an IP address for her wireless network. Disabling SSID broadcasts from the access point or wireless router will prevent the network's name from being sent out, effectively making it invisible to anyone searching for open Wi-Fi networks. Enabling MAC address filtering on the access point or wireless router allows you to enter the MAC, or physical, addresses of all authorized computers into the access point or router and create a rule so that only devices with those physical addresses will be able to connect to the wireless network.

    ☒ **D** is incorrect because you would choose either WEP or WPA2 as encryption options but you would not use them together. Also, WPA2 is the better security option.

2. ☑ **D.** To allow normal Web traffic, the firewall must allow inbound and outbound traffic on port 80. If the customer specifically wants to prevent someone from uploading data from inside the network to an FTP server on the Internet but doesn't specify blocking downloading data from an FTP server into the network, block outgoing traffic on port 21. If you don't specifically block inbound port 21 traffic, it will likely (but not assuredly, since configuration settings are different on different broadband modems) be allowed by default.

    ☒ **A, B,** and **C** are incorrect. **A** is incorrect because, although Web traffic is allowed in, it isn't known if the default setting for outbound port 80 traffic will be allowed by default, since it's not specifically expressed. If not, people inside the network wouldn't be able to send requests for specific Websites, preventing the employees from accessing the Internet. Also, blocking incoming port 21 traffic wasn't one of the customer's requirements. **B** is incorrect because, while the port 80 rules are consistent with the customer's requirements, blocking incoming port 21 traffic wasn't one of the customer's requirements. **C** is incorrect because this rule would completely block both Web and FTP traffic and no one would be able to access Websites on the Internet.

3. ☑ **D.** Port triggering is the best option. This firewall feature works similarly to port forwarding in that you can create a rule that directs incoming traffic from the gaming port on the Internet to a specific IP address in the internal network, but you can also specify that the port be opened, or "triggered," only when traffic from the specified port is detected.

    ☒ **A, B,** and **C** are incorrect. **A** is incorrect because assigning a port number to be opened or closed in the firewall won't meet the customer's specific requirements, because traffic will be allowed or denied all of the time. **B** is incorrect because port forwarding will allow traffic from a specific port number to be directed to a specific IP address, but it won't let the port be opened or closed by the presence or absence of traffic from the specified port number. **C** is incorrect because a port rule is a generic description of a set of conditions relative to traffic for a port number, but it doesn't meet any of the particular requirements.

4. ☑ **C.** 802.11n wireless networking has only two 40 MHz channel possibilities: 3 or 11. Of these, channel 3 is not recommended for use in the United States due to interference issues, so channel 11 is the best option.

☒ **A, B,** and **D** are incorrect. **A** is incorrect because channel 1 only provides 20 MHz of bandwidth. **B** is incorrect because channel 3 is not recommended for use in the United States due to interference issues. **D** is incorrect because channel 13 only provides 20 MHz of bandwidth.

5. ☑ **D.** The demilitarized zone (DMZ) network is the appropriate location for servers that must be accessed by the general public. This network is shielded by the firewall but also isolated from the internal network.

☒ **A, B,** and **C** are incorrect. **A** and **B** are incorrect because the server should not be placed on the private internal (intranet) network. This network is reserved for trusted systems. If the Web server is placed here and compromised by an attacker, the entire network will be at risk. **C** is incorrect because placing the server outside the firewall on the Internet will leave it unprotected and vulnerable to attack.

6. ☑ **B.** The tool shown in the illustration is a crimper, a tool used to attach connecters to network cables.

☒ **A, C,** and **D** are incorrect. **A** is incorrect because the tool is not a toner probe, a tool used to identify cables. **C** is incorrect because the device shown is not a multimeter, a device used to measure electrical characteristics. **D** is incorrect because the tool is not a wire stripper, used to remove the protective casing from a cable.

7. ☑ **A.** You are trying to measure the resistance of the terminators, and measuring resistance is one of the functions of a multimeter.

☒ **B, C,** and **D** are incorrect. **B** is incorrect because a crimper is used to attach connectors to wires and cannot measure resistance. **C** is incorrect because a stripper is used to remove the protective casing from wires and cannot be used to measure resistance. **D** is incorrect because a toner probe is used to identify wires and cannot be used to measure resistance.

8. ☑ **D.** The toner probe (also known as a tone and probe kit) is used to generate and detect a tone being transmitted on a wire. You can use it to generate a tone on the cable at the network jack and then use the probe to identify it in the data closet.

☒ **A, B,** and **C** are incorrect. **A** is incorrect because a multimeter can't be used by itself to identify the cable. **B** is incorrect because a crimper is used to attach connectors to wires and cannot identify wires. **C** is incorrect because a stripper is used to remove the protective casing from wires and cannot be used to identify wires.

9. ☑ **D.** Given the limitation of range for each access point and the size of the room, you will need to place access points in each major cubicle area, plus an access point in the center to cover the greatest area for a total of five. The rule of thumb of access points in such situations is that you need about 20 percent signal overlap between access points to provide sufficient coverage. Other factors that affect access point placement include the specific 802.11 protocol being used, the overall power of the radio transmitter, and any obstructions or interference. For instance, objects such as metal cabinets can block or restrict radio waves, and the operation of microwave ovens can cause interference. Often a site survey is conducted before a plan is created for wireless device placement so that the environment can be examined with specific testing devices and software in order to define specific problems with the environment.

☒   **A, B,** and **C** are incorrect. **A** is incorrect because a single access point in the center will only cover the middle of the floor, servicing only those users in each of the four cubicle areas closest to the room's center. **B** is incorrect because this placement will only cover the two cubicle areas on the left side of the floor. **C** is incorrect because it will cover most of the room, but there may be users near the middle of the room who won't have wireless access.

10.   ☑   **C.** The maximum effective cable length for Ethernet cable is 100 meters, or about 328 feet, and if you are running cable from the center of the room to the edges, you shouldn't need repeaters or switches, but you will also be using a lot of cable length conforming to the position and shape of all of the individual cubicles in each area. Accordingly, you'll likely need one device per major quarter of the floor to make sure all of the cubicles can be networked.

☒   **A, B,** and **D** are incorrect. **A** is incorrect because, to cable all of the cubicles in all four areas, you'll need more than 300 meters of cable running in each direction from the center of the room. **B** is incorrect because the column is close enough to the center of the floor that the left and right sides of the room are more or less equally spaced. **D** is incorrect because the effective cable length for Ethernet is 100 meters, not 50 meters.

11.   ☑   **A and D.** You can adjust the power level of the wireless network radio to limit spread into adjoining buildings. You can also orient the antennas so that the majority of the signal is radiated into the business. These methods will not prevent the signal from leaking but will minimize how far outside the business it reaches.

☒   **B and C** are incorrect. **B** is incorrect because the use of static IP addresses will prevent the business' customers from using the network without configuration assistance. **C** is incorrect because the business owner specified that the network must not have a password.

12.   ☑   **B, C,** and **D.** The use of static IP addresses means that unauthorized devices that connect to the network will not function unless properly configured. This is not a foolproof technique but will deter the casual user seeking a wireless network. WPA2 encryption will provide confidentiality for data transmitted over the network, while the firewall will protect against Internet-based attackers.

☒   **A** is incorrect because the WEP encryption standard is insecure and should not be used for confidential information.

13.   ☑   **B, C,** and **D.** Disabling unused switch ports prevents unauthorized users from accessing the network via an unused jack. MAC address filtering prevents the addition of unapproved devices to the network. Static addressing requires that someone connecting a device to your network has knowledge of your IP addressing scheme.

☒   **A** is incorrect because WPA2 encryption is only used on wireless networks.

14.   ☑   **A** and **C.** Switches should always be housed in a physically secure location because an attacker who gains physical access to the switch will be able to take it over. Administrators should always change switch account passwords from their default values before installing them on the network

☒   **B** and **D** are incorrect. **B** is incorrect because WPA2 encryption is performed by wireless access points, not switches. **D** is incorrect because port blocking is performed by firewalls, not switches, and blocking port 80 would block all Web traffic on the network.

16

Troubleshooting
Networks

❑   **802: 4.5**   Given a scenario, troubleshoot wired and wireless networks with appropriate tools.

QUESTIONS

The one plaintive cry from end users that most network engineers don't like to hear is, "The network is down!" Fortunately, as an A+ technician, you won't be expected to solve every problem that can possibly occur in a network infrastructure, but you will be asked to diagnose and fix many of the common problems users have when their computers can't connect to a file share or the Internet.

Objective 802: 4.5   Given a Scenario, Troubleshoot Wired and Wireless Networks with Appropriate Tools

1. You work for a small city IT department, and you have a customer in city hall who can print to a network printer and access a shared folder on a coworker's computer but who can't connect to a remote file share in another city department across town. She also can't connect to the Internet. What do you suspect?

   A. The DHCP settings on the customer's computer are wrong.

   B. The DNS settings on the customer's computer are wrong.

   C. The gateway settings on the customer's computer are wrong.

   D. The subnet mask settings on the customer's computer are wrong.

2. You have just installed a new network printer in a customer's office. You connect your laptop to the printer using a USB cable, and it prints fine. However, when your customer attempts to connect and print over the network, he can't do so. You check the computer's network configuration and physical network connections, and everything is fine. You check the IP address you've given the printer as well as its physical connections, and they are correct. You try to ping the printer's IP address from the customer's computer, but the request times out. Of the following, what could be wrong?

   A. The printer is configured to use the wrong DHCP server.

   B. The printer is configured to use the wrong DNS server.

   C. The printer is configured to use the wrong NAT server.

   D. The printer is configured to use the wrong subnet mask.

3. You have a customer who says one of the computers in her office can't connect to the local network or to the Internet. You check, and the network configuration settings on the computer are correct. You open a command-line window and at the prompt, you type **ping loopback** and then press ENTER. What are you testing?

A. You are testing the NIC on the computer.

B. You are testing the network cable.

C. You are testing the connection to the gateway.

D. You are testing the connection to the DHCP server.

4. You have a customer who has installed an FTP client on her Windows 7 computer and wants to use it to update a number of Websites she administers. She says she has a good Internet connection and is able to surf the Web and send and receive e-mails, but she can't get her FTP client to connect to any of the required Websites. She has verified that her user name and password for those sites is good, and she can ping the IP addresses and domain names for each of the required servers. What should you check?

A. Check the security settings on the FTP client to make sure they aren't blocking Internet access.

B. Check the Windows firewall to see if it's blocking port 21.

C. Use the tracert utility to check for problems on the Internet that could be preventing access to the required sites.

D. Access the domain name mapping for the DNS records for the Websites using nslookup.

5. You have a customer who says one of the computers in his office can't connect to the local network or the Internet. The network configuration settings seem correct. You want to check the number of bytes and packets sent and received by the computer's NIC card using a command-line tool and produce output such as what is illustrated in the accompanying screenshot. What utility do you use?

```
C:\WINDOWS\system32\cmd.exe                                    _ □ ×

                        Received            Sent
Bytes                 1451318888       4151579234
Unicast packets         10098761         15565969
Non-unicast packets       643450            18617
Discards                       0                0
Errors                         0                0
Unknown protocols            167

C:\Documents and Settings\jmp>_
```

A. tracert

B. nslookup

C. netstat

D. net use

6. You have a small-office customer who complains that some of her mapped drives on her Windows computer keep becoming disconnected. You want to use a command-line tool to see all network connections to her PC, including any disconnected network shares, such as illustrated in the accompanying screenshot. Which command-line utility do you use?

```
C:\WINDOWS\system32\cmd.exe                                    _ □ ×

Status          Local      Remote              Network
_____

                K:         \\filesrv1\shared        Microsoft Windows Network
Disconnected M:            \\filesrv1\development   Microsoft Windows Network
Disconnected Y:            \\filesrv1\home\jmp       Microsoft Windows Network
                Z:         \\Filesrv1\shared\Kou
                                                     Microsoft Windows Network
The command completed successfully.


C:\Documents and Settings\jmp>_
```

A. netstat

B. net use

C. ipconfig

D. telnet

7. You want to use a command-line utility that's designed to view, update, and fix network settings from a host computer on the network, but you aren't sure of the exact syntax options that can be used with this command. Of the following, what should you type at the command prompt to get help with this command?

A. net /?

B. netstat /?

C. net use /?

D. net view /?

8. You are troubleshooting a network issue on a Windows 7 computer and wish to check the traffic reaching the network firewall from that computer. You want to use a command-line tool that produces output similar to the following illustration that includes the IP addresses assigned to each network interface. What tool do you use?

```
C:\Windows\system32\cmd.exe
   Node Type . . . . . . . . . . . : Hybrid
   IP Routing Enabled. . . . . . . : No
   WINS Proxy Enabled. . . . . . . : No
   DNS Suffix Search List. . . . . : localdomain

Ethernet adapter Local Area Connection:

   Connection-specific DNS Suffix  . : localdomain
   Description . . . . . . . . . . : Intel(R) PRO/1000 MT Network Connection
   Physical Address. . . . . . . . : 00-1C-42-0F-27-36
   DHCP Enabled. . . . . . . . . . : Yes
   Autoconfiguration Enabled . . . : Yes
   Site-local IPv6 Address . . . . : fec0::fea9:bcbc:3686:7da0:f975%1(Preferre
d)
   Link-local IPv6 Address . . . . : fe80::bcbc:3686:7da0:f975%11(Preferred)
   IPv4 Address. . . . . . . . . . : 10.211.55.4(Preferred)
   Subnet Mask . . . . . . . . . . : 255.255.255.0
   Lease Obtained. . . . . . . . . : Sunday, May 06, 2012 7:42:01 PM
   Lease Expires . . . . . . . . . : Monday, May 07, 2012 12:47:01 PM
   Default Gateway . . . . . . . . : 10.211.55.1
   DHCP Server . . . . . . . . . . : 10.211.55.1
   DNS Servers . . . . . . . . . . : 10.211.55.1
   NetBIOS over Tcpip. . . . . . . : Enabled

Tunnel adapter isatap.localdomain:
```

A. netstat

B. nbtstat

C. ipconfig

D. arp

9. You are troubleshooting an issue on an end user's Windows 7 computer that cannot seem to access any resources on the network. When you check the machine's IP address, you see that it is 169.254.0.4. What type of IP address is this?

A. Class A

B. Class E

C. DHCP

D. APIPA

10. You receive a call at your help desk from a user reporting that her network connection goes down occasionally. She reports that physically jostling the computer can cause it to come back up. Which of the following problems might be occurring?

A. The network cable is defective.

B. The HDMI adapter is loose.

C. The switch port is not soldered properly.

D. The CPU is not properly seated in its socket.

11. You receive the following screenshot from a user who is reporting intermittent connectivity problems on his computer. Which of the following might be the issue? (Choose two.)

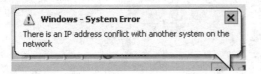

   A. The machine is assigned a static IP address on a DHCP network.

   B. The network firewall does not have the appropriate rules for this computer.

   C. This computer was not properly configured to use DNS.

   D. The DHCP server is malfunctioning.

12. Several users complain that when they are using a conference room at the end of the hallway, their wireless connections drop sporadically. What is the likely cause of this problem?

   A. The conference room is specially shielded to block wireless signals.

   B. The access points in the area are not directing enough RF power toward the conference room.

   C. The users do not have their computers configured properly for the wireless network.

   D. The antennas on the user's computers are not oriented in the correct direction.

QUICK ANSWER KEY

1. C		**5.** C		**9.** D	
2. D		**6.** B		**10.** A	
3. A		**7.** A		**11.** A, D	
4. B		**8.** C		**12.** B	

IN-DEPTH ANSWERS

1. ☑ **C.** Since the customer can connect to devices on the local network segment but not to file shares on remote network segments, the most likely problem is that the computer isn't accessing the correct gateway router to connect to remote network hosts, including those on the Internet. A computer must be either manually or dynamically configured to use the IP address of a gateway router directly connected to its network segment in order to be able to send and receive network traffic to and from remote networks.

   ☒ **A, B,** and **D** are incorrect. **A** is incorrect because if the computer is receiving dynamic addressing via DHCP, it should be able to network remotely, unless the DHCP server itself were misconfigured to give out the wrong IP address to the gateway router. If the computer has been configured manually, then DHCP is irrelevant. **B** is incorrect because not being able to use DNS services would not explain why the computer could network locally to a file share but not connect to a remote file share. **D** is incorrect because if the computer was receiving an incorrect subnet mask, either by manual configuration or dynamically, it wouldn't be able to network at all.

2. ☑ **D.** A subnet mask defines the specific network to which an IP address belongs. It is expressed similarly to the way an IPv4 address is expressed. A common subnet mask is 255.255.255.0. If this setting is missing or entered incorrectly onto a device that has a manual network configuration, the device will not be able to be reached over the network.

   ☒ **A, B,** and **C** are incorrect. **A** is incorrect because network resources such as printers are assigned an IP address manually, not via DHCP. **B** is incorrect because hostname-to-IP address translation wouldn't prevent you from being able to ping the printer. **C** is incorrect because NAT is a service that maps the external, or Internet, IP address of a network to the internal IP addresses of computers in a LAN, and wouldn't affect the connection between two devices on the same LAN network segment.

3. ☑ **A.** Although a computer is assigned an IP address either manually or dynamically, each network interface card, or NIC, on a computer can be tested by pinging the loopback address, which is typically 127.0.0.1 for IPv4 and ::1 for IPv6. You can ping the loopback address by issuing either the command "ping loopback" or "ping 127.0.0.1." If there's a problem with the computer's NIC, you won't receive a ping reply.

   ☒ **B, C,** and **D** are incorrect. **B** is incorrect because you can't specifically test a network cable using ping. You must use specialized equipment for this task. **C** is incorrect because to test the connection to the gateway, you typically ping the gateway's IP address. **D** is incorrect because to ping the DHCP server, you typically ping the server's IP address.

4. ☑ **B.** Since the customer can surf the Web and check e-mail, she's able to connect to the Internet, and assuming her credentials for the required sites are good, it's likely the Windows Firewall is blocking port 21, which is the port used for FTP.

☒ **A, C,** and **D** are incorrect. **A** is incorrect because FTP clients don't have security settings that would prevent an Internet connection. **C** is incorrect because if the sites can be pinged, using tracert to determine the route to the sites wouldn't be helpful. **D** is incorrect because name-to-IP address issues aren't the problem if the sites can be pinged by their hostnames, and you can configure an FTP client to connect to a Website using an IP address rather than a hostname.

5. ☑ **C.** Netstat (the name stands for Network Statistics) is a command-line utility used to display network connections, routing tables, and interface statistics for a computer. The command netstat -e command specifically produces output about the Ethernet statistics related to the computer's NIC.

☒ **A, B,** and **D** are incorrect. **A** is incorrect because tracert is a command-line tool used to show the route taken by packets across a network, including the Internet, between source and destination. **B** is incorrect because nslookup is a command-line tool used for querying DNS servers in order to acquire domain name–to–IP address mappings. **D** is incorrect because Net use is a command-line tool used to connect a computer to a shared resource on the network or to display information about computer connections.

6. ☑ **B.** If you type **net use** at the command prompt with no parameters, you'll see output detailing the mapped drives on the computer, including those that are currently disconnected.

☒ **A, C,** and **D** are incorrect. **A** is incorrect because netstat is a command-line utility used to display network connections, routing tables, and interface statistics for a computer. **C** is incorrect because ipconfig is a command-line utility that is used to display the IP configuration settings for a computer, such as IP address, subnet mask, and default gateway. **D** is incorrect because telnet is a command-line utility used to provide a bidirectional, interactive virtual terminal connection between a local computer and a remote host.

7. ☑ **A.** The net command can take a variety of syntax options, such as net config, net diag, net use, and net view. Typing **net /?** at the command-line prompt will show all of the different options available. Once you choose a specific option, such as net use, you can type **net use /?** to view the parameters specific to this command.

☒ **B, C,** and **D** are incorrect. **B** is incorrect because it only gets help information for the netstat command and not any of the variations on the net command. **C** is incorrect because it only gives you the parameters for the net use command and not all of the syntax options for the net command. **D** is incorrect because it only gives you the parameters for the net view command and not all of the syntax options for the net command.

8. ☑ **C.** The ipconfig command provides detailed information about the network interfaces on a Windows system, including the IP addresses assigned to network adapters.

   ☒ **A, B,** and **D** are incorrect. **A** and **B** are incorrect because, while the netstat and nbtstat commands will provide the machine's IP address, they do not include interface information and do not provide the detailed configuration information in the screenshot. **D** is incorrect because the arp command displays information about MAC and IP address pairs stored in the system's ARP table.

9. ☑ **D.** Addresses that begin with 169 are assigned by the Automatic Private IP Addressing (APIPA) mechanism. APIPA is used to provide machines with addresses when a DHCP server cannot be found. The technician should use this information to troubleshoot the DHCP process.

   ☒ **A, B,** and **C** are incorrect. **A** is incorrect because Class A IP addresses have values between 1 and 126 in the first octet. **B** is incorrect because Class E IP addresses have initial octets in the range 240 to 254. **C** is incorrect because the presence of an APIPA address indicates that the system could not locate a DHCP server.

10. ☑ **A.** The fact that jostling the computer restores the connection indicates that the network cable or network interface card is probably faulty. Replacing the connector or the cable itself may resolve the problem.

   ☒ **B, C,** and **D** are incorrect. **B** is incorrect because the HDMI interface affects video, not network connectivity. **C** is incorrect because a faulty switch port would not be affected by the user jostling the computer. **D** is incorrect because the computer would not start if the CPU was not properly seated.

11. ☑ **A and D.** The error shown in the illustration occurs when two machines on the network have the same IP address. This may be caused by a machine on the network that is improperly using a static address from a dynamically assigned range. It also may occur if the DHCP server is inappropriately handing out the same address twice.

   ☒ **B and C** are incorrect. **B** is incorrect because the network firewall is not normally involved in the assignment of IP addresses. **C** is incorrect because DNS does not provide IP addresses to computers, but rather allows systems to look up the addresses of other systems.

12. ☑ **B.** The most likely explanation for this scenario is that the access point is not radiating enough RF power down to the end of the hallway. This may be corrected by realigning the access point's antennas, adjusting the power on the access point, or adding an access point.

   ☒ **A, C,** and **D** are incorrect. **A** is incorrect because it is unlikely that the building designers would intentionally shield a conference room against wireless signals outside of a secure government facility. **C** is incorrect because there is no indication that users are having this problem in other rooms in the same building. **D** is incorrect because most mobile devices do not have user-adjustable antennas.

17

Computer Security
Fundamentals

QUESTIONS

While there may be no such thing as 100 percent security in the world of information technology, there are still multiple techniques available to improve the security of machines and information. As an A+ technician, you will be expected to be familiar with the basics.

Objective 802: 2.1   Apply and Use Common Prevention Methods

1. You are configuring a wireless network for a business that is extremely concerned with the confidentiality of information transmitted over the network. Their federal contracts require them to choose a wireless security mode that supports the Advanced Encryption Standard (AES). What mode should you choose?
    A. WEP
    B. WEP2
    C. WPA
    D. WPA2

2. You want to allow the firewall on your Windows 7 computer to pass traffic for a specific online game. The port number for the game is 65535, and it uses the TCP protocol. How do you open the firewall and allow access?
    A. Add an exception by clicking Add Exception.
    B. Add a port by clicking the Add Port button.
    C. Unblock a port by clicking the Unblock Port button.
    D. Remove the block for the game in the firewall rules by clicking Remove Block.

3. You work for a small city IT department, and you are providing training to new hires on authorized computer usage and security. Of the following, what part of your training will most help the new employees detect when an unauthorized person is attempting to get the employee to release information?
    A. Compliance with information security policies
    B. Understanding the different levels of data security
    C. Comprehending the nature of social engineering
    D. Developing a secure user name and password

4. You are evaluating a popular antivirus product for a customer's home computer. Of the following, what threats do you tell her that her computer will be protected from by the antivirus application? (Choose three.)

   A. Viruses
   B. Trojans
   C. Worms
   D. Spam

5. Members of your organization's sales force travel constantly and are concerned about the risk of people looking over their shoulders and reading their laptop screens while they are on airplanes. What technology can assist with mitigating this risk?

   A. Strong passwords
   B. File-based encryption
   C. Password-protected screen saver
   D. Privacy filters

6. You find a user's computer has been infected with a type of malicious code that transmits her keystrokes back to a remote location. What type of malware is this?

   A. Trojan horse
   B. Adware
   C. Spyware
   D. Logic bomb

Objective 802: 2.2   Compare and Contrast Common Security Threats

7. The Stuxnet malicious code spread from computer to computer without any user intervention required. What type of malicious code is Stuxnet?

   A. Virus
   B. Worm
   C. Trojan horse
   D. Logic bomb

8. When a hacker gains access to a system, he or she normally first gets access to a user-level account and then uses a special set of tools to elevate that access to administrator-level privileges. What is this set of tools called?

A. Logic bomb

B. Rootkit

C. Privilege escalator

D. Port scanner

9. One of your users received an e-mail informing him that his Webmail account was expiring and that he needed to visit a Website to renew it. He logged into that Website with his e-mail user name and password. Shortly thereafter, his account was used to send massive quantities of spam. What type of attack did this user fall victim to?

A. Phishing

B. Shoulder surfing

C. Piggybacking

D. SMiShing

10. The president of your company recently installed a new game of solitaire on his computer. Immediately thereafter, the computer began to exhibit slow performance, missing files, and other signs of a malware infection. What type of attack do you suspect?

A. Social engineering

B. Worm

C. Trojan horse

D. Logic bomb

Objective 802: 2.4   Given a Scenario, Use the Appropriate Data Destruction/Disposal Method

11. You recently replaced the hard drive of a user's computer in the accounting department because the drive would not power up. The drive is known to contain sensitive data, and you wish to make sure it is disposed of securely. What methods can you use to ensure data on the drive is completely inaccessible? (Choose two.)

A. Low-level format the drive.

B. Degauss the drive.

C. Drill holes in the drive.

D. Use a secure wiping tool.

QUICK ANSWER KEY

1.	D	**5.**	D	**9.**	A	
2.	B	**6.**	C	**10.**	C	
3.	C	**7.**	B	**11.**	B, C	
4.	A, B, C	**8.**	B			

IN-DEPTH ANSWERS

1. ☑ **D.** Wi-Fi Protected Access v2 (WPA2) is the only wireless security mode that supports the use of AES encryption.

   ☒ **A, B,** and **C** are incorrect. **A** is incorrect because Wired Equivalent Privacy (WEP) is an insecure security mode that does not support AES encryption. **B** is incorrect because a second version of WEP was never released. **C** is incorrect because the first version of WPA used the Temporal Key Integrity Protocol (TKIP) and did not support AES encryption.

2. ☑ **B.** To unblock a port in the Windows Firewall, you add a port, specifying the program name, port number, and protocol (TCP or UDP). When you add the port, you open it in the firewall. Note: The port number 65535 is used just for this example.

   ☒ **A, C,** and **D** are incorrect. **A** is incorrect because you can click Add Program to add an exception for the program, but there is no Add Exception button. **C** is incorrect because there is no Unblock Port button. You can only open a port by adding it. **D** is incorrect because there is no Remove Block button.

3. ☑ **C.** Social engineering, in general, is when a party without access to confidential information attempts to trick or convince a person with access to the desired data to divulge that data to the unauthorized party.

   ☒ **A, B,** and **D** are incorrect. **A** is incorrect because anyone working for any company with an information security policy would be expected to comply with all of the conditions contained within the policy, but policy compliance may not be specific to social engineering attempts. **B** is incorrect because understanding the different levels of security applied to data, such as low, medium, or high, won't assist in helping a person resist a social engineering attempt. **D** is incorrect because developing and using a secure user name and password won't be effective in a social engineering scenario.

4. ☑ **A, B,** and **C.** Most antivirus programs created for home computer use will detect and block known viruses, Trojans, and worms but will not be able to protect the customer from receiving e-mail spam. Usually, an upgrade to the vendor's "Internet security" product will offer spam protection. In general, a computer virus is a malicious program that can infect a computer, make copies of itself, and infect other computers, doing some kind of damage to the operating system or applications on the computer. A Trojan is a specific type of malicious software that initially appears as a desirable or useful type of application but then, once it's on your computer, runs and harms your computer's software. A worm is a self-replicating type of malicious software that is specifically designed to take advantage of a vulnerability on a computer to invade the system and then do damage. Worms almost always cause at least some harm to the network, if only by consuming bandwidth, whereas viruses almost always corrupt or modify files on a targeted computer.

   ☒ **D** is incorrect because typical antivirus programs won't block spam e-mails.

5. ☑ **D.** Privacy filters use optical filtering to make it difficult for people not looking at the screen from directly in front of it to read the contents. They are well-suited for computer use in public environments such as airplanes and coffee shops.

   ☒ **A, B,** and **C** are incorrect because all of these technologies would prevent the sales force from viewing the content at the same time. Files must be decrypted before they are useable. The screensaver must be disengaged and passwords entered before the individual can use the computer.

6. ☑ **C.** The malware described in the scenario is a keylogger, which is a form of spyware. Computers should be equipped with antispyware software (which may be a module of their antivirus software) to protect against these threats.

   ☒ **A, B,** and **D** are incorrect. **A** is incorrect because while a Trojan horse might install a keylogger, it is not necessary for a keylogger to be a Trojan horse. **B** is incorrect because the purpose of adware is to display unwanted advertising on the user's computer. **D** is incorrect because a logic bomb is software that waits until certain conditions are met before delivering its malicious payload.

7. ☑ **B.** Worms are malicious code objects that are able to propagate from system to system without any user action required.

   ☒ **A, C,** and **D** are incorrect. **A** is incorrect because viruses require some user action to spread, such as sharing infected media or opening an infected attachment. **C** is incorrect because Trojan horses spread by posing as legitimate software. **D** is incorrect because logic bombs are planted in a system by the programmer and trigger when certain conditions are met.

8. ☑ **B.** Rootkits are used to gain privileged access on a system where the attacker already has a user-level account. They derive their name from the "root" superuser account on Linux systems.

   ☒ **A, C,** and **D** are incorrect. **A** is incorrect because logic bombs are malicious code planted in a system by the programmer and trigger when certain conditions are met. **C** is incorrect because privilege escalators do not exist. **D** is incorrect because port scanners are security reconnaissance tools.

9. ☑ **A.** In a phishing attack, the attacker sends out false e-mails claiming to require a user's password or other sensitive information to perform some important activity. That information is then later used for some malicious purpose.

   ☒ **B, C,** and **D** are incorrect. **B** is incorrect because shoulder surfing attacks occur when an individual looks over the shoulder of someone using a computer to read what is on their screen. **C** is incorrect because piggybacking attacks involve someone physically entering a building when the person in front of them does not let the door securely shut behind them. **D** is incorrect because SMiShing is a special type of phishing attack sent via text message.

10. ☑ **C.** Trojan horses are a type of malicious code that spreads by posing as legitimate software. It is likely in this scenario that the solitaire game was a Trojan horse.

    ☒ **A, B,** and **D** are incorrect. **A** is incorrect because social engineering attacks occur when an individual convinces another person to divulge sensitive information. **B** is incorrect because worms are malicious code that spreads from system to system independently of user action. **D** is incorrect because logic bombs are planted in a system by the programmer and trigger when certain conditions are met.

11. ☑ **B and C.** You may choose to physically destroy the drive by drilling holes in it or using an industrial shredder. You may also magnetically destroy the information on the drive platters using an electromagnet or degaussing tool.

    ☒ **A and D** are incorrect. **A** is incorrect because, while a low-level format may remove the data, it is not possible to low-level format a drive that will not spin up. Standard formatting, it should be noted, does not remove data from the drive. **D** is incorrect because the fact that it is not possible to power up the drive prevents the use of a secure overwriting or drive wiping tool.

18
Implementing Digital Security

❑   **802: 4.7**   Given a scenario, troubleshoot common security issues with appropriate tools and best practices.

❑   **802: 2.3**   Implement security best practices to secure a workstation.

QUESTIONS

Murphy's Law tells us that "Anything that can go wrong, will." Whenever something goes wrong with a computer, as an A+ technician, you will be responsible for fixing it, particularly in the area of security. If proper prevention methods are not implemented, you may find yourself spending a great deal of time repairing PCs suffering from malware infections and securing computers from unauthorized use.

Objective 802: 4.7 Given a Scenario, Troubleshoot Common Security Issues with Appropriate Tools and Best Practices

1. You work for a small city IT department, and one of the customers in the vehicle maintenance department is complaining that her computer has become very slow, unusual icons have spontaneously appeared on her desktop, and whenever she opens a Web browser, an endless stream of pop-ups and browser windows open uncontrollably. It seems obvious that her computer is infected by malware, and you are concerned that the infection could spread to other computers on the network. How can you quarantine the infected PC while you are trying to remove the malware?

    A. Use the computer's antivirus software to quarantine the virus.

    B. Use the computer's software firewall to block all ports.

    C. Unplug the Ethernet cable from the computer's network port.

    D. Shut down the computer and unplug the power cord.

2. You work for a small city IT department, and one of the customers in the vehicle maintenance department is complaining that his computer has become very slow, unusual icons have spontaneously appeared on his desktop, and the system is locking up periodically. It seems obvious that his computer is infected by malware, but the infection has also disabled the computer's onboard antivirus program. First, you disconnect the computer from the rest of the network to keep other computers from being infected. How can you then clean the infection off the computer? (Choose two.)

    A. Run a stand-alone antivirus computer scan from a USB drive on the compromised computer.

    B. Reboot the computer into Safe Mode and run the onboard antivirus program.

    C. Create a boot disc using the onboard antivirus program and scan the BIOS.

    D. Put the hard disk drive from the infected computer into another PC, boot that PC from the infected system's hard disk, and then run the antivirus software.

3. You have just installed an antivirus program on a home user's new computer. What are the next steps you must perform before the user's computer is protected? (Choose two.)

A. Manually update the program to the latest version.

B. Set the antivirus program to automatically scan the computer starting tomorrow at a time when the computer is not normally in use.

C. Manually update the virus signatures to the latest version.

D. Set the antivirus program to automatically look for program and signature updates every day when the computer is not normally in use.

4. You work for a small city IT department, and a policy of your department states that you do not allow any users to belong to a security group on a computer with greater permissions than they require in performing their job. You have a user in city hall who needs to be able to create other user accounts and local groups on her Windows XP Professional computer but does not require permissions to delete any other accounts or groups on the computer, except those she's created. Of the following, which is the appropriate security group to assign her?

A. Administrators

B. Power Users

C. Users

D. Guests

5. You want to install the Recovery Console on a customer's Windows XP Professional computer so that it will appear as an option in the Start menu rather than, in an emergency, having to locate the Windows XP installation CD. You want to perform this task using the command prompt. You insert the Windows XP installation CD into the customer's computer and, if necessary, stop the setup program. Assuming the computer's CD drive uses the D drive letter, what is the correct command to use to start the Recovery Console installation process?

A. d:\i386\winnt32 /console

B. d:\i386\winnt32.exe /cmdcons

C. d:\windows\winnt32 /console

D. d:\windows\winnt32 /cmdcons

6. You receive a telephone call from a user who is complaining about Internet connectivity problems. Whenever he opens Internet Explorer, it opens seemingly random Websites rather than the ones he requested. You believe that his system is infected with malware. What type of attack should you suspect?

   A. Browser redirection

   B. Distributed denial of service

   C. Phishing

   D. Social engineering

7. You receive a phone call from a user who is looking at a message on her screen indicating a security alert. She sends you a screenshot of the message, and it does not appear to be from your organization's antivirus software. What could be causing this message? (Choose three.)

   A. Rogue antivirus software

   B. Spam e-mail

   C. Keylogger

   D. Pop-up advertisement

8. A user asks you to visit his desktop and shows you that his computer is reporting repeated Windows Update failures. You explore the system in further detail and discover that several system files have been renamed. What should be your next step?

   A. Reinstall the operating system.

   B. Wipe the hard drive.

   C. Run antivirus software.

   D. Rerun Windows Update.

9. You are examining a system and attempting to determine whether it is infected with malware. Which of the following symptoms would indicate a potential malware infection? (Choose three.)

   A. Presence of a master boot record

   B. User files disappearing

   C. Unexpected permission changes on files

   D. Access Denied errors on the desktop

10. A user contacts your help desk and reports that he is receiving a large number of undeliverable e-mail messages. The returned messages appear to have been sent from his e-mail address and are selling illegal pharmaceuticals. What should you recommend the user do first?

   A. Run an antivirus scan.

   B. Change his password.

   C. Ignore the messages.

   D. Contact the telephone number provided in the spam messages.

11. You are attempting to use Windows 7 System Restore (see the next Illustration) to restore a computer's settings. In what Control Panel category can you find the option to restore?

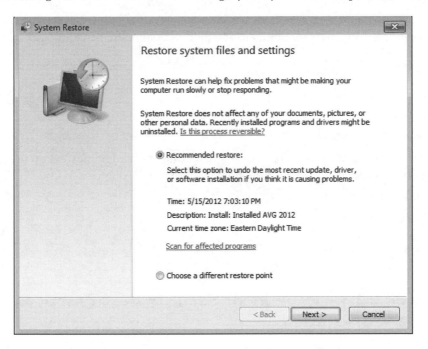

   A. Network and Internet
   B. Hardware and Sound
   C. Programs
   D. System and Security

12. You would like to create a USB flash drive that you can use when repairing computers with security issues. The drive should contain a bootable operating system that provides you with native Windows tools at the command line only. What operating system is most suitable?
   A. Windows 7
   B. WinPE
   C. Ubuntu
   D. Windows Server 2008 R2

13. Your supervisor is conducting an investigation and asked you to determine the users who logged onto a specific Windows 7 computer over the past few days. You recognize that Event Viewer provides this information. What section of Event Viewer contains these logs?
   A. Hardware events
   B. Security

C. System

D. Application

14. You are trying to remove a virus from a Windows system and receive a message that the antivirus software cannot remove a virus found in the System Volume Information folder. What should be your next step?

A. Restore the system from last night's backup.

B. Rerun the antivirus scan.

C. Rebuild the system from scratch.

D. Disable System Restore.

15. You are configuring antivirus software on a new computer and are setting up the frequency of virus definition updates. Which of the following is the best choice?

A. Manual updates

B. Daily updates

C. Weekly updates

D. Monthly updates

Objective 802: 2.3   Implement Security Best Practices to Secure a Workstation

16. You are creating a new security policy for your organization that requires that all workstations be secured with strong passwords. Which one of the following passwords would provide the highest level of security?

A. RottenApple

B. Yna9xmg!

C. gniees2

D. 5mOlmaf

17. You are creating a standard for securing new workstations when they are received from the manufacturer with the operating system preinstalled. Which of the following actions should you take? (Choose three.)

A. Disable any guest accounts.

B. Change any default passwords.

C. Modify registry entries.

D. Disable autorun.

QUICK ANSWER KEY

1.	C	**7.**	A, B, D	**13.**	B
2.	A, B	**8.**	C	**14.**	D
3.	A, C	**9.**	B, C, D	**15.**	B
4.	B	**10.**	B	**16.**	B
5.	B	**11.**	D	**17.**	A, B D
6.	A	**12.**	B		

IN-DEPTH ANSWERS

1. ☑ **C.** You will need the computer to be powered up in order to work on it, but you can protect the rest of the hosts on the network and prevent malware on the PC from installing more malicious software by unplugging the Ethernet cable from the computer.
   ☒ **A, B,** and **D** are incorrect. **A** is incorrect because, even if the antivirus program on the computer is still functioning, it will take time to use it to contain the infection and, in the meantime, the rest of the network is at risk. **B** is incorrect because the firewall on a compromised computer cannot be trusted, as the virus may have opened ports or will not allow ports to be closed to prevent further intrusion. Also, this is not the most efficient means by which you can isolate the computer. **D** is incorrect because you cannot work on the computer to rid it of the infection if the PC is shut down.

2. ☑ **A and B.** You can download a stand-alone antivirus program on another, noninfected computer, save it to a USB thumb drive, and then run the program on the infected computer. Usually, portable antivirus programs aren't a substitute for a full-featured antivirus application, but they can work well enough to remove the more serious aspects of the viruses and allow the onboard program to finish the job. You can also boot the computer into Safe Mode, where only a minimal group of programs is loaded. This will usually prevent viruses from launching and may let the onboard antivirus program remove them.
   ☒ **C and D** are incorrect. **C** is incorrect because if the antivirus program on the computer can't launch, you won't be able to use it to create an antivirus boot disc. You would use a boot disc created by an antivirus program to allow the computer to boot into a clean boot environment so that the virus can be removed if the boot sector of the computer were compromised. **D** is incorrect because putting an infected hard disk in another computer won't let the antivirus program remove the virus any more than leaving the hard drive in its original location will.

3. ☑ **A and C.** Once you install an antivirus program, you must manually update it to the most current version of the program and with the most recent virus signatures to make sure the program is able to detect and stop the latest threats from compromising the computer. The next steps after these would be to manually run the first scan to make sure the computer isn't compromised (even brand-new computers have sometimes been found to be infected), and then set the schedules for the program to automatically scan the computer as well as automatically check for virus signature and program updates on a regular basis.
   ☒ **B and D** are incorrect. **B** is incorrect because you will need to manually trigger a scan immediately to make sure the computer isn't compromised. **D** is incorrect because you will set up the schedule to automatically check for updates only after all of the manual tasks have been performed and you know the computer is immediately clear of threats.

4. ☑ **B.** Members of the Windows XP Power Users group can create user accounts and local groups, but can modify or delete only the accounts and groups they created. They also can remove users from the Power Users, Users, and Guests groups.

☒ **A, C,** and **D** are incorrect. **A** is incorrect because members of the Administrators group have full rights on a computer and can delete users and local groups that they have not created. **C** is incorrect because members of the Users group can create local groups but not user accounts. **D** is incorrect because members of the Guests group have the least permissions on a computer and can perform only limited tasks; they cannot create user accounts or local groups.

5. ☑ **B.** The correct executable is located in the i386\winnt32 directory and is called cmdcons.

☒ **A, C,** and **D** are incorrect. **A** is incorrect because console is not the name of the Recovery Console executable. **C** and **D** are incorrect because the winnt32 directory is not contained in the Windows directory.

6. ☑ **A.** The scenario describes a classic example of a browser redirection attack, where the malware is intentionally redirecting the user to unwanted Websites to generate advertising revenue or for other nefarious purposes.

☒ **B, C,** and **D** are incorrect. **B** is incorrect because a system participating in a distributed denial of service attack would likely see system slowdowns as the primary symptom. **C** and **D** are incorrect because phishing and social engineering are attacks against user behavior and would not redirect a Web browser.

7. ☑ **A, B,** and **D.** The message could be the result of a type of malware installed on the computer called rogue antivirus software that displays false security alert messages and then demands a fee to resolve the problem. Rogue antivirus software can often be removed using a legitimate antivirus or antimalware package. It could also be a spam e-mail message or advertising pop-up with the same desired effect.

☒ **C** is incorrect because a keylogger does not display messages but, rather, remains inconspicuous and logs a user's keystrokes to mine sensitive information. Keyloggers can often be removed with antispyware software.

8. ☑ **C.** The symptoms described usually indicate a malware infection. You should run a full antivirus scan on the system as your first attempt to resolve the issue.

☒ **A, B,** and **D** are incorrect. **A** and **B** are incorrect because they are too drastic. While wiping the drive and reinstalling the operating system may prove necessary eventually, you should first try to resolve the issue with an antivirus scanner. **D** is incorrect because Windows Update has already failed repeatedly. Rerunning it is unlikely to have a different result.

9. ☑ **B, C,** and **D.** Systems infected with malware often display symptoms involving user files, including permission changes that result in Access Denied errors and disappearing files.

☒ **A** is incorrect because the presence of a master boot record is normal and should be expected.

10. ☑ **B.** The user should first change his password, as it is possible that the spammers have gained access to his e-mail account. Changing the password will cut off that access.
☒ **A, C,** and **D** are incorrect. **A** is incorrect because, while the user should definitely run an antivirus scan, changing his password is more urgent, as the account may be compromised. **C** is incorrect because while the messages may be the result of spoofed e-mail rather than a hijacked e-mail account, changing the account password is a prudent safeguard and the messages should not be ignored. **D** is incorrect because the user should not attempt to engage in an investigation without consulting law enforcement.

11. ☑ **D.** System Restore is found in the System and Security section of the Windows 7 Control Panel.
☒ **A, B,** and **C** are incorrect because System Restore is found in the System and Security section of the Windows 7 Control Panel.

12. ☑ **B.** The Windows Preinstallation Environment (WinPE) is a command-line version of Windows often used for this purpose.
☒ **A, C,** and **D** are incorrect. **A** and **D** are incorrect because Windows 7 and Windows Server 2008 R2 are full-featured operating systems not suitable for this purpose. **C** is incorrect because Ubuntu is a Linux-based operating system and does not provide native Windows utilities.

13. ☑ **B.** The Security section within Event Viewer contains information about successful and unsuccessful login attempts.
☒ **A, C,** and **D** are incorrect. **A** is incorrect because Hardware events contains information related to hardware issues. **C** is incorrect because the System log contains messages generated by the operating system but does not include logon attempts. **D** is incorrect because the Application log contains messages generated by Windows applications and would not contain login information generated by the operating system.

14. ☑ **D.** The fact that the System Volume Information folder is infected indicates that System Restore has been compromised by the malware. You should disable System Restore and rerun the antivirus scan.
☒ **A, B,** and **C** are incorrect. **A** is incorrect because last night's backup likely contains the malware as well and restoring from it will not help. **B** is incorrect because rerunning the antivirus scan without disabling System Restore first will have the same unsuccessful result. **C** is incorrect because rebuilding the system is too drastic for a first step.

15. ☑ **B.** Security professionals recommend daily updates of virus definitions to protect systems against newly created malware.
☒ **A, C,** and **D** are incorrect. **A** is incorrect because antivirus software should not be configured to require manual updates. Users often forget to do so, and this puts the system at risk. **C** and **D** are incorrect because virus definitions should be updated on a daily basis to provide maximum protection.

16. ☑ **B.** This password combines characters from the most classes (uppercase letters, lowercase letters, digits, and punctuation, so it is the most secure.

    ☒ **A, C,** and **D** are incorrect. **A** is incorrect because it consists of two dictionary words. **C** is incorrect because it only contains characters from two classes and it contains a dictionary word spelled backwards. **D** is incorrect because it only contains characters from three classes.

17. ☑ **A, B,** and **D.** You should always disable any guest accounts and change any passwords that are set to default values by the manufacturer. Also, disabling autorun prevents malicious code installed on DVDs or other removable media from automatically executing when the DVD is inserted into the system.

    ☒ **C** is incorrect because it is not necessary to change registry entries when securing a new computer.

19

Configuring and Troubleshooting Windows Clients

❑   **802: 1.6**   Set up and configure Windows networking on a client/desktop.

❑   **802: 1.8**   Explain the differences among basic OS security settings.

QUESTIONS

A+ technicians often find themselves resolving issues on Windows client systems. These issues often involve setting up and configuring networking and security options to provide users with secure, reliable connections to the organization's networked resources. You should be able to work with basic Windows network and security options in your role as an A+ technician.

Objective 802: 1.6 Set Up and Configure Windows Networking on a Client/Desktop

1. You work for a small city IT department and you are configuring a Windows XP Professional computer for a new hire in the office. You've attached the patch cable to the computer's NIC port and noticed that the indicator light on the NIC is flashing. Now you need to provide an alternative IP address, subnet mask, DNS server, and default gateway. How do you configure this?

   A. In the Control Panel, open Network Connections, right-click Local Area Connection, and select Properties; on the Local Area Connection Properties box, select Client For Microsoft Networks, and then click Properties.

   B. In the Control Panel, open Network Connections, right-click Local Area Connection, and select Properties; on the Local Area Connection Properties box, select Internet Protocol (TCP/IP), and then click Properties.

   C. In the Control Panel, open Network Connections, right-click Local Area Connection, select Status, select the Support tab, and then select Details.

   D. In the Control Panel, open Network Connections, right-click Local Area Connection, select Status, select the General tab, and then select Details.

2. You have just set up a Windows 7 computer for a home customer and connected it to the Internet. You refer to the network status indicator in the computer's notification area. What should you see?

   A. A network icon with a red X

   B. A network icon with a green exclamation point

   C. A network icon glowing yellow

   D. A network icon with a cable

3. You work for a small city IT department. One of the other technicians is configuring networking for a Windows computer and is prompted to select between a workgroup and a domain. He asks you which option he should select. Your workplace uses a network environment where a trusted group of computers share security, share access control, and receive data passed down from a centralized server. Given this environment, how do you answer the tech's question?

A. Select the workgroup option because a workgroup is a collection of computers that connects to a central Active Directory server for DHCP and DNS.

B. Select the workgroup option because a workgroup is a collection of computers that connects to a workgroup controller server.

C. Select the domain option because a domain is a group of computers that connects to a central domain controller that manages security and data for the domain.

D. Select the domain option because a domain is a group of computers that connects directly to DHCP and DNS services without requiring the use of a domain controller.

4. You are reviewing basic network communications functions and features with a new tech at your workplace. In describing full-duplex communications versus half-duplex communications, which of the following do you say are accurate? (Choose two.)

A. Half-duplex communications works like a walkie-talkie, where only one party has control of the entire communications conduit at any one time.

B. Full-duplex communications works like a telephone, where both parties have equal access to the communications conduit and can both speak simultaneously.

C. Half-duplex communications works like a telephone, where both parties have equal access to the communications conduit and can both speak simultaneously.

D. Full-duplex communications works like a walkie-talkie, where only one party has control of the entire communications conduit at any one time.

5. You are setting up a dial-up connection for a rural customer who is using a Windows 7 computer. You know you must configure the connection by clicking the Setup button on the Internet Properties box as shown in the accompanying screenshot. How do you get to this dialog box? (Choose three.)

A. In Control Panel in Category view, click Network And Internet, click Network And Sharing Center, click Internet Options, and then, on the Internet Properties box, click the Connections tab.

B. In Control Panel in Category view, click Network And Internet, click HomeGroup, click Internet Options, and then, on the Internet Properties box, click the Connections tab.

    C. In Control Panel in Category view, click Network And Internet, click Internet Options, and then, on the Internet Properties box, click the Connections tab.

    D. In Control Panel in Large Or Small Icons view, click Network And Sharing Center, click Internet Options, and then, on the Internet Properties box, click the Connections tab.

6. You are setting up a customer's home office to use wireless networking and are configuring a Windows XP laptop to join the wireless network. You have launched the Wireless Network Setup Wizard in Windows XP as shown in the accompanying illustration. Of the selections available, which will provide the best wireless security?

    A. Give your network an SSID name.

    B. Automatically assign a network key.

    C. Manually assign a network key.

    D. Use WPA encryption instead of WEP.

7. You are setting up a small network in your boss' home and he asked you to network the computers together. You choose to use Windows 7 HomeGroup to create the network. What operating systems may be used to create the HomeGroup? (Choose two.)

 A. Windows 7 Enterprise

 B. Windows 7 Starter

 C. Windows 7 Home Basic

 D. Windows 7 Home Premium

8. Your network requires the use of a proxy server for outbound Web traffic. This server is used to filter objectionable content and boost performance. You recognize that you need to configure the proxy server for Windows 7 systems in the LAN Settings page (shown here). On what tab of Internet Properties will you find the button to access these settings?

 A. Security

 B. Privacy

 C. Content

 D. Connections

9. You are attempting to configure Windows Remote Desktop to allow remote access to a Windows 7 Enterprise system but are having difficulty allowing the connection through a network firewall. What port should you ensure is allowed to pass through the firewall?

 A. 80

 B. 1433

 C. 3389

 D. 8080

10. You are configuring a laptop computer so that it is able to connect to your organization's virtual private network (VPN). The system is running Windows 7 Enterprise, and you are using the Connect to a Workplace wizard to configure the VPN connection, as shown here. It is asking you for the Internet address. Which of the following may you use? (Choose two.)

- **A.** Fully qualified domain name of the VPN server
- **B.** IP address of the VPN server
- **C.** Fully qualified domain name of the DNS server
- **D.** IP address of the DNS server

Objective 802: 1.8 Explain the Differences Among Basic OS Security Settings

11. You are configuring a Windows XP system account and need to give the user permission to install drivers on the computer. What type of account should you create to provide the minimum level of permission that can make this change?
- **A.** Administrator
- **B.** Power user
- **C.** Guest
- **D.** Standard user

12. Mary is a member of two groups: Accounting and Accounts Payable. There is a file stored on an NTFS partition that has the following permission settings:

- The Accounting group is denied permission to access the file.
- Mary's account is granted permission to access the file.
- There is no permission statement made for the Accounts Payable group.

What will happen when Mary tries to access the file?

A. She will be allowed to see it because the permission granted to her is the most specific.

B. She will be allowed to see it because allow permissions always override deny permissions.

C. She will not be allowed to see it because there are an equal number of allow and deny permissions that apply to Mary's account.

D. She will not be allowed to see it because deny permissions always override allow permissions.

13. Which of the following statements about Windows file permissions is not correct?

A. When moving a file within the same NTFS partition, the file retains its permission settings.

B. When copying a file within the same NTFS partition, the file retains its permission settings.

C. When moving a file between different NTFS partitions, the file inherits the destination permission settings.

D. When copying a file between different NTFS partitions, the file inherits the destination permission settings.

14. You are exploring the file shares on a Windows 7 system and find the four shares listed here. Which one is an administrative file share?

A. ADMINS$

B. C$

C. My Documents

D. System

15. You suspect that system files may be corrupted on a Windows 7 system. What utility can you use to verify the integrity of system files?

A. SFC

B. CHKDSK

C. Disk Cleanup

D. Disk Defragmenter

QUICK ANSWER KEY

1.	B	**6.**	D	**11.**	B
2.	D	**7.**	A, D	**12.**	D
3.	C	**8.**	D	**13.**	B
4.	A, B	**9.**	C	**14.**	B
5.	A, C, D	**10.**	A, B	**15.**	A

IN-DEPTH ANSWERS

1. ☑ **B.** On the Internet Protocol (TCP/IP) Properties box, select Obtain An IP Address Automatically and Obtain DNS Server Address Automatically to have addressing information assigned dynamically to the computer via the DHCP server. You can also configure static IP address information manually on this box.

   ☒ **A, C,** and **D** are incorrect. **A** is incorrect because this will open the Client for Microsoft Networks Properties box, where you can only select the name service provider for the Remote Procedure Call (RPC) service. **C** is incorrect because clicking the Details button on the Support tab will only show the network connection details, such as the computer's physical address, IP address, gateway address, and so on, but you can't configure any information here. **D** is incorrect because there is no Details button on the General tab. If you were to click the Properties button on the General tab, though, it would take you to the Local Area Connection Properties box, where you could select Internet Protocol (TCP/IP) and then click Properties to configure dynamic or manual addressing for the computer.

2. ☑ **D.** When a Windows 7 computer is connected to the network, you should see a network icon with a little cable displayed in the notification area.

   ☒ **A, B,** and **C** are incorrect. **A** is incorrect because this icon indicates no network connection. **B** and **C** are incorrect because they are fictitious network icons.

3. ☑ **C.** A domain is a trusted collection of computers that share access control, security, software distribution, and user management as managed by one or more domain controllers. Microsoft's implementation of domain controllers runs Active Directory Services.

   ☒ **A, B,** and **D** are incorrect. **A** and **B** are incorrect because a workgroup is a peer-to-peer collection of computers all connected on the same network segment but without any central control. Each computer in the workgroup can share its resources with the other computers in the workgroup, but no one host manages the network environment. **D** is incorrect because domain systems do require the use of a domain controller.

4. ☑ **A** and **B.** Half-duplex network communications describes two devices networked together where only one device may communicate at any one time. The other device must wait until the first device is finished before initiating communications. Full-duplex describes a situation where two networked devices may transmit information to each other simultaneously, much in the same way two people can speak at the same time during a phone conversation.

   ☒ **C** and **D** are incorrect because each description is of the opposite communications type.

5. ☑ **A, C,** and **D.** To reach the Internet Properties dialog box, in Control Panel Category view, click Internet Options on the Network And Internet screen, and then click the Connections tab. After clicking Setup, if the computer hasn't yet been connected to the Internet, you will be able to enter the required phone number provided by the ISP for the computer to use to connect to a dial-up connection. Enter a user name and password, give the connection a name, and then click Connect. Once the computer connects to the Internet, you can exit the wizard. The Network And Sharing Center has an Internet Options link in the lower-left sidebar.

   ☒ **B** is incorrect because there is no Internet Options selection on the HomeGroup screen.

6. ☑ **D.** Selecting the Use WPA Encryption Instead Of WEP check box will provide better security than the WEP option, but you must verify that the devices on the wireless network support WPA. WPA2 has replaced WPA as a security standard and is mandatory for all devices in order to use the Wi-Fi trademark.

   ☒ **A, B,** and **C** are incorrect. **A** is incorrect because the SSID is the name of the wireless network and does not provide any security features. **B** is incorrect because you must select the encryption method to be used, WEP or WPA, before a key can be automatically assigned. **C** is incorrect because before manually assigning a key, you must still select an encryption method, WEP or WPA.

7. ☑ **A** and **D.** HomeGroup networks may be created with Windows 7 Home Premium, Windows 7 Ultimate, Windows 7 Professional, or Windows 7 Enterprise.

   ☒ **B** and **C** are incorrect because although these operating system editions can join a Windows 7 HomeGroup, they may not be used to create a new HomeGroup.

8. ☑ **D.** LAN Settings is found on the Connections tab of Internet Properties.

   ☒ **A, B,** and **C** are incorrect because the LAN Settings button is found on the Connections tab of Internet Properties.

9. ☑ **C.** Windows Remote Desktop uses port 3389 by default. This port must be allowed to pass through the firewall for Remote Desktop to function properly.

   ☒ **A, B,** and **D** are incorrect. **A** is incorrect because port 80 is used by HTTP for Web traffic. **B** is incorrect because port 1433 is used by Microsoft SQL Server. **D** is incorrect because port 8080 is commonly used for Web proxy servers.

10. ☑ **A** and **B.** You must provide an address for the VPN server and may choose to enter either a fully qualified domain name or an IP address.

    ☒ **C** and **D** are incorrect because you must provide the address of a server running a VPN, not the DNS server.

11. ☑ **B.** The Power user account type is the lowest level of privilege that can install drivers on a Windows XP system.

☒ **A, C,** and **D** are incorrect. **A** is incorrect because it is an unnecessarily high privilege level. Power users can install drivers with a much lower permission level. **C** and **D** are incorrect because Guests and Standard users do not have the ability to install drivers.

12. ☑ **D.** Mary will not be allowed to view the file because deny permissions always override allow permissions.

☒ **A, B,** and **C** are incorrect because a single deny permission always overrides any allow permission statements that apply to the same account.

13. ☑ **B.** When copying a file within the same NTFS partition, the file inherits the permissions of the destination folder.

☒ **A, C,** and **D** are incorrect. **A** is incorrect because when moving a file within the same NTFS partition, the file retains its permission settings. **C** is incorrect because when moving a file between different NTFS partitions, the file inherits the destination permission settings. **D** is incorrect because when copying a file between different NTFS partitions, the file inherits the destination permission settings.

14. ☑ **B.** The only administrative shares on a Windows system are those created by Microsoft by default: ADMIN$ and the single-letter shares (e.g., C$) created for each nonremovable drive.

☒ **A, C,** and **D** are incorrect. **A** is incorrect because, while all administrative file shares end with a $, not all shares ending with a $ are administrative. The ADMINIS$ share, although similar in name to the ADMIN$ administrative share, is not an administrative share created by default. **C** and **D** are incorrect because all administrative shares end with a $ character.

15. ☑ **A.** The SFC (System File Checker) utility verifies the integrity of operating system files.

☒ **B, C,** and **D** are incorrect. **B** is incorrect because CHKDSK finds errors on the hard disk but does not verify the integrity of system files. **C** is incorrect because the Disk Cleanup tool removes unneeded files. **D** is incorrect because the Disk Defragmenter optimizes the organization of files on your disk.

20

Supporting
Mobile Devices

QUESTIONS

Today's users often require access to information and resources while mobile. Smartphone and tablet computing options provide the "always on" access needed to keep them productive while traveling on business, at home, or on vacation. As an A+ technician, you must know how to support these mobile devices.

Objective 802: 3.1 Explain the Basic Features of Mobile Operating Systems

1. You are troubleshooting a user's smartphone and see the home screen shown here. What operating system is the phone running?

- A. Windows Mobile
- B. Apple iOS
- C. Google Android
- D. BlackBerry OS

2. Where can you purchase applications for a smartphone running the Android operating system? (Choose two.)

  A. iTunes Store

  B. Google Play

  C. Third-party marketplaces

  D. App World

3. Where can you purchase applications for a smartphone running the iOS operating system?

  A. iTunes Store

  B. Google Play

  C. Third-party marketplaces

  D. App World

Objective 802: 3.2   Establish Basic Network Connectivity and Configure E-mail

4. Which of the following networks will provide the fastest data transfer speed for Internet browsing under normal circumstances?

  A. 3G cellular network

  B. 4G cellular network

  C. Wi-Fi network

  D. Bluetooth

5. You are attempting to pair a Bluetooth headset with a mobile phone and are having difficulty. The device is prompting you to enter a Bluetooth PIN, and you do not have one assigned and cannot locate the documentation. What value should you try first?

  A. 0000

  B. 1111

  C. 4444

  D. 9999

6. You are configuring an e-mail account on an Apple iPhone and need to set the account settings. Which of the following statements is not true?

  A. IMAP accounts don't download messages from the server until you are ready to read them.

  B. POP3 accounts download all of your messages from the server.

  C. IMAP accounts with SSL security use port 993.

  D. POP3 accounts without SSL security use port 143.

Objective 802: 3.3 Compare and Contrast Methods for Securing Mobile Devices

7. A user approaches you, concerned about the fact that his mobile phone may be lost or stolen. What security features can help protect a lost or stolen device? (Choose two.)

    A. Bluetooth

    B. Remote wipe

    C. Passcode

    D. Biometric authentication

8. You wish to apply a security control to a mobile device to prevent an unauthorized user who discovers the device from guessing the passcode. What security feature should you use?

    A. Antivirus software

    B. Failed login attempt restriction

    C. Locator application

    D. Passcode lock

9. One of your users has misplaced her Android smartphone and wants your help remotely wiping it so that anyone who finds it cannot access her data. What application must she have installed to allow you to wipe the device from your Google Control Panel?

    A. Google Remote Wipe

    B. Android Wiper

    C. Google Apps Device Policy

    D. Mobile Device Manager

10. What methods may commonly be used to install updates on mobile phones? (Choose three.)

    A. Update via mobile device management software

    B. Update via desktop sync

    C. Update over the air

    D. Update via CompactFlash

Objective 802: 3.4 Compare and Contrast Hardware Differences in Regards to Tablets and Laptops

11. What type of storage device is typically used for the primary storage on a tablet computer?

    A. Magnetic hard drive

    B. USB drive

    C. SD cards

    D. Solid-state drive

12. Which of the following are common characteristics of a tablet computer? (Choose two.)
   A. Field serviceable
   B. Multitouch interface
   C. Upgradeable
   D. Handheld form factor

Objective 802: 3.5 Execute and Configure Mobile Device Synchronization

13. What calendar options are commonly supported by smartphones? (Choose three.)
   A. Synchronization with Microsoft Exchange Calendar
   B. Synchronization with Google Calendar
   C. Synchronization with desktop calendar
   D. Synchronization with day planners

14. What software and services can you use to synchronize music directly with an Android device? (Choose three.)
   A. Windows Media Player
   B. iTunes
   C. Android apps from Google Play
   D. Amazon MP3 store

15. You wish to synchronize music between iTunes and your iPad. What options do you have? (Choose three.)
   A. Use a local Wi-Fi network shared between the iPad and computer running iTunes.
   B. Use a direct USB connection to a computer running iTunes.
   C. Use a 4G cellular connection and iTunes Match.
   D. Use a 4G cellular connection to a computer running iTunes.

A

QUICK ANSWER KEY

1.	B	**6.**	D	**11.**	D
2.	B, C	**7.**	B, C	**12.**	B, D
3.	A	**8.**	B	**13.**	A, B, C
4.	C	**9.**	C	**14.**	A, C, D
5.	A	**10.**	A, B, C	**15.**	A, B, C

IN-DEPTH ANSWERS

1. ☑ **B.** The screenshot is from an Apple iPhone running the iOS operating system.
    ☒ **A, C,** and **D** are incorrect because the screenshot is from an Apple device, which is only capable of running the iOS operating system.

2. ☑ **B** and **C.** Android users may purchase apps from the Google Play store (formerly known as the Android Marketplace) or from third-party sites, such as the Amazon Appstore. This is part of Google's open source approach for Android devices.
    ☒ **A** and **D** are incorrect. **A** is incorrect because the iTunes Store sells only iOS apps. **D** is incorrect because App World sells only BlackBerry apps.

3. ☑ **A.** iPhone and iPad users may only purchase apps from the Apple iTunes Store unless they jailbreak their phones, voiding the license agreement.
    ☒ **B, C,** and **D** are incorrect because Apple iOS only allows users to download apps from the iTunes Store.

4. ☑ **C.** Wi-Fi networks provide high-speed Internet connectivity for mobile devices when the user is within range of an available network.
    ☒ **A, B,** and **D** are incorrect. **A** and **B** are incorrect because the 3G and 4G cellular networks provide slower connections than Wi-Fi networks, although they are more widely available. **D** is incorrect because Bluetooth networks are not normally used for Internet connectivity.

5. ☑ **A.** Most manufacturers use the default PIN of 0000 for Bluetooth devices. Once you have enabled Bluetooth and pairing on both the mobile phone and headset, you should find the headset on the mobile phone, try the default 0000 PIN, and test connectivity.
    ☒ **B, C,** and **D** are incorrect because most manufacturers use the default PIN of 0000 for Bluetooth devices.

6. ☑ **D.** POP3 accounts configured to use unencrypted connections use port 110. Port 143 is used for unencrypted IMAP connections.
    ☒ **A, B,** and **C** are incorrect because those statements about POP3 and IMAP are accurate.

7. ☑ **B** and **C.** Remote wipe features allow administrators or the end user to remove data from the phone when it is reported lost or stolen. A passcode lock prevents someone who finds the phone from accessing it.
    ☒ **A** and **D** are incorrect. **A** is incorrect because Bluetooth technology allows the use of wireless peripherals and does not provide security for lost or stolen devices. **D** is incorrect because smartphones do not commonly support biometric authentication.

8. ☑ **B.** Adding a failed login attempt restriction limits the success of brute force password guessing attacks by disabling the phone after a designated number of failed attempts.
☒ **A, C,** and **D** are incorrect. **A** is incorrect because antivirus software protects against malicious code, not password guessing attacks. **C** is incorrect because locator applications help locate a phone that is lost or stolen but do not prevent password guessing. **D** is incorrect because enabling passcode lock would not prevent someone from guessing the passcode.

9. ☑ **C.** Android devices with the Google Apps Device Policy app installed may be wiped from the Devices tab of the Google Apps Control Panel.
☒ **A, B,** and **D** are incorrect because they are not legitimate apps.

10. ☑ **A, B,** and **C.** Smartphones, depending upon the model, may be updated by a variety of means. In many cases, administrators may push updates through mobile device management software. It is also possible to update a phone via sync with desktop software, such as iTunes. Some phones also support over-the-air updates.
☒ **D** is incorrect because smartphones do not commonly support CompactFlash cards.

11. ☑ **D.** Tablet computers typically use solid-state storage devices to provide maximum speed.
☒ **A, B,** and **C** are incorrect. **A** is incorrect because tablet computers typically do not use traditional magnetic hard drives, as laptop and desktop computers do. **B** and **C** are incorrect because they are not commonly found on tablets and are not primary storage devices.

12. ☑ **B** and **D.** Tablet computers typically use multitouch interfaces that allow the use of complex, multifinger gestures. They also have handheld form factors. Laptop and desktop computers do not normally have multitouch interfaces.
☒ **A** and **C** are incorrect. **A** is incorrect because tablet computers, unlike laptop and desktop computers, are normally not field serviceable and must be returned to the manufacturer for repair. **C** is incorrect because, unlike laptop and desktop computers, tablet computers are typically not upgradeable.

13. ☑ **A, B,** and **C.** Smartphones generally allow synchronization with both Microsoft Exchange and Google Calendar, as well as many popular desktop calendaring programs.
☒ **D** is incorrect because it is not possible to synchronize a smartphone with a written day planner.

14. ☑ **A, C,** and **D.** Android devices may synchronize music using Windows Media Player, a variety of third-party Android apps, and the Amazon MP3 store.
☒ **B** is incorrect because iTunes cannot synchronize music directly to an Android device. Third-party applications are available to perform this migration indirectly.

15. ☑ **A, B,** and **C.** You may synchronize music between iOS devices and iTunes on a computer either using a USB connection or having the two devices on the same Wi-Fi network. You may also use the iTunes Match service to download music directly to your phone from iCloud over a cellular or Wi-Fi network.
☒ **D** is incorrect because you can't directly synchronize your iPad with your computer over a cellular connection.

21

Using and Supporting Printers

❏ **801: 4.1** Explain the differences between the various printer types and summarize the associated imaging process.

❏ **801: 4.2** Given a scenario, install and configure printers.

❏ **801: 4.3** Given a scenario, perform printer maintenance.

❏ **802: 4.9** Given a scenario, troubleshoot printers with appropriate tools.

QUESTIONS

In spite of promises of a "paperless society," technology hasn't removed the necessity for people and businesses to print documents, images, and other material output. As an A+ technician, you will be required to install, configure, and maintain printers on local PCs and networks, and to figure out what's happened when a printer doesn't print as expected. You'll also have to possess a basic understanding of how different printers work. The following questions will ensure you are up to speed on all of these topics.

Objective 801: 4.1 Explain the Differences Between the Various Printer Types and Summarize the Associated Imaging Process

1. Of the following, what is the first part of the process a laser printer goes through in producing a print job?
   A. Cleaning
   B. Conditioning
   C. Writing
   D. Developing
   E. Transferring
   F. Fusing

2. What are the rollers responsible for doing in an inkjet printer? (Choose all that apply.)
   A. Moving the ink cartridges into position
   B. Moving the print head into position
   C. Moving paper into position
   D. Moving the duplexing assembly into position

3. Of the following, what distinguishes a thermal printer from other printer types?
   A. Feeder assembly
   B. Temperature-sensitive paper
   C. Heating element
   D. Ink-based printing

4. Of the following, what are features unique to impact printers not shared by other printer types? (Choose all that apply.)
   A. Print head
   B. Ribbon
   C. Tractor feed
   D. Impact paper

Objective 801: 4.2 Given a Scenario, Install and Configure Printers

5. You are installing a network printer for one of the branch offices of your business. The printer has both wired and wireless network capacities. You check the available ports on the printer. What wired network port type is most commonly used?

   A. Ethernet

   B. Parallel

   C. Serial

   D. USB

6. You are installing a network printer for one of the branch offices of your business, which has both wired and wireless network capacities. You are required to set up the printer to use a form of wireless networking that requires a line-of-sight connection between the computer and the printer. Of the following, which network port type are you configuring?

   A. 802.11x

   B. Bluetooth

   C. Infrared (IR)

   D. No wireless network technology requires a line-of-sight connection.

7. You have a business client who feels she needs a print server for her office. You assess her company's needs and suggest different print server hardware types that might fill her requirements. Of the following, what devices are most likely to be used as a print server in a stable office environment? (Choose all that apply.)

   A. A dedicated server computer

   B. A desktop PC

   C. A laptop PC

   D. A printer

8. You have just installed a new printer on your Windows 7 computer and you want to share it so the other computers in your home network can print to it. In Windows 7, you click the Windows Start button and then click Devices And Printers. You then right-click the new printer. In the menu that appears, what do you click next?

   A. Networking

   B. Properties

   C. Printer Properties

   D. Sharing

Objective 801: 4.3   Given a Scenario, Perform Printer Maintenance

9. You are visiting the offices of a small business customer and performing routine maintenance on his laser printer. You discover the toner is running low and needs to be replaced. Of the following, which is the correct procedure?

    A. Pour the correct liquid toner for the customer's laser printer into its toner port until the holding tank is at the full mark.

    B. Locate and insert the toner ribbon for the model of laser printer you are working on into the device.

    C. Remove the old toner cartridge and replace it with one that is correct for your customer's laser printer.

    D. You cannot replace laser toner in the customer's office. You must send the printer to the local shop of the company that produced the device and have the toner replaced there.

10. You are visiting the offices of a small business customer and performing routine maintenance on his laser printer. You have brought a maintenance kit for the customer's laser printer so you can service the device. What do you expect to find in the maintenance kit? (Choose all that apply.)

    A. Fuser assembly

    B. Transfer rollers

    C. Pickup rollers

    D. Laser paper

11. You are visiting the retail offices of a small business customer and performing routine maintenance on their credit card processing devices. These devices use a thermal printer to generate receipts for credit card customers. The receipt paper is running low on several of these devices. How can you replace it?

    A. Open the device; remove the older, spent roll; and replace it with a compatible fresh roll of thermal paper.

    B. Open the device; remove the older, spent paper cartridge; and replace it with a compatible fresh cartridge of thermal paper.

    C. Open the device and add more sheets of compatible thermal paper to the paper feeder tray.

    D. Open the device; disassemble the thermal print head and remove it; remove the integrated paper container; replace it with a fresh, compatible container; reassemble the print head; and close the device.

12. You are visiting a business customer who runs a warehouse that uses several impact printers to produce multicopy invoice documents. You are going to perform routine maintenance on the impact printers and you have the necessary tools and supplies handy for the task. Of the following, what tasks do you expect to perform? (Choose all that apply.)

    A. Replace the ink cartridges.

    B. Replace the paper.

    C. Replace the print heads.

    D. Replace the ribbons.

Objective 802: 4.9 Given a Scenario, Troubleshoot Printers with Appropriate Tools

13. You are visiting a business customer and you are about to perform maintenance and repair work on several printers in their offices. You are about to use a toner vacuum. What printer type are you working on?

    A. Impact

    B. Inkjet

    C. Laser

    D. Thermal

14. You are visiting a business customer and you are about to perform maintenance and repair work on several printers in their offices. You are about to use a can of compressed air in an inkjet printer. What are you most likely trying to do?

    A. Clean excess ink off the print head.

    B. Remove excess bits of paper from the interior of the printer.

    C. Spray excess ink off the print rollers.

    D. Remove excess dust off the printer's exterior.

15. You are visiting a business customer and you are about to perform maintenance and repair work on several printers in their offices. Your customer informs you that she has been receiving an error message when trying to use one of the inkjet printers referring to the printer spooler. What sort of problem is this?

    A. The printer spooler assembly in the device is misaligned.

    B. The paper tray feeding spooler is jammed.

    C. There is a problem with the spooling RAM used to store printer configuration data.

    D. There is a problem with the area on the disk where print jobs are stored before printing.

QUICK ANSWER KEY

1. B
2. C, D
3. B
4. B, C, D
5. A

6. C
7. A, B, D
8. C
9. C
10. A, B, C

11. A
12. B, C, D
13. C
14. B
15. D

IN-DEPTH ANSWERS

1. ☑ **B.** At the start of a laser printer print job, the print drum is conditioned to contain a high electrical charge.

    ☒ **A, C, D, E,** and **F** are incorrect. **A** is incorrect because cleaning is the last step in the print job process where the drum is cleaned of its residual electrical charge and any leftover toner is removed. **C** is incorrect because this step takes place right after conditioning and is the part of the process where the laser beam reduces the high charge down to a lower charge on the drum where the toner will be applied. **D** is incorrect because developing happens right after writing and is the step where toner is applied to the drum where the charge has been reduced. **E** is incorrect because transferring occurs right after developing and is the part of the process where toner is drawn off the print drum onto the paper. **F** is incorrect because fusing happens immediately after transferring and is the step where heat and pressure are used to fuse the toner to the paper.

2. ☑ **C and D.** The rollers in an inkjet printer pull the paper from the feeder tray and advance the paper under the print head as the print head sprays ink to create the print image. Rollers are also used in duplex printing to move the paper so it is printed first on one side and then on the other.

    ☒ **A and B** are incorrect. **A** is incorrect because the ink cartridges are inserted onto the print head, which moves the cartridges into position. **B** is incorrect because the print head stepper motor moves the print head.

3. ☑ **B.** Thermal printers, such as those used to produce receipts at gas pumps and slot machines, require that a special heat-sensitive paper be used in order to produce an image by selectively heating coated paper as it passes over the printer's thermal heads. This is different from a laser printer, which charges the print drum electrically and then transfers the charged print toner onto "regular" print paper, and inkjet printers, which spray heated ink drops onto print paper.

    ☒ **A, C,** and **D** are incorrect. **A** is incorrect because the vast majority of printers have an assembly to feed paper into the printer. **C** is incorrect because although the heating assembly in a thermal printer is unique, inkjet printers heat ink in order for it to be used. **D** is incorrect because inkjet printers are also ink-based.

4. ☑ **B, C,** and **D.** Unlike other printer types, an impact printer uses a set of hard pins or keys to create an impression on paper through an ink ribbon, similar to how old typewriters used to work. For some kinds of impact printers, such as dot matrix printers, special multicopy impact paper is fed continually across the print head using a tractor sprocket feed, where the sprockets grab hold on either side of the paper to pull it through the printer.

    ☒ **A** is incorrect because although the print head of an impact printer is of a different design than other printer types, all printers use some kind of print head.

5. ☑ **A.** An Ethernet port is the most commonly used wired networking port you will find on the printer.

   ☒ **B, C,** and **D** are incorrect because these wired port types are more likely used to connect to a local computer rather than directly to the network.

6. ☑ **C.** Infrared (IR) wireless connections send and receive data over a short-range infrared light beam, but this type of connection requires line-of-sight, since unlike radio waves, light travels in a generally straight line and cannot bend around obstacles.

   ☒ **A, B,** and **D** are incorrect. **A** and **B** are incorrect because both 802.11x and Bluetooth technology use radio waves that propagate or spread out from the transmission point, like an FM radio signal is transmitted, and do not require a direct line-of-sight link. **D** is incorrect because infrared (IR) networking does require line-of-sight.

7. ☑ **A, B,** and **D.** A dedicated server computer can be configured to operate as a print server, and this is the sort of device most people think of when they think of a print server. However, a desktop PC can also be set up as a dedicated print server device. Some printers have a built-in print server integrated into their system.

   ☒ **C** is incorrect because, although a laptop PC could be set up to function as a print server, as a mobile device, it is unlikely to be used as such in a stable business office setting.

8. ☑ **C.** Click Printer Properties and then on the Printer Properties dialog box, click the Sharing tab and proceed to share the printer.

   ☒ **A, B,** and **D** are incorrect. **A** and **D** are incorrect because there is not a Networking or Sharing option on the menu that appears. **B** is incorrect because clicking Properties will open the Properties dialog box for the device but only present the General and Hardware tabs, which do not offer you the ability to share the printer.

9. ☑ **C.** Verify the make and model of the laser printer and that you have a toner cartridge that is correct for the device. Remove the old toner cartridge and replace it with the new one. You will need to follow the specific directions for the make and model of laser printer to correctly perform this task.

   ☒ **A, B,** and **D** are incorrect. **A** is incorrect because laser printer toner is a powder, not a liquid, and it is contained in a cartridge, not poured into a holding tank. **B** is incorrect because laser toner is contained in a cartridge, not supplied by a ribbon. **D** is incorrect because replacing a laser printer's toner cartridge is a relatively simple procedure and does not require that it be done at a commercial facility.

10. ☑ **A, B,** and **C.** Although the contents of a laser printer maintenance kit will vary depending on the make and model, you can expect to find items such as a fuser assembly, various roller types, possibly a separation pad, and transfer corona assembly.

    ☒ **D** is incorrect because printer paper is not typically included in a maintenance kit and most laser printers use "regular" printer paper rather than special "laser paper."

11. ☑ **A.** Most credit card processing devices print receipts on a roll of thermal paper that is fed through the device. When the roll is nearly gone, you can open the device and replace the roll. The specific process of opening the device and removing the roll will vary from device to device, so you will need to read the instructions for the specific device you are servicing.

☒ **B, C,** and **D** are incorrect. B and C are incorrect because most credit card processing devices use paper fed from rolls and not from a paper cartridge or as individual sheets from a paper tray. **D** is incorrect because this sort of device uses a paper roll instead of an integrated paper container, and typically, you don't have to deconstruct the printer head just to add a new roll of paper.

12. ☑ **B, C,** and **D.** Paper is fed through on tractor sprockets, so replacing paper is not quite as easy as performing the same task on an inkjet. Replacing worn print heads is an expected task, as is used-up printer ribbon.

☒ **A** is incorrect because impact printers typically use ink ribbons rather than ink cartridges to produce an image on paper.

13. ☑ **C.** Over time, laser printer toner can contaminate the interior of the printer, resulting in smudged or otherwise unacceptable printer output. You can use a toner vacuum to safely clean out the device's interior.

☒ **A, B,** and **D** are incorrect because this specialized device is not typically used to clean out the interiors of other types of printers.

14. ☑ **B.** Over time, small bits of paper begin to litter the interior of the inkjet printer and can cause rollers and gears to jam or become misaligned. Use a can of compressed air to gently remove this debris.

☒ **A, C,** and **D** are incorrect. **A** is incorrect because you would typically use isopropyl alcohol and either a Q-Tip or cloth to gently remove ink and debris from the print head. **C** is incorrect because you would typically use isopropyl alcohol and a cloth to clean the rollers. **D** is incorrect because you do not need to blow dust off the printer's exterior. Just rub it with a moist cloth.

15. ☑ **D.** The printer spooler is a service that provides temporary storage of print jobs from a computer to a printer before a print job is processed by the printer.

☒ **A, B,** and **C** are incorrect. **A** and **B** are incorrect because the printer spooler is not a physical component of the printer. **C** is incorrect because the printer spooler stores print jobs, not printer configuration data.

A

Pre-Assessment Test: Exam 220-801

INSTRUCTIONS

This pre-assessment test is designed to help you prepare to study for the CompTIA A+ 220-801 examination. You should take this test to identify the areas where you should focus your study and preparation.

This pre-assessment test includes 50 questions that are similar in style and format to the questions you will see on the actual exam. As you prepare to take this test, you should try to simulate the actual exam conditions as closely as possible. Go to a quiet place and be sure that you will not be interrupted for the full length of time it will take to complete the test. Do not use any reference materials or other assistance while taking the pre-assessment—remember, the idea is to help you determine what areas you need to focus on during your preparation for the actual exam.

The pre-assessment test contains questions divided in proportion to the 220-801 exam itself. Here is a breakdown of the exam content:

Domain	Exam Weight	Number of Pre-Assessment Questions
1.0 PC Hardware	40%	22
2.0 Networking	27%	13
3.0 Laptops	11%	5
4.0 Printers	11%	5
5.0 Operational Procedures	11%	5

Complete the entire pre-assessment test before checking your results. Once you have finished, use both the "Quick Answer Key" and the "In-Depth Answers" sections to score your pre-assessment test. You can use the table in the "Analyzing Your Results" section to determine how well you performed on the test. The objective map at the end of the appendix will help you identify those areas that require the most attention while you prepare for the exam.

Are you ready? Go ahead and set your clock for 45 minutes and begin!

QUESTIONS

1. A customer complains that his laptop's battery isn't recharging when it's plugged into a wall socket. He knows the wall socket is good because he's plugged a lamp into it and the lamp lit up. What is the first and easiest component to check?

    A. Replace the detachable power cord with a known good power cord and see if power gets to the battery.

    B. Check the LED on the power adapter "brick" and if it is not lit, replace the adapter with a known good adapter and see if power gets to the battery.

    C. Replace the battery with a known good battery and see if it charges.

    D. Open the laptop and check the power connector to see if it is loose or damaged.

2. You get a call from a laptop customer who says that her laptop fans are running all of the time while she's using her laptop. You investigate and discover she uses the laptop primarily late in the evening after she's gotten ready to go to bed. What do you suspect?

    A. The laptop has been on all day and has been accumulating heat.

    B. She is using the laptop in bed and the sheets and blankets on the bed are blocking the laptop's cooling vents.

    C. The laptop's cooling fans are going bad.

    D. The battery is overheating.

3. You are giving a presentation at a technology workshop to a group of high school students. You are discussing the main components in a laptop's video system. Of the following, which components do you say make up the video system in a laptop? (Choose three.)

    A. DC controller

    B. Inverter

    C. LCD display

    D. Video adapter

4. You are helping a customer who has trouble receiving a Wi-Fi signal on her laptop computer in the basement of her house. What is the easiest solution to her problem?

    A. Use an external Wi-Fi antenna on the laptop.

    B. Run a wired network into the basement.

    C. Add a new access point in the basement.

    D. Relocate the wireless router to the basement.

5. You are concerned about the theft of laptop equipment from your offices. What is the lowest cost and most practical option to control this problem?

   A. Hire a security guard.

   B. Use physical cable locks for the laptops.

   C. Purchase tracking software and a monitoring service.

   D. Permanently affix the laptops to users' desks.

6. You are reviewing the cable types used for networking and particularly for the Internet's backbone. Of the following cable types, which transmit data via light? (Choose two.)

   A. RG-6 coaxial

   B. Single-mode fiber

   C. RG-59 coaxial

   D. Multimode fiber

7. You are reviewing different DSL services with a small business customer to determine which type of service he should purchase. You tell him that some services offer the same maximum upload and download speeds, while others offer different maximum upload and download speeds. Of the following, which services offer different maximum upload and download speeds? (Choose two.)

   A. ADSL

   B. HDSL

   C. SDSL

   D. VDSL

8. You are a technician for a small city IT department, and you have just repaired and brought up a DHCP server that recently went down. You get a complaint from a customer serviced by this DHCP server that he cannot connect to the network. You suspect his computer has not automatically acquired an IP address since the DHCP server was restored. You go to his computer and open a command prompt. What command do you issue to get the computer to request an IP address?

   A. ipconfig

   B. ipconfig /all

   C. ipconfig /renew

   D. ipconfig /restore

9. You are installing an analog modem in a computer for a customer who doesn't have access to any form of broadband Internet and who must use a dial-up connection. The modem is designed to accommodate a particular connector used by standard phone lines. Of the following, what is the proper connector?

   A. RJ-11
   B. BNC
   C. RJ-45
   D. F-connector

10. You are talking to a customer who wants to add a wireless network component to his small office environment of ten computers. He uses DSL for an Internet connection and has a DSL modem that was provided by his ISP. What do you say he needs in order to build a wireless network?

    A. He can only use a wireless access point (WAP).
    B. He can only use a wireless router.
    C. His DSL modem may have a wireless router as part of its functionality; otherwise, he'll need a similar, stand-alone solution such as a WAP or wireless router.
    D. He can use an ad hoc wireless network.

11. You are attempting to determine whether some RG-6 in your environment is faulty. What tool should you use?

    A. Cable tester
    B. Punchdown tool
    C. Loopback plug
    D. Crimper

12. You have a computer with IP address 192.168.12.15. What technology must be in use on your network for this computer to communicate with the Internet?

    A. DNS
    B. DHCP
    C. Firewall
    D. NAT

13. You are helping a user set up a wireless network in her home and find that her computer and wireless router both support a technology that allows you to set up the network with the press of a button on the router. What is this technology?

    A. WEP
    B. WPA
    C. WPS
    D. WPA2

14. You are debating the merits of parity versus nonparity memory in PC use with a coworker. While parity memory has the capacity to check and correct errors, she doesn't believe it's worth the additional bit width on PC systems, which increases drastically as the pin count for a stick of DIMM increases. For instance, on a 168-pin DIMM, she says nonparity memory uses 64 bits to store eight bytes of data. How many bits does a 168-pin DIMM with parity use to store eight bytes of data?

    A. 68

    B. 72

    C. 76

    D. 80

15. You are replacing two failed sticks of memory in a server. The server has ECC RAM installed because of the error-checking feature available. The only replacement RAM you have available is non-ECC RAM, which is otherwise identical to the RAM in the server. Should you replace the failed ECC RAM sticks with non-ECC RAM, mixing both ECC and non-ECC RAM in the same server machine?

    A. Yes. As long as there are at least two pairs of ECC RAM in the server, the error-checking feature will remain active.

    B. Yes, but although all of the RAM will be recognized by the server and work with no problems, error checking will not be available.

    C. No, because the server will not recognize the non-ECC RAM. All of the RAM needs to be either ECC or non-ECC.

    D. No, because none of the RAM will be recognized and the server will fail to boot.

16. You work for a small city IT department, and you are going over the inventory of RAM modules with a new employee. He notices that some of the RAM modules have chips only on one side while others have chips on both sides. How do you explain the difference to him?

    A. All single-sided RAM chips are DRAM, or dynamic random access memory, while all double-sided chips are SRAM, or static random access memory.

    B. All double-sided RAM chips have exactly twice the memory capacity as their single-sided counterparts.

    C. All single-sided RAM chips have one "rank" and the computer can access all their memory at once, while all double-sized chips have two "ranks" and the computer can access only one rank at a time.

    D. All single-sided RAM chips have one "rank" and the computer can access all their memory at once, while all double-sized chips have two "ranks" and the computer can access all the memory in both ranks at the same time.

17. You have been asked to upgrade the memory on a desktop computer. It currently uses two modules of 512 MB PC-2700 memory and only has two memory sockets available. The customer has asked you to upgrade the computer with two sticks of 1 GB PC-3200 memory, expecting not only to have twice as much RAM available but that the RAM will be faster. What do you tell her?

   A. You tell her that the computer will have twice as much memory as before and it will run at 3200 MHz rather than 2700 MHz.

   B. You tell her that the computer will have twice as much memory as before but it will only run at the faster 3200 MHz speed if the bus speed on the motherboard supports it.

   C. You tell her that the computer will only recognize twice as much memory as before if the motherboard supports that much memory but will run at the higher 3200 MHz speed.

   D. You tell her that the computer will only recognize twice as much memory as before if the motherboard supports that much memory but will run faster only if the motherboard bus speed supports the faster speed.

18. You have a customer who has a failed graphics card on his new computer. He can get a new one under warranty from the manufacturer, but while he waits for it to arrive, he wants you to temporarily install an AGP graphics card so that he can still use his computer for gaming. You tell him this is not a good technical option because of what?

   A. Installing a card other than the one provided as a replacement by the manufacturer could void his warranty.

   B. Not all AGP cards use the same type of AGP slot, and it may not fit the AGP slot on his brand-new motherboard.

   C. His brand-new computer does not have an AGP slot, since AGP support on new motherboards has been phased out in place of PCIe support.

   D. His AGP card is older and is too slow to support the AGP bus on his brand-new motherboard.

19. You get a call from one of your older home customers who uses a single PC to connect to the Internet via a DSL modem. He wants to buy another computer for his wife and put it in the same home office he uses for the first computer. He asks if he has to add a NIC (network interface card) to his current computer to connect the two and share his Internet connection with his wife's PC. What do you tell him is his best option?

   A. You tell him that you can add a PCI Express NIC to his computer and use a crossover cable to connect the two computers, thus enabling his computer to share its Internet connection with his wife's computer.

   B. You tell him that you can add a USB wireless NIC to his wife's PC and then turn on wireless networking on the DSL modem so that his wife can use the Internet.

C.   You tell him that if the DSL modem doesn't have two Ethernet ports, he can buy a small two- or four-port switch and an Ethernet cable; then you can connect the two PCs to the switch and connect the switch to the DSL modem, so that both PCs can network to each other and connect to the Internet.

D.   You tell him that he needs to replace the DSL modem with a wireless router and connect his PCs wirelessly to the Internet.

20.   You have a customer who would like to be able to connect his laptop to a cellular phone network so he can surf the Web and check e-mail. What does he need to do to accomplish this?

A.   Laptops cannot connect to cellular phone networks.

B.   He needs to purchase a WWAN adapter for his laptop plus a data plan from his cellular provider.

C.   He needs to purchase a WLAN adapter for his laptop plus a data plan from his ISP.

D.   He needs to enable the wireless card in his laptop for WWAN in the BIOS and purchase a data plan from his telephone provider.

21.   You have a customer who usually watches DVDs on her computer but would also like to watch TV shows directly on her PC. In addition, she'd like the ability to record some of the TV shows on her computer. Her computer is new but doesn't have these capacities. What is the most common upgrade she needs to fulfill her requirements?

A.   She needs to have a PCI Express TV tuner card installed, which will satisfy all her requirements.

B.   She needs to have a PCI Express TV tuner card and a PCI Express video capture card installed to meet her requirements.

C.   She needs to have a SCSI TV tuner card installed, which will satisfy all her requirements.

D.   She needs to have a SCSI TV tuner card and a SCSI video capture card installed to meet her requirements.

22.   You are helping a customer back up her data, and she suggests using CDs for storage. What do you tell her is the storage capacity of a standard CD?

A.   700 MB

B.   1.4 GB

C.   3.2 GB

D.   4.7 GB

23.   What is the standard SCSI ID for a host adapter?

A.   0

B.   1

C.   7

D.   15

24. You have a small business customer who wants you to install a bar code scanner on his computer so that he can use it to scan items for sale. Of the following, what is true about installing a bar code scanner on a computer? (Choose two.)

    A. You can connect the bar code scanner via a 40-pin parallel port.

    B. You can connect the bar code scanner via a USB port.

    C. Bar code scanners are plug and play and require no software configuration.

    D. Bar code scanners require software to be installed on the computer to understand the meaning of the bar codes.

25. You get a call from a customer who has just bought a new computer with an LCD flat monitor. He is confused because the monitor came with two video cables, a VGA cable, and a cable with a connection that is depicted in the accompanying illustration. There are connections for both on the back of his new computer. What is the unknown connector?

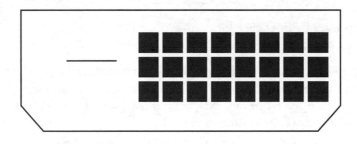

    A. It is a DVI-I (single link) connector.

    B. It is a DVI-D (single link) connector.

    C. It is a DVI-D (dual link) connector.

    D. It is an HDMI connector.

26. You are helping a new technician at work understand motherboard busses and bus speeds. There are numerous busses on a motherboard, which connect one component or chipset on a motherboard to another. Of the following, which bus do you say is used to determine a motherboard's bus speed?

    A. The front side bus (FSB), which connects the CPU to the Northbridge

    B. The PCI bus, which connects the PCI slots to the Southbridge

    C. The ATA bus, which connects the ATA hard drive to the Southbridge

    D. The Memory bus, which connects the RAM slots to the Northbridge

27. You are a technician who supports the computer and printer maintenance and repair needs of a number of small business customers. You get a call from one of your customers saying that a "service required" message is being displayed on her laser printer. What should you do?

A. Replace the printer since it is faulty.

B. Change the toner and reset the printer.

C. Apply the printer maintenance kit.

D. Send the printer to the manufacturer for servicing.

28. You are a technician who supports the computer and printer maintenance and repair needs of a number of small business customers. You get a call from one of your customers saying that her color laser printer is malfunctioning. The colors on printouts are "off" and words of text are overlapping. Based on these symptoms, what do you need to do?

A. Clean the printer.

B. Change the black toner cartridge.

C. Apply the printer maintenance kit.

D. Calibrate the printer.

29. You are a technician who supports the computer and printer maintenance and repair needs of a number of small business customers. You are providing a routine cleaning of a customer's laser printer at his office. Of the following, what printer components or elements do you clean and how do you clean them? (Choose all that apply.)

A. Clean the corona wires with a specialized vacuum or metal brush.

B. Clean the paper feed rollers with a cloth.

C. Clean the interior assembly that contains the toner cartridge with a cloth or specialized vacuum.

D. Clean the fan vents with compressed air.

30. You are a technician who supports the computer and printer maintenance and repair needs of a number of small business customers. You are servicing a number of thermal printers a customer uses for producing bar code labels. Of the following, what should you do to clean the thermal printers? (Choose all that apply.)

A. Clean the print head with a no-lint cloth moistened with isopropyl alcohol.

B. Remove any small paper debris and dust from the interior of the printer.

C. Clean the ribbon with a swab lightly moistened with water.

D. Use a dry cloth to wipe any dust off the paper roll that feeds through the thermal printer.

31. You are reviewing basic networking devices with a new trainee at your computer support business. You describe a device that is known as a multiport repeater and is unable to learn which device is connected to which port in a wired network. Of the following, which device is being described?

  A. Access point

  B. Hub

  C. Router

  D. Switch

32. You are configuring a firewall to allow traffic associated with Web browsing from users on your network. What ports should you allow? (Choose all that apply.)

  A. 80

  B. 25

  C. 443

  D. 23

33. You are reviewing basic networking with a new trainee at your computer support business and are currently discussing network topologies, which are logical or physical arrangements of network devices. You are currently describing a topology that sends messages either clockwise or counterclockwise and where a failure in any one device can bring down the entire network. Which topology is this?

  A. Mesh

  B. Ring

  C. Bus

  D. Star

  E. Hybrid

34. You are reviewing computer CPU types with a new trainee at your computer support business and you give the trainee a list of socket types and ask the trainee to identify the manufacturers. Of the following, which socket types are associated with Intel CPUs? (Choose all that apply.)

  A. AM2+

  B. LGA

  C. 775

  D. 940

35. You recently flashed the BIOS of your computer and now it will not boot properly. You want to reset the BIOS to its default settings so you can boot your computer again. Of the following, which method will most likely accomplish your goal?

A. Reset the jumper on the computer's hard drive.

B. Reset the jumper on the computer's motherboard.

C. Reset the jumper on the computer's power supply.

D. Press the reset button on the front of your computer.

36. You have just bought a new ATX form factor motherboard and are planning to build a new customer computer. You are reviewing the various features and connections on the motherboard, including the fan connections. How many pins should you expect to see for the different types of fan connections? (Choose all that apply.)

A. 2-pin

B. 3-pin

C. 4-pin

D. 5-pin

37. You have just bought a new ATX form factor motherboard and are planning to build a new customer computer. You are reviewing the various features and slots on the motherboard. Of the following, which expansion slot are you least likely to work with in building your new PC?

A. CNR

B. PCI

C. PCIe

D. SATA

38. You are setting up a small home RAID server for your own use. The server needs to supply excellent read/write speeds, as you'll be using it to create and edit video and audio content. You also have limited funds so you need to use the least number of hard drives possible. Data redundancy is not a requirement. Of the following, which RAID level would serve your purposes?

A. 0

B. 1

C. 5

D. 10

39. You have a customer who has one SATA1 drive installed in her computer. She wants to add one or possibly two more SATA drives to expand storage space but is wondering if she can have you install a SATA2 or SATA3 drive in the same computer with a SATA1 drive. What do you tell her?

    A. SATA2 and SATA3 drives cannot be installed in a computer that has a SATA1 drive installed, as the different physical SATA connectors are incompatible.

    B. SATA2 drives can be installed in a computer with a SATA1 drive because SATA2 drives can use SATA1 physical connectors, but SATA3 drives aren't compatible with that physical connector type.

    C. The SATA controller connector will physically work for SATA1, SATA2, and SATA3 since the only difference in these specifications is data transfer speed. Each drive will be able to transfer its data to and from the motherboard at its rated transfer speed.

    D. The SATA controller connector will physically work for SATA1, SATA2, and SATA3, but the data transfer speed for all SATA drives will be that of the SATA connector type on the motherboard.

40. You are visiting the computer of an employee in your company and notice a file on the desktop labeled "Porn Files." What should you do?

    A. Ignore the files, as they are none of your business.

    B. Open the folder and inspect the files.

    C. Report the incident to your supervisor.

    D. Ask the customer about the files.

41. You are doing an inventory at your computer repair shop and counting the different display cable types you have available. Of the following, which cables in your inventory can be used for computer displays? (Choose all that apply.)

    A. DVI

    B. Ethernet

    C. SATA

    D. VGA

42. You are doing an inventory at your computer repair shop and counting the different drive connectors and cables you have available. In examining the device connectors, of the following, which ones have a seven-pin connector? (Choose all that apply.)

    A. eSATA data connector

    B. Floppy data connector

    C. SATA data connector

    D. USB standard A connector

43. You recently replaced a customer's laptop battery and want to dispose of the old battery. What method should you use?
    A. Throw it in the trash.
    B. Place it in a recycling bin.
    C. Follow special disposal procedures for your area.
    D. Physically destroy the battery and then throw it in the trash.

44. While you are working on a computer, another employee approaches you and says that he is bothered that one of his coworkers is accessing pornographic Websites at work. What should you do?
    A. Report the incident to your supervisor.
    B. Confront the accused user.
    C. Check logs to determine if the complaint is accurate.
    D. Tell the user that you are not responsible for inappropriate-use complaints.

45. You are reviewing safety procedures with a new intern in your computer support business. Of the following, which one do you say protects against severe electrical shock that could potentially lead to death?
    A. Cable management
    B. CRT safety
    C. ESD straps
    D. ESD mats

46. You are identifying the supplies that you need to stock in your computer supply closet. You want to make sure you have an adequate inventory of toner. What type of printer uses toner?
    A. Inkjet
    B. Laser
    C. Thermal
    D. Dot matrix

47. You are building a wireless network for a customer's SOHO, or small office/home office, environment. What basic service do you recommend be turned off to improve wireless network security?
    A. DHCP
    B. DMZ
    C. DNS
    D. FTP

48. You were dispatched to visit a customer's home and perform a lengthy repair job on her hard drive. While you are there the customer requests that you show her how to visit a Website. This is not on your work order, and you estimate it will take five minutes. What should you do?

    A. Contact your supervisor for instructions.

    B. Request that the customer contact your office to pay for the service.

    C. Tell the customer you are not authorized to perform additional work.

    D. Show the customer how to visit the Website.

49. You are working with a home customer who is unfamiliar with basic computers and explaining how devices can be connected to her computer. Of the following, which connection types do you say she can use to connect a keyboard and mouse to her computer? (Choose all that apply.)

    A. PS/2

    B. RJ-45

    C. USB

    D. Wi-Fi

50. What is the purpose of a computer's power supply?

    A. Convert DC power to AC power

    B. Convert AC power to DC power

    C. Store power for later use

    D. Protect the computer against surges in power

QUICK ANSWER KEY

1.	A	18.	C	35.	B
2.	B	19.	C	36.	B, C
3.	B, C, D	20.	B	37.	A
4.	A	21.	A	38.	A
5.	B	22.	A	39.	D
6.	B, D	23.	C	40.	C
7.	A, D	24.	B, D	41.	A, B, D
8.	C	25.	C	42.	A, C
9.	A	26.	A	43.	C
10.	C	27.	C	44.	A
11.	A	28.	D	45.	B
12.	D	29.	B, C, D	46.	B
13.	C	30.	A, B	47.	A
14.	B	31.	B	48.	D
15.	B	32.	A, C	49.	A, C, D
16.	C	33.	B	50.	B
17.	D	34.	B, C		

IN-DEPTH ANSWERS

1. ☑ **A.** While any of the options can be the problem, the first and easiest thing to check is the power cord that plugs into the wall socket. Even if it doesn't look damaged, it can be the victim of being stepped on, mashed under the wheels of a rolling chair, and so forth. If the cord is the problem, it is a quick and easy fix.

    ☒ **B, C,** and **D** are incorrect. **B** is incorrect because, while this can be the problem, the first thing to check is the power cord. **C** is incorrect because, although the battery can be the problem, the first thing to verify is if the power cord is good. **D** is incorrect because, although the power connector on the motherboard can be the problem, the first and easiest component to check is the power cord.

2. ☑ **B.** People commonly use their laptops in bed, but the presence of thick blankets or other bedding can block the cooling fan vents, causing the machine to overheat and the fans to continually run to try to cool the unit.

    ☒ **A, C,** and **D** are incorrect. **A** is incorrect because under normal circumstances, the laptop cooling system should keep the laptop interior cool, even if the unit has been running all day. Also, most laptops are set to go into some form of Sleep mode, which drastically reduces the machine's heat output, if left unused for long periods of time, so heat wouldn't have "accumulated" by the evening when the customer started using the laptop. **C** is incorrect because, although possible, the circumstances of the problem strongly indicate a situational rather than a systemic problem. **D** is incorrect because it is unlikely the battery is overheating under these circumstances.

3. ☑ **B, C,** and **D.** The inverter supplies power to the backlight of the LCD display, while the video adapter controls the laptop's video output.

    ☒ **A** is incorrect because a DC controller is an internal component in a laptop that manages minor changes in DC electrical current.

4. ☑ **A.** Adding an external Wi-Fi antenna to the laptop is an effective technique to boost wireless range and, of the options listed, is the easiest to implement.

    ☒ **B, C,** and **D** are incorrect because, while they might improve the reception problem, they are much more difficult to implement than adding an external antenna to the laptop.

5. ☑ **B.** Cable locks are the most effective and inexpensive way to solve this problem. They have a small, one-time cost and will deter most thieves.

    ☒ **A, C,** and **D** are incorrect. **A** and **C** are incorrect because, while they might be effective, they are more expensive than cable locks. **D** is incorrect because permanently attaching laptops to desks is not a practical solution, as it removes their mobility.

6.   ☑   **B** and **D.** Both single-mode and multimode fiber-optic cable use light to transmit data and are capable of far faster speeds and bandwidth than coaxial cable, which uses electrical impulses.
☒   **A** and **C** are incorrect because coaxial cable uses electrical impulses, rather than light, to transmit data.

7.   ☑   **A** and **D.** ADSL, or asymmetric DSL, offers maximum download speeds of between 1.5 and 9 Mbps and maximum upload speeds of between 16 and 640 Kbps. VDSL, or very high data-rate DSL, offers maximum download speeds of between 13 and 52 Mbps and maximum upload speeds of between 1.5 and 6.0 Mbps.
☒   **B** and **C** are incorrect because high data-rate DSL (HDSL) and symmetric DSL (SDSL) offer the same maximum upload and download speeds.

8.   ☑   **C.** Technically, you'd issue the ipconfig /release command first to make sure the NIC isn't bound to an incorrect IP address, but to specifically request a new IP address from a DHCP server, use the ipconfig /renew command.
☒   **A, B,** and **D** are incorrect. **A** is incorrect because this will provide limited configuration information for the computer, such as its IP address and subnet mask. **B** is incorrect because this will provide more detail about the computer's network configuration, including the IP addresses of the DHCP server and the DNS servers, and when the computer's IP address was obtained. However, it will not remedy the situation. **D** is incorrect because /restore is an invalid switch for the ipconfig command and will return an error message along with the ipconfig help menu.

9.   ☑   **A.** An RJ-11 connector is used for standard phone jacks and is the proper connector for the port of an analog modem installed in a computer to be used for dial-up Internet connections.
☒   **B, C,** and **D** are incorrect. **B** and **D** are incorrect because they are used on coaxial cables. **C** is incorrect because this is the standard connector for Ethernet ports.

10.   ☑   **C.** There are a few options your customer can use to add a wireless network to his environment. The DSL modem he is currently using may have a wireless access point (WAP) as part of its functionality. Such devices may have an external antenna for this purpose. If not, he will need to purchase a WAP or wireless router to use to add the wireless network.
☒   **A, B,** and **D** are incorrect. **A** is incorrect because there are other devices that can be used besides a WAP. **B** is incorrect because there are other devices that can be used besides a wireless router. **D** is incorrect because an ad hoc wireless network, one in which wireless computers connect to each other directly, is an inadequate solution for more than just a few computers.

11. ☑ **A.** RG-6 is a form of coaxial cable, and a cable tester will determine whether there are any faults present.

☒ **B, C,** and **D** are incorrect. **B** is incorrect because a punchdown tool is used to insert wires into patch panel connectors. **C** is incorrect because a loopback plug is used to test a network interface. **D** is incorrect because a crimping tool is used to attach connectors to cable.

12. ☑ **D.** All IP addresses beginning with 192.168 are private IP addresses and cannot be used on the Internet without the use of Network Address Translation (NAT).

☒ **A, B,** and **C** are incorrect. **A** is incorrect because DNS is used to translate domain names to IP addresses. This is not necessary for Internet communication, although it does facilitate it. **B** is incorrect because DHCP is used to assign IP addresses to hosts and this system already has an IP address. **C** is incorrect because although a firewall is advisable, it is not necessary for communication.

13. ☑ **C.** Wi-Fi Protected Setup (WPS) allows you to create a secure wireless network by pressing a button on the router.

☒ **A, B,** and **D** are incorrect because WEP, WPA, and WPA2 are encryption technologies used to secure Wi-Fi networks but they must be configured either manually or through the use of WPS.

14. ☑ **B.** Parity memory uses eight bits to store a byte of data, plus one bit for parity, so a total of nine bits per byte. To store eight bytes of data, parity memory uses 72 bits.

☒ **A, C,** and **D** are incorrect. **A** and **C** are incorrect because there is no reasonable way to add parity bits to come to those values. **D** is incorrect because it would require eight bits per byte and two bits for parity to come to the stated value.

15. ☑ **B.** You can substitute non-ECC RAM for ECC RAM and mix both types together, but all the memory will run as non-ECC and error checking will not occur.

☒ **A, C,** and **D** are incorrect. **A** is incorrect because all of the RAM must be ECC for the error-checking feature to operate. **C** and **D** are incorrect because both the ECC and non-ECC RAM will be recognized by the server.

16. ☑ **C.** Ranks on memory modules share the same bus on the computer, so only one rank can be accessed by the computer at any given time. The other rank is deactivated while the first rank is accessed, and then the first rank is deactivated while the other rank is accessed.

☒ **A, B,** and **D** are incorrect. **A** is incorrect because you do not distinguish between DRAM and SRAM modules by whether or not they are single or double sided. **B** is incorrect because double-sided memory modules don't automatically contain twice the memory of single-sided modules. **D** is incorrect because only one rank on a memory module can be accessed by the computer at any one time.

17. ☑ **D.** Motherboards are designed to recognize only a certain amount of memory and memory speed, depending on a variety of factors. In this case, the motherboard in the computer owned by the customer may only recognize up to 1 GB of RAM and up to 2700 MHz of memory speed.

    ☒ **A, B,** and **C** are incorrect because the amount of RAM and the speed of the RAM recognized by the computer are dependent on the amount and speed of memory the motherboard is designed to run. Unless you have checked the motherboard specifications in advance, you cannot say exactly how much memory a motherboard will support or what memory speeds it is capable of using.

18. ☑ **C.** Almost no modern motherboards support AGP, even though new AGP video cards continue to be made. Most likely, the original video card in his computer is PCIe compliant and his replacement graphics card will need to be a PCIe card.

    ☒ **A, B,** and **D** are incorrect. **A** is incorrect because although installing a card not provided by the manufacturer may void the computer's warranty under these circumstances, this is not a good technical reason for not installing a new card. **B** and **D** are incorrect because his brand-new motherboard most likely does not have an AGP slot.

19. ☑ **C.** The best option is to connect the two computers using a small switch and then connect the switch to the DSL modem and thus connect both computers to each other through the switch and to the Internet.

    ☒ **A, B,** and **D** are incorrect. **A** is incorrect because although it would work, it is unnecessarily complicated. **B** is incorrect because even though it would work, it would be an uncommon solution unless his wife's computer is located in a different part of the house. **D** is incorrect because the two computers can be networked to connect to the Internet without replacing the current DSL modem with a different piece of hardware for wireless networking, particularly if the two computers are in the same room with the DSL modem.

20. ☑ **B.** While you can request a WWAN (wireless wide area network) card be added to your laptop at the time of purchase, a WWAN adapter can also be added later via USB or as a Mini PCI Express card. As with any other cellular service, you will also need to purchase a data plan from your cellular provider before you can make the appropriate connection.

    ☒ **A, C,** and **D** are incorrect. **A** is incorrect because laptops can be connected to cellular WANs or WWANs. **C** is incorrect because a WLAN (wireless local area network) adapter cannot be used to connect to a cellular network and your ISP is not likely to be able to provide the required service. **D** is incorrect because you cannot enable a wireless (WLAN) card for WWAN in the BIOS, and your telephone company cannot provide this service unless they provide cellular as well as landline-based services.

21. ☑ **A.** The simplest and most common upgrade is to have a PCI Express TV tuner card installed in her PC. This card will allow her to receive and watch TV shows on her computer, and most TV tuner cards also function as video capture cards, so she can also record TV shows onto the PC's hard drive.

☒ **B, C,** and **D** are incorrect. **B** is incorrect because you do not need to have two PCI Express cards installed to fulfill both functions in most cases. **C** and **D** are incorrect because although SCSI TV tuner cards exist, they are not the most common solution to the customer's request.

22. ☑ **A.** CD capacities vary somewhat based upon the type of CD, but the standard capacity is approximately 700 MB.

☒ **B, C,** and **D** are incorrect because the standard capacity of a CD is approximately 700 MB.

23. ☑ **C.** SCSI host adapters are traditionally assigned SCSI ID 7.

☒ **A, B,** and **D** are incorrect because SCSI host adapters are traditionally assigned SCSI ID 7.

24. ☑ **B** and **D.** You can attach a bar code scanner to a computer using either a USB or a serial connection, and software needs to be installed on the computer so that it understands the meaning of the bar codes and how to process the data.

☒ **A** and **C** are incorrect. **A** is incorrect because you cannot connect a bar code scanner to a computer using a 40-pin parallel port, though you can make the connection using a serial port. **C** is incorrect because without software, the hardware components may scan bar codes, but the computer won't understand the input or how to process it.

25. ☑ **C.** DVI, or Digital Visual Interface, is a video interface standard that is replacing VGA for flat-panel LCD computer displays. The DVI-D single-link connector is used for only digital signals; however, other DVI connectors, such as DVI-I, can be used for integrated analog and digital signals. While it is possible to connect a male DVI-D cable to a female DVI-I connector, a male DVI-I to female DVI-D connection is not possible due to pin incompatibility.

☒ **A, B,** and **D** are incorrect because the connector pinouts do not match the illustration accompanying the question.

26. ☑ **A.** A motherboard's bus speed refers to the front-side bus, which connects the computer's CPU to the Northbridge and is typically measured in megahertz (MHz). The bus speed determines how fast information is moved to and from the CPU for processing.

☒ **B, C,** and **D** are incorrect. **B** is incorrect because how quickly information moves across the PCI bus is not a measure of a motherboard's bus speed. Also, in modern computers, you are much more likely to find PCI-E slots than archaic PCI slots, so the PCI bus is not relevant. **C** is incorrect because the ATA bus is also not a measure of a motherboard's bus speeds. In addition, it is more likely for modern computers to use SATA drives rather than ATA (also known as IDE) drives. **D** is incorrect because the memory bus is not an indicator of a motherboard's bus speed.

27. ☑ **C.** A laser printer maintenance kit contains all of the parts required to provide regular maintenance to the printer. When a "service required" or "perform printer maintenance" message is displayed on the printer, use the official printer maintenance kit provided by the printer's manufacturer to replace worn parts such as the transfer roller, pickup roller, and separation pad. You may also have to replace the fuser and install a fresh toner cartridge.

☒ **A, B,** and **D** are incorrect. **A** is incorrect because the printer needs routine maintenance, not replacement. **B** is incorrect because replacing the toner cartridge is only one part of applying the maintenance kit. **D** is incorrect because with the maintenance kit, a technician can service the printer on site, and it does not have to be sent back to the manufacturer for routine maintenance.

28. ☑ **D.** Generally, when color is off or discoloration is occurring and words and letters are overlapping in laser printer output, the printer needs to be calibrated. Depending on the printer, this can be a software and/or hardware process, which includes updating the printer drivers. Most likely, you will use the software calibration option on the printer and test the calibration by printing a color calibration test sheet. Regular calibration of a laser printer will ensure that the colors of a document or image you see on the computer's screen are what actually print.

☒ **A, B,** and **C** are incorrect. **A** is incorrect because cleaning the printer won't correct a discoloration and text overlap problem. **B** is incorrect because changing the black toner cartridge won't correct the symptoms. **C** is incorrect because this will provide routine maintenance for the printer, but will not replace calibration of the laser printer.

29. ☑ **B, C,** and **D.** Cleaning a laser printer can be very messy and potentially hazardous. Spilled toner is a very fine substance and should not be inhaled. You may want to consider wearing a facial mask to filter out the toner. Also spread a cloth around your work area. Use a soft cloth to clean the rollers. You can also use a cloth or a specialized vacuum cleaner to remove toner residue from the printer's interior (never use an ordinary household vacuum cleaner, as it can damage the printer). Also, just as with computer fans, laser printer fans can become clogged with dust and you can use a can of compressed air to blow the dust free.

☒ **A** is incorrect because using a vacuum or metal brush on the thin, delicate corona wire can break it. Instead, clean the wire using a soft cloth moistened with a little isopropyl alcohol, and gently run the cloth along the length of the wire.

30. ☑ **A** and **B.** The print head is the single most expensive replacement item on a thermal printer, so clean it carefully. Gently rub a lint-free cloth moistened with isopropyl alcohol across the print head after removing the ribbon. Allow to dry before replacing the ribbon and paper. Make sure you have removed any loose bits of paper debris or other contaminants from inside the printer.

☒ **C** and **D** are incorrect. **C** is incorrect because the ribbon on a thermal label printer is a consumable and it is replaced rather than cleaned. **D** is incorrect because the paper is also a consumable and should not need to be cleaned.

31. ☑ **B.** A hub is also known as a multiport repeater and is used to connect two or more computers to a local network segment with Ethernet patch cables. A hub is a very simple device and, unlike a switch, cannot "learn" which computer is connected to which of its ports. Hubs are almost unknown in modern networking, but some legacy devices may still be found.
☒ **A, C,** and **D** are incorrect. **A** is incorrect because an access point is a device used to connect multiple devices wirelessly. **C** is incorrect because a router connects computers that belong to two or more network segments. **D** is incorrect because it is capable of learning which device is connected to which port in the same wired network segment.

32. ☑ **A and C.** Web browsing takes place using two ports. HTTP connections take place over port 80, while HTTPS connections take place over port 443.
☒ **B and D** are incorrect. **B** is incorrect because port 25 is used by the SMTP protocol. **D** is incorrect because port 23 is used by the telnet protocol.

33. ☑ **B.** A ring topology is a circular network design where any device sends a message to one of its two neighbors on the ring. Each device passing the message along is used as a repeater, but any break in the ring due to a malfunctioning device can potentially bring the entire ring network down.
☒ **A, C, D,** and **E** are incorrect. **A** is incorrect because a mesh topology is one that provides redundant paths between devices, so a breakdown on one device would not disable the entire network. **C** is incorrect because a bus topology describes a series of devices all connected to a single backbone. Because devices are not used as repeaters, a disabled device would not bring down the network. **D** is incorrect because a star topology also provides redundant network paths, just as a mesh topology does, so the network would continue to operate if a device were disabled. **E** is incorrect because a hybrid topology is a combination of any of the other two topology types.

34. ☑ **B and C.** Intel socket types are largely identified by three- or four-digit numbers, such as 775, 1155, and 1156, but the LGA socket type is also Intel.
☒ **A and D** are incorrect. **A** is incorrect because many AMD socket types are identified by letter and number combinations, such as AM2, AM2+, and AM3. **D** is incorrect because it is an exception to the "rule" that most numeric socket types are Intel. The 940 socket type is AMD.

35. ☑ **B.** On many motherboards, there is a three-pin jumper near the CMOS battery that is sometimes labeled "clear cmos" or "reset bios." Removing the jumper and resetting the jumper to cover the second and third pins, pressing the computer's power button, waiting, then replacing the jumper to the original position, and then powering up the computer will usually reset the BIOS. Check the manual for your computer's motherboard to make sure of the proper procedure, since no single process applies to all motherboards.
☒ **A, C,** and **D** are incorrect. **A** is incorrect because the jumpers on an IDE hard drive (SATA drives have no jumpers) will not reset the BIOS. **C** is incorrect because a computer's power supply doesn't have jumpers. **D** is incorrect because even if your

computer has a reset button, all it does is put your computer through a restart sequence in the event that a program hangs or other similar error occurs. Many modern computers do not have a reset button.

36. ☑ **B and C.** On a modern ATX form factor motherboard, you are most likely to see three-pin power fan connectors and four-pin CPU fan connectors.

☒ **A and D** are incorrect because there are no computer fan connectors that use two-pin or five-pin connections on an ATX motherboard.

37. ☑ **A.** The CNR, or Communication and Networking Riser, was included on motherboards largely for OEM manufacturers to include devices such as modems on an expansion card rather than integrate them onto the motherboard so that only the CNR card had to meet FCC certification and not the motherboard. Unlike PCI or PCIe slots, you are unlikely to add an expansion card in this slot when custom-building your own computer. Also, CNR cards are somewhat difficult to come by.

☒ **B, C,** and **D** are incorrect. **B** and **C** are incorrect because you are very likely to add devices to your new computer using PCI and/or PCIe expansion slots, which are commonly used for this purpose. **D** is incorrect because SATA is a hard drive type, and a motherboard's SATA connectors are not considered expansion slots but instead, channels that allow the SATA drive to connect to and communicate with the computer's motherboard and motherboard components.

38. ☑ **A.** RAID 0, or striping, provides excellent read/write speeds because the data is written across different blocks in the RAID array so data can be written to and read from different disks simultaneously. Speed is further enhanced if each RAID disk has its own controller on the motherboard. RAID 0 requires a minimum of two disks, so the requirement of the fewest number of hard disks is also met by this RAID type. RAID 0 provides no data redundancy.

☒ **B, C,** and **D** are incorrect. **B** is incorrect because RAID 1, or mirroring, provides redundancy by writing the same data to two sets of disks, but it is not an effective use of a limited number of disks and it isn't particularly fast. **C** is incorrect because RAID 5 requires a minimum of three disks, so it doesn't meet the requirement of the fewest number of disks possible. It does provide good speed performance, but also provides redundancy, which isn't a requirement. **D** is incorrect because RAID 10 requires a minimum of four disks and so it doesn't meet the requirement of the fewest possible number of disks. This RAID level provides excellent performance and redundancy, but is more expensive than the other options.

39. ☑ **D.** Connecting a SATA2 or SATA3 drive to a SATA motherboard connector is physically possible, but the drives will only transfer data at the speed of the motherboard.

☒ **A, B,** and **C** are incorrect. **A** and **B** are incorrect because the physical connector types are all the same. The only difference is data transfer speed. **C** is incorrect because the data transfer rate for a SATA2 or SATA3 drive will not be able to transfer data at their expected speeds.

40. ☑ **C.** You should report all suspected cases of inappropriate computer use to your supervisor immediately.

    ☒ **A, B,** and **D** are incorrect. **A** is incorrect because you are obligated to report suspicions of inappropriate use to your supervisor. **B** is incorrect because you should never open a file without the customer's permission. **D** is incorrect because you should never confront a user about suspicions of inappropriate use.

41. ☑ **A, B,** and **D.** DVI and VGA cables are commonly used with computer displays. Ethernet cables can be used with displays with RJ-45 connectors to receive video content across a network.

    ☒ **C** is incorrect because video content cannot be sent across a SATA cable, which is used to transfer data to and from a SATA hard drive.

42. ☑ **A** and **C.** Both the eSATA and SATA data connectors have seven pins.

    ☒ **B** and **D** are incorrect. **B** is incorrect because the floppy drive data connector has 34 pins. **D** is incorrect because the USB standard A connector has four pins.

43. ☑ **C.** Batteries contain environmentally sensitive chemicals and must be disposed of using special processes. You should contact your local authorities to determine the proper disposal procedures for your area.

    ☒ **A, B,** and **D** are incorrect. **A** is incorrect because batteries should be recycled. Placing them in the trash exposes the landfill to dangerous chemicals and may be illegal. **B** is incorrect because normal recycling procedures are not capable of handling the dangerous chemicals in batteries. **D** is incorrect because opening a laptop battery can be very dangerous.

44. ☑ **A.** You should inform your supervisor of any reports of inappropriate computer use that you receive without performing any other investigation.

    ☒ **B, C,** and **D** are incorrect. **B** and **C** are incorrect because you should never perform your own investigation of inappropriate use. **D** is incorrect because you are obligated to inform your supervisor when you receive a report of inappropriate computer use.

45. ☑ **B.** A CRT, or cathode ray tube, monitor is an extremely hazardous piece of equipment if you attempt to open it up and work inside. Even when unplugged from a power source, without proper equipment and training, you could receive a strong and potentially fatal electrical shock. Never open a CRT monitor under any circumstances.

    ☒ **A, C,** and **D** are incorrect. **A** is incorrect because cable management refers to the collection and organization of power, network, and other cables in a computing environment, such as a server room, in order to prevent a tripping hazard. **C** and **D** are incorrect because these are devices used to prevent electrostatic discharge hazards, which are dangerous to delicate electronic components inside a computer but not to a person.

46. ☑ **B.** Laser printers require the use of toner to create an image on paper.

   ☒ **A, C,** and **D** are incorrect. **A** is incorrect because inkjet printers use ink cartridges instead of toner. **C** is incorrect because thermal printers use special thermal paper instead of toner. **D** is incorrect because dot matrix printers use ribbons instead of toner.

47. ☑ **A.** DHCP is a service provided by a server or other device on the network, such as a wireless router, that automatically assigns IP addresses to network devices. If this service is left on, a person trying to hack into a wireless network could receive an IP address that would allow them to communicate with the rest of the network. If you turn off DHCP in the Wi-Fi and configure IP addresses on each wireless device manually, then an intruder will not be as likely to connect to your network. This is only effective if you have a small number of wireless computers to manually configure with addresses.

   ☒ **B, C,** and **D** are incorrect. **B** is incorrect because DMZ stands for demilitarized zone and is an area of a network that insulates your local wired or wireless network from a larger and uncontrolled network such as the Internet. It is not a service. **C** is incorrect because DNS, or Domain Naming Service, is a service that resolves computer hostnames and domain names to their IP addresses and lets you connect to a host by name rather than having to specify the IP address. **D** is incorrect because FTP, or File Transfer Protocol, is used to send and receive large files between hosts across networks, including the Internet. It's not particularly common to run an FTP server on a small, wireless network, and disabling FTP is not a traditional part of securing a SOHO's Wi-Fi environment.

48. ☑ **D.** In this case, the customer is making a simple request that will take very little time and poses no risk. In the spirit of good customer service, you should simply help her.

   ☒ **A, B,** and **C** are incorrect because they are not examples of good customer service. While it is true that the customer did not pay for this assistance and it is technically outside the scope of the work order, common courtesy dictates that you should provide an extra five minutes of help after performing a lengthy, paid repair job.

49. ☑ **A, C,** and **D.** Although not commonly used anymore, a PS/2 connection can be used to attach mouse and keyboard to a computer. USB or wireless connections are common for this use.

   ☒ **B** is incorrect because an RJ-45 connection is used to link a computer to a network using an Ethernet patch cable.

50. ☑ **B.** The purpose of a power supply is to convert the AC power received from the wall outlet to the DC power used by the computer.

   ☒ **A, C,** and **D** are incorrect. **A** is incorrect because it reverses the process. Power supplies convert AC power to DC power, not the opposite. **C** is incorrect because power supplies do not store power. This is the function of the battery. **D** is incorrect because power supplies do not protect against surges. This is the purpose of a surge suppressor.

ANALYZING YOUR RESULTS

Congratulations on completing the 220-801 pre-assessment. You should now take the time to analyze your results with two objectives in mind:

- Identifying the resources you should use to prepare for the 220-801 exam.
- Identifying the specific topics that you should focus on in your preparation.

First, use this table to help you gauge your overall readiness for the 801 examination:

Number of Answers Correct	Recommended Course of Study
1–25	If this had been the actual exam, you probably would not have passed. We recommend that you spend a significant amount of time reviewing the material in the *CompTIA A+® Certification Study Guide, Eighth Edition (Exams 220-801 & 220-802)* before using this book.
26–37	If this had been the actual 220-801 exam, you might have passed, but there is a significant risk that you would not. You should review the following objective map to identify the particular areas that require your focused attention and use the *CompTIA A+® Certification Study Guide, Eighth Edition (Exams 220-801 & 220-802)* to review that material. Once you have done so, you should proceed to work through the questions in this book.
38–50	Congratulations! If this was the actual 220-801 exam, it is likely that you would have passed. You should use this book to refresh your knowledge and prepare yourself mentally for the actual exam.

Once you have identified your readiness for the exam, you may use this table to identify the specific objectives that require your focus as you continue your preparation.

Domain	Weight	Objective	Chapter(s)	Question Number in Pretest
1.0 PC Hardware	40%	1.1 Configure and apply BIOS settings	3	35
		1.2 Differentiate between motherboard components, their purposes, and properties	3, 6	26
		1.3 Compare and contrast RAM types and features	4, 6	14, 15, 16, 17
		1.4 Install and configure expansion cards	4, 6	18, 37
		1.5 Install and configure storage devices and use appropriate media	4, 6	22, 23, 38, 39

Domain	Weight	Objective	Chapter(s)	Question Number in Pretest
		1.6 Differentiate among various CPU types and features, and select the appropriate cooling method	3, 6	34
		1.7 Compare and contrast various connection interfaces and explain their purpose	4	25, 42, 49
		1.8 Install an appropriate power supply based on a given scenario	5	50
		1.9 Evaluate and select appropriate components for a custom configuration to meet customer specifications or needs	5, 6	19
		1.10 Given a scenario, evaluate types and features of display devices	5	41
		1.11 Identify connector types and associated cables	4, 5	36
		1.12 Install and configure various peripheral devices	5	21, 24
2.0 Networking	27%	2.1 Identify types of network cables and connectors	14	6
		2.2 Categorize characteristics of connectors and cabling	14	9
		2.3 Explain properties and characteristics of TCP/IP	14	8, 12
		2.4 Explain common TCP and UDP ports, protocols, and their purpose	14	32
		2.5 Compare and contrast wireless networking standards and encryption types	14	13
		2.6 Install, configure, and deploy a SOHO wireless/wired router using appropriate settings	15	10, 47
		2.7 Compare and contrast Internet connection types and features	14	7, 20
		2.8 Identify various types of networks	14	33
		2.9 Compare and contrast network devices, their functions, and features	14	31

Domain	Weight	Objective	Chapter(s)	Question Number in Pretest
		2.10 Given a scenario, use appropriate networking tools	3, 15	11
3.0 Laptops	11%	3.1 Install and configure laptop hardware and components	7	1, 2, 5
		3.2 Compare and contrast the components within the display of a laptop	7	3
		3.3 Compare and contrast laptop features	7	4
4.0 Printers	11%	4.1 Explain the differences between the various printer types and summarize the associated imaging process	21	46
		4.2 Given a scenario, install and configure printers	21	27
		4.3 Given a scenario, perform printer maintenance	21	28, 29, 30
5.0 Operational Procedures	11%	5.1 Given a scenario, use appropriate safety procedures	1	45
		5.2 Explain environmental impacts and the purpose of environmental controls	1	43
		5.3 Given a scenario, demonstrate proper communication and professionalism	1	48
		5.4 Explain the fundamentals of dealing with prohibited content/activity	1	40, 44

B

Pre-Assessment
Test: Exam 220-802

INSTRUCTIONS

This pre-assessment test is designed to help you prepare to study for the CompTIA A+ 220-802 examination. You should take this test to identify the areas where you should focus your study and preparation.

The pre-assessment test includes 50 questions that are similar in style and format to the questions you will see on the actual exam. As you prepare to take this test, you should try to simulate the actual exam conditions as closely as possible. Go to a quiet place and be sure that you will not be interrupted for the full length of time it will take to complete the test. Do not use any reference materials or other assistance while taking the pre-assessment—remember, the idea is to help you determine what areas you need to focus on during your preparation for the actual exam.

The pre-assessment test contains questions divided in proportion to the 220-802 exam itself. Here is a breakdown of the exam content:

Domain	Exam Weight	Number of Pre-Assessment Questions
1.0 Operating Systems	33%	17
2.0 Security	22%	11
3.0 Mobile Devices	9%	4
4.0 Troubleshooting	36%	18

Complete the entire pre-assessment test before checking your results. Once you have finished, use both the "Quick Answer Key" and the "In-Depth Answers" sections to score your pre-assessment test. You can use the table in the "Analyzing Your Results" section to determine how well you performed on the test. The objective map at the end of the appendix will help you identify those areas that require the most attention while you prepare for the exam.

Are you ready? Go ahead and set your clock for 45 minutes and begin!

QUESTIONS

1. You are configuring the software firewall on the broadband modem used by one of your small business customers. The customer wants all incoming and outgoing Web and e-mail traffic allowed, wants incoming and outgoing .NET Messenger Service connections blocked, and wants only incoming telnet connections blocked. You know that the .NET Messenger Service uses port 1863. Of the following, which is the correct firewall configuration?
   A. Allow incoming and outgoing connections on ports 25, 80, 110, and 143; block inbound and outbound connections on port 1863; and filter incoming TCP packets on port 23.
   B. Allow incoming and outgoing connections on ports 23, 25, 110, and 143; block inbound and outbound connections on port 1863; and filter incoming TCP packets on port 80.
   C. Allow incoming and outgoing connections on ports 23, 25, 80, and 143; block inbound and outbound connections on port 1863; and filter incoming TCP packets on port 110.
   D. Allow incoming and outgoing connections on ports 23, 25, 80, and 110; block inbound and outbound connections on port 1863; and filter incoming TCP packets on port 143.

2. You are going over network troubleshooting basics with a new technician in your department. Of the following, which do you say are command-line utilities used to troubleshoot network problems? (Choose three.)
   A. DIR
   B. IPCONFIG
   C. PING
   D. NETSTAT

3. You are talking to a small business customer who has offices in an area that suffers from frequent electrical power outages. This causes all of his network equipment to fail when the power goes out, interrupting file transfers and sometimes causing data corruption. While you can't prevent power outages, what solution can you suggest that will keep his equipment from immediately quitting when the power goes out?
   A. Better power strips
   B. Professional surge protectors
   C. A UPS
   D. Car batteries

4. You are sorting through your network toolkit and come across the tool shown here. What is this tool?

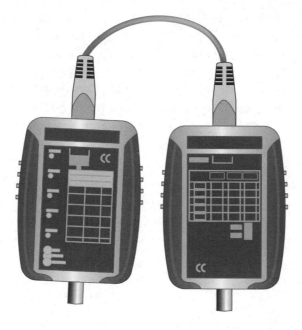

   A. Punchdown tool
   B. Cable tester
   C. Loopback plug
   D. Studfinder

5. You receive a report from a user that he is experiencing intermittent network connectivity problems on his laptop computer that is attached to an Ethernet network. What do you suspect might be the problem?
   A. Incorrectly configured wireless access point
   B. Wireless network adapter has incorrect drivers
   C. Network cable is not connected
   D. Network cable is loose

6. You are concerned about the physical security of your office and decide to enforce a locked door policy with automatically locking doors. Which of the following security risks is most likely to undermine your new policy?
   A. Failure of employees to engage the locks
   B. Phishing
   C. Tailgating
   D. Fake ID badges

7. You discover a set of physical documents that appear to contain passwords for your organization's computing systems. After determining that they are not needed, what should be your next course of action?

   A. Recycle them.
   B. Store them in a secure, locked location.
   C. Shred them with a cross-cut shredder.
   D. Degauss them.

8. You are designing a new access control system and are in the process of assigning access rights to the individuals in your organization for files that may contain confidential business information. What principle should you follow?

   A. Least privilege
   B. Two-person control
   C. Security through obscurity
   D. Separation of duties

9. You are securing a Windows 7 desktop computer and wish to implement the principle of least privilege. The computer account you are creating will be used by an end user. What permission should you restrict?

   A. The ability to read and write files
   B. The ability to set the desktop background
   C. The ability to install software on the computer
   D. The ability to perform a desktop login

10. You are inspecting the security settings on a Windows Vista desktop computer assigned to an end user in your business. Which of the following settings should you alter?

    A. Security logging is enabled.
    B. Windows Firewall is configured to not allow inbound connections.
    C. There is a local administrator account.
    D. The guest account is enabled.

11. You work for a small city IT department, and you have been tasked with securing the servers that provide all the services for city employees and for city residents. You have configured the firewall, installed and configured an intrusion detection device, and set very strong passwords on the servers. You believe the servers are safe from malicious intruders. Of the following, what else should you do to protect the servers? (Choose three.)

    A. Set up BIOS security.
    B. Use antiphishing software.
    C. Use antivirus software.
    D. Lock the server room door.

12. You work for a small city IT department, and you have a customer who repeatedly violates security policy by walking away from his computer without first locking the desktop or logging off. The policy is in place to prevent an unauthorized person from gaining access to his computer and its sensitive data or from sending e-mails posing as the customer. What can you do to enforce company policy with this customer? (Choose two.)

   A. Talk to your supervisor and suggest your supervisor speak with the customer's supervisor and have the customer advised of proper security behaviors.

   B. Reprimand the customer directly.

   C. Set the screensaver on his computer to activate when the computer is inactive for a very short time.

   D. Set the screensaver on his computer to activate when the computer is inactive for a very short time and require a password to turn off the screensaver.

13. You have a rural customer who connects to the Internet via a dial-up connection and is complaining that she hasn't been able to get to the Internet in the last few days. She has checked with her ISP and their service is normal in her area. Her home phone also is working fine. You check the IRQ settings and I/O addresses for the computer's dial-up modem and find no conflict. Where should you go on her Windows XP computer to check the dialing settings?

   A. Network Connections

   B. Phone and Modem Options

   C. Windows Firewall

   D. Wireless Network Setup Wizard

14. You suspect the NIC on a customer's Windows XP computer is not receiving data. Where in Windows XP can you go to check the NIC's status as displayed in the accompanying screenshot?

   A. Go into Control Panel in Classic view, right-click Network Connections, and then click Status.

   B. Go into Control Panel in Classic view, open Network Connections, right-click Local Area Connection, and then click Properties.

   C. Go into Control Panel in Classic view, open Network Connections, right-click Local Area Connection, and then click Status.

   D. Go into Control Panel in Classic view, open Internet Options, and then click the Status tab.

15. You receive a call from an end user who is frustrated by the number of steps that she must follow to access the departmental server from her Windows 7 desktop. She is typing the address of the server into Windows Explorer each time she needs to access a file. How could you help her improve this process?

    A. Defragment the disk.

    B. Map a drive to the server from the desktop.

    C. Use a shortcut key to improve the speed of typing the server address.

    D. On the server, create a shortcut for the desktop user.

16. You are attempting to locate a file on a disk formatted to use the NTFS file system under Windows Vista. You are certain the file is present, but it does not appear in Windows Explorer. You suspect that the hidden attribute might be set on the file. How can you confirm its presence?

    A. Use the DIR command from the command prompt.

    B. Enable the Show Hidden Files And Folders setting in the Folder Options section of the Appearance And Personalization control panel.

    C. Browse to the folder containing the hidden file in Windows Explorer.

    D. Delete the file and re-create it.

17. Beth is attempting to access a file contained within the Accounts Payable subfolder of the Accounting folder on a Windows 2008 Server. There is a deny permission on the Accounting folder for her account that is inherited by the Accounts Payable folder and an allow permission on the specific file for her account. What will happen when she tries to access the file?

    A. She will be allowed to access the file because explicit permissions always override inherited permissions.

    B. She will be allowed to access the file because allow permissions always override deny permissions.

    C. She will not be allowed to access the file because inherited permissions always override explicit permissions.

    D. She will not be allowed to access the file because deny permissions always override allow permissions.

18. You work for a small city IT department and are training a class of new hires on computer security. You are discussing password security, and you identify several user behaviors that indicate the use of insecure passwords. Of the following, what are some of those behaviors? (Choose two.)

    A. Using multiple passwords

    B. Being unable to remember all of your passwords

    C. Using special symbols in your passwords

    D. Having a favorite password

19. You work for a small city IT department, and one of your coworkers has forgotten the administrator password to the BIOS of a server and now can't gain access to the BIOS settings or boot the server. What options do you have that could fix this problem? (Choose three.)

    A. Use the user password if it provides access to the BIOS and will boot the server.

    B. Try the default BIOS password set by the motherboard maker.

    C. Clear the CMOS memory to reset the password to the default or to clear the BIOS passwords.

    D. Power down the server, remove all power connections to clear the BIOS memory, and then plug the server back in and power it up.

20. You work for a small city IT department and are giving a presentation on correct employee computer and network use to a group of new hires. You are currently describing various security issues in relation to the Internet and are describing a type of attack directed at a server computer by a massive number of computers for the purpose of making the services provided by that server unavailable. What are you describing?

    A. DoS

    B. DDoS

    C. Rootkit

    D. Grayware

21. You power up your computer and although the PC seems to be running, there is no image on the screen. What should you check? (Choose all that apply.)

    A. Is the monitor on?

    B. Is the monitor plugged in?

    C. Is the power supply bad?

    D. Is the video card bad?

22. You work for a small city IT department, and you are going over your network infrastructure with a new technician. You tell her that the city employees are able to collaborate using the city's intranet. How do you describe an intranet?

    A. It is a private Internet-like network owned by your organization and only accessible by employees while still allowing access to the Internet by employees.

    B. It is a private Internet-like network owned by your organization and used by the vendors from which the city purchases goods and services.

    C. It is the city's Internet access but over a dial-up WAN connection.

    D. It is the city's Internet access but over a satellite WAN connection.

23. You are discussing various Internet access methods with a business customer. Of the following, which do you say are valid Internet access technologies? (Choose three.)

    A. Fiber

    B. Satellite

    C. T-carrier

    D. VPN

24. You have installed a PCIe wireless NIC in a computer desktop in a small office environment that cannot be wired for an Ethernet network. Despite the fact that the nearest access point is well within range, the computer still receives a poor Wi-Fi signal. What can you do to improve the computer's reception?

    A. Turn up the sensitivity on the PCIe wireless NIC.

    B. Install a PCIe wireless NIC with a stronger receiver.

    C. Install an external USB wireless NIC that can have its antenna placed to get better reception.

    D. Change the entire wireless network to use an 802.11 standard that has greater range.

25. You are setting up two laptops in a small business to network wirelessly during a meeting for collaboration purposes. The computers don't have to connect to the Internet. This will be a temporary wireless connection just for this conference. What is your best and quickest option?

    A. Set up the computers to use an ad hoc wireless setup.

    B. Set up the computers to use an infrastructure wireless setup.

    C. Bring a wireless router into the room and have the laptops associate with the router.

    D. You must connect the two computers together using a crossover cable.

26. You get a call from a customer who is an avid gamer. She complains that her video output flickers and flashes and that sometimes her computer spontaneously shuts down. You suspect the problem is her computer's graphics card. What should you look for? (Choose all that apply.)

    A. A clogged or broken fan on the graphics card.

    B. The graphics card is poorly seated in the expansion slot on the motherboard.

    C. The computer's CPU is overclocked.

    D. The BIOS for the graphics card is misconfigured.

27. You are trying to install a new application on your Windows 7 computer and you receive a message saying, "This program has known compatibility issues." You want to be able to use the application you are trying to install. How can you solve this problem?

    A. Click Check For Solutions Online and see if Windows can find a solution that will allow you to successfully install the program.

    B. Click Run Program to install the application and then, after it is installed, update the drivers for the application.

    C. Click Cancel and then install the application anyway.

    D. Run Windows Update to install the latest patches issued from Microsoft in order to repair the compatibility issue.

28. You get a call from a customer who has started his Windows XP computer this morning and received an "NTLDR is missing" error message. You go over to his office to troubleshoot the problem. What should you check for? (Choose all that apply.)

    A. Check the BIOS and see if the computer is trying to load Windows from a drive that does not contain the operating system.

    B. The master boot record may be the problem. Enter the Windows XP Recovery Console and use the fixmbr utility to repair it.

    C. If the NTLDR and ntdetect.com files are corrupt or missing, you will have to replace them using the Windows XP installation disc.

    D. Check the BOOTMGR file to see if it is damaged. If it is, you'll need to use Startup Repair to fix it.

29. You have a customer who says her Windows 7 computer is having difficulties upon startup, but the operating system will load. You want to run a diagnostic startup routine where only basic devices and services are used. You configure this tool in the GUI and then reboot the computer. What utility are you using?

    A. MSCONFIG

    B. Recovery Console

    C. REGEDIT

    D. Windows 7 installation disc

30. You are partitioning a Windows 7 computer and you want to make a partition bootable. What specific partition type (as opposed to a disk type) can you make bootable?

    A. Dynamic

    B. Basic

    C. Primary

    D. Extended

    E. Logical

31. You want to take a quick look at the hosts running on your local network using the command line. Of the following, which command with the switch "view" (such as "command" view) will let you do this?

    A. nbtstat

    B. net

    C. netstat

    D. nslookup

32. You are trying to look at the "help" information for various operating system–related command-line tools before using them to work on a Windows 7 computer. Of the following, which command will return a message stating that it is "not recognized as an internal or external command, operable program or batch file"?

   A. shutdown /?

   B. del /?

   C. diskpart /?

   D. /? /?

33. You are performing a number of administrative tasks on a Windows 7 computer using various utilities. Which of the following requires that you restart the computer before it will run?

   A. Local security policy

   B. Performance monitor

   C. Services

   D. Windows memory diagnostics

34. You are on a Windows 7 computer in the Computer Management utility attempting to perform some diagnostic and repair tasks. When you expand the System Tools tree, which of the following do you find?

   A. System configuration

   B. Task scheduler

   C. Component services

   D. Data sources

35. You are on a Windows 7 computer attempting to perform some diagnostic and repair tasks. You have Administrative Tools open. Of the following, which utilities do you see? (Choose all that apply.)

   A. Advanced Security

   B. Device Manager

   C. Print Management

   D. Windows Firewall

36. You have just added a second hard disk to a Windows 7 computer to increase the amount of data the PC can store. You have started the PC, clicked Start, and then clicked Computer, but you don't see the new drive. Where else can you look for it?

   A. In Administrative Tools

   B. In Computer Management

   C. In Control Panel

   D. In Disk Management

37. You have just physically added a basic disk to a Windows 7 computer that was previously in another Windows 7 PC. It is already partitioned and formatted. You've powered up the PC, and it recognizes the new hardware. Of the following, what will you have to do in Disk Management?

- **A.** Add a disk.
- **B.** Add the disk to a disk array.
- **C.** Initialize the disk.
- **D.** Make it online.

38. You are responsible for a desktop PC migration project in which 300 people in a department where you work are getting new Windows 7 computers. You want to migrate all of their data as well as the user profiles that exist on the old computers. Which tool should you use for this job?

- **A.** Windows Easy Transfer Wizard
- **B.** User State Migration Tool (USMT)
- **C.** Preboot Execution Environment (PXE) Tool
- **D.** File Transfer Protocol (FTP) Tool

39. You are performing routine maintenance on a Windows 7 computer. In the search box, you type MSTSC and press ENTER. What happens?

- **A.** The Remote Desktop Connection utility opens.
- **B.** A console window for Microsoft Management Console opens.
- **C.** The Services utility opens.
- **D.** A command-line window opens with administrator rights.

40. You are in the MSCONFIG tool and you want to select and launch the Event Viewer. What tab must you be on?

- **A.** General
- **B.** Services
- **C.** Startup
- **D.** Tools

41. You are attempting to diagnose a problem with a customer's PC that spontaneously reboots. You suspect an overheating problem. Of the following, what are some possible causes of a computer overheating? (Choose all that apply.)

- **A.** Internal dust contamination
- **B.** Case fans underperforming
- **C.** Power supply fan failure
- **D.** RAM stick overheating

42. You have a customer who has just called you because his Windows XP computer has just experienced the "Blue Screen of Death" (BSOD), which is otherwise known as a STOP error.

As you are talking to him, you try to find out what the user may have been doing to cause this error. Of the following, what are some likely causes? (Choose all that apply.)

A. Installing a new piece of hardware

B. Updating a device driver

C. Using System Restore

D. Filling up the hard drive's primary partition

43. You get a call from a customer who says that when she pressed the power button on her gaming PC to turn it on this morning, she saw a brief flash of light and then smoke came out of the computer. Given these symptoms, what is the most likely cause?

A. CPU

B. Motherboard

C. Power supply fan

D. RAM stick

44. You get a call from a customer who says he tried to turn on his Windows Vista computer this morning and received a "No OS Found" message. He's had the computer for several years and it has always worked fine up until this point. What could be some possible causes of this error? (Choose all that apply.)

A. Corrupt boot manager.

B. Faulty motherboard chipset.

C. General hard drive failure.

D. This was a bug with early editions of Windows Vista and was corrected in SP1.

45. You have just completed building a PC for a customer and are testing it. You press the power button and hear the CPU fan spin up, but nothing else turns on. You suspect the computer isn't getting enough electricity to power all of its components and allow it to boot. Of the following what tools can you use to see if this is true? (Choose all that apply.)

A. Loopback plug

B. Multimeter

C. POST card

D. Power supply tester

46. You have been working on a spare PC and have added two more drives. You have configured the computer to use a RAID array, but when you boot the computer, you get an error message saying, "RAID not found." What could be the problem? (Choose all that apply.)

A. Bad RAID controller card

B. Damaged hard disk data cable

C. Power supply produces insufficient current to power the RAID array

D. RAID type not specified in the BIOS

47. You are installing a Bluetooth device for pairing on a Windows 7 computer so they will be able to communicate with each other. The Windows 7 computer also uses a Wi-Fi connection to communicate with the rest of the computers in your home network. What will you need to do to successfully set up the Bluetooth device?

A. You must disable Wi-Fi on the computer since Wi-Fi and Bluetooth are incompatible.

B. You must plug the Bluetooth device into the Bluetooth adapter on the computer.

C. You must enter a passkey during the installation process if prompted.

D. You must open the Device Pairing Wizard using the Search box.

48. You want to sync your MP3 player with Media Player in your Windows 7 desktop computer. You connect the MP3 player to your computer using a cable attached to one of the computer's USB ports. What action must you perform on the MP3 player?

A. Make the device discoverable.

B. Open Windows Media Player.

C. Give the device a name on the Device Setup screen.

D. Automatically select an optimal sync method.

49. You are setting up your new mobile phone to use e-mail. In configuring the incoming mail server information, you configure the phone to use a POP server without SSL. What port number do you use?

A. 110

B. 143

C. 993

D. 995

50. You are setting up your Windows 7 phone to send and receive e-mails from your Gmail account. What are the correct steps to configure your phone to use Gmail? (Choose all that apply.)

A. On the Start screen, open the Settings list and then select Applications.

B. Select Add An Account and then use the Gmail option.

C. Enter your Gmail e-mail address in the Email Address box.

D. Select Sign In as the last step in the process.

QUICK ANSWER KEY

1.	A	18.	B, D	35.	A, C, D
2.	B, C, D	19.	A, B, C	36.	D
3.	C	20.	B	37.	D
4.	B	21.	A, B, D	38.	B
5.	D	22.	A	39.	A
6.	C	23.	A, B, C	40.	D
7.	C	24.	C	41.	A, B
8.	A	25.	A	42.	A, B, D
9.	C	26.	A, C	43.	A
10.	D	27.	A	44.	B, C
11.	A, C, D	28.	A, B, C	45.	B, D
12.	A, D	29.	A	46.	A, B, D
13.	B	30.	C	47.	C
14.	C	31.	B	48.	A
15.	B	32.	D	49.	A
16.	B	33.	D	50.	C, D
17.	A	34.	B		

IN-DEPTH ANSWERS

1. ☑ **A.** You allow incoming and outgoing traffic on port 25, which is SMTP and used for outgoing e-mail; ports 110 and 143, which are POP3 and IMAP and used for incoming e-mail; and port 80, which is HTTP and used for Web connections. You block port 1863, which is used for .NET Messenger Service, and you set the firewall to filter incoming TCP packets on port 23, which is used for telnet.

   ☒ **B, C,** and **D** are incorrect. **B** is incorrect because this configuration would block incoming Web traffic and allow unrestricted telnet connections. **C** is incorrect because it would allow unrestricted telnet connections and block incoming POP3 e-mails. **D** is incorrect because it would allow unrestricted telnet connections and block incoming IMAP e-mail.

2. ☑ **B, C,** and **D.** IPCONFIG is a command-line utility used to display network configuration information about a computer and to refresh dynamic addressing. PING is a command-line utility used to test network connectivity with a remote host. NETSTAT is a command-line tool that displays network connections, routing tables, and a number of network interface statistics.

   ☒ **A** is incorrect because DIR is a command used at the command prompt to list the names and characteristics of directories in the current working directory on a computer.

3. ☑ **C.** A UPS, or uninterruptible power supply, is a device that stores power in an onboard battery that will provide electricity for any machine plugged into the UPS when main power fails. This will let your customer gracefully shut down all his equipment. It won't necessarily stop the network connections from being dropped, but it will prevent data corruption.

   ☒ **A, B,** and **D** are incorrect. **A** is incorrect because a power strip has no ability to provide electricity in a power outage. **B** is incorrect because a surge protector, while preventing power surges, doesn't have an onboard battery. **D** is incorrect because wiring a car battery to your network equipment either won't work or will provide a dangerous environment.

4. ☑ **B.** The tool shown is a cable tester, used to verify connectivity from one end of a cable to the other.

   ☒ **A, C,** and **D** are incorrect. **A** is incorrect because a punchdown tool is used to make connections in wiring closets and has blades. **C** is incorrect because a loopback plug is used to connect a NIC and is a single-piece component. **D** is incorrect because a studfinder is used in construction and is a single piece.

5. ☑ **D.** A loose network cable is often the cause of intermittent connectivity problems.

   ☒ **A, B,** and **C** are incorrect. **A** and **B** are incorrect because Ethernet networks do not use wireless components. **C** is incorrect because a disconnected cable would cause complete, rather than intermittent, connectivity loss.

6. ☑ **C.** Tailgating is the greatest risk in this environment. In a tailgating attack, the intruder either asks a valid employee to hold the door for the attacker or grabs the door before it shuts fully.

☒ **A, B,** and **D** are incorrect. **A** is incorrect because the doors lock automatically. **B** is incorrect because phishing attacks normally target information, rather than physical access. **D** is incorrect because fake ID badges may be used to impersonate an individual, but it is unlikely that an intruder could create a fake badge that would work in a lock.

7. ☑ **C.** Unneeded documents containing sensitive information should always be destroyed with a cross-cut shredder that makes it very difficult to reassemble the pieces.

☒ **A, B,** and **D** are incorrect. **A** is incorrect because you should not send documents containing sensitive information to a recycling facility without first cross-cut shredding them. **B** is incorrect because you should destroy, rather than retain, unneeded sensitive documents. **D** is incorrect because degaussing removes sensitive information from magnetic media, but is not effective against physical documents.

8. ☑ **A.** The principle of least privilege states that an individual should have only the access necessary to perform his or her job functions. This should be a design principle for all access control systems.

☒ **B, C,** and **D** are incorrect. **B** is incorrect because two-person control is an extremely burdensome security requirement and should only be used in the most sensitive situations, not for general-purpose access to business files. **C** is incorrect because security through obscurity involves relying upon the secrecy of the security mechanism and is not good practice. **D** is incorrect because separation of duties applies to privileges to perform operations and not file access.

9. ☑ **C.** Generally speaking, in an office productivity environment, end users should not have the ability to install software on their computers. This privilege should be reserved for system administrators.

☒ **A, B,** and **D** are incorrect because the ability to read and write files, change the desktop background, and log in from the desktop are reasonable activities for a typical end user.

10. ☑ **D.** The Guest account allows temporary use of a computer by a guest user and should generally not be turned on in a business environment.

☒ **A, B,** and **C** are incorrect. **A** is incorrect because security logging should always be enabled. **B** is incorrect because inbound connections are not normally needed on an end-user computer. **C** is incorrect because the local administrator account is needed for system administrator access to the computer.

11. ☑ **A, C,** and **D.** You should use BIOS security to make sure anyone with physical access to the servers cannot make changes to the BIOS of the servers that would allow a malicious attack. Give the BIOS passwords only to authorized personnel. All servers should have the latest antivirus software installed with updated definitions to prevent infection by malicious software designed to compromise these machines. Often, physical security of servers is ignored. Even if you lock down your server system from remote attacks, the simplest way to take down your system is to go into the server room and start a fire. Lock the server room, use an alarm system, and make sure only authorized personnel have the keys and alarm codes.

☒ **B** is incorrect because a phishing scam will not have an impact on server security; a phishing scam requires a person to respond to a hoax e-mail message or bogus Website.

12. ☑ **A and D.** This isn't a perfect solution, but sometimes you must constructively assist business customers who refuse to comply with company security standards through administrative channels. While having the screensaver lock the computer isn't a perfect solution, it does apply some form of security should the user leave the computer while logged in. Additionally, if this is an Active Directory domain, you can use Group Policies to force the computer to lock the desktop if the computer is inactive for a certain period of time.

☒ **B and C are incorrect. B** is incorrect because it is not your role in the business place to manage or supervise customers in personnel matters. Always go through channels, asking your supervisor to speak to his or her counterpart who does have the responsibility to manage the customer in question. **C** is incorrect because, while the screensaver may become active, all anyone has to do is move the mouse to gain access to the desktop.

13. ☑ **B.** Go into Control Panel in Classic view and open the Phone and Modem Options applet to view and modify the dialing rules for the computer and make sure they are not misconfigured. For instance, a home user will not need to dial "9" to get out of the local phone system before connecting to a public phone line.

☒ **A, C,** and **D** are incorrect. **A** is incorrect because this will allow you to edit the LAN settings and Internet Protocol properties, but not modify the dialing settings. **C** is incorrect because Windows Firewall contains no method of managing dialing settings. **D** is incorrect because this is not a wireless networking issue.

14. ☑ **C.** When you right-click Local Area Connections and click Status, the Local Area Connection Status dialog box appears, and on the General tab, you can see how much data has been sent and received in the Activity area.

☒ **A, B,** and **D** are incorrect. **A** is incorrect because right-clicking Network Connections only gives you options to open the applet, explore, or create a shortcut. **B** is incorrect because clicking Properties opens the Local Area Connections Properties dialog box, not the Status dialog box. **D** is incorrect because there is no Status tab in the Internet Properties dialog box.

15. ☑ **B.** The best solution to this problem is to create a permanent mapped drive on the workstation that accesses the needed location on the server.

☒ **A, C,** and **D** are incorrect. **A** is incorrect because defragmenting the disk may improve file access speed but will not reduce the amount of time needed to connect to the server. **C** is incorrect because using a shortcut key will reduce the typing time but is still a cumbersome process. **D** is incorrect because the mapped drive shortcut must be created on the desktop, not the server.

16. ☑ **B.** You can reveal the presence of hidden files using the Folder Options section of the Appearance and Personalization control panel in Windows Vista.
☒ **A, C,** and **D** are incorrect. **A** and **C** are incorrect because the file will not appear in the output of DIR or Windows Explorer. **D** is incorrect because you do not need to delete and re-create the file to make it visible.

17. ☑ **A.** Beth will be able to access the file because the explicit allow permission for that file overrides the inherited deny permission.
☒ **B, C,** and **D** are incorrect because explicit permissions always override inherited permissions.

18. ☑ **B** and **D.** While using multiple passwords is a good idea, having too many to remember is a problem, since this will inhibit your ability to quickly authenticate. This may also prompt you to write down passwords to remember them, which is a major security "no-no." If you have a favorite password, you probably use it with all of the computer, Web, and other accounts on which you authenticate. If someone discovers this one password, they can compromise every system on which you require security.
☒ **A** and **C** are incorrect. **A** is incorrect because having multiple passwords, as long as you can remember them, prevents a large-scale security breach. If one of your passwords is discovered, only part of your system of security is compromised. **C** is incorrect because using special symbols in your password, such as $, #, and @, makes it more difficult for password-cracking programs, such as a dictionary attack, to discover your password.

19. ☑ **A, B,** and **C.** In some BIOS password configurations, you can set a user password and an administrator password. Sometimes the user password lets the computer boot but won't let you in the BIOS setup, but on other occasions, the user password will do both. The purpose of an administrator password, then, is to have a single administrator's password for the BIOS of all computers or servers in your infrastructure and let you set different BIOS user passwords on each computer to be used by the individuals directly responsible for those machines. If you forget the required BIOS password, sometimes the default BIOS password set at the factory will still work. If not, you can remove the CMOS battery to clear the memory, which will either reset the BIOS password to the factory default password or completely clear the BIOS passwords so that you can enter the BIOS setup without one.
☒ **D** is incorrect because powering down the machine won't clear the CMOS memory or BIOS password.

20. ☑ **B.** A distributed denial-of-service (DDoS) attack is one in which a vast number of compromised computers are directed to request services or otherwise communicate with a specific server at the same time for the purpose of making that server and its services unavailable. Often, the owners of the computers used in this type of attack are unaware that their computers have been compromised and are being used by a malicious person for this purpose.

    ☒ **A, C,** and **D** are incorrect. **A** is incorrect because a denial-of-service (DoS) attack, while similar in nature, uses a small number of compromised computers (often one) to perform the same task. **C** is incorrect because a rootkit is malware installed on a computer that conceals its presence and performs such tasks as allowing a "back door" to be created on the computer to be accessed by the person who covertly installed the rootkit. **D** is incorrect because grayware is a generic term for many different types of malware that aren't specifically designed to harm a computer, such as adware, spyware, and spam.

21. ☑ **A, B,** and **D.** The most common problem causing a blank monitor when everything else seems to be okay is either the monitor switch is turned off or one of the cables is unplugged or bad. If the monitor is getting power but not receiving a signal, the power button on the monitor should glow amber. If it's not getting power, the power button will be dark. Check the power and monitor cables to make sure they're secure. It's also possible the video card in the computer is faulty. You can also unplug the monitor from the computer and turn it on to see what the monitor's self-check routine reveals.

    ☒ **C** is incorrect because if the power supply was bad, it would affect more than just the monitor. Chances are, the computer wouldn't start at all or it would start and then periodically reboot.

22. ☑ **A.** An intranet is a private organization's network, which can be composed of Web servers, file and print servers, and other resources that can only be accessed by company employees for internal collaboration and information sharing. Typically, you can access the Internet from an intranet, but external Internet users cannot access the company's intranet.

    ☒ **B, C,** and **D** are incorrect. **B** is incorrect because this more accurately describes an "extranet," which is a Web interface between an organization and vendors of goods and services. **C** and **D** are incorrect because an intranet is not specified by the method of its Internet connection.

23. ☑ **A, B,** and **C.** Fiber connections are now available for home and small business customers, making speeds of more than 100 Mbps available. Satellite is also available for homes and small businesses, but at more modest speeds than fiber. T-carrier is typically used only by business customers and is offered as full T-1 or partial T-1 plans. A full T-1 circuit offers data, voice, and digital speeds of 1.544 Mbps.

    ☒ **D** is incorrect because a virtual private network (VPN) is a method of creating a virtual private connection between two nodes by encrypting traffic over the public Internet.

24. ☑ **C.** Internal wireless NICs have the antenna directly connected to the NIC so that it sits at the back of the computer. This might not be the ideal location to receive Wi-Fi

signals, even if the computer is within range otherwise. Using a USB wireless NIC with an external antenna that can be moved for better reception is a more workable option.

☒ **A, B,** and **D** are incorrect. **A** is incorrect because the wireless NIC doesn't have sensitivity controls. **B** is incorrect because even if you are able to find such a device, it may still not receive an adequate signal due to the location of the PC. **D** is incorrect because, while this might help, changing the entire network for the sake of one computer will result in increased costs of money and time.

25. ☑ **A.** You can quickly set two computers to network wirelessly using ad hoc mode, which allows them to communicate directly with each other without the presence of a wireless router or access point. This is the best option for a quick and temporary wireless solution.

☒ **B, C,** and **D** are incorrect. **B** is incorrect because infrastructure mode requires the presence of wireless devices such as a router or access point to mediate the wireless communication between the two computers and would take more time to set up. **C** is incorrect because this also describes an infrastructure setup. **D** is incorrect because there is a wireless solution to this situation and you don't have to resort to an Ethernet crossover cable to make the connection.

26. ☑ **A** and **C.** The most obvious cause of an overheating graphics card is a clogged or broken cooling fan; however, an overclocked CPU can overwork a graphics card, causing it to overheat, and gamers often overclock their CPUs to improve performance.

☒ **B** and **D** are incorrect. **B** is incorrect because if the graphics card were improperly seated in the expansion slot, chances are it wouldn't work at all. **D** is incorrect because if there was a problem in the BIOS, the card would not work or would not work correctly, but it wouldn't overheat.

27. ☑ **A.** The best solution for this problem is to click the Check For Solutions Online button in the Program Compatibility Assistant dialog box. Windows will check to see if there is an online solution to this problem. If it exists, follow the instructions provided to install the application.

☒ **B, C,** and **D** are incorrect. **B** is incorrect because clicking Run Program will not fix the compatibility problem, and generally, a software application does not have drivers to update. The best you could hope for would be to find a newer version of the application that is compatible with Windows 7. **C** is incorrect because pressing Cancel and proceeding to install the application will not fix the compatibility problem. The installed program is not likely to work. **D** is incorrect because there is no guarantee that installing the latest patches from Microsoft will fix the compatibility problem.

28. ☑ **A, B,** and **C.** There are a number of reasons why your customer may be receiving this message. NTLDR is the boot loader for Windows XP and is used to load the operating system from disk. If the computer is trying to find NTLDR on a disk that doesn't include the operating system, such as the wrong hard disk or an optical disc, the error will occur. Problems with the master boot record, NTLDR, or ntdetect.com can also result in this error message.

☒ **D** is incorrect because the BOOTMGR file is used by Windows Vista and Windows 7 to load the operating system, but not Windows XP.

29. ☑ **A.** Launch MSCONFIG in Windows 7 and on the General tab, select Diagnostic Startup, click OK, and reboot the computer. Windows 7 will reboot and load only basic device drivers and services, allowing you to diagnose startup problems.
☒ **B, C,** and **D** are incorrect. **B** is incorrect because this is a utility run in Windows XP and is not available in Windows 7. **C** is incorrect because REGEDIT is a utility used to edit the Windows registry, which contains all of the configuration settings for the system. **D** is incorrect because, while the Windows 7 installation disc contains options that let you repair Windows, you can't use it directly from the GUI, and MSCONFIG will let you perform a diagnostic startup as described.

30. ☑ **C.** A primary partition on a basic disk is required for the disk to be bootable.
☒ **A, B, D,** and **E** are incorrect. **A** is incorrect because a dynamic disk is not a partition type, but a type of disk that can be used to create volumes that span multiple disks. Like basic disks, they can use partition styles that can be made bootable, but the disk itself is not a specific partition type that is bootable. **B** is incorrect because, while a basic disk can contain a primary partition that is bootable, the disk itself isn't considered a partition. **D** and **E** are incorrect because these partition types cannot be made bootable.

31. ☑ **B.** The net command is used for network management, such as managing network users, shares, and print jobs. The net view command will let you see which servers and computers are currently active on the local network.
☒ **A, C,** and **D** are incorrect. **A** is incorrect because nbtstat is used to troubleshoot NetBIOS to name resolution problems and does not work with the "view" switch. **C** is incorrect because netstat lets you view network connections, but not all network hosts active on the local network. It also does not work when used with the "view" switch. **D** is incorrect because nslookup is a command-line utility used for acquiring a domain name or IP address mapping by querying the Domain Name System (DNS). It also does not work with the "view" switch.

32. ☑ **D.** The switch /? is only meant to be used to request help information on other commands, but you cannot use it to request help data on the /? switch itself. Doing so returns an error message.
☒ **A, B,** and **C** are incorrect because each of these commands used with the /? switch will return a short description of the command and the various switches that the command uses.

33. ☑ **D.** When Windows detects a problem with the memory on the computer, it will display a notification window prompting you to click Restart. Once you do, the Memory Diagnostics Tool will run and perform a check on the computer's memory. If the tool detects problems, the information will be displayed, but the tool will not attempt to fix the memory problems.

☒ **A, B,** and **C** are incorrect. **A** is incorrect because you can open the local security policy tool from Administrative Tools in Control Panel, but only on Windows 7 Professional, Ultimate, and Enterprise editions. **B** and **C** are incorrect because you can access Performance Monitor and Services from Administrative Tools in Control Panel.

34. ☑ **B.** Only Task Scheduler can be found in Computer Management under the System Tools tree. Other items found in that tree are Event Viewer, Shared Folders, Local Users and Groups, and Performance.
☒ **A, C,** and **D** are incorrect. **A** is incorrect because System Configuration is found in Control Panel. **C** and **D** are incorrect because Component Services and Data Sources are found in Administrative Tools.

35. ☑ **A, C,** and **D.** Windows Firewall with Advanced Security and Print Management are present in Administrative Tools.
☒ **B** is incorrect because Device Manager is found within Computer Management.

36. ☑ **D.** If you cannot see the new disk in Computer, go into Control Panel, open Administrative Tools, open Computer Management, and then open Disk Management. The new drive should be visible there, but you may have to format the disk before you can use it.
☒ **A, B,** and **C** are incorrect. **A** is incorrect because once in Administrative Tools, you have to open Computer Management and then Disk Management. **B** is incorrect because once in Computer Management, you have to open Disk Management. **C** is incorrect because once in Control Panel, you have to open Administrative Tools, then Computer Management, and then Disk Management.

37. ☑ **D.** After physically adding the disk, it will appear in Disk Management as offline. Right-click the disk in Disk Management and click Online.
☒ **A, B,** and **C** are incorrect. **A** is incorrect because the disk will already appear in Disk Management and can be used immediately once it is made online. **B** is incorrect because only a dynamic disk can be added to an array. **C** is incorrect because the disk has already been partitioned and formatted and can be used without being initialized. If the disk has never been used before, it would need to be initialized.

38. ☑ **B.** The User State Migration Tool (USMT) is a command-line utility designed to facilitate large-scale computer migrations from older to newer Windows computers, and allows the transfer of files, directories, and settings between computers. It is recommended for advanced IT professionals only, as it requires a great deal of experience with scripting language.
☒ **A, C,** and **D** are incorrect. **A** is incorrect because the Easy Transfer Wizard is used only for much smaller computer migrations by home or small business users. **C** is incorrect because PXE is a method of booting a computer over the network and can be used to install an operating system remotely. **D** is incorrect because FTP is a file transfer protocol used to move large files across networks, but it cannot facilitate PC data and profile migration.

39. ☑ **A.** MSTSC is the run-line command for the Remote Desktop Connection tool, which lets you connect to a computer across the network and allows you to control and manage other computers.

☒ **B, C,** and **D** are incorrect. **B** is incorrect because the Microsoft Management Console is a framework for managing MMC snap-ins to perform multiple computer management tasks. It is opened by the run-line command MMC. **C** is incorrect because the Services window allows you to see, start, stop, and otherwise configure the services available on the computer. It is opened with the run-line command SERVICES.MSC. **D** is incorrect because the command-line window is opened with the run-line command CMD.

40. ☑ **D.** On the Tools tab, scroll down the list of tools until you find Event Viewer. Select it and click the Launch button.

☒ **A, B,** and **C** are incorrect. **A** is incorrect because the General tab lets you choose a startup method, such as Normal Startup, Diagnostic Startup, or Selective Startup. **B** is incorrect because the Services tab allows you to select services and enable or disable them, but not to launch utilities. **C** is incorrect because the Startup tab lets you select which services are enabled when the computer starts.

41. ☑ **A and B.** Too much dust collecting inside the PC case could limit airflow, resulting in overheating. Also, if the case fan is slow, it may not be dissipating heat from inside the machine.

☒ **C and D** are incorrect. **C** is incorrect because a power supply fan failure would result in the power supply failing, so the computer would shut down and not restart. **D** is incorrect because RAM modules would not heat to such an extent that it would cause the entire computer to overheat and reboot.

42. ☑ **A, B,** and **D.** There are numerous events and activities that can cause a BSOD to occur. Installing a new device or updating device drivers are common causes. Also, if the primary partition used for the Windows operating system has less than 15 percent free space, data corruption can occur, which may result in a BSOD error.

☒ **C** is incorrect because using System Restore is unlikely to cause a BSOD and in fact, is one of the methods that can sometimes recover a Windows computer after a BSOD, if the computer can reboot into Windows after the error.

43. ☑ **A.** The most likely cause given these symptoms is the CPU. CPUs often heat to the point of burning if they are used for processing-intensive activities such as gaming. The CPU was probably already damaged the last time the computer was used. When the customer powered it up this morning and the first surge of power hit the CPU, it burned, emitting smoke. Time to replace the CPU and hope the heat and the smoke didn't damage other motherboard components.

☒ **B, C,** and **D** are incorrect. **B** is incorrect because the entire motherboard and all its components wouldn't spontaneously burn causing these symptoms. The most likely culprits are the CPU and possibly the graphics card. **C** is incorrect because fans do not emit smoke, although they may blow smoke out of a PC from a burning component. **D** is incorrect because RAM sticks do not heat to the point of burning.

44. ☑ **B** and **C.** On occasion the Southbridge chipset on a computer's motherboard can result in multiple bad read and write operations that shift data in the boot sector, resulting in this error. Much more commonly, this type of problem is caused by a mechanical failure of the hard drive containing the boot sector.

    ☒ **A** and **D** are incorrect. **A** is incorrect because a corrupt boot manager problem will result in an error message saying, "Boot manager corrupt or missing." **D** is incorrect because this type of error is not common in Windows Vista.

45. ☑ **B** and **D.** Given the symptoms and what you suspect, you can use a multimeter or power supply tester to determine if the computer's power supply is putting out enough current to power the PC. It's possible the power supply is too small or that it's faulty.

    ☒ **A** and **C** are incorrect. **A** is incorrect because this device is used to test circuits or network connections and to determine if signals are being sent across the link. **C** is incorrect because a POST card is used to display any error codes that are displayed during the POST (Power On/Self Test) portion of a computer's startup routine. In this case, the computer isn't even getting that far.

46. ☑ **A, B,** and **D.** There are any number of possible causes for this error message. The RAID controller card could be bad. Try switching it for a known good card. The data cable from one of the disks could be bad. Switch it for a known good cable and test. Also, since this computer is being configured to use a RAID array for the first time, you'll need to set the BIOS to use the desired RAID array. Check the BIOS to see if that is the problem.

    ☒ **C** is incorrect because if the power supply were faulty or insufficient, chances are the computer wouldn't even start.

47. ☑ **C.** If prompted during the installation process, you must enter a passkey for the device. The default passkey for many Bluetooth devices is 0000, but consult the device's documentation to verify the correct passkey for the device you are installing.

    ☒ **A, B,** and **D** are incorrect. **A** is incorrect because Wi-Fi and Bluetooth are compatible when operating on the same computer. **B** is incorrect because a Bluetooth device can be connected to a computer using a USB port. **D** is incorrect because you can launch the wizard by going to Devices and Printers and then clicking Add A Device.

48. ☑ **A.** After connecting the MP3 device to the computer, you must turn the device on and make it discoverable so Windows can "see" and connect to the device. Consult the MP3 device's documentation to see how to make it discoverable.

    ☒ **B, C,** and **D** are incorrect because you must open Windows Media Player on the Windows 7 machine, and when adding the device in Windows, you must give it a name and let Windows automatically choose the optimal method for syncing.

49. ☑ **A.** To set up a phone to use an incoming mail server for POP without SSL for security, you must use port number 110.

☒ **B, C,** and **D** are incorrect. **B** is incorrect because port number 143 is used if the incoming mail server is using IMAP without SSL. **C** is incorrect because port number 993 is used if the incoming mail server is using IMAP with SSL. **D** is incorrect because port number 995 is used if the incoming mail server is using POP (or POP3) with TLS/SSL.

50. ☑ **C** and **D.** During the setup process, you must enter the e-mail address of your Gmail account and the password associated with that address. The last step is to click Sign In to make sure you can access your Gmail account from the phone.

☒ **A** and **B** are incorrect. **A** is incorrect because you must open the Applications list and then click Settings. **B** is incorrect because after you click Add An Account you must use the Google option. There is no Gmail option.

ANALYZING YOUR RESULTS

Congratulations on completing the 220-802 pre-assessment. You should now take the time to analyze your results with two objectives in mind:

- Identifying the resources you should use to prepare for the 220-802 exam
- Identifying the specific topics that you should focus on in your preparation

First, use this table to help you gauge your overall readiness for the 220-802 examination:

Number of Answers Correct	Recommended Course of Study
1–25	If this had been the actual exam, you probably would not have passed. We recommend that you spend a significant amount of time reviewing the material in the *CompTIA A+® Certification Study Guide, Eighth Edition (Exams 220-801 & 220-802)* before using this book.
26–37	If this had been the actual 220-802 exam, you might have passed, but there is a significant risk that you would not. You should review the following objective map to identify the particular areas that require your focused attention and use the *CompTIA A+® Certification Study Guide, Eighth Edition (Exams 220-801 & 220-802)* to review that material. Once you have done so, you should proceed to work through the questions in this book.
38–50	Congratulations! If this was the actual 220-802 exam, it is likely that you would have passed. You should use this book to refresh your knowledge and prepare yourself mentally for the actual exam.

Once you have identified your readiness for the exam, you may use this table to identify the specific objectives that require your focus as you continue your preparation.

Domain	Weight	Objective	Chapter(s)	Question Number in Pretest
1.0 OS	33%	1.1 Compare and contrast the features and requirements of various Microsoft operating systems	2, 10	36
		1.2 Given a scenario, install and configure the operating system using the most appropriate method	9, 10	30
		1.3 Given a scenario, use appropriate command-line tools	10, 13	2, 31, 32
		1.4 Given a scenario, use appropriate operating system features and tools	9, 13	33, 34, 35, 37, 38, 39, 40
		1.6 Set up and configure Windows networking on a client/desktop	19	13, 22, 23, 25
2.0 Security	22%	2.1 Apply and use common prevention methods	17	1, 6, 8, 11, 12, 17
		2.2 Compare and contrast common security threats	App B	20
		2.3 Implement security best practices to secure a workstation	18	9, 10
		2.4 Given a scenario, use the appropriate data destruction/disposal method	17	7
3.0 Mobile Devices	9%	3.2 Establish basic network connectivity and configure e-mail	20	47, 49, 50
		3.5 Execute and configure mobile device synchronization	20	48
4.0 Troubleshooting	36%	4.2 Given a scenario, troubleshoot common problems related to motherboards, RAM, CPU, and power with appropriate tools	11	3, 41, 42, 43, 45
		4.3 Given a scenario, troubleshoot hard drives and RAID arrays with appropriate tools	11	44, 46
		4.4 Given a scenario, troubleshoot common video and display issues	11	26
		4.5 Given a scenario, troubleshoot wired and wireless networks with appropriate tools	16	4, 5, 14, 15, 16, 24
		4.6 Given a scenario, troubleshoot operating system problems with appropriate tools	13	27, 28, 29

C

Practice
Exam 220-801

QUESTIONS

1. You are replacing a failing CPU heat sink and fan assembly on a customer's laptop. What should you have available when you perform this task? (Choose two.)
   A. A can of compressed air
   B. A soldering iron
   C. Thermal paste
   D. A driver disc

2. A customer complains that he gets no image on the display screen when he opens his laptop lid and turns on the power. The power indicator light is on and he can hear the cooling fan working, so he knows the unit is getting electricity. How do you test the video problem? (Choose three.)
   A. Check the LCD lid close switch.
   B. Attach an external monitor to the VGA port on the laptop.
   C. Check the FN key.
   D. Reseat the laptop battery.

3. You have a customer who says that the keyboard on his laptop has stopped working. You check the laptop and the keyboard appears to be completely dead. Of the following, what troubleshooting methods can you use to investigate the problem? (Choose three.)
   A. Plug an external USB keyboard into the laptop and see if it works.
   B. Check Device Manager and see if any keyboard error messages appear.
   C. Open the laptop and check the keyboard power cable connection.
   D. Open the laptop and check the keyboard data cable connection.

4. You are preparing to install a new DVD drive in a customer's laptop. What should you do to prepare for this task? (Choose two.)
   A. Power down the laptop.
   B. Remove the laptop's battery.
   C. Remove the motherboard.
   D. Place the laptop in an antistatic bag.

5. You get a call from a customer saying that his laptop won't hold a charge, and he asks you if the problem is the battery. Of the following, what do you say could be potential problems? (Choose three.)
   A. The battery could be faulty.
   B. The power cord could be faulty.
   C. The power converter could be faulty.
   D. The motherboard could be faulty.

6. You are installing a device in a customer's laptop and he hands you the device that he purchased. It appears similar to the drawing shown here. What type of card is this?

   A. PCMCIA

   B. ExpressCard/34

   C. ExpressCard/54

   D. CardBus

7. A user walks into your office and hands you a memory card similar to the one shown in the following illustration. She informs you that it contains photos from a recent sales call and that she would like you to put them on the shared file server. What type of memory card is this?

   A. CompactFlash

   B. SD

   C. Memory Stick

   D. MiniSD

8. You are speaking with a user who notes that she is having difficulty using her laptop on airplanes. She notes that the brightness of the screen disturbs those next to her and she has difficulty seeing the keyboard. What laptop features can address these issues? (Choose two.)

   A. Privacy filter

   B. Keyboard backlight

   C. Screen brightness

   D. Bluetooth

9. Your boss recently purchased a Bluetooth headset that is labeled as a Class 1 Bluetooth device. How far should she expect to be able to stray from her computer and still use the device?

   A. 1 meter

   B. 10 meters

   C. 25 meters

   D. 100 meters

10. You are teaching a new user how to control the volume settings on his Windows 7 laptop computer. What options do you suggest? (Choose two.)

   A. Use the Windows volume control.

   B. Use the keyboard volume shortcuts.

   C. Adjust the volume on the laptop's sound card.

   D. Adjust the volume using the volume knob on the speakers.

11. You get a call from a rural customer who uses dial-up as an Internet connection because no other service is available in her area. She wants to know if there is any way to get a faster data speed than 56k. What do you tell her?

    A. You tell her that even with a 56k modem, she likely gets only 40–50k throughput, on average and there's absolutely no way to provide a faster data speed using dial-up.

    B. You tell her that with a 56k modem, she always gets 56k data throughput, but that's the fastest data transfer speed she can ever get using dial-up.

    C. You tell her that even with a 56k modem, she likely gets only 40–50k throughput, on average, but she might be able to exceed the 56k limit using compression.

    D. You tell her that with a 56k modem, she always gets 56k data throughput, but she might be able to exceed that limit using signal acceleration.

12. You are giving a presentation at a technology workshop and speaking to a group of high school students. You are discussing various broadband WAN technologies and the standards on which they are based. Of the following, which broadband technology uses the CDMA and GSM standards in the United States?

    A. Cable

    B. Mobile hotspot

    C. DSL

    D. ISDN

13. You are helping a customer decide between the DSL and cable broadband solutions for home and small business use. What do you say is the biggest disadvantage of using cable for Internet access?

    A. Cable is more prone to service outages.

    B. Since cable also provides television and phone service, Internet access speeds are slow.

    C. Fitting a special coaxial cable connection to computers is expensive.

    D. You have to share the Internet bandwidth with the other cable users in your area.

14. You are working on a fiber-optic network and need to replace a connector similar to the one shown in the following illustration. What type of connector do you need?

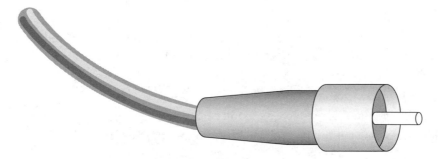

    A. SC connector

    B. ST connector

    C. LC connector

    D. MT-RJ connector

15. You are troubleshooting a problem in a wiring closet and realize that the closet contains a mixture of T568A and T568B patch cables. What effect would this have on the network?

    A. The network is likely to experience intermittent failures due to the mixture of wiring standards.

    B. The network is likely to be severely degraded due to the mixture of wiring standards.

    C. The network will not function at all due to the mixture of wiring standards.

    D. The mixture of wiring standards is not likely to have a significant effect on the network.

16. You are helping a user access several Internet sites and she is having issues. She shows you the following four IP addresses that she wants to connect with, and you point out that two of them are not valid public IP addresses. Which two do you tell her are incorrect? (Choose two.)

    A. 192.168.10.142

    B. 129.24.200.12

    C. 169.254.104.95

    D. 10.8.4.3

17. You are troubleshooting a computer where the user reports that she cannot access any Websites using their standard URLs (e.g., www.mysite.com). However, she can access sites by typing the IP address in her Web browser. What setting do you suspect is incorrect on her computer?

    A. IP address

    B. Default gateway

    C. DNS server

    D. Proxy server

18. You are monitoring a network connection and notice an unusual amount of traffic on TCP port 3389. What service normally runs over this port?

    A. HTTP

    B. HTTPS

    C. SMTP

    D. RDP

19. You are creating a network for an end user's laptop computer, smartphone, and tablet to communicate with each other in close proximity over Bluetooth. What type of network is this?

A. LAN

B. PAN

C. MAN

D. WAN

20. You are working on the Internet connection at your boss' home and realize that the Internet connection uses an antenna mounted high on the home's chimney. What type of Internet service is likely in use?

A. Wi-Fi

B. DSL

C. Line-of-sight

D. Cable

21. You are setting up a wireless access point, or WAP, in a customer's home office. The WAP will be used to connect local computers to each other wirelessly and to connect them to the Internet. There will be no wired component to the network. Of the following, what is required to set up the WAP to meet these requirements? (Choose two.)

A. A permanent wired connection to a broadband modem

B. A permanent wired connection to a computer

C. A temporary wired connection to a broadband modem for configuration only

D. A temporary wired connection to a computer for configuration only

22. You are creating a firewall rule that will block the telnet protocol due to security issues with that service. What port should you block?

A. 21

B. 23

C. 53

D. 80

23. Which of the following is not a standard speed for a magnetic hard disk?

A. 5400 rpm

B. 7500 rpm

C. 10,000 rpm

D. 15,000 rpm

24. You are selecting a router for a small office network environment where the network will be shared by data and VoIP traffic. You are concerned that data traffic could affect the clarity of voice traffic. What feature should you look for on the router to address this issue?

    A. Firewall

    B. DHCP

    C. DNS

    D. QoS

25. You are upgrading a system from dual-channel RAM to triple-channel RAM. What increase in memory speed should you expect?

    A. 33 percent

    B. 50 percent

    C. 100 percent

    D. 200 percent

26. What technology is used to store data on removable data storage cards?

    A. Magnetic

    B. Optical

    C. Chemical

    D. Solid state

27. You are selecting a video capture card for a user's computer. He will use it to access video from a modern camcorder. What connector should you ensure that the card has to allow this connection in the simplest fashion?

    A. RCA

    B. BNC

    C. F-connector

    D. HDMI

28. You are choosing an optical storage medium and are considering the use of dual-layer DVD-RW media. How much data may be stored on a dual-layer DVD-RW?

    A. 640MB

    B. 1.2GB

    C. 4.7GB

    D. 8.5GB

29. You are selecting optical storage media for the backup of data in your organization and want to choose a reusable type of media. Which of the following options could you use? (Choose two.)

A. BD

B. DVD-RW

C. DVD-R

D. BD-RE

30. You are discussing computer security with a group of high school students attending a technology workshop, and you are mentioning the encryption types used on wireless networks. Of the following, which are valid wireless encryption types? (Choose two.)

A. SSID

B. SSL

C. WEP

D. WPA

31. You are looking for a storage solution for your organization that can be directly attached to your Ethernet network and provides a file system accessible to end users. What technology should you choose?

A. USB drive

B. NAS

C. SAN

D. DAS

32. You are configuring a PATA IDE drive for use and want to set the jumper settings so that the drive will function properly wherever it is placed on an IDE connection. What setting should you use?

A. Master

B. Slave

C. Device 0

D. Cable Select

33. Which of the following SCSI IDs has the highest priority during bus arbitration?

A. 0

B. 7

C. 15

D. 32

34. You are selecting an interface for a mass storage device and wish to choose the highest speed connection. Which should you use?

A. USB 2.0

B. USB 3.0

C. FireWire 400

D. FireWire 800

35. You come across the three storage cards shown in the following illustration when digging through a desk drawer. What type of card is Card III?

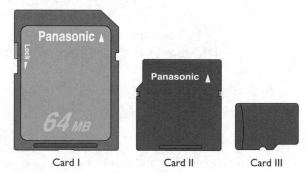

Card I   Card II   Card III

A. SD

B. miniSD

C. microSD

D. tinySD

36. You are helping a real estate agent in your office troubleshoot her digital camera and find that it uses a memory card similar to the one shown in the following illustration. You are unfamiliar with this card format and need to purchase a replacement. What type of card do you need to buy?

A. CF

B. SD

C. xD

D. BD

37. You are helping a friend set up a small computer lab in his home, and he wants to work with different levels of RAID, or redundant array of independent (or inexpensive) disks. He currently wants to configure a RAID level that will create an exact copy of the data from disk 1 onto disk 2. What RAID level is this?

A. RAID 0

B. RAID 1

C. RAID 5

D. RAID 10

38. A customer says he recently purchased a set of floppy drive diskettes and believes they are faulty. He hasn't used the floppy disk drive (FDD) on his computer in quite some time, and when he tried to use a new diskette to save a file, the file became corrupted. You check the problem by inserting a diskette into the FDD, and you are able to successfully save a file to the diskette and then read it. Besides the customer's diskette being faulty, what else could have been the problem?

    A. If the FDD hasn't been used in a long amount of time, dust may have accumulated on the read/write heads, which caused the first diskette to be damaged but also removed the dust so that when you tried another diskette, the FDD worked fine.

    B. The customer inserted the diskette in the FDD upside down, causing the failure but fortunately not damaging the read/write heads so that when you tested the FDD, it worked fine.

    C. FDDs are notorious for working intermittently, so that is the most likely cause of the customer not being able to save his work and you being able to subsequently perform the same function without incident.

    D. The only possible problem is that the customer's first diskette was faulty.

39. You work for a small city IT department, and you've been asked to install a tape drive solution for one of the servers used by the city assessor's office. You look up the specifications and documentation for tape drives to understand the correct installation and configuration procedure. Of the following, what do you discover while doing your research?

    A. The unit can only be attached via an IDE interface.

    B. The unit can only be attached via a SCSI interface.

    C. The unit can only be attached via SCSI or SAS interfaces.

    D. The unit can be attached via all drive interfaces.

40. You are looking for a way to transfer a 2 GB file via optical media. Which of the following technologies will meet your need? (Choose two.)

    A. CD

    B. DVD

    C. Blu-ray

    D. Tape

41. You are designing a manual data transfer process for a 3GB file between two offices. You wish to use a media type that allows reuse of the media. Which of the following formats will work in this scenario? (Choose two.)

    A. CD-RW

    B. DVD-RW

    C. Tape

    D. Floppy

42. You are considering using the dual-layer DVD format for mass distribution of large data files. What is the maximum capacity of DL DVD media?

    A. 2.7 GB

    B. 4.7 GB

    C. 8.0 GB

    D. 12.7 GB

43. You visit a user who is experiencing slow data transfer rates to an external hard drive. You note that the drive is connected via a USB 1.1 interface. What speed increase can the user expect by moving from a USB 1.1 interface to a USB 2.0 interface, provided that both the computer and drive support the maximum USB 2.0 transfer rate?

    A. 2X increase

    B. 10X increase

    C. 20X increase

    D. 40X increase

44. You are sorting through a drawer full of USB cables trying to find a cable to support a device that uses a USB Mini-A connector. Which one of the connectors shown in the following illustration is correct?

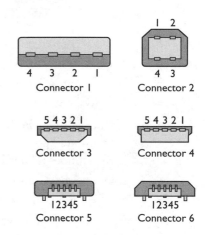

    A. Connector 3

    B. Connector 4

    C. Connector 5

    D. Connector 6

45. You are attaching an external storage device to a computer and need to obtain a data transfer rate of at least 10 Mbps over a distance of 50 feet using a single cable. Which one of the following interfaces will provide this capacity at the lowest cost?

    A. USB 1.1

    B. USB 2.0

    C. USB 3.0

    D. FireWire 800

46. You are teaching a class in basic PC usage to a group of older customers who have little experience with personal computers. You are describing the different connections that are typically made on the front of an average PC. Of the following, which connections are usually found on the front of a PC? (Choose two.)

    A. Audio

    B. Parallel

    C. Serial

    D. USB

47. You are teaching a class in basic PC usage to a group of older customers who have little experience with personal computers. You are describing the different connections that are typically made on the back side of a computer. Using the accompanying photograph, which option is the correct description for these connectors?

    A. 1 is a modem, 2 is a NIC, 3 is a video connection, and 4 are USB connections.

    B. 1 is a NIC, 2 is a modem, 3 is a video connection, and 4 are USB connections.

    C. 1 is a modem, 2 is a NIC, 3 is an audio card connection, and 4 are FireWire connectors.

    D. 1 is a NIC, 2 is a modem, 3 is a parallel connection, and 4 are FireWire connections.

48. You have a customer who has a laptop with an infrared port, and he just bought a PDA that also has an infrared port. He'd like to be able to transfer data from his PDA to his laptop via infrared. What does he need to know to do this?

    A. Infrared connections work like Wi-Fi connections.

    B. Infrared connections require line-of-sight.

    C. Infrared connections work like Bluetooth connections.

    D. Infrared connections work only when the room lights are off.

49. You suspect a customer's computer is infected with the Stuxnet virus, and you need to learn more about the malware's symptoms and behavior. How can you discover this information? (Choose three.)

    A. Use a search engine and search for "computer viruses."

    B. Use a search engine and search for "stuxnet symptoms."

    C. Use a search engine and search for "computer virus encyclopedia stuxnet."

    D. Go to the Website of a reputable antivirus program vendor and search its virus database for "stuxnet."

50. A customer asks you to upgrade the hard drive in his computer and would like you to use a solid-state drive (SSD) rather than a hard disk drive (HDD). He asks if you will need to install an adapter to accommodate the SSD on his motherboard or if he'll need a new motherboard. What do you tell him?

  A. You tell him that HDD-to-SSD adapters are readily available and you'll be able to successfully install the SSD on his current motherboard.

  B. You tell him that if his motherboard was made before 2009, you will need to upgrade the motherboard as well, since earlier motherboards didn't support SSD drives.

  C. You tell him that SSDs use the same interface as HDDs so you will be able to perform the upgrade on his computer without a problem.

  D. You tell him that SSDs are only available when you purchase a computer directly from the manufacturer, and an upgrade is impossible.

51. You want to install a joystick to the game controller on a Windows XP computer to play a game not supported in Windows 7. You've plugged the joystick into the game controller port. What should you do now?

  A. Open USB Controllers in Control Panel.

  B. Open Game Controllers in Control Panel.

  C. Open Printers And Faxes and then click Add A Device.

  D. Nothing. Windows XP will automatically detect and install the joystick.

52. You have just installed a new printer to your Windows 7 computer and you want to share it so others using your home network can print, too. How do you share the printer from the Devices And Printers screen?

  A. Right-click the desired printer and click Properties.

  B. Right-click the desired printer and click Printer Properties.

  C. Right-click the desired printer and click Sharing.

  D. Once you install a printer on a Windows 7 computer, it should be shared automatically.

53. You have a small business customer who uses a network printer in her offices. A new employee needs his computer set up to use the network printer from his Windows 7 computer. From the Devices And Printers screen, what should you do?

  A. Click Add A Printer and in the Add Printer wizard, click Add A Network, Wireless Or Bluetooth Printer.

  B. Click Add A Printer and in the Add Printer wizard, click Add A Network Printer.

  C. Click Add A Printer and in the Add Printer wizard, click A Network Printer Or A Printer Attached To Another Computer.

  D. Click Add A Printer and in the Add Printer wizard, click Automatically Detect And Install Network Printer.

54. You have a home customer who purchased a printer and all of its equipment and documentation from a garage sale and wants you to help install it on his Windows 7 computer. The printer is older and you're not sure if there are drivers available that are supported on Windows 7. Where can you look to see if there are appropriate drivers available?

A. On the driver CD that came with the printer.

B. At the Website for the company that made the printer.

C. At a third-party Website that "collects" drivers for legacy printers.

D. If Windows 7 doesn't natively have the drivers for this printer, trying to install it is a waste of time.

55. You want to install a fingerprint reader in your Windows 7 computer to test this technology for your employer. How do you install this device?

A. Connect the device to your computer and then, in Control Panel, double-click Biometric Devices.

B. Connect the device to your computer and then, in Devices And Printers, click Add A Device.

C. Connect the device to your computer, install the drivers for the device, and then in Devices And Printers, click Add A Device.

D. Connect the device to your computer and let Windows 7 automatically detect and install it.

56. You want to install a second SATA drive in your Windows 7 computer to add to its storage capacity. You go into the BIOS but do not see the second drive. What should you do?

A. Change the CMOS battery.

B. Set the SATA jumper on the motherboard so the BIOS will detect more than one SATA drive.

C. Flash the BIOS.

D. Physically connect the SATA drive to the SATA controller on the motherboard.

57. You are installing a touch screen on a customer's Windows 7 computer. You plug the touch screen into a USB port on the computer as recommended in the instructions. What other steps must you take? (Choose all that apply.)

A. Connect the VGA cable between the computer and the monitor.

B. Install drivers.

C. Configure the touch screen in the BIOS.

D. Calibrate the touch screen after installation.

58. As a member of the IT department for your company, you have discovered another employee has been sending information considered trade secrets by your business to a competitor via e-mail.

You have informed your supervisor and been advised to document what you discovered and the steps you took in response. What will this documentation be used for? (Choose all that apply.)

A. As evidence pursuant to a civil or criminal prosecution

B. As part of human resources documentation for the employee in question

C. To verify that you took the appropriate steps in response to the incident, according to company policy

D. To record the specific trade secrets that were involved as part of a press release

59. As a member of the IT department for your company, you have discovered another employee has been sending information considered trade secrets by your business to a competitor via USB drive. Of the following, what are your responsibilities in this situation? (Choose all that apply.)

A. Identify the suspected employee, the information he has been disclosing, and the media he has been using to commit this act.

B. Present your information to your supervisor and receive appropriate instructions as to your further duties.

C. Make a copy of any data that is suspected of being released and keep it on the hard drive of your computer.

D. If you have possession of the USB drive, follow company policy in releasing the item to your supervisor or the responsible party in your organization.

60. You are trying to help a small business customer with a computer that is heavily compromised with a variety of malware. The customer is upset that the process of "cleaning up" the PC is taking so long. When talking to an upset customer, what activities should you avoid? (Choose all that apply.)

A. Taking personal calls on your mobile

B. Texting on your mobile

C. Explaining in plain terms what the problem is with the computer

D. Suggesting that the customer has himself to blame for the problem

61. You provide printer support for a number of small business customers and you are inventorying your replacement supplies, including different types of printer paper. Of the following, what printer types are likely to require a specialized type of paper? (Choose all that apply.)

A. Laser

B. Impact

C. Inkjet

D. Thermal

62. You are on staff in the IT department in your company and you are explaining the differences between printer types to a new intern. Of the following, which printer type do you say has no print head in the conventional sense?

A. Laser

B. Impact

C. Inkjet

D. Thermal

63. You are on staff in the IT department in your company and you are explaining the capacities of a motherboard's BIOS to a new intern. Of the following, what monitoring abilities are some BIOSs able to perform? (Choose all that apply.)

A. Bus speeds

B. CPU temperature

C. Fan speeds

D. USB activity

64. You have a customer who wants you to wirelessly network his home as an alternative to wiring the home with Ethernet cable. There is one Windows 7 PC that has no wireless capacity. How can you make it able to connect to the wireless network? (Choose all that apply.)

A. Install a FireWire modem card.

B. Install a PCIe wireless NIC.

C. Install a USB wireless NIC.

D. Install a serial cellular card.

65. You are building a gaming computer for a customer and installing a liquid cooling system, since it is superior at removing heat from inside a PC than the traditional air cooling system. How does the liquid cooling system keep the chipsets on the motherboard cool?

A. By using plastic tubes of liquid that flows through the chipsets

B. By using metal blocks containing tubes of liquid that sit on top of the chipsets

C. By using plastic tubes of liquid that are channeled on both sides of the chipsets

D. By using metal blocks containing liquid that are attached under the chipsets

66. You have just finished building a gaming computer for a customer that includes a liquid cooling system. What is the last step in the installation of the cooling system?

A. Run the liquid cooling system with the computer off to check for leaks.

B. Run the liquid cooling system with the computer on to check for leaks.

C. Fill the liquid cooling system reservoir, close the case, and power up the computer.

D. Run air through the liquid cooling system to check for seal integrity, and then fill the reservoir with liquid and start the system and the computer.

67. You are cleaning the inside of a laser printer for one of your small business customers. What parts of this process could present a hazard to you or anyone near you? (Choose all that apply.)

A. Using compressed air

B. Using a vacuum

C. Working in a confined space

D. Wiping toner with a cloth

68. You installed a pair of computer speakers for a customer last week on her Windows XP computer and now she says that they aren't producing any sound when she watches videos on YouTube, plays a music CD, or tries to watch a DVD movie. What do you suspect is the problem? (Choose all that apply.)

A. The speakers are turned off.

B. The sound knob on the speakers is turned to the lowest setting.

C. The speakers are muted in Windows.

D. The sound is muted in YouTube.

69. You have a friend who is an artist and asks you to help her install a digitizer pad on her Windows 7 computer so she can draw on the pad and digitalize her artwork, further processing with various applications. What will you need to install this device? (Choose all that apply.)

A. A cable such as a USB cable to connect the digitizer pad to the computer

B. The drivers for the digitizer device

C. Video software to process the analog content to a digital display

D. A stylus

70. You are giving a training class to the IT staff at your company on personal safety issues. Of the following, which items pertain directly to personal safety and avoiding injury on the job? (Choose all that apply.)

A. Electrical fire safety

B. Lifting techniques

C. Removing jewelry

D. Self-grounding

E. Weight limitations

71. You have a home office/small office customer who lives in an area prone to power outages, power surges, and brownouts. She needs protection for her computers from these variations in electrical power, including the potential for electrical fires. Of the following, which devices provide some measure of protection for electrical threats? (Choose all that apply.)

   A. Power strip

   B. Power supply

   C. Surge protector

   D. Uninterruptable power supply

72. You are installing a Blu-ray drive in a customer's Windows 7 computer. It physically installs pretty much like any other drive. You attach one end of the cable that came with the drive to its data port. Where on the motherboard do you plug in the other end of the cable?

   A. Blu-ray controller

   B. DVD controller

   C. IDE controller

   D. SATA controller

73. You just finished installing Windows 7 on a customer's computer using an installation DVD. To complete this task, the computer had to be set to boot from the optical drive. Now you want to change this setting for security reasons and have the computer look to the hard drive first for the boot sector. Where can you change this setting?

   A. BIOS

   B. Computer

   C. Control Panel

   D. Device Manager

74. You just installed a new Ethernet network card in a customer's Windows 7 computer and now you suspect it is causing a problem. You want to temporarily disable the card in order to troubleshoot the computer. Where can you disable the network card?

   A. BIOS

   B. Computer

   C. Control Panel

   D. Device Manager

75. You are installing an eSATA drive to a Windows 7 computer for a home customer. The computer doesn't have an eSATA port available but does have several USB ports, a serial port, a network cable port, and a parallel port on the back of the PC. Of the following, what are your options? (Choose all that apply.)

   A. eSATA expansion card

   B. eSATA-to-RJ45 port adapter

C. eSATA-to-serial port adapter

D. eSATA-to-USB adapter

76. You have a customer who has only one FireWire port on his computer but he wants to attach several external FireWire devices to his PC. The computer has several USB ports but no external SATA or eSATA connections. What can you suggest? (Choose all that apply.)

A. A FireWire expansion card

B. A FireWire hub

C. A FireWire-to-SATA adapter

D. A FireWire-to-USB adapter

77. You have just installed a new sound card in a customer's Windows 7 computer. You know that the sound card drivers will need to be installed before the sound card will work. What is the most likely source for drivers for this card?

A. The sound card driver disc

B. The sound card manufacturer's Website

C. Windows 7

D. Windows Update

78. You see a newly hired technician carrying a screwdriver and pliers in his shirt pocket while working on the inside of a PC. You pull him aside and explain the safety problem with that practice. What are some of the things you mention? (Choose all that apply.)

A. Loose tools could fall into the computer case, damaging components.

B. Loose tools may stab or otherwise injure the technician if he leans over or moves in a particular way.

C. Loose tools could build up a magnetic charge that could damage a computer when used inside the case.

D. Loose tools may damage the technician's clothing.

79. You are working with a team of technicians decommissioning older Windows computers for a small business customer and installing new Windows 7 computers. As part of this process, team members must pack up each of the old computers in packing boxes, including their monitors, keyboard, and mice. The computers have been left up and running by the customer's employees. What are some safety precautions you should take when getting the older units ready for packing? (Choose all that apply.)

A. Power down the computers completely from the Windows Start menu.

B. Unplug only the power cables before moving.

C. Handle monitors with care.

D. Stack computer cases on top of one another for symmetry.

80. You are teaching a class in safety to the staff of the IT department where you work. Of the following, which components do you say should never be opened due to the danger of potentially lethal electric shock? (Choose all that apply.)

  A. CRT monitor

  B. Laser printer

  C. Power supply

  D. Server computer

81. You are evaluating the environmental conditions in your computer workshop and notice some factors that could contribute to ESD, which can damage delicate internal computer components. What environmental factors are you worried about? (Choose two.)

  A. Low humidity

  B. High humidity

  C. Low temperature

  D. High temperature

82. You are servicing a laser printer for a small business customer and replacing a number of components, including the toner cartridge. You have a large number of similar clients and many of them use laser printers. For this reason, you have accumulated a fair supply of used toner cartridges at your shop and they're taking up valuable space. What should you do with them?

  A. Throw them in a dumpster.

  B. Contact the printer manufacturer.

  C. Contact the store where the customer buys their printer supplies.

  D. Buy new toner and refurbish them.

83. You have decommissioned a large number of PCs in one of the branch offices of the company you work for and now have a large supply of old CRT monitors. What should you do with them?

  A. Disassemble them and salvage the usable parts.

  B. Send them to the local landfill.

  C. Send them to the local recycling company.

  D. Send them back to the manufacturer.

84. You are about to make a number of changes to the BIOS of a customer's computer. You have heard that you should "back up the BIOS" before making such changes in case something goes wrong. How can you do this? (Choose all that apply.)

  A. Use a pencil and paper to copy down all of the BIOS settings.

  B. Use a digital camera to photograph all of the BIOS settings.

  C. Use third-party software to back up the BIOS settings.

  D. Use a Windows-native application to back up the BIOS settings.

85. You are aware that a computer's BIOS is capable of performing several monitoring and testing functions. Of the following, which is the most basic and common test performed by BIOS?

A. CPU temperature monitoring

B. Fan speed monitoring

C. Power-on Self-test

D. Voltage monitoring

86. You are reviewing basic information about computer power supplies with a new intern in your department. Of the following, what do you say a power supply does?

A. Converts direct current into alternating current

B. Converts alternating current into direct current

C. Converts volts into watts

D. Converts watts into volts

87. You are reviewing basic information about computer power supplies with a new intern in your department. Of the following, what specific tasks does a power supply perform? (Choose all that apply.)

A. Provides the computer with the type of power it needs: ±12 VDC, ±5 VDC, or ±3.3 VDC.

B. An auto-switching power supply can detect the incoming voltage and switch to accept either 120 or 240 VAC.

C. Restricts the amount of wattage the computer can use to 800 watts or less.

D. Provides cooling for the interior of the PC.

88. You are reviewing basic information about computer power supplies with a new intern in your department. You say that most motherboards use a 20- or 24-pin connector for electrical power. What is this connector called?

A. P1 connector

B. P4 connector

C. Mini connector

D. Molex connector

89. You are reviewing basic information about computer displays and their resolutions. What do you say is the maximum graphics resolution of VGA?

A. 640 × 480

B. 800 × 600

C. 1024 × 768

D. 1600 × 1200

90. You are reviewing basic information about computer displays and their qualities with an intern in your department. You ask him what the term is for the amount of time in milliseconds (ms) it takes for a single pixel on an LCD screen to go from active (black) to inactive (white). He answers correctly. What does he say?

A. Color quality

B. Display resolution

C. Refresh rate

D. Response time

91. You are about to install a commercial scanner for a small business customer. You are reviewing the documentation for the scanner and notice that the scanner's driver must conform to a specific set of standards. Of the following, what are those standards?

A. FAX

B. OCR

C. TWAIN

D. USB

92. You are in the process of installing several multimedia devices to a customer's computer. Of the devices she has requested to be installed, which one is likely to require the most work?

A. Digital camera

B. MIDI device

C. Video capture card

D. Webcam

93. You have been hired to install a series of computer kiosks at a local business that require multiple keyboards, monitors, and mice to be attached to a single computer. Business customers will be able to use this kiosk setup to look up catalog and other information while visiting the company. What sort of device will you have to install for this type of kiosk setup?

A. Electronic KVM switch

B. KVM over IP switch

C. Local KVM switch

D. Local remote KVM switch

94. You have been hired to install a high mass-printing station for a business customer that requires very fast, high-quality printing results. Of the following, what sort of cable and connection does this printer require to a computer?

A. Ethernet

B. Parallel

C. Serial

D. USB

95. You have been hired to install a specialized printer for a business customer. The printer needs to be installed on a Windows XP computer's serial interface. You have successfully installed the printer, but want to verify the port it is using to make sure it is associated with the correct serial port in Windows. Starting in Printers And Faxes, where can you do this?

A. Right-click the printer, click Printing Preferences, and then click Ports.

B. Right-click the printer, click Printer Properties, and then click Ports.

C. Right-click the printer, click Properties, and then click Ports.

D. Right-click the printer and then click Ports.

96. You are working with a small business customer who has an all-in-one printer, copier, scanner, and fax device. The unit is networked over Wi-Fi and has an embedded Web server so it can be managed in a Web browser. In Windows 7, where can you locate the link to the pages offered by the printer's web server?

A. Right-click the printer, click Printing Preferences, and then click Web Services.

B. Right-click the printer, click Printer Properties, and then click Web Services.

C. Right-click the printer, click Properties, and then click Web Services.

D. Right-click the printer and then click Web Services.

97. You are performing an in-depth review of the BIOS in a customer's computer and making some optimization settings. Of the following, which actions can you take to optimize computer performance in the BIOS? (Choose all that apply.)

A. Disable the computer's USB controller.

B. Reduce CPU performance to prevent heat damage to the processor chip.

C. Turn off printing services for the computer.

D. Control the SATA controller's operating mode.

98. You've just finished performing some routine maintenance inside a customer's computer and you've powered it up. As the BIOS goes through the POST test, you hear two short beeps. What does this mean?

A. Memory error.

B. Video error.

C. System timer failure.

D. The meaning depends on the BIOS type.

99. You are building a computer for a customer and suspect that the motherboard may be faulty. When you boot the computer, the POST test runs but the beep codes are not sufficient to notify you of everything that is happening during POST. You decide to use a POST card to get a detailed list of the events occurring and their result during the test. What will you need to do to use and interpret the POST card? (Choose all that apply.)

A. The card will have to be inserted in one of the computer's USB ports.

B. Only the motherboard, CPU, RAM, and power supply need to be working and properly connected in order to run the POST test and use the POST card.

C. You will need to know the BIOS your computer's motherboard uses.

D. You will need to keep a list of the error and test codes handy so you can interpret them as the test runs.

100. You are part of a team that is deploying desktop computers and phones for a new department at the company you work for. You and your team must install PCs and phones for 30 people, including connecting each computer to an available Ethernet port. The phones are all VoIP, or Voice over IP, which means they need to be connected to the network via an Ethernet cable as well. How can this be done?

A. Each employee's work area will need two Ethernet ports on the wall, one for the computer and one for the phone.

B. Each VoIP phone typically has two Ethernet ports, so you can run a patch cable from the wall to the phone and another patch cable from the second port to the NIC on the computer.

C. You will have to install a NIC expansion card in each computer so you can run a patch cable from the wall to the computer and then run a second cable from the second port on the NIC to the phone.

D. Each VoIP phone connects to the network wirelessly, so you only need to run a patch cable from the wall port to the computer.

QUICK ANSWER KEY

1.	A, C	22.	B	43.	D
2.	A, B, C	23.	B	44.	A
3.	A, B, D	24.	D	45.	D
4.	A, B	25.	B	46.	A, D
5.	A, B, C	26.	D	47.	A
6.	C	27.	D	48.	B
7.	B	28.	D	49.	B, C, D
8.	B, C	29.	B, D	50.	C
9.	A	30.	C, D	51.	B
10.	A, B	31.	B	52.	B
11.	C	32.	D	53.	A
12.	B	33.	B	54.	B
13.	D	34.	B	55.	C
14.	B	35.	C	56.	D
15.	D	36.	C	57.	A, B, D
16.	A, C	37.	B	58.	A, B, C
17.	C	38.	A	59.	A, B, D
18.	D	39.	D	60.	A, B, D
19.	B	40.	B, C	61.	B, D
20.	C	41.	B, C	62.	A
21.	A, D	42.	C	63.	A, B, C

64.	B, C	**77.**	C	**90.**	D
65.	B	**78.**	A, B	**91.**	C
66.	A	**79.**	A, C	**92.**	C
67.	A, C	**80.**	A, C	**93.**	C
68.	A, B, C	**81.**	A, C	**94.**	C
69.	A, B	**82.**	B	**95.**	C
70.	A, B, C, E	**83.**	C	**96.**	C
71.	C, D	**84.**	A, B, C	**97.**	A, B, D
72.	D	**85.**	C	**98.**	D
73.	A	**86.**	B	**99.**	B, C, D
74.	D	**87.**	A, B, D	**100.**	B
75.	A, C, D	**88.**	A		
76.	A, B, D	**89.**	A		

IN-DEPTH ANSWERS

1. ☑   **A** and **C.** When you're replacing a heat sink and fan for a CPU, the old heat sink assembly likely has accumulated a lot of dust, so you'll want to blow the dust out of the laptop interior with compressed air. Once you remove the old heat sink, you'll need to apply some fresh thermal paste on the CPU before attaching the new heat sink.
    ☒   **B** and **D** are incorrect. **B** is incorrect because you shouldn't have to solder the CPU heat sink into place. **D** is incorrect because the heat sink assembly doesn't require drivers.

2. ☑   **A, B,** and **C.** Sometimes the LCD lid "close" switch gets stuck. The screen is actually on but the backlight isn't. You can usually tell because there is a very faint image on the screen. Try tapping on the close switch to loosen it. If the screen comes on and stays on, you've fixed the problem. If you suspect the video card is the issue, try attaching an external monitor to the laptop via the VGA port to see if you get an image. If the customer uses the FN keys for different functions, try tapping the F7 key repeatedly to see if the screen will brighten.
    ☒   **D** is incorrect because a poorly seated laptop battery wouldn't specifically affect the display screen.

3. ☑   **A, B,** and **D.** If you can use a USB keyboard with the laptop, the problem is probably keyboard or motherboard related. Checking Device Manager will show any warnings or errors associated with the keyboard, such as needing updated drivers (assuming the keyboard shows up as installed), and opening the laptop will let you verify that the problem isn't a loose or disconnected data cable link between the motherboard and keyboard.
    ☒   **C** is incorrect because there is no separate power cable connection between the motherboard and keyboard.

4. ☑   **A** and **B.** Before working on any computer, always power down the machine. Before opening any laptop to perform maintenance, always remove the battery to prevent any electrical surges or other damage to the machine.
    ☒   **C** and **D** are incorrect. **C** is incorrect because you shouldn't have to remove the laptop's motherboard in order to remove and replace a DVD drive, though you may have to remove other components, such as the keyboard. **D** is incorrect because, while you will probably place the old DVD unit in an antistatic bag after removing it from the laptop, putting the entire laptop in an antistatic bag would make it impossible to perform maintenance on the unit.

5. ☑ **A, B,** and **C.** There are any number of reasons why a laptop could seem not to hold a charge. The battery could be faulty, requiring a replacement. The power cord itself could be damaged so that the battery is not charging when the unit is plugged into a power strip. The power converter on the cord could be damaged, preventing the battery from receiving a charge.

   ☒ **D** is incorrect because a damaged motherboard wouldn't specifically manifest itself as a failure of the unit to gain or hold a charge.

6. ☑ **C.** The drawing is of an ExpressCard/54. This is the 54mm form factor of the ExpressCard standard for laptop peripherals. The 54mm slot can accept both ExpressCard/34 and ExpressCard/54 cards.

   ☒ **A, B,** and **D** are incorrect. **A** and **D** are incorrect because the L-shape is unique to the ExpressCard format. **B** is incorrect because the ExpressCard/34 uses a 34mm format that is rectangular and 20mm shorter in width.

7. ☑ **B.** The notched rectangle shape is characteristic of an SD memory card.

   ☒ **A, C,** and **D** are incorrect. **A** is incorrect because CompactFlash (CF) cards are rectangular with no notches. **C** is incorrect because memory sticks are rectangular with a USB interface. **D** is incorrect because the miniSD card has a different shape, with a "reverse-7" notch on the left side of the card.

8. ☑ **B** and **C.** The keyboard backlight provides light underneath the keyboard, illuminating the characters on the keys. Adjusting the screen brightness can help reduce the impact on those nearby. Both settings are normally labeled keyboard shortcuts on the keyboard.

   ☒ **A** and **D** are incorrect. **A** is incorrect because a privacy filter will prevent others from reading her screen but does not adjust brightness. **D** is incorrect because Bluetooth technology allows wireless connections but will not affect brightness of the screen or keyboard.

9. ☑ **A.** The maximum range of a class 1 Bluetooth device is one meter.

   ☒ **B, C,** and **D** are incorrect because the maximum range of a class 1 Bluetooth device is one meter. Class 2 devices have a maximum range of 10 meters, and Class 3 devices have a 100-meter maximum range.

10. ☑ **A** and **B.** The volume on a laptop computer running Windows 7 may be adjusted using the Windows volume control or the keyboard volume shortcuts.

    ☒ **C** and **D** are incorrect. **C** is incorrect because laptops do not have accessible sound cards. **D** is incorrect because laptop speakers do not have volume control knobs.

11. ☑ **C.** 56 Kbits/s data throughput is the theoretical maximum data speed anyone using dial-up can expect to attain; however, on average, actual data speeds are more in the 40-to-50k range. Compression algorithms can achieve greater speeds, but the speeds are variable.

☒ **A, B,** and **D** are incorrect. **A** is incorrect because, with compression, it is possible to exceed the 56k limit. **B** is incorrect because it is rare to actually achieve 56k data speeds using dial-up, even though it's the theoretical maximum. **D** is incorrect because it is rare to achieve the theoretical maximum data speed of 56k using dial-up and the signal acceleration solution is fictitious.

12. ☑ **B.** In the United States, digital cellular networks use the Code Division Multiple Access (CDMA) and Global System for Mobile Communications (GSM) standards. Mobile hotspots use these digital cellular networks.
    ☒ **A, C,** and **D** are incorrect because the CDMA and GSM standards are specific to cellular digital networks.

13. ☑ **D.** Cable uses a one-to-many rather than a one-to-one connection, such as DSL; therefore, you have to share the cable bandwidth with other cable customers in your area. The more customers using cable, the slower your Internet speeds. This may not be particularly noticeable most of the time, however, because cable provides very fast Internet speeds.
    ☒ **A, B,** and **C** are incorrect. **A** is incorrect because cable is no more prone to service outages than DSL. **B** is incorrect because the addition of TV and phone services on a cable line does not cause slower Internet speeds. **C** is incorrect because the coaxial cable connects to a special cable modem, but the connection from the modem to the computer is made by Ethernet cable, so no special connector for the computer is required.

14. ☑ **B.** ST connectors use a rounded plug similar to the one shown in the illustration.
    ☒ **A, C,** and **D** are incorrect. **A** is incorrect because SC connectors use square snap couplings. **C** is incorrect because LC connectors are smaller versions of SC connectors. **D** is incorrect because the MT-RJ connector is similar in appearance to the standard RJ-45 connector used for Ethernet networks.

15. ☑ **D.** Mixing T568A and T568B patch cables in a wiring closet is not likely to have a noticeable effect on the network. It may produce some minor signal loss, but no significant degradation would occur.
    ☒ **A, B,** and **C** are incorrect because mixing wiring standards among patch cables is not likely to have an effect. The only time an issue would occur is if a single cable is terminated with T568A wiring at one end and T568B wiring at the other end. In that case, the cable would not function properly.

16. ☑ **A and C.** Addresses that begin with 192.168 are private IP addresses and are not routable over the Internet. They are intended for use on internal networks only. Addresses that begin with 169.254 are used by the Automatic Private IP Addressing (APIPA) service and are similarly not routable.
    ☒ **B and D** are incorrect because these are valid public IP addresses.

17. ☑ **C.** The failure to access sites by domain name indicates that the DNS server address may be incorrectly configured on the computer.

    ☒ **A, B,** and **D** are incorrect. **A** and **B** are incorrect because if the IP address or default gateway were incorrectly configured, the user would not be able to access any remote network sites. **D** is incorrect because an incorrect proxy server would either have no effect or block all Web traffic, depending upon the network configuration.

18. ☑ **D.** The Remote Desktop Protocol (RDP) uses TCP port 3389.

    ☒ **A, B,** and **C** are incorrect. **A** is incorrect because HTTP uses TCP port 80. **B** is incorrect because HTTPS uses TCP port 443. **C** is incorrect because SMTP uses TCP port 25.

19. ☑ **B.** A personal area network (PAN) consists of devices located in close physical proximity and used by the same individual. Bluetooth is commonly used for PANs.

    ☒ **A, C,** and **D** are incorrect. **A** is incorrect because local area networks (LANs) connect multiple systems belonging to different users. **C** is incorrect because metropolitan area networks (MANs) connect multiple networks in a metropolitan area. **D** is incorrect because wide area networks (WANs) connect networks over long distances.

20. ☑ **C.** The antenna mounted high on the chimney is indicative of line-of-sight wireless infrared access. The antenna must have a clear view to the ISP's antenna, usually located on a tall building or tower in the region.

    ☒ **A, B,** and **D** are incorrect. **A** is incorrect because Wi-Fi does not require an antenna mounted high on a building and is generally used for local area networks. **B** and **D** are incorrect because DSL and cable are wired technologies that do not use antennas.

21. ☑ **A** and **D.** The WAP will need to have a permanent cable connection to the broadband modem in order to provide the wireless computers on the network with an Internet connection. You only need to provide a wired connection between a computer and the WAP when you are initially configuring the WAP to set up a new username and password, IP address, and so forth.

    ☒ **B** and **C** are incorrect. **B** is incorrect because one of the requirements is that there be no wired component to the network. All computers will connect wirelessly via the WAP. **C** is incorrect because if the WAP is to continually provide wireless computers with an Internet connection, it must be connected by cable to the broadband modem.

22. ☑ **B.** The telnet protocol uses TCP port 23.

    ☒ **A, C,** and **D** are incorrect. **A** is incorrect because port 21 is used by the File Transfer Protocol (FTP). **C** is incorrect because port 53 is used by the Domain Name Service (DNS). **D** is incorrect because port 80 is used by the Hypertext Transfer Protocol (HTTP).

23. ☑ **B.** 7500 rpm is not a standard hard drive speed. The standard speeds are 5400 rpm, 7200 rpm, 10,000 rpm, and 15,000 rpm.

☒   **A, C,** and **D** are incorrect because the standard speeds are 5400 rpm, 7200 rpm, 10,000 rpm, and 15,000 rpm.

24. ☑   **D.** Quality of Service (QoS) features allow you to prioritize voice traffic and prevent high levels of data traffic from interfering with VoIP calls.
☒   **A, B,** and **C** are incorrect because while firewalls, DNS, and DHCP are standard features of SOHO routers, they do not allow you to prioritize voice traffic.

25. ☑   **B.** You should expect a 50 percent increase in memory transfer speed because you are increasing the number of channels by 50 percent.
☒   **A, C,** and **D** are incorrect because adding a third channel increases the potential memory transfer rate by 50 percent.

26. ☑   **D.** Removable storage cards typically use solid-state technology to store data.
☒   **A, B,** and **C** are incorrect. **A** is incorrect because magnetic technology is used in hard drives and floppy disks but not removable storage cards. **B** is incorrect because optical technology is used on CDs, DVDs and Blu-ray Discs. **C** is incorrect because chemical technology is not normally used to store data.

27. ☑   **D.** Most modern camcorders provide an HDMI video output, so you should ensure that the card has an HDMI input.
☒   **A, B,** and **C** are incorrect because modern camcorders do not typically have RCA, BNC, or F-connector output options.

28. ☑   **D.** Dual-layer DVD-RW media can store up to 8.5GB of data, compared to 4.7GB for a single-layer DVD-RW.
☒   **A, B,** and **C** are incorrect because dual-layer DVD-RW media can store up to 8.5GB of data, compared to 4.7GB for a single-layer DVD-RW.

29. ☑   **B and D.** The DVD-RW and BD-RE formats provide erasable and rewritable DVDs and Blu-ray Discs, respectively.
☒   **A and C** are incorrect. **A** is incorrect because the standard Blu-ray Disc is not rewriteable. **C** is incorrect because DVD-R media is not rewriteable.

30. ☑   **C and D.** WEP, or Wireless Equivalent Privacy, is a method of encryption that is considered insecure due to its vulnerability to compromise. WPA, or Wi-Fi Protected Access, is considered the more secure of the two encryption methods, with WPA2 being the most recent implementation.
☒   **A and B** are incorrect. **A** is incorrect because SSID, or Service Set Identifier, is considered the network name of a wireless network. As long as SSID broadcasts are enabled on a wireless network, the SSID name is visible to every Wi-Fi compatible device within range. SSID provides no wireless network protection. **B** is incorrect because SSL, or Secure Sockets Layer, is an encryption method, but not one used specifically with wireless networks.

31. ☑ **B.** Network Attached Storage (NAS) provides Ethernet-connected storage and a client-accessible file system.

☒ **A, C,** and **D** are incorrect. **A** is incorrect because USB drives cannot be directly attached to an Ethernet network. **C** is incorrect because Storage Area Network devices do not provide a file system. **D** is incorrect because Direct Attached Storage devices are connected directly to servers, rather than the network.

32. ☑ **D.** In Cable Select mode, the drive will determine its location on the IDE interface and configure itself appropriately as a master or slave.

☒ **A, B,** and **C** are incorrect. **A** and **C** are incorrect because a drive configured in master mode will not function properly if placed in the slave position on the interface. Device 0 is a synonym for master mode. **B** is incorrect because a drive configured in slave mode will not function properly if placed in the master position on the interface.

33. ☑ **B.** The device with SCSI ID 7 is always given the highest priority, as this ID is normally set aside for the host adapter.

☒ **A, C,** and **D** are incorrect. **A** and **C** are incorrect because a device with SCSI ID 7 has the highest priority. **D** is incorrect because the highest valid SCSI ID is 15.

34. ☑ **B.** USB 3.0 interfaces have a maximum theoretical bandwidth of 5 Gbps.

☒ **A, C,** and **D** are incorrect. **A** is incorrect because USB 2.0 interfaces have a maximum theoretical bandwidth of 480 Mbps. **C** is incorrect because FireWire 400 interfaces have a maximum theoretical bandwidth of 400 Mbps. **D** is incorrect because FireWire 800 interfaces have a maximum theoretical bandwidth of 800 Mbps.

35. ☑ **C.** All three cards are versions of the Secure Digital card format. The smallest card is the microSD format.

☒ **A, B,** and **D** are incorrect. **A** is incorrect because the standard SD card is Card I. **B** is incorrect because the miniSD card is Card II. **D** is incorrect because there is no existing tinySD format.

36. ☑ **C.** The curved bottom on the card is characteristic of the xD memory card format. Although cameras are no longer made using this format, many are still in use and replacement cards are available.

☒ **A, B,** and **D** are incorrect. **A** is incorrect because CompactFlash cards are rectangular. **B** is incorrect because SecureDigital cards have a notched rectangular format. **D** is incorrect because Blu-ray Disc media is circular.

37. ☑ **B.** RAID 1, also called mirroring, creates an exact copy of a set of data on two or more disks.

☒ **A, C,** and **D** are incorrect. **A** is incorrect because RAID 0, or striping, distributes data evenly across two or more disks and provides no redundancy. It increases performance but cannot be used as a measure to prevent loss of data in a disaster. **C** is incorrect because RAID 5 uses block-level striping with parity to distribute data across a series of three or more disks, providing low-cost redundancy. **D** is incorrect because RAID 10 uses a combination of block mirroring and striping across a minimum of four disks.

38. ☑ **A.** If a floppy drive isn't used frequently, dust can accumulate on the FDD's read/write heads and cause damage to the first diskette inserted. However, once the diskette is inserted and run, it cleans off the heads, allowing subsequent diskettes to be successfully used. The solution if you use an FDD infrequently is to make sure you insert a cleaning diskette first, or even a known faulty diskette, just to clean the heads.
☒ **B, C,** and **D** are incorrect. **B** is incorrect because a floppy drive diskette cannot be completely inserted in an FDD when the diskette is upside down. **C** is incorrect because FDDs in general are not excessively unreliable. **D** is incorrect because there are other reasons for such a problem besides a faulty diskette.

39. ☑ **D.** Tape drive units usually offer you a choice of all different drive interfaces, although SCSI and SAS are more common interfaces.
☒ **A, B,** and **C** are incorrect because tape drive interfaces are not limited to just the interfaces described in those options.

40. ☑ **B** and **C.** DVD media, with a capacity of 4.7GB or more, and Blu-ray media, with a capacity of 25GB or more, are capable of storing a 2GB file.
☒ **A** and **D** are incorrect. **A** is incorrect because there is no CD format with a capacity of 2GB or more. **D** is incorrect because tapes are magnetic, rather than optical, media.

41. ☑ **B** and **C.** DVD-RW media can hold 4.7GB of data. Tapes come in a variety of formats, many of which are capable of storing a 3GB file.
☒ **A** and **D** are incorrect. **A** is incorrect because CD-RW media is limited to 700MB of capacity. **D** is incorrect because no floppy disk has a capacity in excess of 200 MB.

42. ☑ **C.** The maximum capacity of a DL DVD is 8.0 GB.
☒ **A, B,** and **D** are incorrect because the maximum capacity of a DL DVD is 8.0 GB.

43. ☑ **D.** When upgrading from the full capacity of USB 1.1 to the full capacity of USB 2.0, you can expect a 40-fold increase in throughput, from 12 Mbps to 480 Mbps.
☒ **A, B,** and **C** are incorrect because you can expect a 40-fold increase in throughput.

44. ☑ **A.** Connector 3 is the USB Mini-A format.
☒ **B, C,** and **D** are incorrect. **B** is incorrect because Connector 4 is the USB Mini-B format. **C** is incorrect because Connector 5 is the USB Micro-A format. **D** is incorrect because Connector 6 is the USB Micro-B format. Connector 1 is the USB Type A format, and Connector 2 is the USB Type B format.

45. ☑ **D.** FireWire 800 is the only listed interface capable of this distance. FireWire 800 can carry 800 Mbps of data over distances up to 330 feet.

☒ **A, B,** and **C** are incorrect. **A** and **C** are incorrect because USB 1.1 and 3.0 connections are limited to 3 meters (9.8 feet) in length. **B** is incorrect because USB 2.0 connections are limited to 5 meters (16.4 feet) in length.

46. ☑ **A** and **D.** You usually will find an audio connection for headsets on the front of a computer and a few USB connections as well, along with a microphone connection.

☒ **B** and **C** are incorrect because parallel and serial connections, if they are on a PC, are usually found on the back end of the computer.

47. ☑ **A.** 1 is an RJ-11 connector used to connect a modem to a standard telephone line, 2 is a NIC used to connect to an Ethernet cable's RJ-45 connector, 3 is a video connection used for a monitor, and 4 are USB connections.

☒ **B, C,** and **D** are incorrect. **B** is incorrect because it switches the modem and NIC ports. **C** is incorrect because it misidentifies the video and USB connectors as audio and FireWire connectors. **D** is incorrect because it misidentifies all of the connectors.

48. ☑ **B.** Unlike radio waves, infrared transmission requires line-of-sight between the infrared port of the PDA and the infrared port of the laptop in order to make a connection. The devices also have to be reasonably close together. Infrared transfers data at a rate of 4 Mbps and has largely been replaced by Bluetooth because Bluetooth has faster data transmission rates and does not require line-of-sight.

☒ **A, C,** and **D** are incorrect. **A** and **C** are incorrect because infrared connections require line-of-sight and don't propagate in waves like radio-based transmissions. **D** is incorrect because the room lights do not have to be dark in order for an infrared connection to be made.

49. ☑ **B, C,** and **D.** If you know the name of the virus you want to learn about, the easiest way to discover its symptoms is to search for the virus name. If you don't know the name, you can search for an online virus encyclopedia, or use the virus database maintained by a known antivirus application vendor.

☒ **A** is incorrect because searching for "computer viruses" will return too many unspecified results that won't help you narrow down your specific virus problem.

50. ☑ **C.** SSDs use the same motherboard interfaces as HDDs, and if his motherboard otherwise supports SSDs, the upgrade should proceed without a problem.

☒ **A, B,** and **D** are incorrect. **A** is incorrect because you do not need an adapter to install an SSD on a motherboard that previously used an HDD. **B** is incorrect because motherboards made before 2009 are able to support SSDs. **D** is incorrect because SSDs are available as individual units and do not have to be purchased exclusively from a computer vendor as a completed PC.

51. ☑ **B.** Open Game Controllers in Control Panel, click Add, and then in the Game Controllers list, select the controller you just added and click OK.

☒ **A, C,** and **D** are incorrect. **A** is incorrect because there is no USB Controllers item in the Windows XP Control Panel. **C** is incorrect because in Windows XP Printers And Faxes, there is no Add A Device link. **D** is incorrect because Windows XP will not just detect and install the joystick automatically.

52. ☑ **B.** Right-click the printer, click Printer Properties, select the Sharing tab, and complete the steps to share the printer.

☒ **A, C,** and **D** are incorrect. **A** is incorrect because the Properties box only allows you to access the General and Hardware tabs, neither of which allows you to share the printer. **C** is incorrect because there is no Sharing option on this menu. **D** is incorrect because Windows 7 does not automatically share a printer once it is installed.

53. ☑ **A.** In all versions of Windows 7, click Add A Printer and when the Add Printer wizard launches, click Add A Network, Wireless Or Bluetooth Printer, and then proceed through the rest of the wizard.

☒ **B, C,** and **D** are incorrect. **B** is incorrect because this option does not exist in Windows 7. **C** is incorrect because this option is available when adding a network printer for Windows XP. **D** is incorrect because this option does not exist.

54. ☑ **B.** The most reliable place to look for the correct drivers is the Website for the company that made the printer. If they do not have drivers for the printer that are supported on Windows 7, chances are the printer is obsolete and will not work with your customer's computer.

☒ **A, C,** and **D** are incorrect. **A** is incorrect because the drivers on the CD were probably written before Windows 7 existed and will not work on a Windows 7 computer. **C** is incorrect because the site may or may not have the appropriate drivers, and it is possible the third-party site's drivers will either be defective or even a trick to convince you to download malware when you think you're downloading drivers. **D** is incorrect because drivers external to Windows 7 may be available from the printer manufacturer.

55. ☑ **C.** After connecting the device to your computer, Windows 7 may not be aware of the device until you install the drivers for it. Then it will probably detect it when you click Add A Device in Devices And Printers. After installation, the device will appear in Devices And Printers along with any other installed devices such as printers, fax machines, and cameras.

☒ **A, B,** and **D** are incorrect. **A** is incorrect because Biometric Devices doesn't appear by default in the Windows 7 Control Panel. **B** is incorrect because even after connecting the device to your computer and clicking Add A Device in Devices And Printers, Windows 7 will likely not be able to detect the device. **D** is incorrect because Windows 7 will not automatically detect and install the biometric device.

56. ☑ **D.** If you don't first connect the SATA drive to the SATA drive controller on the computer's motherboard, the BIOS will not be able to detect the drive.

☒ **A, B,** and **C** are incorrect. **A** is incorrect because you have no reason to believe a bad CMOS battery is the cause of this issue. **B** is incorrect because there is no SATA jumper on a computer's motherboard, and this is not the proper way to have the BIOS detect an additional SATA drive. **C** is incorrect because there is a low probability that the BIOS needs to be flashed in order to detect the drive, especially if you haven't connected the drive to the computer first.

57. ☑ **A, B,** and **D.** In addition to connecting the USB cable, you will need to connect a video cable, such as VGA, between the monitor and the cable. You'll also need to install the appropriate drivers and, after installation, you will need to calibrate the screen to define the limits of the monitor.

☒ **C** is incorrect because the typical touch screen installation does not require that you perform any setup in the BIOS.

58. ☑ **A, B,** and **C.** Documentation in the case of an employee committing a crime or violation of company policy is critical as evidence for any court or administrative review of this activity. It also can be used as part of a human resources action regarding the employee and establishes that you took the proper steps when you encountered the matter.

☒ **D** is incorrect because the disclosure of trade secrets to a competitor is not something a company will present in a press release.

59. ☑ **A, B,** and **D.** When you discover evidence of any wrongdoing in the workplace, you should verify what the nature of the wrongdoing is, who is involved, and if relevant, what physical media is involved. You should disclose this information to your supervisor and respond to any further instructions you may be given. If you are in possession of any physical evidence, you should release it to your supervisor, another responsible party in your company, or if required, to law enforcement.

☒ **C** is incorrect because you should not keep any personal copies of information deemed trade secrets or property of the company. It should be kept by the appropriate party according to company policy and other procedures and laws.

60. ☑ **A, B,** and **D.** As part of treating a customer with respect, you should indicate that you are paying attention to him and taking the situation seriously. Avoid any personal distractions, such as unnecessary phone calls or texting during the transaction. Also, even if you suspect that the customer may have participated in creating the computer problem, avoid attributing blame.

☒ **C** is incorrect because it is appropriate to explain to the customer in terms he is familiar with what is wrong with the computer and the actions that it will take to fix the problem.

61. ☑ **B** and **D.** Impact printers often use paper that must be fed into the device using sprockets, so the paper will need to have attached sprocket holes at each edge. Also, impact printer paper can be multilayer to produce several copies of the printout. Thermal printers require paper that is heat-sensitive as part of the printing process.

☒   **A** and **C** are incorrect because most laser and inkjet printers can use standard printer paper.

62.   ☑   **A.** Laser printers don't have what you would think of as a traditional print head, since the image is "drawn" on the drum with a laser, toner is attracted to the "drawn" areas of the drum, and then the image is transferred to the paper and affixed with the fuser.

☒   **B, C,** and **D** are incorrect because each of these printer types has a conventional print head, which is used to create the print image on the print media.

63.   ☑   **A, B,** and **C.** Some, but not all, BIOSs have the ability to monitor a variety of functions on a PC, including bus speeds, CPU temperature, fan speeds, and voltage. This information is not available for display in the operating system without installing additional third-party software.

☒   **D** is incorrect because the BIOS is not known to be able to monitor USB activity on a computer.

64.   ☑   **B** and **C.** You can install a PCIe wireless NIC expansion card or a wireless adapter via USB.

☒   **A** and **D** are incorrect. **A** is incorrect because a modem card is typically used for dial-up Internet access. **D** is incorrect because a cellular card is typically used to connect a computer to a cellular phone network.

65.   ☑   **B.** Since electronic components can't tolerate direct contact with liquids, liquid cooling systems use water blocks, which are heat-conductive metal pieces that contain hollow tubes of liquid and sit on top of the chips that need to be cooled. Thermal paste is applied between the chip and the block to improve heat transfer.

☒   **A** and **C** are incorrect because plastic tubes containing liquid coming into direct contact with hot chipsets are not particularly safe, as the heat might melt the plastic enough to release liquid onto the motherboard components. **D** is incorrect because water blocks contain their water inside tubes, not holding the liquid directly, nor are they attached underneath the chips, which would put the water blocks on the underside of the motherboard, between it and the PC case.

66.   ☑   **A.** When the hardware installation is finished, including the liquid cooling system, keep the computer powered down to minimize any potential for damage, fill the reservoir, and run the cooling system to check for leaks.

☒   **B, C,** and **D** are incorrect. **B** is incorrect because if a leak occurs while the computer is running, you are increasing the potential for damaging the computer's mechanical and electronic components. **C** is incorrect because this doesn't test the cooling system for leaks. **D** is incorrect because there is no process for running air through a liquid cooling system, particularly as a test to check for seal leaks.

67. ☑   **A and C.** If you use compressed air to spray clean the inside of the laser printer, you will most likely spray loose toner into the air, creating a breathing hazard for you and anyone around you. This is made worse if you are working in a confined space where the toner is concentrated. If you know you are going to be exposed to potentially hazardous particles in the air, consider wearing a face mask to filter out the particles.

    ☒   **B and D** are incorrect. B is incorrect because using a vacuum that is designed for the inside of electronic units like printers is a safer way to clean up loose toner, dust, and debris. **D** is incorrect because wiping up loose toner and dust with a cloth minimizes the possibility of this material becoming airborne and creating a breathing hazard.

68. ☑   **A, B, and C.** The most common problem in this circumstance is that the speakers are turned off or the volume is turned all the way down. It's also possible that sound for the speakers is set to mute in Windows. It's also possible that the speakers could be unplugged from the computer.

    ☒   **D** is incorrect because a muted YouTube video wouldn't cause sound to not work with CDs and DVDs.

69. ☑   **A and B.** You will need a physical connection between the device and the computer, such as a USB cable, and the drivers for the device so you can install them on the computer. Consult the documentation that came with the digitizer pad for more detailed instructions.

    ☒   **C and D** are incorrect. C is incorrect because the digitizer device drivers should be all of the software you need, and video software won't add anything to the performance of this device. **D** is incorrect because although a stylus is useful in order to draw on the digitizer pad, it's not required for the installation process.

70. ☑   **A, B, C, and E.** Since you work around electronic components and machines that reach high temperatures, you should take precautions to avoid burning yourself and possibly starting an electrical fire. Many on-the-job injuries are the result of improper lifting techniques, and IT technicians are asked to lift computers, packing boxes containing heavy equipment, and similar items. Also, be aware of the weight limitations of surfaces such as tables and racks when setting heavy items on them or installing them in structures. Since you sometimes work inside machines while they are running, you may want to remove loose jewelry and make sure loose clothing items cannot be snagged by running machinery. Also, jewelry can sometimes come in contact with live electrical circuits, resulting in electric shock.

    ☒   **D** is incorrect because self-grounding is the process of touching the metal frame of a computer before reaching inside the case. This equalizes the static potential between you and the machine in the event you don't have an ESD strap handy. This is for the protection of the sensitive electronic components in the computer; static shock does not pose a personal safety hazard.

71. ☑   **C and D.** A surge protector provides some measure of protection, in that it can be turned off by power surges, protecting computers and other devices plugged into them.

Uninterruptable power supplies (UPSs) can perform a similar function along with "treating" the electrical current that flows through them, making the current more "even" for computer use. UPS devices can also supplement a computer's power in the event of a blackout, allowing your customer the opportunity to gracefully power down her computers.

    ☒   **A** and **B** are incorrect. **A** is incorrect because a power strip only allows you to plug in multiple devices to a strip that's connected to a single power outlet. It provides no protection for devices on the power strip. **B** is incorrect because a power supply is an internal unit in a computer that converts AC current from the wall outlet to DC current used by the computer, and it offers little or no protection for the computer from electrical mishaps.

72. ☑ **D.** It's typical to install the Blu-ray drive by attaching its data cable to an available SATA controller port.

    ☒   **A, B,** and **C** are incorrect. **A** and **B** are incorrect because Blu-ray and DVD controllers do not exist on motherboards. **C** is incorrect because it is common for modern Blu-ray drives to be treated like SATA drives rather than attach to the computer using IDE.

73. ☑ **A.** You have to go into the BIOS to change the boot order of the drives so that the computer will know to look at the hard drive first and not the optical drive.

    ☒   **B, C,** and **D** are incorrect because you cannot change the boot order of a computer from inside an operating system. It must be performed in the BIOS.

74. ☑ **D.** Go into Device Manager, expand Network Adapters, right-click the adapter name, and then click Disable.

    ☒   **A, B,** and **C** are incorrect. **A** is incorrect because you do not have to perform this task in the BIOS. The device is easily accessible from the operating system. **B** and **C** are incorrect because you cannot directly access devices to disable from either Computer or Control Panel. From Control Panel, you can open System and then click Device Manager.

75. ☑ **A, C,** and **D.** You can install a PCIe card with an eSATA port, use an eSATA-to-serial port adapter on the computer's serial port, or use an eSATA-to-USB adapter on one of the computer's USB ports.

    ☒   **B** is incorrect because there is not an eSATA-to-RJ45 (Ethernet port) adapter. Also, since computers typically have only one RJ45 port, if you use it for the eSATA drive, you would have to find a different way to network the computer, such as Wi-Fi.

76. ☑ **A, B,** and **D.** You can install a PCIe card with FireWire ports, connect a FireWire hub to the computer via its FireWire or USB ports so that the hub can provide additional FireWire connections, or use a FireWire-to-USB adapter.

    ☒   **C** is incorrect because the computer has no external SATA connections. Typically, if a computer is going to have a SATA-related external port, it will be eSATA.

77. ☑ **C.** Once you install the sound card and power up the computer, Windows 7 will install the necessary drivers in the vast majority of cases. In the unlikely event that this does not occur, check Windows Update for the latest drivers for the sound card.

☒ **A, B,** and **D** are incorrect. **A** and **B** are incorrect because Windows will install the card's drivers in most instances. Only in extremely unlikely cases will you need to resort to these options. **D** is incorrect because you will only have to go to Windows Update if Windows 7 doesn't install the drivers.

78. ☑ **A** and **B.** Tools carried in a shirt pocket could fall into the computer, damaging motherboard components or other parts of the computer. They could also be a personal hazard if the technician bends or moves in a way that would cause the tools to press or stab against his body. Tools should always be carried in an appropriate carrying case.

☒ **C** and **D** are incorrect. **C** is incorrect because tools will not build up a "magnetic charge" while being carried in a shirt pocket. **D** is incorrect because although tools may damage the technician's clothing, this is not a safety hazard.

79. ☑ **A** and **C.** Rather than just unplugging a running computer or pressing the power button while Windows is operating, first gracefully power down the computer by clicking the Windows Start button and going through the shutdown routine. If the computers are to be repurposed, this will save wear and tear on the PCs. Also, regardless of whether the monitors are LCD or CRT, they are fragile, so handle with care.

☒ **B** and **D** are incorrect. **B** is incorrect because you should disconnect all cables attached to the computer before moving the unit. If cables are still attached to other components, you could pull these components, damaging them or their cables. Also, dangling cables could represent a safety hazard if you step on them while moving the PC. **D** is incorrect because stacking heavy computer cases on top of one another could damage the computers.

80. ☑ **A** and **C.** Both CRT monitors and power supplies can be extremely hazardous. Even when left unplugged for long periods of time, they still can carry lethal electrical charges and are highly dangerous if opened.

☒ **B** and **D** are incorrect. **B** is incorrect because while it can be dangerous to open a laser printer soon after it has been operating due to the heat it generates, after a reasonable cooling period, it's okay to work inside the device. **D** is incorrect because opening a server computer case is no more dangerous than opening a PC computer case.

81. ☑ **A** and **C.** A cool, dry room can contribute to ESD shock if that's where you are working inside computers. It's best if the humidity is kept between 50 and 80 percent.

☒ **B** and **D** are incorrect because neither of these factors promotes ESD, although a room that is too moist could contribute to moisture condensation, which can also damage the internal components of computers.

82. ☑ **B.** Most companies that make laser printers have buy-back programs for accepting and refurbishing spent toner cartridges.

☒ **A, C,** and **D** are incorrect. **A** is incorrect because toner is an environmental hazard due to the chemicals and fine particles that make up the toner. **C** is incorrect because you can send spent toner cartridges directly to the manufacturer. You do not need to go through a retail outlet. **D** is incorrect because there is no process for you to refurbish old toner cartridges, but the printer maker can reuse the old units.

83. ☑ **C.** Since CRT monitors contain toxic substances such as lead and cannot be thrown away, they should be recycled, as they also contain various useful metals.

☒ **A, B,** and **D** are incorrect. **A** is incorrect because it is very dangerous to take a CRT monitor apart due to the risk of electric shock. **B** is incorrect because the materials inside CRT monitors are highly toxic. **D** is incorrect because there is no buy-back or recycling program for CRT monitors operated by monitor manufacturers.

84. ☑ **A, B,** and **C.** Often technicians recommend either copying the settings down by hand or photographing them as they appear on the screen, but depending on the BIOS you are using, there are some methods of backing up the BIOS and, in case of a serious incident that destroys the BIOS, recover the original BIOS settings.

☒ **D** is incorrect because no Windows application allows you to back up the BIOS settings of the computer.

85. ☑ **C.** Every time a computer is powered up, the BIOS runs the Power-On Self-Test, or POST, which is a collection of tests that checks for the presence and status of required computer components such as keyboard, mouse, hard disk, RAM, and so on. If there is a problem the BIOS will issue an alert in the form of a beep code or as a message on the monitor.

☒ **A, B,** and **D** are incorrect because while BIOS can run these tests and monitor these components, the POST test is by far the most commonly run test for which the BIOS is responsible.

86. ☑ **B.** Electricity travels to homes and businesses as alternating current, or AC, but computers use direct current, or DC. A power supply converts AC current that arrives from the wall outlet through the surge protector and converts it to DC.

☒ **A, C,** and **D** are incorrect. **A** is incorrect because electricity arrives from the power company as AC and the power supply converts it to DC. **C** and **D** are incorrect because watts cannot be converted into volts or vice versa, and not only can a power supply not perform this function, but it makes no sense for it to do so.

87. ☑ **A, B,** and **D.** Different computer components require different amounts of voltage in DC or VDC: ±12 VDC, ±5 VDC, or ±3.3 VDC. Some power supplies can detect incoming voltage from the wall socket and automatically switch it to the type used by the computer in case the computer is operating in a region where the electrical power standards are different from what it was built to use. The power supply fan also assists in keeping the inside of the computer cool.

    ☒ **C** is incorrect because power supplies are made to produce different wattage depending on the needs of the device in which they are installed. Some computers use well above 1000 watts.

88. ☑ **A.** The P1 power connector is the primary electrical connection between the power supply and ATX motherboard, using 20 or 24 pins.

    ☒ **B, C,** and **D** are incorrect. **B** is incorrect because the P4 connector is used in addition to the P1 if the motherboard needs additional power. **C** and **D** are incorrect because the mini and Molex connectors provide power to peripheral devices.

89. ☑ **A.** The maximum resolution for VGA, or Video Graphics Array, is 640 ×480 pixels.

    ☒ **B, C,** and **D** are incorrect. **B** is incorrect because this does not correspond to the maximum resolution of VGA or any other display standard. **C** is incorrect because this corresponds with the maximum resolution of the XGA and EVGA display standards. **D** is incorrect because this resolution corresponds to the SVGA display standard.

90. ☑ **D.** For LCD displays, the response time is the time in milliseconds it takes for one pixel to go from active to inactive.

    ☒ **A, B,** and **C** are incorrect. **A** is incorrect because color quality is a setting in the Windows XP display applet that lets you adjust the number of colors used by the display. **B** is incorrect because display resolution is the number of displayable pixels on a monitor. **C** is incorrect because refresh rate is the rate per second at which an image appears on a CRT monitor screen.

91. ☑ **C.** TWAIN (not an acronym) is a standard software protocol used by imaging devices such as scanners and digital cameras.

    ☒ **A, B,** and **D** are incorrect. **A** is incorrect because FAX stands for facsimile and usually refers to a machine that can send and receive documents as images. **B** is incorrect because OCR, or optical character recognition, is a type of software that must be TWAIN-compliant and allows devices to interpret bitmap images and determine which images are alphanumeric characters. **D** is incorrect because USB refers to devices that comply with the Universal Serial Bus standard for device communication and is commonly used by everything from mice, to printers, to portable storage media.

92. ☑ **C.** Although most multimedia devices are relatively simple to install, video capture cards require that they be installed as expansion cards (typically PCIe) with drivers for the

card plus specialized software to allow the card to perform the function of capturing video input and storing it on the computer.

☒ **A, B,** and **D** are incorrect because these devices usually connect to a computer using USB and only require that the drivers be installed (and often, Windows will already have the drivers) before they work.

93. ☑ **C.** This type of switch has two models: the "many devices to one computer" model, which is described in the question, and the "many computers to one keyboard, monitor, and switch" model, which is still the standard in many server rooms.

☒ **A** is incorrect because it doesn't specify a type of KVM model as much as a control mechanism. KVM switches can be switched either electronically or mechanically (inactive KVM switch). **B** is incorrect because this type of switch is used to control a remote computer over an Ethernet connection using IP packets to encode and transmit data. **D** is incorrect because this is another method of remotely controlling a computer, but uses a proprietary protocol for the data mechanism and not IP.

94. ☑ **C.** This particular printer type requires a serial printer cable that uses a 9-pin or 25-pin serial connector because the connection is faster than either the old parallel printer cables or USB.

☒ **A, B,** and **D** are incorrect. **A** is incorrect because this connection would be required for a network printer. **B** is incorrect because parallel printer connections are used with older printers and are too slow for the needs of the printer described in the question. **D** is incorrect because USB, although used commonly for printer connections, is too slow for this printer's needs.

95. ☑ **C.** On the Ports tab of the Properties box, you can view, add, change, or configure a port for the printer.

☒ **A, B,** and **D** are incorrect. **A** is incorrect because Printing Preferences allows you to configure the layout and paper/quality features of how a page prints. **B** is incorrect because Printer Properties is not an option when you right-click a printer in Windows XP. **D** is incorrect because this option doesn't exist.

96. ☑ **C.** On the Web Services tab of the Properties box, click the IP address next to Web Page, which should look something like http://192.168.0.1. A Web browser will open with the printer's "Home" page displayed, which may allow you to view the printer's status, ink levels, network status, and other information. Depending on the type of device and the manufacturer, there may be tabs at the top to manage scanning, faxing, networking, and other options.

☒ **A, B,** and **D** are incorrect. **A** is incorrect because Printing Preferences allows you to configure the layout and paper/quality features of how a page prints. **B** is incorrect because Printer Properties provides you with a great deal of information about the printer, but not a way to access Web Services. **D** is incorrect because this option doesn't exist.

97. ☑ **A, B,** and **D.** There are a wide variety of settings and services that you can enable, disable, and configure in a computer's BIOS. These include being able to manage the performance of the USB controller, the SATA drive controller, and CPU performance.
☒ **C** is incorrect because there is no option in the BIOS for enabling or disabling the printing service on a computer. This is usually controlled in the operating system.

98. ☑ **D.** Each type of BIOS has its own alert of beep codes. In this case, if the BIOS is AMI, two short beeps means a memory error, but it can also mean a POST error (if you've just upgraded the computer's RAM as part of your maintenance, that could be a clue). Award BIOS doesn't issue two short beeps for any error, but will beep in long and short beeps together or in repeating beeps. Phoenix BIOS beeps will be in combination such as one beep-one beep-two beeps.
☒ **A, B,** and **C** are incorrect because unless you know the BIOS type, you can't be sure what the beep codes mean. Either enter your BIOS setup to discover the BIOS type or consult your computer's motherboard manual.

99. ☑ **B, C,** and **D.** You do not even need a monitor, keyboard, mouse, or any other components of the computer to be attached or working. The minimum the computer needs to boot is a working motherboard, CPU, power supply, and RAM. The computer will boot, the POST will run, and the POST card will display the output as hexadecimal characters on its display. You will need to know the BIOS the computer runs and have a list of the test and error codes the BIOS uses to be able to interpret the codes the card will display during the test.
☒ **A** is incorrect because the POST card must be inserted into an expansion slot on the motherboard.

100. ☑ **B.** It's fairly normal for VoIP phones to have two Ethernet ports so both the phone and the computer can share a single Ethernet port on the wall.
☒ **A, C,** and **D** are incorrect. **A** is incorrect because while this is not unheard of, it's really unnecessary. **C** is incorrect because most VoIP phones come with two Ethernet ports by default. **D** is incorrect because, as previously explained, the phone and computer can share the same wired connection.

D

Practice Exam
220-802

QUESTIONS

1. Your customer wants you to set up a wireless network for her office. She works with confidential business documents and wants to make sure no one compromises the security of her wireless access point in order to breach network security. Of the following, which suggestions do you make to improve access point security? (Choose three.)
   A. Change the default SSID, user name, and password.
   B. Update the access point's firmware to the most current version.
   C. Turn off DNS in the access point.
   D. Enable WPA2 encryption.

2. You are speaking to a group of high school students in a technology workshop about network security. You are describing a protocol that uses public-key cryptography to authenticate between a local computer and a remote computer. Of the following, what security protocol are you describing?
   A. FTP
   B. HTML
   C. SSH
   D. TCP/IP

3. You receive a phone call from a user who keeps seeing pop-ups with the error message "Limited or no connectivity: The connection has limited or no connectivity. You might be unable to access the Internet or some network resources." No other users in the same office are having problems. What three troubleshooting steps should you try first? (Choose three.)
   A. Reboot the computer.
   B. Check the network cable.
   C. Restart the network firewall.
   D. Check for a valid IP address.

4. You are helping a user select a smartphone device. Which of the following features is not commonly found in smartphones?
   A. Accelerometer
   B. GPS
   C. Remote backup
   D. VGA port

5. Your supervisor would like to have a mobile phone that allows for a wireless connection to the audio system in his car. What technology is most appropriate?
   A. Bluetooth
   B. Infrared

   C. VoIP

   D. IPv6

6. One of your users is experiencing slow wireless connection speed on a laptop that is often used outside of the office in many different locations. The user has administrative permission on the computer, and you notice that he has installed a large amount of downloaded software. What do you suspect might be the problem?

   A. Faulty wireless access point

   B. Failed Ethernet interface

   C. Malware infection

   D. IP address conflict

7. You are troubleshooting a NetBIOS connection issue and would like to see a list of all active NetBIOS connections. What command can you use?

   A. nbtstat -c

   B. nbtstat -n

   C. nbtstat -r

   D. nbtstat -s

8. You are concerned about the potential presence of rogue wireless access points on your network. What tool can you use to detect these devices?

   A. Wireless locator

   B. Punchdown tool

   C. Toner probe

   D. Ping

9. You work in the IT department of a highly secure government facility, and you are evaluating different biometric methods of computer authentication. Of the following, which method of biometric authentication is considered the least reliable?

   A. Fingerprint scan

   B. Hand geometry scan

   C. Retina scan

   D. Voice analysis

10. You receive a call from the company CEO informing you that he lost his smartphone and it contains sensitive information. What safeguards should you suggest to protect information on the phone? (Choose two.)

   A. Remote wipe

   B. Geolocation via GPS

   C. Password change

   D. Patching

11. A user brings his tablet computer into your help desk and notes that it is not functioning properly. After diagnosing the situation, you suspect that the solid-state memory in the device has experienced a hardware failure. What do you suggest?

   A. Replacement of the SSD

   B. Reformatting the memory

   C. Returning the device to the manufacturer

   D. Rebooting the device

12. You are studying the differences between FAT32 and NTFS file systems. One thing you discover is that, regardless of which file system is used on a Windows computer, files can be marked with the same attributes. Which attributes can you use with files in either a FAT32 or NTFS file system? (Choose three.)

   A. Read-only

   B. Hidden

   C. System

   D. Full control

13. You are working with a user who travels quite a bit and you suggest to her that a privacy filter may be an appropriate security control. What risk is this designed to mitigate?

   A. Phishing

   B. Shoulder surfing

   C. Wi-Fi eavesdropping

   D. Viewing inappropriate content

14. After troubleshooting a computer, you notice that it contains software that monitors the Websites a user visits and reports them back to a central server. What type of malicious software is this?

   A. Virus

   B. Adware

   C. Spyware

   D. Trojan horse

15. You are concerned about the security implications of having a default administrator account on your Windows 7 computer. The account is currently enabled. What tool can you use to disable it?

   A. Local Users and Groups

   B. Policy Editor

C. REGEDIT

D. Group Policy Editor

16. Your company's IT department has a policy that says all employees are to lock their computer desktops whenever their computers are turned on and they have to leave their cubicles, even for short breaks. Of the following options, in a small business setting, what is the most likely method to make users comply with this policy?

A. Manually locking their desktops

B. Having their desktops become locked when the screensaver is activated

C. Using Active Directory Servers Group Policies

D. Having security staff lock unattended computers

17. You are concerned that users may bring infected media into the office and transmit a virus to your computers. What actions should you take to protect against this threat? (Choose two.)

A. Disable Autorun.

B. Require passwords on all computers.

C. Install antivirus software.

D. Use a password-protected screensaver.

18. You are reviewing computer security issues with a new technician in your department. You are currently discussing computer malware. What sort of malicious software sends a copy of what the computer user types to a remote location to harvest passwords and other private information?

A. A virus

B. A worm

C. A keystroke logger

D. A password cracker

19. You get a call from a home customer complaining that his computer is behaving strangely. Some of the symptoms include strange icons and shortcuts appearing on the PC's taskbar, new programs appearing in Add/Remove Programs, and an unusual number of favorites appearing in Internet Explorer. What is the most likely cause of these events?

A. The computer is infected with malware.

B. A hacker has logged into the customer's computer remotely.

C. Microsoft Automatic Updates is reconfiguring the computer.

D. The computer's antivirus program is installing protective applications.

20. The boot block on a customer's Windows XP machine has been corrupted by a virus. Of the following, what methods can you use to repair it? (Choose two.)

  A. Download a standalone antivirus product onto a USB drive and run the program on the affected computer from the thumb drive using the boot-sector virus removal and repair tools.

  B. Run the onboard antivirus program on the computer and select the fix boot block option when prompted.

  C. Boot the computer from the Windows XP boot CD or DVD and repair the boot block with Recovery Console.

  D. Boot the computer into Safe Mode and then run the antivirus product to repair the boot block.

21. You have just removed a number of viruses from a home customer's Windows XP computer and repaired the corrupted boot block. You have scanned the computer after updating the antivirus program and virus signatures to the latest versions, and no threats were found, so the computer is currently threat free. What is your next step to reduce the risk of the computer being infected again?

  A. Advise the customer that he is using a poor antivirus product and suggest a better solution.

  B. Advise the customer that his computer's operating system is vulnerable and suggest he update it to the latest version of Windows.

  C. Advise the customer that his ISP provides insufficient protection and suggest he change ISPs.

  D. Advise the customer to avoid opening e-mail attachments from unknown sources, to avoid visiting "dangerous" Websites, and to avoid engaging in other behaviors that could put his computer at risk of infection.

22. You work for a small city IT department and have just deployed several new Windows 7 workstations in city hall. One of your customers complains about the User Account Control (UAC), which dims the desktop and prompts her to click Yes in a dialog box whenever she installs a program such as a PDF reader. She asks if you can turn this feature off, since she promises to install only programs that are safe and that she absolutely needs to do her job. What do you tell her?

  A. You tell her that the UAC feature cannot be configured and must be used the way it is.

  B. You tell her that this is the least restrictive setting for the UAC feature, and more restrictive settings would prevent her from installing any software on the computer.

  C. You tell her that you could change the setting so that it wouldn't dim the desktop, but there's no way to completely remove the requirement of the dialog box prompt.

  D. You tell her that you could change the setting to be less restrictive in the way she requests, but company policy requires that you leave the UAC configuration at its default setting as part of the organization's strict adherence to company security policy.

23. You work for a small city IT department, and you get a call from a customer who says he cannot write to documents in the City shared folder on an NTFS volume. He had read and write permissions to this folder last week. He's a member of the Managers group and was just recently added as a member of the Auditors group. These groups were specifically created in your organization to manage access to different NTFS volumes on the network. Of the following, what is the problem?

   A. The Managers group has Allow permissions for read and write for the folder, but the Auditors group does not have any Allow permissions for the folder.

   B. The Auditors group has Allow permissions for read and write for the folder, but the Managers group does not have any Allow permissions for the folder.

   C. The Managers group has Allow permissions for read and write for the folder, but the Auditors group has Deny permissions for read and write for the folder.

   D. The Managers group has Deny permissions for read and write for the folder, but the Auditors group has no Allow or Deny permissions for the folder.

24. You have a customer who has been the victim of an online scam that caused him to input his user name and password on a site he believed was his bank's Website but in fact was a copy of the site. As a result, his bank account has been compromised. What sort of scam does this describe? (Choose two.)

   A. Cookies

   B. Phishing

   C. Social engineering

   D. War driving

25. You work for a small city IT department, and you get a call from a customer in city hall saying she can't log in to her computer. You've gotten several such calls in the past 30 minutes, and you explain that the domain controller is having a problem and is not accepting authentication credentials from end users. The customer states that she needs to get to a Word file on her hard drive to prepare for a meeting with the mayor. What do you tell her she can do to log in to her computer and access her documents?

   A. You tell her the domain controller will be repaired soon and then she'll be able to log in to her computer.

   B. You give her the local administrator user name and password used by IT to access computers for maintenance, as long as she promises not to reveal this information to anyone else.

   C. You tell her to log in to the computer locally using the Guest account.

   D. You tell her to log in to the computer locally using her own user account.

26. You work for a small city IT department, and you are reviewing computer security procedures with a new technician. You are currently reviewing the special hidden administrative shares on Windows machines. What is the share used for temporary connections for remotely administering a computer?

   A. ADMIN$
   B. FAX$
   C. IPC$
   D. PRINT$

27. You get a call from a user who has just purchased a Windows 7 computer. She was installing a PDF reader when her desktop dimmed and a dialog box appeared asking her if she wanted to continue. What just happened?

   A. Her antivirus program detected malware that was about to be installed.
   B. This is the default action of User Account Control.
   C. User Account Control detected malware that was about to be installed.
   D. She does not have permissions to install this program and must log in as an administrator.

28. You have a customer who tells you his Windows 7 computer has been experiencing problems for the past week or so. You troubleshoot the computer and decide to restore it to a restore point that was created before the computer started having problems. Your customer is concerned because he deleted several applications that were causing other types of problems on his computer a few weeks ago and he doesn't want those programs restored. What can you do to find out which programs a particular restore point will affect? (Choose two.)

   A. In the System Restore dialog box, double-click the desired restore point.
   B. In the System Restore dialog box, click the desired restore point to select it and then click Scan For Affected Programs.
   C. On the System Properties dialog box on the System Protection tab, click System Restore Options.
   D. There is no method for making this determination. You'll just have to select the most likely restore point.

29. You are helping a user configure a smartphone for the first time. He asks you to describe the types of content that can be easily synchronized between a computer and a smartphone. What do you tell him can be synchronized easily and used on both devices? (Choose three.)

   A. Contacts
   B. Photos

    C. Music

    D. Applications

30. You are discussing user authentication technology with your coworkers and someone suggests adopting a system that allows users to use the same passwords across systems. What technology is he referring to?

    A. SSL

    B. SSD

    C. SSH

    D. SSO

31. You are selecting a wireless device for one of your users and would like to find a cellular WWAN device that allows you to connect multiple computers through the same connection easily. What device do you choose?

    A. Integrated WWAN adapter

    B. USB broadband card

    C. PCMCIA broadband card

    D. Mobile hotspot

32. You are configuring a Windows 7 computer for your small office network and are asked to choose a network connection. You want to choose an option that enables Network Discovery. Which of the following options will enable this feature? (Choose two.)

    A. Home

    B. Work

    C. Enterprise

    D. Public

33. You are configuring the Windows firewall on a customer's Windows 7 computer, and you want to allow certain programs to have access to the Public and Home/Work (Private) networks as shown here. Of the following, what is this form of firewall configuration called?

A. Exceptions.

B. Port forwarding.

C. Port security.

D. You must call the manufacturer and have them remotely connect to the firewall to allow the desired traffic to pass.

34. You would like to configure the Wake-on-LAN feature of a network device in Windows 7 and know that you need to enable the Allow This Device To Wake The Computer setting of the Network Adapter Properties. On what tab is this found?

   A. General

   B. Power Management

   C. Driver

   D. Resources

35. You are deploying Voice over IP telephones in your organization and wish to use a single connection for both power and data. What technology must your network support to provide this capability?

   A. PPP

   B. PoE

   C. RADIUS

   D. VPN

36. Your organization allows the use of streaming media by employees at work but you are concerned about the impact this will have on the speed of other network traffic. What technology can you use to limit the amount of bandwidth consumed by this type of activity?

   A. QoS

   B. Content filtering

   C. IDS

   D. SSL

37. You are configuring the NTFS attributes for a folder that will be searched frequently. What attribute should you enable?

   A. Hidden

   B. Read-only

   C. Indexed

   D. Encrypted

38. You are configuring group membership for a computer user and want to make sure that she only has access to her files. Which of the following groups grant members the ability to access the files of other users?

   A. Administrators

   B. Power Users

   C. Guest

   D. Users

39. You have a customer using a Windows 7 computer who says he cannot connect to the Internet. You ping the gateway and get a response, but you cannot ping a domain name such as www.google.com on the Internet. When you look at the Internet Protocol (TCP/IP) Properties box on the computer, you see manual settings for both the IP address and the DNS server. What is the problem?

A. The computer isn't configured to use a manual IP address.

B. The IP address, subnet mask, and default gateway fields are blank.

C. The computer is pointed to the wrong DNS server IP address.

D. The DHCP server is down.

40. You work for an ISP, and you are providing phone support, helping a customer set up Microsoft Office Outlook to connect to your company's mail servers. You provide the name mail.company .com so that the customer can configure Outlook to connect to the ISP's outgoing mail server, allowing the customer to send e-mails. In Outlook, what field must the customer use to enter the outgoing mail server name?

A. DNS

B. IMAP

C. POP

D. SMTP

41. You work for a small city IT department and receive a complaint from a new hire saying he is unable to use Internet Explorer 8 on his Windows Vista computer to connect to a secure site using HTTPS. He is able to connect to all HTTP protocol sites. You check and verify that this is the first time he's tried to connect to an HTTPS site since being hired last week. You use another computer in the same office and are able to connect to the HTTPS site the customer needs to access. What do you suspect?

A. The corporate firewall is blocking HTTPS connections.

B. Internet Explorer on the hire's computer needs to have its proxy settings changed.

C. The proxy settings on the hire's Windows Vista computer need to be changed in Administrative Tools.

D. The HTTPS site was down when the hire tried to access it but was back up when you accessed it a few minutes later.

42. You work for a small city IT department and you have a customer in city hall who complains that the network is slow. What do you tell her about how network speeds can be affected?

A. The network bandwidth varies throughout the day because the ISP serving city hall manually adds or subtracts bandwidth based on overall customer use in the Internet backbone.

B. The network bandwidth always remains at its peak capacity and the network slowness is only perceived by the customer, since she is downloading several large data files from the Internet and she believes they should download faster.

C. The network bandwidth remains the same but is affected by different factors that cause delays or latency on the network, such as heavy traffic or network equipment that is temporarily down.

D. Network traffic consists of two components, bandwidth and latency, where bandwidth is the speed at which the computer works to produce data and latency is the limitation of how quickly the computer's NIC can transfer computer data to the network.

43. You are using the Recovery Console to repair a damaged Windows XP machine. You want to write a new partition table from the backup Master File Table. What command do you use in Recovery Console?

A. DISKPART

B. FIXBOOT

C. FIXMBR

D. SYSTEMROOT

44. You are reviewing computer security issues with a new technician in your department. You are currently discussing your company's strong password policy and how to teach customers to use strong passwords. Of the following, which represents a strong password that a customer will be likely to remember?

A. password

B. Pa$$wo5d

C. 4s&7yrsaO

D. 5gh90j6r9v94f$2&&

45. You work for a small city IT department, and you are currently teaching a class to employees on computer and network security. You are describing some methods of preventing computers from being compromised by viruses, spyware, and adware. Of the following, what are some valid methods that will still allow customers to perform normal tasks on the Internet? (Choose two.)

A. Don't open attachments from an unknown sender.

B. Use a pop-up blocker on your Web browser.

C. Set the Windows Firewall to allow no exceptions.

D. Disconnect the Ethernet cable from the computer.

46. You get a call from a Windows 7 home user who has forgotten her user password and now can't log in to her computer. What do you tell her to do?

A. Use the Password Reset Disk that shipped with the computer.

B. Log in to the computer as Guest and reset her user password.

C. Reboot the computer from an installation DVD to the repair mode command prompt and reset the password at the command line.

D. Reinstall Windows 7.

47. You work for a small city IT department and you have a customer who complains that she is unable to delete any of the files in a folder called Subfoo, which is contained in a shared folder named Foo on an NTFS volume on the network. She has all Allow permissions to the Foo folder except Full Control, the highest being Modify. She is able to create and delete documents from directly within Foo but is not able to delete files in Subfoo. What is the problem?

A. The Allow permission for Modify does not include the Traverse Folder/Execute File Allow permission.

B. The Allow permission for Modify does not include the Create Folders/Append Data Allow permission.

C. The Allow permission for Modify does not include the Delete Subfolders And Files Allow permission.

D. The Allow permission for Modify does not include the Delete Allow permission.

48. You share a Windows XP workstation with a coworker, and you both have created a number of documents in a shared folder on the PC so that you can collaborate on your work efforts. You created a text file called "test" in a shared folder, but your coworker says she can't find it. You check and you can't find the file either. You do a search and come up with nothing. You know you created the file and saved it in the shared folder. What could have happened?

A. The file is marked hidden.

B. The file is marked read-only.

C. The file is marked for archiving.

D. The file is marked for compression.

49. You are navigating through the directory system of a Windows XP computer and come across a screen as illustrated in the accompanying screenshot. What has been hidden in this directory?

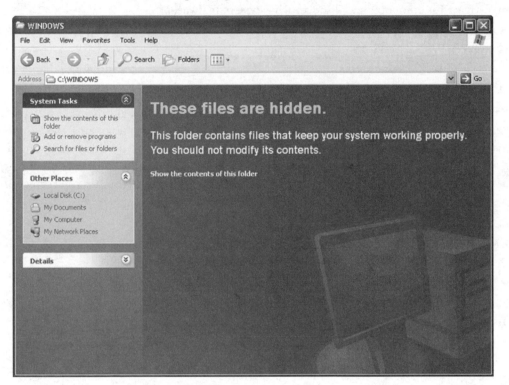

A. Archived files

B. Compressed files

C. Program files

D. System files

50. You work for a small city IT department and you are assisting a customer secure data on a Windows Vista laptop he is about to take on a business trip. You want to make sure that if the laptop is stolen, the data will not be compromised. Which security measure do you use that works before the Windows operating system is even loaded and encrypts the entire volume?

A. BitLocker

B. EFS

C. Intrusion detection

D. TPM

51. You have a rural dial-up customer who complains that a large number of phone calls have been made to "dangerous" sites on the Internet from his computer but he didn't make these calls. You investigate his computer and discover what type of malware?

    A. Adware

    B. Dialer

    C. Keystroke logger

    D. Spim

52. You want to install Windows 7 on a PC that does not have an optical drive, so you have decided to install Windows 7 from a bootable USB drive. You need to acquire the Windows 7 installation files from a computer currently running Windows 7. To do this, you insert a USB thumb drive into a USB port on a Windows 7 computer. You need to use a command-line utility to format the thumb drive and make it bootable. Of the following, which is the correct utility?

    A. diskpart

    B. fdisk

    C. format

    D. xcopy

53. You want to install Windows 7 on several PCs over an Ethernet connection at the office where you work rather than having to manually install the OS on each machine one by one. Which installation method will allow you to do this?

    A. CD

    B. DVD

    C. PXE

    D. USB

54. You are reviewing the various methods for installing Windows 7. You want to select a method of installing Windows 7 on a PC that lets you preselect the configuration selections required during the installation process. Of the following, what installation type are you describing?

    A. Clean install

    B. Repair installation

    C. Unattended installation

    D. Upgrade

55. You are reviewing disk partitioning procedures with another member of the IT staff where you work. You are planning to perform some partitioning tasks on the hard drives of several Windows XP computers. Of the following, which scenarios can you successfully accomplish? (Choose two.)

   A. In the Disk Management tool, right-click the unallocated area of the basic disk and then click New Partition.

   B. In the Disk Management tool, right-click the free space in an extended partition on a basic disk and then click New Logical Drive.

   C. In the Disk Management tool, right-click the unallocated area of a dynamic disk and then click New Partition.

   D. In the Disk Management tool, right-click the free space in an extended partition on a dynamic disk and then click New Logical Drive.

56. You've opened Internet Options in the Control Panel of a Windows 7 computer. You want to set the home page for the computer's Web browser. What tab must you be on?

   A. General

   B. Security

   C. Privacy

   D. Programs

57. You have opened the Display tool in Control Panel on a Windows 7 computer. You click Adjust Resolution. What can you do on this screen? (Choose all that apply.)

   A. Select the type of display device if more than one is available.

   B. Adjust the resolution.

   C. Adjust the orientation to settings such as landscape or portrait.

   D. Set a custom text size.

58. You have opened User Accounts on a Windows 7 computer and want to perform some tasks to manage your account on the PC. Of the following, what options are available to you directly from the User Accounts screen if you are an administrator? (Choose all that apply.)

   A. You can change your password.

   B. You can change your picture.

   C. You can create a new account.

   D. You can change the User Account Control (UAC) settings.

59. You have opened up the Folder Options tool in Control Panel on a Windows 7 computer. You want to adjust the folder settings that control the sharing wizard, viewing hidden files, hiding file extensions, and the layout of folders. On what tab can you accomplish all of these tasks?

A. General

B. Search

C. View

D. You can't perform all of these tasks on only one tab.

60. You are performing some routine maintenance on your Windows 7 computer. You are in Control Panel and you open the System item. On the System screen, when you click Advanced System Settings, which of the following can you manage?

A. Performance (virtual memory)

B. Hardware profiles

C. Remote settings

D. System protection

61. You have opened the Action Center in the Control Panel of your Windows 7 computer. In the pane on the left side of the screen, what options can you select? (Choose all that apply.)

A. Change Action Center Settings

B. Change User Account Control Settings

C. Change Performance (Virtual Memory)

D. View Performance Information

62. You have just opened Windows Firewall in the Control Panel of a Windows 7 computer. You click Advanced Settings. When the Windows Firewall with Advanced Settings screen opens, what options are available in pane on the left? (Choose all that apply.)

A. Turn Windows Firewall On Or Off

B. Monitoring

C. Inbound Rules

D. Outbound Rules

63. You opened the Power Options item in the Control Panel of a Windows 7 computer. What is displayed in the main pane of the Power Options screen?

A. Select A Power Plan

B. Select Hibernate Options

C. Select Sleep/Suspend Options

D. Select Standby Options

64. Your Windows 7 computer belongs to a HomeGroup. You open the HomeGroup screen in Control Panel. What are you able to share on this screen under Share Libraries And Printers? (Choose all that apply.)

  A. Directories

  B. Music

  C. Pictures

  D. Videos

65. You have opened up the Troubleshooting screen in the Control Panel of your Windows 7 computer. What are your available options? (Choose all that apply.)

  A. Video Performance

  B. Programs

  C. Hardware And Sound

  D. Appearance And Personalization

66. You are providing computer and printer support services for a small business customer and are currently working on a laser printer. The printer is displaying symptoms that lead you to believe that a residual electric charge is being left on the drum after printing. What is the common symptom for this problem?

  A. Faded prints

  B. Ghost images

  C. Streaks

  D. Vertical lines on the page

67. You are providing computer and printer support services for a small business customer and are currently trying to install a new printer on a Windows 7 computer as a local printer. You receive an error message stating "Unable to install printer. Either the printer name was typed incorrectly, or the specified printer has lost its connection to the server. For more information, click Help." Of the following, what are the most likely causes of this error? (Choose all that apply.)

  A. Faulty USB cable.

  B. Incompatible drivers.

  C. The printer service was not installed in Windows 7.

  D. You forgot to insert valid ink cartridges in the printer.

68. You are providing computer and printer support services for a small business customer. The screen on his printer has issued the error message "Error 13." What does this mean?

A. Black ink cartridge empty.

B. Paper jam.

C. Paper out.

D. Consult the printer's documentation. There are too many error codes for all of the various makes and models of printers available for you to memorize them all.

69. You are troubleshooting a customer's Windows 7 computer that has experienced a serious system error. Of the following, which tools or utilities can you use for diagnosis and repair? (Choose all that apply.)

A. Automated System Recovery

B. System Repair Disc

C. Event Viewer

D. Safe Mode

70. You have a customer who uses Windows XP SP3 as her home computer. She calls you and complains that when she started the computer this morning, the computer's startup routine behaved normally until the graphical user interface (GUI) failed to load. She said that yesterday, she started the computer and got a "blue screen" but rebooted and it was fine. You go to her home and try to diagnose the problem. You are unable to boot into Safe Mode, as the GUI continues to not load. What could be causing this problem? (Choose all that apply.)

A. Bad hard drive.

B. Bad motherboard.

C. Bad network interface card.

D. A music CD left in the computer's optical drive is causing the computer to fail to boot.

71. You have a customer who uses a Windows XP computer in his small home office. He says that when he attempted to shut down the computer last night, it spontaneously rebooted. Of the following, what do you suspect?

A. Windows Startup and Recovery is set to reboot the computer upon detecting a serious OS error.

B. Windows Startup and Recovery is set to reboot upon a power supply failure.

C. Windows hangs on Saving Your Settings as it tries to shut down and spontaneously reboots.

D. Windows hangs when trying to erase virtual memory at shutdown and spontaneously reboots.

72. You are working in the IT department for a mid-sized business and are responsible for managing all of the software updates for the Windows servers in the server room. Of the following, which tool will you use to accomplish the task of overseeing software updates for all of the servers?

A. Antivirus updates

B. Driver/firmware updates

C. Patch management

D. Windows Updates

73. You suspect that the hard drive on a customer's Windows 7 computer contains file system errors, and you want to use a tool that will check for those errors and attempt to repair them. Which tool should you use?

A. System Restore

B. Check Disk

C. Recovery Image

D. Defrag

74. You are in the Control Panel of a customer's Windows XP computer performing some routine maintenance tasks. In the Control Panel in Classic View, which of the following items are immediately visible? (Choose all that apply.)

A. Network connections

B. Printers and faxes

C. Automatic updates

D. Network setup wizard

75. You are in the Control Panel of a customer's Windows Vista computer performing some routine maintenance tasks. Of the following, what items do you expect to find only in Vista's Control Panel? (Choose all that apply.)

A. HomeGroup

B. Offline files

C. Pen and input devices

D. Tablet PC settings

76. In Windows XP, when you needed to install third-party drivers for RAID during the OS installation, when prompted, you would press the F6 function key and proceed. How is this same task performed during the Windows 7 installation?

A. The same as in Windows XP.

B. When prompted during installation, press F5 instead.

C. On the Where Do You Want To Install Windows screen, select the disk and partition and then click Load Driver.

D. You can only install the drivers after the Windows 7 installation is complete.

77. You want to install two operating systems on the same computer so that when your customer starts her computer, she can choose which operating system to load and use. What installation-related process must you use?

   A. Multiboot

   B. Remote network installation

   C. Image deployment

   D. Partitioning

78. You are planning to install Windows 7 on a customer's computer and are reviewing the various steps of the installation process. Of the following, which is not part of the normal Windows installation routine?

   A. Workgroup versus domain setup

   B. Time/date/region/language settings

   C. Driver installation, software, and Windows Updates

   D. Factory recovery partition

79. You are performing routine maintenance tasks on a customer's Windows XP computer. You have clicked the Start button and want to launch several tools from the run box. Which names can you type into the run box, press ENTER, and expect to launch? (Choose all that apply.)

   A. Control Panel

   B. Explorer

   C. Network Connections

   D. Notepad

80. You are troubleshooting a customer's computer that is making a loud "whirring" sound. The sound started off fairly soft but has been getting louder over the past several days. If this problem isn't diagnosed and repaired, what other problems could it cause? (Choose all that apply.)

   A. Complete computer shutdown

   B. Intermittent device failures

   C. Monitor damage

   D. Overheating

81. You get a call from a customer saying that when he pressed the power button on his computer this morning, absolutely nothing happened. The computer is completely dead. What are some things you tell the customer over the phone to try before you come out to check his PC? (Choose all that apply.)

   A. Make sure the computer is plugged in to a power strip or surge protector.

   B. Make sure the power strip or surge protector is plugged in and turned on.

    C. Make sure the computer's power supply is not faulty.

    D. Make sure the computer's power switch is not faulty.

82. You get a call from a customer saying that her older Windows XP computer is running slowly. When you get more details about the problem, you discover that the hard drive read/write performance is slow and sometimes fails altogether. The computer only has one IDE hard disk. What could be causing this sort of problem? (Choose all that apply.)

    A. Bad BIOS setting

    B. Bad IDE cable

    C. Bad IDE drive

    D. Bad power supply

83. You get a call from a customer saying that when he tried to play a DVD movie on his Windows Vista computer, the DVD drive was not recognized. You go out to his home to troubleshoot the problem. What is the most likely first step you take to solve the problem?

    A. Uninstall and reinstall the drivers for the DVD drive.

    B. Uninstall and reinstall the movie player used on the computer.

    C. Uninstall and reinstall the operating system.

    D. Edit the Registry.

84. You have a RAID array configured in a Windows 7 computer for testing. After rebooting the computer, RAID stops working and the drives read as unformatted. Of the following, what is the most likely cause?

    A. A problem in the BIOS.

    B. A problem with all of the hard drives in the array.

    C. A problem with the hard drive cables.

    D. The hard drive controller has failed.

85. You have a customer whose Windows XP computer has experienced a "Blue Screen of Death," or BSOD. You troubleshoot the STOP error code on the screen and discover that it is related to the video card or video card drivers. Of the following, what could cause this type of error? (Choose all that apply.)

    A. The CPU needs to be overclocked.

    B. The video drivers need to be updated.

    C. The video card is overheating.

    D. Windows needs to "redetect" the video card.

86. You are troubleshooting a customer's monitor problem. The monitor image is displaying green, dotted lines in some places, some blinking at a high rate of speed. What do you think this is, and what could be the cause? (Choose all that apply.)

    A. Dead pixels

    B. Video artifacts caused by bad video drivers

    C. Bad video cable

    D. Failing CPU

87. You have installed two hard disks on a Windows 7 computer for testing purposes and configured the computer to use RAID 0. During installation of the operating system you get the error "RAID not detected." What could be the problem? (Choose all that apply.)

    A. Bad RAID controller.

    B. Both hard disks are bad.

    C. Windows 7 is not designed to use RAID.

    D. Bad drivers for the RAID controller.

88. You are rebooting a computer after installing a new device. The computer boots normally, but you get a "This device cannot start" error message. What could be the cause?

    A. Bad drivers.

    B. Bad RAM stick.

    C. Missing .dll file.

    D. Your account has insufficient permissions to use the device.

89. You are troubleshooting a computer that always boots directly into Safe Mode. Your customer says that he installed a new video card recently and now every time he reboots the computer, it goes into Safe Mode. What do you suspect? (Choose all that apply.)

    A. The video drivers could be bad.

    B. The video settings could be misconfigured.

    C. The computer is suffering from keylogger malware.

    D. Windows has experienced a serious STOP error.

90. A customer's older laser printer is displaying a low memory error. It gives the total memory capacity of the printer, but says only a very small amount of that memory is available. What can you do to fix this problem? (Choose all that apply.)

    A. Add more memory to the computer.

    B. Clear any documents such as saved faxes stored on the machine.

    C. Physically reseat the printer memory.

    D. Restore the printer to its default settings.

91. You have a small business customer who says that the print output of her laser printer is a mess. The toner seems to just fall off the paper after the print job is complete. Of the following, what part of the laser print process seems to be failing?

    A. Cleaning

    B. Conditioning

    C. Writing

    D. Developing

    E. Transferring

    F. Fusing

92. You are servicing a small business customer's printer, and during the process, she explains that she's had a lot of problems with paper jams and similar issues. You talk with her about the specifics of the printer issues and suspect that the printer needs to have the paper feeder and rollers replaced. Of the following, which problems should this solve? (Choose all that apply.)

    A. Creased paper

    B. Paper not feeding

    C. Paper jams

    D. Print queue backed up

93. You get a call at the help desk of your company's IT department saying that a new employee wasn't able to add a network printer to his Windows 7 computer as instructed by his supervisor, and is receiving an "Access Denied" error. What could be the problem?

    A. The user doesn't have proper permissions on the Windows 7 computer.

    B. The user doesn't have proper permissions on the print server.

    C. The user doesn't have proper permissions to the network.

    D. Only members of the IT department can add a network printer to Windows 7.

94. You get a call at the help desk of your company's IT department saying that the network printer for one of the departments isn't printing. Today is one of the days when most of the employees must print their end-of-month reports so the printer is getting heavy use. Given these conditions, what could be the problem?

    A. The network printer is disconnected from the network.

    B. The access permissions to the printer have been changed and no one has access rights to print.

    C. Print jobs are stuck in the queue.

    D. The printer overheated due to heavy use.

95. You get a call from one of your small business customers saying that when she prints color content, all of the colors are wrong, compared to what she sees on her monitor. What do you suspect is the cause? (Choose all that apply.)

    A. The color ink cartridges are all empty.

    B. The print head is jammed.

    C. The printer color needs to be calibrated.

    D. A problem with the color profile of the printer.

96. You get a call from a small business customer saying that she just installed a printer locally to her Windows 7 computer but all it's printing out is "garbage" or garbled characters. The printer and print cable were a unit she found in a store. What problems do you suspect? (Choose all that apply.)

    A. The print heads are clogged.

    B. The printer cable is damaged.

    C. The ink cartridges are faulty.

    D. The print drivers are bad.

97. You are working inside a customer's PC and you need to remove the hard drive. Of the following, which tool are you most likely to use?

    A. Hammer

    B. Pliers

    C. Screwdriver

    D. Tweezers

98. You have a home customer who deleted a file that he badly needs. The problem is, after he deleted it, he also emptied his computer's Recycle Bin. He has never backed up his computer. Is there any way to recover the file?

    A. No, it's gone forever.

    B. Yes, right-click the Recycle Bin and select Restore Recently Deleted Files.

    C. Yes, you can use the Windows onboard recovery program to restore recently deleted files.

    D. Yes, but you'll have to use a third-party application.

99. You boot a customer's Windows XP computer and receive an "OS not found" error. Of the following, what are valid methods of attempting to recover the computer from this error? (Choose all that apply.)

    A. Verify that the BIOS is looking at the correct hard disk to boot.

    B. Use the Windows XP Recovery Console.

    C. If the master boot record (MBR) is damaged, repair it with fixmbr.

    D. Deactivate the partition containing the MBR.

100. You notice that your computer's date and time have reset and are completely inaccurate. You manually reset the date and time, but later notice that they are inaccurate again. What could be the likely cause?

    A. Your computer has a virus.

    B. Time and date are misconfigured in the BIOS.

    C. The computer is set to automatically use Internet time for its date and time.

    D. The CMOS battery is dying.

QUICK ANSWER KEY

1. A, B, D	22. D	43. B
2. C	23. C	44. C
3. A, B, D	24. B, C	45. A, B
4. D	25. D	46. C
5. A	26. C	47. C
6. C	27. B	48. A
7. D	28. A, B	49. D
8. A	29. A, B, C	50. A
9. D	30. D	51. B
10. A, C	31. D	52. A
11. C	32. A, B	53. C
12. A, B, C	33. A	54. C
13. B	34. B	55. A, B
14. C	35. B	56. A
15. A	36. A	57. A, B, C
16. A	37. C	58. A, B, D
17. A, C	38. A	59. C
18. C	39. C	60. A
19. A	40. D	61. A, B, D
20. A, C	41. B	62. B, C, D
21. D	42. C	63. A

64.	B, C, D	77.	A	90.	B, C, D
65.	B, C, D	78.	D	91.	F
66.	B	79.	A, B, D	92.	A, B, C
67.	A, B	80.	A, B, D	93.	B
68.	D	81.	A, B	94.	C
69.	B, C, D	82.	A, B, C	95.	C, D
70.	A, B	83.	A	96.	B, D
71.	A	84.	A	97.	C
72.	C	85.	B, C, D	98.	D
73.	B	86.	B, C	99.	A, B, C
74.	A, B, C	87.	A, D	100.	D
75.	B, C, D	88.	A		
76.	C	89.	A, B		

IN-DEPTH ANSWERS

1. ☑ **A, B,** and **D.** All access points are set with a default SSID, user name, and password, configured by the manufacturer. An unauthorized person can look up that information on the Internet and use it to log in to your access point and change its settings. Always change the default settings on wireless devices to prevent security breaches. An access point is like any other computer, and making sure its firmware is updated to the most current version will improve security by fixing any existing bugs or other vulnerabilities. Enabling WPA2 encryption prevents intruders from eavesdropping on network communications.

   ☒ **C** is incorrect because turning off the DNS service in the access point won't affect the device's security level.

2. ☑ **C.** SSH, or Secure Shell, is a network protocol that allows data to be exchanged using a secure channel between two network hosts.

   ☒ **A, B,** and **D** are incorrect. **A** is incorrect because FTP is a network protocol that is used to copy files from one host to another host across a network. **B** is incorrect because HTML is the primary markup language used for writing Web page content and elements. **D** is incorrect because TCP/IP is a set of protocols that allow communications across networks, including the Internet.

3. ☑ **A, B,** and **D.** Rebooting the computer may reset the error with the network connection. A faulty network cable may be causing this problem. If the machine has an APIPA IP address beginning with 169.254, this may also be the source of the problem.

   ☒ **C** is incorrect because resetting the network firewall would be extremely disruptive to other users and there is no sign that anyone else is experiencing problems.

4. ☑ **D.** Smartphones do not contain VGA ports. These are normally used to connect monitors to laptop and desktop computers.

   ☒ **A, B,** and **C** are incorrect. **A** is incorrect because accelerometers are devices commonly used to control screen orientation in smartphones. **B** is incorrect because most smartphones include GPS location services, including geotracking and location tracking. **C** is incorrect because many smartphones include remote backup services, such as Apple's iCloud.

5. ☑ **A.** Bluetooth technology allows short-range pairing between devices and is commonly used in car audio systems.

   ☒ **B, C,** and **D** are incorrect. **B** is incorrect because infrared connections do not allow for audio transmission. **C** is incorrect because the VoIP protocol does not provide a way to connect to an external audio system. **D** is incorrect because IPv6 is a networking protocol and does not connect devices for audio pairing.

6. ☑   **C.** The large amount of downloaded software is a clue that the system may be infected by malicious software. This is a common cause of slow connections.

☒   **A, B,** and **D** are incorrect. **A** and **D** are incorrect because a faulty wireless access point or IP address conflict would only affect connections in a single location. **B** is incorrect because wireless connections do not use Ethernet interfaces.

7. ☑   **D.** The nbtstat –s command shows all active NetBIOS sessions.

☒   **A, B,** and **C** are incorrect. **A** is incorrect because the nbtstat –c command shows the contents of the NetBIOS name cache. **B** is incorrect because the nbtstat –n command shows the local name registrations on the system. **C** is incorrect because the nbtstat –r command displays the count of resolved NetBIOS names.

8. ☑   **A.** A wireless locator can be used to identify unauthorized wireless access points in a facility.

☒   **B, C,** and **D** are incorrect. **B** is incorrect because punchdown tools are used to create connections in a wiring closet. **C** is incorrect because toner probes are used to locate wires. **D** is incorrect because ping is a system command used to test network connectivity.

9. ☑   **D.** While voice recognition software can't be fooled by a person imitating the voice of another person, a recording of the authorized person's voice could be used to authenticate.

☒   **A, B,** and **C** are incorrect. **A** is incorrect because a fingerprint scan is very reliable, since no two people have the same fingerprints, not even identical twins. **B** is incorrect because hand geometry is considered unique, plus hand geometry scanners have the advantage of working in harsh and unclean industrial environments. **C** is incorrect because the pattern of the blood vessels in a person's retina is unique, and there's no known method of duplicating a retina.

10. ☑   **A** and **C.** You should attempt to perform a remote wipe to remove data from the device. You should also ask the CEO to change his password to prevent future connections to the corporate servers from the device.

☒   **B** and **D** are incorrect. **B** is incorrect because GPS geolocation may locate the phone but it will not do anything to protect data stored on the device. **D** is incorrect because patching the phone will not do anything to secure data on the device.

11. ☑   **C.** Generally speaking, tablet computers do not contain field serviceable parts and you must return the device for repair.

☒   **A, B,** and **D** are incorrect because the only way to correct a hardware memory failure is to replace the memory, which is not field serviceable in a tablet device.

12. ☑   **A, B,** and **C.** Regardless of the file system, all Windows files can be marked with the Read, Hidden, and System file attributes.

☒   **D** is incorrect because Full Control is a permission setting for a file in an NTFS file system using standard permissions.

13. ☑ **B.** Privacy filters protect against individuals looking at the screen of someone sitting next to them, an attack known as shoulder surfing.

☒ **A, C,** and **D** are incorrect. **A** is incorrect because privacy filters do nothing to protect against users responding to phishing attacks they receive via e-mail or other means. **C** is incorrect because privacy filters do not protect against wireless eavesdropping. Encryption would be the appropriate control for this. **D** is incorrect because privacy filters do not screen the content visited by users. A content filter would perform this task.

14. ☑ **C.** Spyware monitors user activity and sends reports back to the command and control server.

☒ **A, B,** and **D** are incorrect. **A** is incorrect because a virus generally slows down a system, steals data, or performs some other malicious activity, but spyware is the specific type of software that monitors user activity. **B** is incorrect because adware displays unwanted ads on the user's computer. **D** is incorrect because a Trojan horse is a type of malicious software that poses as a desired program but then performs malicious activity.

15. ☑ **A.** You may disable any Windows account in the Local Users and Groups tool.

☒ **B, C,** and **D** are incorrect because accounts are disabled in the Local Users and Groups tool.

16. ☑ **A.** In a small business setting with this requirement, the most likely option is to train employees to have the habit of manually locking their desktops by pressing CTRL-ALT-DEL and then selecting Lock Computer whenever they get up to leave their desks.

☒ **B, C,** and **D** are incorrect. **B** is incorrect because screensavers don't usually activate the moment a person stops working on their computer, so there would be an interval of time when the computer desktop would be unlocked. **C** is incorrect because it's unlikely that a small business environment would be using Microsoft Windows Active Directory Services. **D** is incorrect because it wouldn't be cost or time effective to have separate staff members manually lock all unattended computers.

17. ☑ **A and C.** Disabling Autorun prevents the automatic execution of programs stored on media when inserted into a computer. Installing antivirus software allows the scanning of media for malware upon use.

☒ **B and D** are incorrect. **B** is incorrect because requiring passwords would not prevent an authorized user from accidentally infecting the system. **D** is incorrect because a password-protected screensaver would not prevent a user from accessing the system and accidentally infecting it.

18. ☑ **C.** Keystroke loggers are a form of malware that records every key the computer user presses to harvest user names, passwords, Social Security numbers, and other confidential information and then send that data to the person who caused the malware installation.
☒ **A, B,** and **D** are incorrect. **A** is incorrect because a virus is a more or less generic term for a type of malware designed to perform various malicious acts on a computer, up to and including destroying data and permanently incapacitating the computer. **B** is incorrect because worms are self-replicating viruses that, once installed on a machine, make duplicates of themselves and send the duplicates on to other machines, usually via the user's e-mail address book. Worms can have a number of different effects, including severely incapacitating computers once they have sent their copies out. **D** is incorrect because a password cracker is a specific type of malware that is designed to harvest passwords from computers.

19. ☑ **A.** The most likely cause of these events is that the customer's computer has become infected with some form of malware, which is installing new programs and adding unwanted favorites in the Web browser.
☒ **B, C,** and **D** are incorrect. **B** is incorrect because it's unlikely a hacker would invade a home user's computer to install malicious programs. **C** is incorrect because Microsoft Automatic Updates would install recognizable Windows, Office, or other Microsoft-related programs. **D** is incorrect because an antivirus program is usually configured to update its own program or its antivirus signatures, not to install unrecognizable programs and icons.

20. ☑ **A and C.** Symantec, MacAfee, and Avira have all created boot sector virus removal and repair tools that can be downloaded and run on a compromised computer. Boot the computer using the Windows XP Repair Disc, choose the repair option when prompted, and use the Recovery Console to repair the corrupted boot block.
☒ **B and D** are incorrect because running antivirus programs in this manner will not allow you to repair a damaged or corrupted boot block.

21. ☑ **D.** Usually, the weakest link in a computer's chain of security is the user. Educating the user in how to avoid risks that could harm his computer and how to maintain his antivirus program is the best way to protect the PC.
☒ **A, B,** and **C** are incorrect. **A** is incorrect because if you cleaned the computer using the current antivirus product, chances are it's at least adequate. **B** is incorrect because although Windows XP is aging, properly updated, it is still reasonably secure. **C** is incorrect because an ISP cannot guarantee that its customers will never encounter a virus when connected to the Internet.

22. ☑ **D.** The UAC default setting dims the desktop and prompts the user to click Yes when installing a new program but not when the user is modifying Windows settings. The dimming of the desktop is deliberate and prevents an unauthorized spoofing of the UAC by a malicious program seeking to be installed. You can set the UAC to offer no prompt at all, to offer a prompt but not dim the desktop, or to use the most restrictive setting and have it offer a prompt both when the user is trying to install software and when the user changes any settings in Windows.

    ☒ **A, B,** and **C** are incorrect. **A** is incorrect because you can change the degree of restrictions available in the UAC. **B** is incorrect because the default setting is not the least restrictive setting. **C** is incorrect because you can remove the prompt by setting the UAC to its least restrictive setting.

23. ☑ **C.** The customer originally belonged to only the Managers group, which has Allow permissions for read and write for the City folder on the NTFS volume. The Auditors group has Deny permissions for read and write on the same folder. When the customer was added to the Auditors group, the Deny permissions overrode the Allow permissions, cutting off the customer's ability to read and write to documents in the City folder.

    ☒ **A, B,** and **D** are incorrect. **A** is incorrect because if the customer had Read and Write Allow permissions from the Managers group but no permissions selected at all for the Auditors group, the Allow Read and Write permissions from the Managers group would continue to let him write to documents in the City folder. **B** is incorrect because this configuration would have resulted in the customer not being able to write to documents in the City folder until he was added to the Auditors group. **D** is incorrect because this configuration would result in the customer never having been able to write to documents in the City folder and continuing to be denied that ability.

24. ☑ **B and C.** Phishing is a scam where a customer receives an e-mail (or instant message), supposedly from a trusted source such as a bank, stating that his user name and password data has been lost and that the customer must click a link provided in the e-mail to re-enter this data. Once the link is clicked, the customer is taken to a copy, sometimes a very bad copy, of the banking Website, where the customer enters his user name and password, giving it to the malicious person who created the phishing scheme. Advise customers to never click a link in such an e-mail but to check this information by calling the bank or other trusted source and talking to a representative of that organization. Social engineering is a method a malicious person uses, sometimes over the phone, to attempt to convince you to release confidential information to that person. Phishing is a specific example of social engineering.

    ☒ **A and D** are incorrect. **A** is incorrect because cookies are small files saved in your Web browser that contain certain bits of information about you and that can be read by certain Websites. For example, Amazon can install a cookie on your Web browser so that, when you visit Amazon's site, it reads the cookie, determines your shopping preferences, and displays items you might want to buy based on those preferences. **D** is incorrect because war driving is a method used by malicious people to roam an area on foot or by car, seeking unsecured wireless networks for the purpose of using that network connection to surf the Internet or to hack into your home computer.

25. ☑ **D.** Each Windows computer, even if it is a member of an Active Directory domain, also has a local account that can be used to log in to the machine. The user should have a local account on the machine under her name that will let her log in and retrieve the required Word file.

☒ **A, B,** and **C** are incorrect. **A** is incorrect because this does not address the customer's immediate needs and is not a good example of customer service. **B** is incorrect because although the IT department has a separate local administrators account configured on the machine for maintenance purposes, it would be a breach of security to give the login details to this account to a customer. **C** is incorrect because logging in to the computer's local Guest account won't give the customer access to her Documents folder.

26. ☑ **C.** The IPC$ share is used most commonly for remote administration of servers.

☒ **A, B,** and **D** are incorrect. **A** is incorrect because this is the share on the computer's root folder share used by administrators to quickly access this folder across the network. **B** is incorrect because FAX$ is used by fax clients to send faxes, storing fax pages, including cover pages, on a server. **D** is incorrect because PRINT$ is used for printer administration across the network.

27. ☑ **B.** User Account Control (UAC) is a feature introduced in Windows Vista and present in Windows 7 that detects changes about to be made on the computer requiring administrator permissions. The default behavior dims the desktop and prompts you to give permission to install the program with administrator privileges as a security measure.

☒ **A, C,** and **D** are incorrect. **A** is incorrect because this isn't a behavior of the antivirus program installed on the computer. **C** is incorrect because this is the default behavior of UAC when any change is about to be made to a Windows 7 computer, not just when malware is detected. **D** is incorrect because the user does not have to log in as an administrator to install the program. UAC is specifically designed so that when a user is logged in under a general user account, UAC gives the user the option to install a program using administrator permissions without the user having to be logged in as an administrator.

28. ☑ **A** and **B.** In the System Restore dialog box, you can either double-click the desired restore point or select the desired restore point and then click the Scan For Affected Programs button. The system will scan your computer and generate a report on the programs that will be impacted by restoring to that particular restore point.

☒ **C** and **D** are incorrect. **C** is incorrect because there is no System Restore Options selection at this location. **D** is incorrect because there is a method of making this determination.

29. ☑ **A, B,** and **C.** Many types of content can be synchronized between smartphones and computers, including e-mail, contacts, pictures, music, and videos.
☒ **D** is incorrect because although computers can be used to transfer applications between mobile devices, mobile applications generally cannot run on a computer.

30. ☑ **D.** Single Sign-On (SSO) technology allows users to sign on to multiple systems with the same credentials.
☒ **A, B,** and **C** are incorrect. **A** is incorrect because Secure Sockets Layer (SSL) is used to encrypt network communications. **B** is incorrect because solid-state drives (SSDs) are a type of storage device. **C** is incorrect because Secure Shell (SSH) is a utility that allows encrypted connections between systems.

31. ☑ **D.** A mobile hotspot creates a Wi-Fi network in the area that can be used by any device with the wireless network key. It is the easiest way to connect multiple computers through a single WWAN connection.
☒ **A, B,** and **C** are incorrect because they are all valid ways to connect a single computer to a cellular WWAN, but that connection is not easily shared among multiple devices.

32. ☑ **A** and **B.** Network Discovery is enabled for the Home and Work network locations on Windows 7 systems.
☒ **C** and **D** are incorrect. **C** is incorrect because there is no Enterprise network location. **D** is incorrect because the Public network location disables Network Discovery.

33. ☑ **A.** You can use the interface shown in the accompanying screenshot to specify a particular program and then determine which network or networks you want this program to be able to access.
☒ **B, C,** and **D** are incorrect. **B** is incorrect because port forwarding is mapping a service entering a network from the external port of the gateway to multiple IP addresses inside the firewalled system. This is usually done to hide the structure of an interior network from the Internet. **C** is incorrect because this involves changing the access rules for specific ports that control services on the firewall. **D** is incorrect because firewall devices can be configured by a knowledgeable technician or engineer.

34. ☑ **B.** You can enable Wake-on-LAN on the Power Management tab of the network adapter properties.
☒ **A, C,** and **D** are incorrect because the setting is found on the Power Management tab.

35. ☑ **B.** Power over Ethernet (PoE) technology allows you to transmit both electricity and data over a network connection.
☒ **A, C,** and **D** are incorrect. **A** is incorrect because the Point-to-Point Protocol (PPP) is used to connect network nodes. **C** is incorrect because the Remote Access Dial-In User Service (RADIUS) is used for user authentication. **D** is incorrect because virtual private networks (VPNs) are used to securely connect to remote networks.

36. ☑ **A.** Quality of Service (QoS) allows you to limit the amount of bandwidth used by any particular service, such as streaming media, so that it does not impact the rest of the network.

☒ **B, C,** and **D** are incorrect. **B** is incorrect because content filtering can restrict the type of traffic on a network but cannot perform bandwidth rate limiting. **C** is incorrect because intrusion detection systems (IDSs) are used to detect network attacks. **D** is incorrect because Secure Sockets Layer (SSL) is used to encrypt network traffic.

37. ☑ **C.** The Indexed attribute instructs the Windows Indexing Service to crawl the contents of the directory and speeds up search results.

☒ **A, B,** and **D** are incorrect. **A** is incorrect because the hidden attribute hides the files from view. **B** is incorrect because the read-only attribute prevents users from editing files. **D** is incorrect because the encrypted attribute secures the contents of the files.

38. ☑ **A.** Members of the Administrators group can access any file on the computer.

☒ **B, C,** and **D** are incorrect because only administrators can access the files of other users.

39. ☑ **C.** The computer is configured to use an IP address manually, and the IP address for the DNS server is configured manually. This can lead to errors if the wrong IP address for the DNS server is used. The computer will still be able to network, but it will not be able to use address–to–domain name translation services.

☒ **A, B,** and **D** are incorrect. **A** is incorrect because the computer isn't intended to have its IP address configured manually, since it can network with a dynamically assigned IP address. **B** is incorrect because these fields are blank and grayed out when the computer is receiving these settings dynamically. **D** is incorrect because if the DHCP server were down, the computer couldn't ping the gateway server, since it is receiving its network configuration settings dynamically.

40. ☑ **D.** The SMTP, or Simple Mail Transfer Protocol, server manages all outgoing mail. When the customer sends an e-mail, this server will manage that message. If the wrong name is entered into the SMTP field, the customer will be unable to send e-mails from Outlook.

☒ **A, B,** and **C** are incorrect. **A** is incorrect because DNS is a service that provides IP address–to–hostname translation and has nothing to do with providing mail services. **B** and **C** are incorrect because these are both protocols for providing incoming mail services. POP, or Post Office Protocol, stores your incoming e-mails and, when requested, will send e-mail to your computer's e-mail client without keeping a copy, unless you specifically request the server to do so. IMAP, or Internet Message Access Protocol, works similarly to POP, except when it sends you incoming e-mail, it always stores a copy on the server.

41. ☑ **B.** Many corporate environments use a proxy server between customers and the Internet to improve performance by storing local copies of frequently accessed Websites. Many times, you can set Internet Explorer to use a proxy server in a single action, but some organizations use different proxy addresses for HTTP, HTTPS, and FTP. In this case, you will need to add those specific addresses using Internet Options by clicking the Connections tab, clicking LAN Settings, selecting the Use A Proxy Server For Your LAN check box, and then clicking the Advanced button. It is likely that when the new hire's computer was set up last week, the proxy settings in Internet Explorer were not configured correctly.

☒ **A, C,** and **D** are incorrect. **A** is incorrect because if the corporate firewall were blocking all HTTPS connections, then no computer in the office would be able to access an HTTPS site; however, you were able to connect to the desired HTTPS site using a coworker's computer. **C** is incorrect because there is no option to configure proxy settings for Windows Vista in Administrative Tools. **D** is incorrect because it is very unlikely that the site would be down at just the time the customer needed to access it but up when you tried to access it. Also, the HTTPS site is the only site type the customer couldn't access.

42. ☑ **C.** Bandwidth describes the data transmission capacity of a network connection, but just because your network is supposed to operate at a particular speed, that doesn't mean you will always experience that speed. A network's bandwidth is limited by a number of factors that are collectively referred to as latency. Network latency is anything that tends to slow traffic down, including the number of users that have to share a network segment, the amount of traffic traversing the gateway, and any network equipment, either locally or on the Internet, that may not be operating or not operating correctly.

☒ **A, B,** and **D** are incorrect. **A** is incorrect because an ISP, or Internet service provider, should provide a constant bandwidth capacity based on a contractual arrangement. However, latency on the network can affect the actual amount of bandwidth experienced by the customer. **B** is incorrect because customers do not always experience the total amount of bandwidth and actual slowdowns do occur. They're not merely tricks of perception. **D** is incorrect because the explanations for bandwidth and latency are fictitious.

43. ☑ **B.** FIXBOOT lets you perform the desired task.

☒ **A, C,** and **D** are incorrect. **A** is incorrect because DISKPART lets you perform disk partitioning. **C** is incorrect because FIXMBR repairs the master boot record. **D** is incorrect because SYSTEMROOT sets the current directory to the location of the Windows system files.

44. ☑ **C.** One method of teaching customers to use strong passwords that they will remember is to have them base their password on a phrase rather than a word. For instance, 4s&7yrsaO is based on the famous phrase used by Abraham Lincoln, "Four score and seven years ago, our." While you may not want to use a phrase that is so famous, having a customer use the lyrics to a song or the words to a favorite poem, shifting it to be represented by letters, numbers, and special characters, is better than using a single word and changing a few of the characters.

☒ **A, B,** and **D** are incorrect. **A** is incorrect because it is a plain word that can easily be figured out or compromised by a dictionary attack. **B** is incorrect because this is a plain word that just has a few characters replacing letters but is still easily discovered. **D** is incorrect because while it is a very strong password, it is unlikely that a customer will be able to remember this character combination.

45. ☑ **A** and **B.** If you receive an e-mail from an unknown source or from a known source that seems otherwise suspicious and the e-mail has an attachment or link, do not open the attachment or link. This is a common ploy to either compromise your computer by tricking you into running malicious software or to visit a Website capable of running malware on your computer. Also, if your computer is compromised by adware, enabling your Web browser's pop-up blocker can minimize the effects until you can have the adware removed.

☒ **C** and **D** are incorrect. **C** is incorrect because while setting the Windows firewall to allow no exceptions, such as for Outlook or your antivirus program, may improve security, the programs you need to be able to access the Internet will not be able to do so and this will reduce or eliminate your productivity. **D** is incorrect because unplugging the Ethernet cable from your computer will remove all networking. While your computer will be safe from remote threats, you won't be able to take advantage of the benefits of a networked environment.

46. ☑ **C.** If the user has a Windows 7 installation DVD, she should boot the computer from that DVD, select Repair Your Computer and then Command Prompt from the menu, and then use the net user command to change the user account password.

☒ **A, B,** and **D** are incorrect. **A** is incorrect because the Password Reset Disk does not ship with the computer, but the customer can create such a disk in User Accounts in Control Panel so that if she forgets her password in the future, she can use the disk to reset the password and log in to the computer. **B** is incorrect because logging in as Guest will not give her the ability to reset her user password, since the Guest account has extremely limited privileges. **D** is incorrect because, although it would work, the customer would lose all of her data and the process is extremely time consuming and, in this case, unnecessary.

47. ☑ **C.** While the Modify Allow permission for the NTFS folder on the network does allow the customer to perform many tasks, it does not include an Allow permission for Delete Subfolders And Files, preventing the customer from being able to delete Subfoo inside of Foo or from deleting any files within Subfoo. To see these specific permissions, right-click the necessary NTFS shared folder and click Properties. Then, select the Security tab, select the group to which the user belongs, and then click Advanced. In the Advanced Security Settings box, select the customer's name and then select Edit. The list of specific permissions will appear. Note that this path varies slightly by OS.

☒ **A, B,** and **D** are incorrect. **A** is incorrect because the customer does possess the Traverse Folder/Execute File Allow permission, which allows the customer to browse through a folder's subfolders, such as Subfoo, where the customer may not otherwise have access. **B** is incorrect because the Allow Modify permission does include the Create Folders/Append Data Allow permission, which allows the customer to add information to an existing file in a situation where he wouldn't have permission to create a brand-new file. **D** is incorrect because the Modify Allow permission does include the Delete Allow permission, letting the customer directly delete files contained in the Foo folder.

48. ☑ **A.** If the hidden file attribute is marked on the file's Properties box, it will not appear in the directory, or even in a standard search. You would have to select the Advanced Search option to search for hidden folders and files to be able to find it and then remove the hidden attribute to have it appear in the directory. In order for the user-created text file to have the hidden attribute, it would have to manually and almost deliberately be marked hidden by the user. In this case, the user would have had to make the attribute hidden and then forgotten he had done so.

☒ **B, C,** and **D** are incorrect. **B** is incorrect because a file marked as read-only would be visible but you or your coworker would not be able to write to the file and then save the changes. **C** is incorrect because, by default, files are already marked as ready for archiving. On the file's Properties box, click Advanced to see this selection. **D** is incorrect because if the file were marked for compression, it would still be visible in the directory, but the text indicating the filename would be colored blue, telling you that it is compressed.

49. ☑ **D.** By default, when you attempt to view the computer's system files in the C:\ Windows directory, the files are hidden to prevent accidental damage, which could result in the computer becoming unstable or unbootable. You can view the contents by clicking the Show The Contents Of This Folder link on the screen or by clicking the link of the same name under System Tasks in the sidebar on the left.

☒ **A, B,** and **C** are incorrect. **A** is incorrect because archived files are not contained in a hidden directory. **B** is incorrect because compressed files are not kept in a hidden directory. **C** is incorrect because program files are kept in the Program Files directory just under the C drive.

50. ☑ **A.** BitLocker is new with Windows Vista and continues to be used with Windows 7. It is a low-level mechanism that encrypts an entire volume, regardless of who owns the data on the volume, and works before the Windows operating system loads.

☒ **B, C,** and **D** are incorrect. **B** is incorrect because EFS, or Encrypted File System, is an encryption method that works at the file system level and does not work until Windows loads. Both BitLocker and EFS can be used together to enhance data security. **C** is incorrect because intrusion detection refers to a system that is used to prevent or detect when an unauthorized person attempts to physically access the inner workings of a computer. **D** is incorrect because TPM, or Trusted Platform Module, is a chip or security module used to contain multiple encryption keys for utilities such as BitLocker.

51. ☑ **B.** Dialers are types of malicious programs installed on computers that cause the dial-up modem to call dangerous or pay-per-call locations on the Internet, often resulting in extremely high phone bills for the customer.

☒ **A, C,** and **D** are incorrect. **A** is incorrect because adware is a type of malware that generates banners or other unwanted advertisements on the customer's computer. **C** is incorrect because a keystroke logger is a type of malware that records the customer's keystrokes on the computer, often to steal the customer's user name and password to protected online accounts such as online banking accounts. **D** is incorrect because spim is spam for instant messaging.

52. ☑ **A.** Diskpart is a command-line disk partitioning utility that creates partitions on storage drives, including USB drives. It can make the USB thumb drive bootable and format it in either FAT32 or NTFS, preparing it to be used as the boot drive to install Windows 7 on another PC.

☒ **B, C,** and **D** are incorrect. **B** is incorrect because fdisk is a command-line utility that partitions disks and writes to the master boot record, but in spite of the similarity between the two tools, diskpart is more powerful and has replaced fdisk in Windows systems. **C** is incorrect because format is primarily used to erase content on a disk and format it with a file system, but does not specifically make a disk bootable. **D** is incorrect because xcopy is a utility used to copy files, and even whole directory trees, but it cannot format a drive and make it bootable.

53. ☑ **C.** PXE stands for Pre-Boot Execution Environment and it allows a PXE-enabled PC to connect to a server over a network and have an operating system installed on the PC. This is an effective method of installing an OS on multiple PCs rather than having to visit each machine with an optical installation disc and installing the OS on each machine one at a time.

☒ **A, B,** and **D** are incorrect because each of these methods requires that the technician physically visit each machine to install the OS using physical installation media.

54. ☑ **C.** An unattended installation is an installation method that lets you select responses to all of the information requested during a normal operating system installation process. It lets you automate the installation process so you don't have to be physically present at the computer while Windows is being installed.

☒ **A, B,** and **D** are incorrect. **A** is incorrect because a clean install is the process of installing an operating system on a computer with either no operating system or an operating system you are going to overwrite. This method requires that you be physically present at the computer for the entire installation process. **B** is incorrect because this installation type is used to repair Windows when it has become damaged or unresponsive. **D** is incorrect because this method is used to upgrade a previous version of Windows to a later version and requires your presence during the installation process.

55. ☑ **A** and **B.** You can create a new partition in the unallocated space on a basic disk but not a dynamic disk. You can also create a new logical drive in an extended partition on a basic disk but not a dynamic disk.

☒ **C** and **D** are incorrect because these operations can only be performed on a basic disk but not on a dynamic disk.

56. ☑ **A.** On the General tab, under Home Page, you can type the URL of the site you want to display as the Web browser's home page in the available field. You can also open the browser, navigate to the desired site, and then under Home Page on the General tab, click the Use Current button.

☒ **B, C,** and **D** are incorrect. **B** is incorrect because this tab lets you choose the security settings for different zones such as Internet, local intranet, trusted sites, and restricted sites. **C** is incorrect because the Privacy tab lets you manage privacy settings for zones, manage privacy settings for sites, and manage the pop-up blocker. **D** is incorrect because the Programs tab lets you select the default Web browser for the computer, manage add-ons, and choose which program you want to use as an HTML editor.

57. ☑ **A, B,** and **C.** The Screen Resolution screen lets you manually select the display device, adjust the screen resolution, and select the screen orientation. In most cases, if Windows hasn't automatically recognized the display, you can click Detect to manually detect the monitor attached to the computer.

☒ **D** is incorrect because on the Display screen, instead of clicking Adjust Resolution, you must click Set Custom Text Size (DPI) to perform this action.

58. ☑ **A, B,** and **D.** You can click links directly on this screen that will let you change your password, change your picture, and change the settings for the UAC for this account.

☒ **C** is incorrect because you have to click the Manage Another Account link and go to another screen before you can directly create a new user account.

59. ☑ **C.** The View tab under Advanced Settings lets you control how folders are displayed, including showing or hiding different features or elements of files and folders; whether or not to use the sharing wizard; and how or if preview panes, drive letters, file extensions, and other file and folder features are displayed and laid out.

☒ **A, B,** and **D** are incorrect. **A** is incorrect because the General tab controls how folders are browsed, setting single or double clicks to open items, and controlling the Navigation pane. **B** is incorrect because the Search tab lets you control how file and folder searching works. **D** is incorrect because you can perform all of these tasks from the View tab.

60. ☑ **A.** Clicking Advanced System Settings opens the System Properties dialog box on the Advanced tab. By clicking the Settings button under Performance, you can manage the computer's virtual memory settings.

☒ **B, C,** and **D** are incorrect. **B** is incorrect because on the System Properties box, you need to be on the Hardware tab. **C** is incorrect because on the System Properties box, you need to be on the Remote tab. **D** is incorrect because on the System Properties box, you need to be on the System Protection tab.

61. ☑ **A, B,** and **D.** You can click Change Action Center Settings, which lets you control which types of messages you get about problems with the computer. You can edit the settings for the User Account Control (UAC), making them more or less strict. You can view performance data about the computer, such as the performance scores for the processor, memory, graphics, and so on.

☒ **C** is incorrect because this option isn't available in the Action Center. To adjust virtual memory, go to the System screen and click the Advanced tab.

62. ☑ **B, C,** and **D.** Selecting Monitoring lets you see the general state and statistics generated by the firewall. Selecting Inbound Rules lets you see and configure all of the inbound connection rules. Selecting Outbound Rules lets you see and configure all of the rules for outbound connections.

☒ **A** is incorrect because this option is on the main Windows Firewall screen.

63. ☑ **A.** You are prompted to select a power plan and can change the settings for each plan displayed.

☒ **B, C,** and **D** are incorrect because you cannot make any of these selections from the main pane on the Power Options screen.

64. ☑ **B, C,** and **D.** You can select check boxes for Pictures, Music, Videos, Documents, and Printers.

☒ **A** is incorrect because there is no selection for Directories.

65. ☑ **B, C,** and **D.** Options appearing in the Troubleshooting screen include Programs, Hardware And Sound, Network And Internet, Appearance And Personalization, and System And Security.

☒ **A** is incorrect because Video Performance is not an available option to troubleshoot.

66. ☑ **B.** When a residual charge is left on the drum of a laser printer, the underlying problem can be associated with either the toner cartridge or the fuser. The result is that "ghost images" of the print job are fused to the paper along with the desired image. Once you locate the specific printer part that's causing the problem, it will have to be replaced.
☒ **A, C,** and **D** are incorrect. **A** is incorrect because faded prints are usually caused when ink or toner is running low in the printer. **C** is incorrect because streaking in a laser printer is most commonly caused by excess toner collecting under the cartridge and sticking to pages as they are fed through the printer. The fuser then impresses the actual print job along with the excess toner on the page. **D** is incorrect because vertical lines in a laser printer are typically caused by dirty or dusty rollers and feeds in the printer. To fix this, clean the interior of the printer and replace the toner cartridge.

67. ☑ **A** and **B.** The most likely cause is that you are trying to install the printer using printer drivers that are incompatible with Windows 7. The USB cable connecting the printer to the computer could also be damaged or unplugged.
☒ **C** and **D** are incorrect. **C** is incorrect because the printer service is installed in Windows 7 by default, although it can be disabled. **D** is incorrect because invalid or third-party ink cartridges in the printer would not result in such an error.

68. ☑ **D.** Although this error message for an HP printer indicates a paper jam, it is impossible to memorize all possible error codes for all of the different printers on the market, as well as any legacy printers your customers may still be using. Either consult the printer's documentation or use a search engine to look up the error codes for the printer in question.
☒ **A, C,** and **D** are incorrect. **A** and **C** are incorrect because unless you have memorized all of the error codes for this type of printer, you most likely won't know what the code means. **B** is incorrect because while this is the correct error code for a paper jam, you wouldn't immediately know this unless you were extremely familiar with the error codes for this particular make and model of printer.

69. ☑ **B, C,** and **D.** You can create a System Repair Disc for Windows 7, which will help you recover the computer from a serious error. You can use Event Viewer to look at various logs for warning and error messages related to the computer's problem. Sometimes booting into Safe Mode, where only basic services and drivers are loaded, will help you diagnose a computer's issues.
☒ **A** is incorrect because Automated System Recovery (ASR) is a utility specific to Windows XP and is not available in Windows 7.

70. ☑ **A** and **B.** These sorts of symptoms usually indicate a serious hardware problem, either in the motherboard's circuitry or a fault in the hard drive containing the operating system.
☒ **C** and **D** are incorrect. **C** is incorrect because a faulty network interface card might cause a serious problem, but chances are you'd still be able to boot into Safe Mode, since

networking isn't loaded in Safe Mode. **D** is incorrect because if the computer were looking to boot from the optical drive and trying to look for the MBR on a music CD, the boot wouldn't get as far as the GUI before failing and the error message would be more like "Missing operating system," "Invalid boot disk," or "Missing boot.ini." Also, this type of problem isn't associated with a "Blue Screen of Death" (BSOD).

71. ☑ **A.** Startup and recovery settings in Windows XP can be set to reboot the computer if it detects a serious system error.

☒ **B, C,** and **D** are incorrect. **B** is incorrect because there is no Startup and Recovery setting for rebooting the computer if the power supply fails. **C** is incorrect because in Windows XP, if the system was hanging at the Saving Your Settings portion of the shutdown sequence, the computer would not proceed to shut down and then restart. It would hang. **D** is incorrect because a problem with erasing virtual memory during shutdown would result in an extremely slow shutdown sequence, but the computer would finally shut down and not spontaneously reboot.

72. ☑ **C.** You will need to use some sort of patch management application to monitor which patches have been applied to which servers and to generate administrative reports. It is often difficult to organize and keep track of how or if various updates, hotfixes, and service packs have been installed across a large number of servers, and a patch management system can assist you in performing this job.

☒ **A, B,** and **D** are incorrect. **A** is incorrect because antivirus updates will keep an individual computer's antivirus protection current, but will not manage all software updates across a server room. **B** is incorrect because driver/firmware updates refer to keeping a computer current on all of its device drivers and similar software, but does not perform the required task of software management across a number of servers. **D** is incorrect because while Windows Updates are part of what a patch management system oversees, it is not the comprehensive utility required.

73. ☑ **B.** Check disk, or chkdsk, is a utility that, when run, will show the status of a hard drive's file system integrity and, if so directed, will attempt to repair any problems.

☒ **A, C,** and **D** are incorrect. **A** is incorrect because System Restore is a utility run from the Windows 7 installation disc or OS that attempts to repair the hard drive or operating system in the event of a serious problem. **C** is incorrect because a recovery image allows you to restore your computer after a serious problem, using a backup or image of the computer to return it to a former state. **D** is incorrect because Defrag is a process of moving portions of data files on a hard disk so the fragments for the same file are located continuously on the drive.

74. ☑ **A, B,** and **C.** Automatic Updates, Network Connections, and Printers And Faxes are all readily available in Control Panel.

☒ **D** is incorrect because to get to the Network Setup wizard from Control Panel, you must Open Network Connections and double-click Create A New Connection to launch the wizard.

75. ☑ **B, C,** and **D.** The Control Panel items Offline Files, Pen And Input Devices, and Tablet PC Settings are unique to the Windows Vista Control Panel.

☒ **A** is incorrect because HomeGroup is unique to the Windows 7 Control Panel.

76. ☑ **C.** During the installation process, when you are selecting the drive on which to install Windows 7, click the Load Driver link to load any necessary third-party drivers.

☒ **A, B,** and **D** are incorrect. **A** is incorrect because the process is very different than in Windows XP. **B** is incorrect because during the installation process, when you are selecting the drive on which to install Windows 7, click the Load Driver link to load any necessary third-party drivers. **D** is incorrect because you can install third-party drivers during the Windows 7 installation process.

77. ☑ **A.** A computer configured to multiboot during the OS installation process will have the ability to boot into different operating systems. The user will be presented with a menu as the computer starts, prompting them to choose an operating system. The computer can run only one operating system at a time.

☒ **B, C,** and **D** are incorrect. **B** is incorrect because remote network installation is the process of installing an operating system on one or more computers over an Ethernet connection. The PCs connect to a server to initiate an automatic process that will install the operating system. **C** is incorrect because image deployment is the process of installing an operating system on multiple computers from a single "image," effectively installing the same OS with the same configuration settings on several PCs. **D** is incorrect because partitioning is the process of dividing areas of a hard disk drive into more than one logical storage units. This is typically done to isolate the operating system from the part of the drive or drives that contain data.

78. ☑ **D.** The factory recovery partition is usually included by the computer hardware manufacturer on the computer's hard disk and is a separate partition that can be used to assist in recovering a computer from a serious problem or to reinstall the basic operating system.

☒ **A, B,** and **C** are incorrect because making decisions about the computer joining a workgroup or a domain; setting the time, date, region, and language information; and installing drivers, Windows Updates, and other software are all part of the usual Windows installation process.

79. ☑ **A, B,** and **D.** Typing Control Panel, Explorer, or Notepad in the run box and then pressing ENTER will launch these dialog boxes or utilities without having to navigate to them using some other process.

☒ **C** is incorrect because typing Network Connections in the run box produces an error. You can launch this in Windows XP from Control Panel.

80. ☑ **A, B,** and **D.** The loud "whirring" sound is most likely a cooling fan that's going bad, either because of lack of lubrication or dust contamination. If the fan isn't cleaned, lubed, and restored to good working order, the computer will likely overheat, which can cause numerous problems, including spontaneous reboots, intermittent failures, and possibly even frying the CPU and shutting down the computer.

☒ **C** is incorrect because a dying fan in a computer will not damage the monitor, although the graphics card could overheat and stop working.

81. ☑ **A** and **B.** The most common cause of this kind of problem is either the computer isn't plugged in or the power strip switch has been accidently moved to the off position. These are things a customer with little or no troubleshooting experience can check.

☒ **C** and **D** are incorrect. **C** is incorrect because checking to see if a power supply is faulty requires a multimeter, power supply tester, and technical skills, all of which the customer may not have. **D** is incorrect because checking to see if the power button is faulty requires opening the PC case and "jumping" the power switch on the motherboard.

82. ☑ **A, B,** and **C.** The most common causes for this sort of problem are either a bad IDE data cable or a failing drive. There is also the possibility that the BIOS is misconfigured for this drive to use the wrong data transfer mode, which will also slow down performance.

☒ **D** is incorrect because a bad power supply will cause a number of symptoms, including spontaneous reboots or failure of the computer to boot upon startup, but not hard drive performance issues.

83. ☑ **A.** The most likely problem is the DVD device drivers. Uninstall and reinstall the drivers and see if the DVD drive shows up (although not listed in the possible options, the problem could be that the drive's data cable is bad, the drive isn't getting any power, or the drive itself is bad).

☒ **B, C,** and **D** are incorrect. **B** is incorrect because the drive would still be recognized by the computer even if Windows Media Player or some other movie playing application were corrupted or missing. **C** is incorrect because reinstalling the operating system is an extreme troubleshooting step and there are other things you can check before being so drastic. **D** is incorrect because, although a registry problem can be the cause, it is not the most common cause of this problem.

84. ☑ **A.** RAID drives will stop being recognized as RAID if the settings in the BIOS change. This can happen if the CMOS battery fails and the OnChip SATA type is changed from RAID to AHCI. Go into your BIOS and verify this. Change the setting. If the setting isn't saved, replace the CMOS battery.

☒ **B, C,** and **D** are incorrect. **B** and **C** are incorrect because while drive and drive cable failures may make the drives unrecognized or result in "not found" errors, they wouldn't result in the drives being "seen" but RAID not being recognized. Also, it is unlikely that all of the drives in the array should go bad at the same time. **D** is incorrect because if the hard drive controller has failed, chances are the motherboard wouldn't be able to communicate with the OS boot sector on the primary drive and the computer would fail to boot.

85. ☑ **B, C,** and **D.** There are any number of causes for this STOP error, including obsolete video drivers, a bad video card, and an overheating video card. The error may be more difficult to identify, but one possible solution is to disable the video card in Device Manager and then re-enable it and let Windows "detect" the "new hardware."

☒ **A** is incorrect because overclocking the CPU can cause this sort of STOP error, not correct it.

86. ☑ **B** and **C.** These video artifacts are most likely caused by a problem with the video card, and updating the drivers may fix it. It could also be an issue with the video cable. Try a known good cable to see if that fixes the issue.

☒ **A** and **D** are incorrect. **A** is incorrect because dead pixels would show up as dark spots on the LCD monitor since they show no light. **D** is incorrect because a failing CPU wouldn't cause these symptoms.

87. ☑ **A** and **D.** The most likely cause is either the hardware RAID controller is bad or the drivers need to be updated. Although it's not an option, some computers use a software RAID instead of a hardware controller, which could also be the problem.

☒ **B** and **C** are incorrect. **B** is incorrect because if both drives were bad, the server probably wouldn't be able to initiate the installation of the OS. **C** is incorrect because Windows 7 can use RAID.

88. ☑ **A.** The most likely cause is that the drivers for the device need to be updated.

☒ **B, C,** and **D** are incorrect. **B** is incorrect because if a stick of RAM was bad, a beep code would have alerted you to a memory problem during boot. **C** is incorrect because a missing .dll file would likely result in a failure to boot normally and you would get a "missing .dll file" error message. **D** is incorrect because devices usually don't require special permissions to run.

89. ☑ **A** and **B.** Since the customer recently installed a video card, the most likely cause is either bad drivers or the video settings are misconfigured. Usually, a computer will spontaneously boot into Safe Mode, which loads minimal drivers, including video, when there is a video problem. Check the video settings for the card, and if they seem fine, update the video drivers.

☒ **C** and **D** are incorrect. **C** is incorrect because a keylogger is a type of malware designed to covertly record the keystrokes of the computer user and transmit them to the virus writer, usually so passwords to secure accounts such as online banking accounts can be harvested. **D** is incorrect because if the computer had experienced a serious STOP error, the computer would have displayed a STOP message. If a serious problem caused a boot into Safe Mode, chances are subsequent reboots would have displayed more problematic symptoms or the computer would fail to boot completely.

90. ☑ **B, C,** and **D.** The printer may be showing a low memory error because jobs such as saved fax jobs may be consuming most of the memory. There could also be an undetectable error that can be cleared by restoring the device to its factory default settings. You can also try reseating the physical memory in the printer.

☒ **A** is incorrect because a low memory error for a printer refers to the printer's memory, not the memory of any computer accessing the printer.

91. ☑ **F.** The toner isn't being fused to the paper, resulting in the symptoms described by the customer. The fuser unit most likely needs to be replaced.

☒ **A, B, C, D,** and **E** are incorrect. **A** is incorrect because this step cleans residual toner and removes the electrical charge after the print job is complete. **B** is incorrect because this step conditions the drum to contain the electrical charge. **C** is incorrect because this step uses a laser to change the charge on the drum from higher to lower where the toner is to be applied. **D** is incorrect because this step places the toner onto the drum where the charge has been reduced by the laser. **E** is incorrect because this step draws toner from the drum onto the paper, but is not designed to fix the toner to the paper.

92. ☑ **A, B,** and **C.** Paper jams, paper feed problems, and creased paper are all caused by physical problems with the printer, such as worn paper feeder, worn paper guides, and problem rollers.

☒ **D** is incorrect because the print queue is the area of printer memory where print jobs are stored between the time the computer sends them to the printer and the printer executes the jobs. A backed-up print queue would result in print jobs not being performed, but would have no affect on physical media.

93. ☑ **B.** The most likely problem is that the user doesn't have access rights to the print server to add a network printer. You will have to give the new employee proper permissions or add the printer yourself using your credentials.

    ☒ **A, C,** and **D** are incorrect. **A** is incorrect because the new employee should have access rights to log on to the Windows 7 computer. If an activity requires greater permissions, the UAC should appear and all the user has to do is to select Yes to proceed. **C** is incorrect because the user should have access to the network, just not all of the devices connected to the network. **D** is incorrect because the user wouldn't have been directed to install the network printer if only IT staff were allowed to do so.

94. ☑ **C.** If a large number of users are sending print jobs to the network printer all at once, it's possible the print queue is jammed and unable to process the jobs. Usually, clearing the queue and cycling power on the printer will fix the problem.

    ☒ **A, B,** and **D** are incorrect. **A** is incorrect because heavy printer use wouldn't kick the printer off the network. Also, if the printer were off the network, when users tried to print, they would find that the printer was offline or unable to be located. **B** is incorrect because there's no reason under the circumstances that everyone's permissions to the printer should be invalidated at the same time. **D** is incorrect because overheating might shut the printer down, but that would be obvious to the users in the department. It's also pretty unlikely.

95. ☑ **C and D.** Colors you see on your monitor may not be what the color printer actually prints. Color printers need to be calibrated so that they will print the colors you see on the monitor when previewing your print job. Also, the color profile settings in the printer may be misconfigured.

    ☒ **A and B** are incorrect. **A** is incorrect because if all of the ink cartridges were empty, it wouldn't print color at all. **B** is incorrect because if the print head were jammed, it probably wouldn't be printing at all.

96. ☑ **B and D.** This sort of problem is most commonly caused by bad print drivers and corrected by updating the drivers. It can also be caused if the printer data cable is damaged, sending erroneous information between the computer and the printer.

    ☒ **A and C** are incorrect. **A** is incorrect because if the print heads were clogged, nothing would print at all, or the print job would be legible but faint. **C** is incorrect because faulty ink cartridges would produce a recognizable set of characters but cause other problems such as streaking.

97. ☑ **C.** This isn't always the case, but often a hard drive is secured inside the computer by screws and you'll need a screwdriver to release it.

    ☒ **A, B,** and **D** are incorrect. **A** is incorrect because there is virtually no occasion where using a hammer inside a computer case is appropriate. **B and D** are incorrect because tweezers or needle nose pliers could be used to move dip switches and jumpers, but not to remove a hard drive.

98. ☑ **D.** Files that have been deleted and then recently emptied from the Recycle Bin are often still present on the computer's hard drive. There are a number of free file recovery programs available that can recover these files. It helps if computer activity has been kept to a minimum after the files have been deleted.

☒ **A, B,** and **C** are incorrect. **A** is incorrect because there are ways to recover recently deleted files. **B** is incorrect because this option doesn't exist in the Recycle Bin. **C** is incorrect because there is no onboard Windows program capable of this action.

99. ☑ **A, B,** and **C.** If the BIOS isn't pointed to the disk containing the OS, you will receive this error. You can change the boot order in the BIOS to correct this problem. Windows XP Recovery Console has a number of utilities that can help repair this type of error. If you suspect the master boot record (MBR) is damaged, you can use the fixmbr tool to fix it.

☒ **D** is incorrect because the partition containing the MBR must be set as active.

100. ☑ **D.** The computer's date and time settings are stored in the BIOS. If the CMOS battery is dying, the time settings will become slower or reset completely. Replace the CMOS battery on the motherboard.

☒ **A, B,** and **C** are incorrect. **A** is incorrect because it is unlikely that a virus would be written to specifically reset your computer's date and time. **B** is incorrect because once the computer date and time are saved in the BIOS, they should never change, unless the CMOS battery, which maintains those settings, is dying. **C** is incorrect because having your computer use an Internet time server will keep the date and time on the computer accurate and you won't notice that it is drastically inaccurate.

E

About the CD-ROM

The CD-ROM included with this book comes complete with MasterExam practice exam software, featuring two practice exams—one for the 220-801 exam and one for the 220-802 exam—and a link to download the Secure PDF copy of the book. The software is easy to install on any Windows 2000/XP/Vista/7 computer and must be installed to access the MasterExam feature. To register for the two bonus MasterExams, simply click the Bonus MasterExam link on the main launch page and follow the directions to the free online registration.

System Requirements

Software requires Windows 2000 or higher and Internet Explorer 6.0 or above and 20 MB of hard disk space for full installation. The Secure PDF copy of the book requires Adobe Digital Editions.

Installing and Running MasterExam

If your computer CD-ROM drive is configured to auto run, the CD-ROM will automatically start up upon inserting the disk. From the opening screen you may install MasterExam by clicking the MasterExam link. This will begin the installation process and create a program group named LearnKey. To run MasterExam, select Start | All Programs | LearnKey | MasterExam. If the auto run feature did not launch your CD-ROM, browse to the CD-ROM and click the LaunchTraining.exe icon.

MasterExam

MasterExam provides you with a simulation of the multiple-choice portion of the actual exams. You have the option to take an open book exam, including hints, references, and answers, a closed book exam, or the timed MasterExam simulation.

Note: MasterExam does not provide simulations of the exams' performance-based question type. For further discussion on this question type, please see the book's Introduction.

When you launch MasterExam, a digital clock display will appear in the bottom right-hand corner of your screen. The clock will continue to count down to zero unless you choose to end the exam before the time expires.

Secure PDF Copy of the Book

The contents of this book are available as a free download in the form of a secured Adobe Digital Editions PDF file, the Secure PDF.

The CD-ROM contains links to both Adobe Digital Editions and to the Secure PDF download Web page. First, download and install Adobe Digital Editions on your computer. Next, follow the link to the Secure PDF download Web page listed below. You are required to provide your name, a valid e-mail address, and your unique access code in order to download the Secure PDF.

Your unique access code can be found on the label that is adhered to the inside flap of the CD-ROM envelope. The CD-ROM envelope is inside the paper sleeve bound into the back of this book.

Upon submitting this information, an e-mail message will be sent to the e-mail address you provided. Follow the instructions included in the e-mail message to download your Secure PDF.

To download your copy, please visit:

http://books.mcgraw-hill.com/ebookdownloads/9780071792295

Note: The unique access code entitles you to download one copy of the Secure PDF to one personal computer. The unique access code can only be used once, and the Secure PDF is only usable on the computer on which it was downloaded. Be sure to download the Secure PDF to the computer you intend to use.

You need a copy of Adobe Digital Editions installed to open, view, and navigate the Secure PDF. You can download the latest version of Adobe Digital Editions for free from Adobe's Website, www.adobe.com, or use the version included on the CD-ROM. Remember, it is highly recommended that you download and install Adobe Digital Editions before attempting to download the Secure PDF.

Help

A help file is provided through the help button on the main page in the lower left-hand corner. An individual help feature is also available through MasterExam.

Removing Installation(s)

MasterExam is installed to your hard drive. For best results removing this program, select Start | All Programs | LearnKey | Uninstall.

Technical Support

For questions regarding the operation of the Adobe Digital Editions download, e-mail techsolutions@mhedu.com or visit http://mhp.softwareassist.com.

For questions regarding the book or MasterExam content, please e-mail customer.service@mcgraw-hill.com. For customers outside the United States, e-mail international_cs@mcgraw-hill.com.

LearnKey Technical Support

For technical problems with the software (installation, operation, removing installations), please visit www.learnkey.com, e-mail techsupport@learnkey.com, or call toll free (800) 482-8244.

INDEX

H

I